AF708570

CREATING COOL™ POWERPOINT® 97 PRESENTATIONS

The IDG Books *Creating Cool™* Series Advantage

We at IDG Books Worldwide created *Creating Cool PowerPoint 97 Presentations* to meet your growing need for quick access to the most complete and accurate computer information available. Our books work the way you do: They focus on accomplishing specific tasks — not learning random functions. Our books are not long-winded manuals or dry reference tomes. In each book, expert authors tell you exactly what you can do and how to do it. Easy to follow, step-by-step sections; comprehensive coverage; and convenient access in language and design — it's all here.

The authors of IDG books are uniquely qualified to give you expert advice as well as to provide insightful tips and techniques not found anywhere else. Our authors maintain close contact with end users through feedback from articles, training sessions, e-mail exchanges, user group participation, and consulting work. Because our authors know the realities of daily computer use and are directly tied to the reader, our books have a strategic advantage.

Our authors have the experience to approach a topic in the most efficient manner, and we know that you, the reader, will benefit from a "one-on-one" relationship with the author. Our research shows that readers make computer book purchases because they want expert advice. Because readers want to benefit from the author's experience, the author's voice is always present in an IDG book.

In addition, the author is free to include or recommend useful software in an IDG book. The software that accompanies each book is not intended to be casual filler but is linked to the content, theme, or procedures of the book. We know that you will benefit from the included software.

You will find what you need in this book whether you read it from cover to cover, section by section, or simply one topic at a time. As a computer user, you deserve a comprehensive resource of answers. We at IDG Books Worldwide are proud to deliver that resource with *Creating Cool PowerPoint 97 Presentations.*

Brenda McLaughlin
Senior Vice President and Group Publisher

Internet: YouTellUs@idgbooks.com

CREATING COOL™ POWERPOINT® 97 PRESENTATIONS

Glenn E. Weadock and Emily Sherrill Weadock

IDG BOOKS WORLDWIDE™

IDG Books Worldwide, Inc.
An International Data Group Company

Foster City, CA ♦ Chicago, IL ♦ Indianapolis, IN ♦ Southlake, TX

Creating Cool™ PowerPoint® 97 Presentations

Published by
IDG Books Worldwide, Inc.
An International Data Group Company
919 E. Hillsdale Blvd.
Suite 400
Foster City, CA 94404

Library of Congress Catalog Card No.: 96-78772

ISBN: 0-7645-3017-8

Printed in the United States of America

10 9 8 7 6 5 4 3 2 1

1B/SW/RR/ZW/FC

Distributed in the United States by IDG Books Worldwide, Inc.

Distributed by Macmillan Canada for Canada; by Computer and Technical Books for the Caribbean Basin; by Contemporanea de Ediciones for Venezuela; by Distribuidora Cuspide for Argentina; by CITEC for Brazil; by Ediciones ZETA S.C.R. Ltda. for Peru; by Editorial Limusa SA for Mexico; by Transworld Publishers Limited in the United Kingdom and Europe; by Al-Maiman Publishers & Distributors for Saudi Arabia; by Simron Pty. Ltd. for South Africa; by IDG Communications (HK) Ltd. for Hong Kong; by Toppan Company Ltd. for Japan; by Addison Wesley Publishing Company for Korea; by Longman Singapore Publishers Ltd. for Singapore, Malaysia, Thailand, and Indonesia; by Unalis Corporation for Taiwan; by WS Computer Publishing Company, Inc. for the Philippines; by WoodsLane Pty. Ltd. for Australia; by WoodsLane Enterprises Ltd. for New Zealand.

For general information on IDG Books Worldwide's books in the U.S., please call our Consumer Customer Service department at 800-762-2974. For reseller information, including discounts and premium sales, please call our Reseller Customer Service department at 800-434-3422.

For information on where to purchase IDG Books Worldwide's books outside the U.S., contact IDG Books Worldwide at 415-655-3021 or fax 415-655-3295.

For information on translations, contact Marc Jeffrey Mikulich, Director, Foreign & Subsidiary Rights, at IDG Books Worldwide, 415-655-3018 or fax 415-655-3295.

For sales inquiries and special prices for bulk quantities, write to the address above or call IDG Books Worldwide at 415-655-3200.

For information on using IDG Books Worldwide's books in the classroom, or ordering examination copies, contact the Education Office at 800-434-2086 or fax 817-251-8174.

For authorization to photocopy items for corporate, personal, or educational use, please contact Copyright Clearance Center, 222 Rosewood Drive, Danvers, MA 01923, or fax 508-750-4470.

About the Authors

Glenn Weadock is president of Independent Software, Inc., a consulting firm he founded in 1982 after graduating from Stanford University's engineering school. One of the country's most popular technical trainers, Glenn is a Microsoft Certified Professional on both Windows 95 and Windows 3.1. He has developed six intensive, two-day seminars for Data-Tech Institute, most recently "Supporting and Troubleshooting Windows 95." He has also written and presented four technical Data-Tech videos.

As a presenter, Glenn has taught Windows troubleshooting to thousands of students in the U.S., U.K., and Canada in more than 150 seminars since 1988. He has been using PowerPoint for years in his seminars and videos. Glenn is the author of *Bulletproof Your PC Network*, *Bulletproofing Windows 95*, and *Exploding the Computer Myth*, and is coauthor of *Bulletproofing NetWare* and *Bulletproofing Client/Server Systems.*

Emily Weadock is the Director of Independent Software's Digital Art Studio. An award-winning computer artist whose work has been featured in international contests and magazines, Emily's talent ranges from technical illustration to broadcast-quality 3-D animation and multimedia development.

An expert on both Macintosh and PC platforms, Emily creates the PowerPoint slide shows for Glenn's seminars and videos. She is also an experienced illustrator, with five books to her credit. Before trading brushes for mice, Emily enjoyed success as a mixed-media construction artist and studied art at SMU and Baylor University.

ABOUT IDG BOOKS WORLDWIDE

Welcome to the world of IDG Books Worldwide.

IDG Books Worldwide, Inc., is a subsidiary of International Data Group, the world's largest publisher of computer-related information and the leading global provider of information services on information technology. IDG was founded more than 25 years ago and now employs more than 8,500 people worldwide. IDG publishes more than 275 computer publications in over 75 countries (see listing below). More than 60 million people read one or more IDG publications each month.

Launched in 1990, IDG Books Worldwide is today the #1 publisher of best-selling computer books in the United States. We are proud to have received eight awards from the Computer Press Association in recognition of editorial excellence and three from *Computer Currents'* First Annual Readers' Choice Awards. Our best-selling *...For Dummies®* series has more than 30 million copies in print with translations in 30 languages. IDG Books Worldwide, through a joint venture with IDG's Hi-Tech Beijing, became the first U.S. publisher to publish a computer book in the People's Republic of China. In record time, IDG Books Worldwide has become the first choice for millions of readers around the world who want to learn how to better manage their businesses.

Our mission is simple: Every one of our books is designed to bring extra value and skill-building instructions to the reader. Our books are written by experts who understand and care about our readers. The knowledge base of our editorial staff comes from years of experience in publishing, education, and journalism — experience we use to produce books for the '90s. In short, we care about books, so we attract the best people. We devote special attention to details such as audience, interior design, use of icons, and illustrations. And because we use an efficient process of authoring, editing, and desktop publishing our books electronically, we can spend more time ensuring superior content and spend less time on the technicalities of making books.

You can count on our commitment to deliver high-quality books at competitive prices on topics you want to read about. At IDG Books Worldwide, we continue in the IDG tradition of delivering quality for more than 25 years. You'll find no better book on a subject than one from IDG Books Worldwide.

John Kilcullen
President and CEO
IDG Books Worldwide, Inc.

Eighth Annual Computer Press Awards 1992

Ninth Annual Computer Press Awards 1993

Tenth Annual Computer Press Awards 1994

Eleventh Annual Computer Press Awards 1995

To our newborn twins, Cecily and Carina, for graciously lying quietly in your cribs while we gave birth to this book.

Credits

Senior Vice President and Group Publisher
Brenda McLaughlin

Acquisitions Manager
Gregory S. Croy

Software Acquisitions Editor
Tracy Lehman Cramer

Marketing Manager
Melisa M. Duffy

Managing Editor
Andy Cummings

Editorial Assistant
Timothy J. Borek

Production Director
Andrew Walker

Supervisor of Page Layout
Craig A. Harrison

Development Editor
Susan Pines

Copy Edit Coordinator
Barry Childs-Helton

Copy Editors
Kerrie Klein
Judy Brunetti

Technical Reviewers
Margie Hart
Paul M. Summitt

Project Coordinator
Katy German

Layout and Graphics
Ritchie Durdin
Elsie Yim

Quality Control Specialist
Mick Arellano

Proofreader
Christine Sabooni

Indexer
David Heiret

Production Administration
Christopher Pimentel

Book Design
Diann Abbott
Theresa Sánchez-Baker
Kurt Krames

Acknowledgments

We're pleased to thank particularly the following individuals and companies for helping make this project both possible and better:

Our literary agent and friend, Mike Snell; Greg Croy, Sue Pines, Kerrie Klein, Judy Brunetti, Margie Hart, Tracy Cramer, and their colleagues at IDG Books Worldwide; and, in alphabetical order by company, Dave Walters of 3D/Eye; Christy Cameron and Patricia Pane of Adobe Systems; Steven Chan of Caligari Corp.; Debbie Derana of Crystal Graphics; Daryl Wise of Fractal Design; Tammy Wing of Image Club; Holly Fisher of MetaTools; Christine Dykstra of MindPath Technologies; Shannon Brown of Micrografx; Dave Martinez of Microsoft; Sophia McShea of PhotoDisc; Jennifer Gervasi of Publishers Depot; Stacey Moran of Sonic Foundry; and Michele D'Amour of Waggener Edstrom.

(The publisher would like to give special thanks to Patrick J. McGovern, who made this book possible.)

Foreword

This book is what every PowerPoint presenter has been waiting for. It is an invaluable guide for presenters who want to jump out of the box of canned PowerPoint presentations and reach new heights of excellence. *Creating Cool PowerPoint 97 Presentations* is more than just another book to adorn the presenter's bookshelf — it is one of those rare books meant to be read and reread. It is meant to have penciled notes in the margins and paper clips on important pages.

When I was invited to write the Foreword for *Creating Cool PowerPoint 97 Presentations,* I was skeptical about the value of another book on PowerPoint. PowerPoint itself comes with good user and technical support, and for those readers desiring additional ideas, numerous books are available on giving effective presentations — in fact, Claudyne Wilder and I had just published a tome on using a laptop for that task. Thus, I had doubts about the need for another PowerPoint book. How wrong I was!

Creating Cool PowerPoint 97 Presentations takes the reader on a voyage of discovery into the world of presentations, where many people venture — but often with disastrous results. It guides the reader to a higher level of presentation quality. It includes hundreds of tips and practical ideas on visual design, working with sound and video, improving speed and transition smoothness, transporting files, and more. The chapters on visual design alone make this book required reading for every presenter.

The book never loses sight of the purpose of a presentation — to communicate a clear set of messages to the audience. Electronic presentations are not meant to show off technology or graphic design talent. They are not ego-extensions of the presenter. They are, however, incredibly powerful tools to convey messages and stir the emotions of the audience. My favorite chapter on this subject is "Enough Versus Too Much." It will challenge you to rethink elements of your presentation — guaranteed!

This book is required reading for everyone who uses PowerPoint and aspires to create truly great presentations. Keep it close at hand — you will refer to it frequently!

David Fine
Toronto, Canada
Coauthor of *Point, Click, and Wow! A Guide to Brilliant Laptop Presentations* (written with Claudyne Wilder)

Contents at a Glance

Table of Contents

Introduction

In 1988, when we got started in the business of writing and presenting technical seminars, the standard presentation involved lots of black-and-white overhead transparencies, a couple of flip charts, and perhaps a markerboard or whiteboard. When we introduced *color* transparencies, our audiences were duly impressed and thought we were very slick professionals indeed.

Today, the increased power of portable PCs and advances in computer projection devices have made computer-based slide shows the preferred method of communicating in all types of meetings, from sales presentations to seminars. Overhead transparencies, flip charts, and 35mm slides are becoming passé in the wake of the more flexible, powerful, and visually dynamic PC slide show. And audiences are not so easily impressed as they were several years ago.

Programs for creating PC slide shows were many and varied only three years ago, but Microsoft's PowerPoint for Windows is clearly today's computerized presentation standard, having sold millions of copies. Why? PowerPoint has steadily improved over the years, but it is not a perfect product by any stretch. Its great popularity today owes much to the strength of Microsoft Word and Excel, which PowerPoint comes bundled with the market-leading Microsoft Office software suite.

PowerPoint has also become popular because a non-artist can easily and quickly prepare an acceptable-looking slide show with PowerPoint's built-in color schemes, backgrounds, and templates. And that's what most PowerPoint slide shows are: acceptable, even attractive, but with a definite "canned" feel. Although that doesn't necessarily matter to someone who has never seen a PowerPoint slide show before, the canned look does reduce the impact for those people who have, and they are fast becoming the majority.

When most people attempt to vary from the preset templates and designs, however, the result unfortunately looks like it was done by someone with no background in art, color, or design — which is almost always the case.

Just as desktop publishing software doesn't work without some attention to traditional page layout principles, PC presentation software doesn't succeed if users do not have any background to help them discern what looks sharp and what looks clunky, cluttered, or just plain ugly.

Why This Book?

We wrote this book to help the general user do two things: (1) break free from the canned slide show styles to create some original-looking presentations, and (2) do so in a pleasing, attractive, and impressive manner that conveys the presenter's points clearly and professionally. *Creating Cool PowerPoint 97 Presentations* will help persons with no artistic background maximize PowerPoint's capabilities and design informative, persuasive, and impressive slide shows.

Several books on PowerPoint are in print, but they mainly focus on the mechanics of the product and read much like detailed user manuals. This book is different in four main ways:

- We're concerned with you creating and delivering knock-'em-dead presentations, using PowerPoint as your main tool. We therefore include topics that most other books don't, such as presentation hardware and tips for presenters.
- We're not here to tell you how to use every single PowerPoint feature in complete detail (other books do that). We're here to help you use PowerPoint to create slide shows that look great. So, throughout the book, we offer a grab bag of aesthetic suggestions that will help your work look professional.
- We take you "outside the box" and show you how to combine PowerPoint with other tools — such as Photoshop, Kai's Power Tools, and Premiere — to create presentations with that extra polish and shine that distinguish the impressive from the mundane, and that leave an audience saying "Wow!" instead of just "OK."
- This book covers both the Windows 3.1 version of PowerPoint, which has sold more than 6 million copies, as well as the two versions for Windows 95, Version 7 (released with Microsoft Office 95) and Version 8 (also known as PowerPoint 97, released with Office 97).

Intended Audience

Creating Cool PowerPoint 97 Presentations is for anyone who needs to prepare a PC presentation, from an entrepreneur courting investors to a project manager seeking management support for a new product or service.

This book is written for not-necessarily-technical PC users who are familiar with Windows 3.1 or Windows 95 and who already know their way around PowerPoint's menus and views, at least at the beginner level. If you've already taken a stab at creating your first slide show, you're probably ready for this book.

This book presumes no reader familiarity with the basics of visual design: color, screen layout, and so on. Though written by a technical expert (Glenn) and a graphics artist (Emily), this book is not *for* technical experts or graphics artists.

Organization

The broad organization of the book moves from design to presentation and (generally) from simpler topics to more complex ones. You can read it straight through and it will make sense; many of the later chapters build on the earlier ones. Or you can use this book as a reference, consulting each chapter as needed.

Part I of this book takes you from the beginner to the intermediate level in as short a time as practical. (After all, we want to get to the cool stuff as soon as we can!) Parts II, III, and IV build on the foundation laid in Part I to show you how to use PowerPoint more creatively and effectively. The topics covered here include PowerPoint's building blocks: templates, backgrounds, text, clip art, charts, graphs, and drawings.

Those of you who've already used PowerPoint to create slide shows should probably not skip Part I entirely, because you may find some capabilities you didn't know about or haven't used yet. You may want to skim it and read what interests you. If you've worked with Version 4 but not Versions 7 or 8, you may find reading Part I worthwhile in order to begin understanding what's new and different with the Windows 95 versions. And if you've worked with PowerPoint but it has been awhile, Part I provides a convenient and concise refresher course.

In Part II, we do two things: Show you how to *combine* PowerPoint's building blocks in a visually sophisticated way and demonstrate how you can *jazz up* the basic elements with the help of third-party software. The end result is customized presentations that break away from the canned feel of so many boilerplate PowerPoint slide shows. The topics covered here include customizing your presentations' screen layout, bitmaps, illustrations, clip art, special text effects, and builds and transitions.

Most of what's covered in Part II is well within what PowerPoint's designers had in mind: that is, displaying still graphics. In Part III, we sail adventurously away from the shore and into the uncharted waters of integrating multimedia (sound, animation, and digital video) into PowerPoint slide shows by using Windows' OLE (object linking and embedding) technology.

Part IV concerns itself with preparing and delivering the actual presentation. This part covers moving PowerPoint files between computers, getting your presentation hardware ready for action, tuning PowerPoint for speed, handling troubleshooting situations, and applying some presentation tips for the day of the show.

Appendix A provides detailed information on companies mentioned in the book, as well as on books and magazines of interest.

Icons

Here are some of the icons used throughout the book, along with their meanings:

warning — Warnings have to do with PowerPoint bugs, limitations, non-intuitive or counter-intuitive procedures, or simply common mistakes that PowerPoint users tend to make. Whenever possible, we give you the workaround or solution.

tip — Tips are pointers that we've found valuable. Often, they consist of clever or unusual applications of existing PowerPoint tools or features. Other times, they are bits of advice on slide show aesthetics.

version 8 — The Version 8 icon indicates that the associated comment only applies to PowerPoint 8 for Windows 95, also known as PowerPoint 97.

version 7 — The Version 7 icon indicates a comment applying only to PowerPoint 7 for Windows 95, also known as PowerPoint 95.

versions 7 & 8 — The Versions 7 & 8 icon indicates a comment applying to both PowerPoint Versions 7 and 8.

version 4 — The Version 4 icon indicates a comment applying only to PowerPoint 4 for Windows 3.*x*.

versions 4 & 7 — The Versions 4 & 7 icon indicates a comment applying to both PowerPoint Versions 4 and 7.

versions 4, 7 & 8 — The Versions 4, 7, & 8 icon indicates a comment applying to all three PowerPoint versions.

CD-ROM

The enclosed CD-ROM is full of very cool stuff, from tryout versions of top graphics programs to sample images from graphics vendors. We've also included PowerPoint slides that illustrate many of the concepts presented in the book. Appendix B provides some more information on the contents of the CD-ROM.

Feedback

We'd be delighted to know how you liked this book and to hear about any PowerPoint tips you've discovered that you think we should mention in the next edition. You can reach us at 71140,2031 on CompuServe. (Internet users, send e-mail to `71140.2031@compuserve.com`.)

Glenn & Emily Weadock
Evergreen, Colorado

PART I

POWERPOINT BASICS

Part I familiarizes you with PowerPoint's core features in as short a time as practical. Parts II, III, and IV build on Part I's foundation to show you how to use PowerPoint more creatively and effectively. The topics covered in this part include PowerPoint's building blocks: templates, backgrounds, text, clip art, charts, graphs, and drawings.

If you've already used PowerPoint to create slide shows, you should probably not skip Part I entirely, because you may find some capabilities you didn't know about or haven't used yet. You may just want to skim it and read what interests you. If you've worked with Version 4 but not Versions 7 or 8, read Part I to learn what's new and different with the Windows 95 versions. And if you've worked with PowerPoint but it's been awhile, Part I provides a convenient and concise refresher course.

Masters, Templates, and Presentations

1

In This Chapter

Discovering the jobs for which PowerPoint is well suited and its limitations

Learning how to use PowerPoint masters to save development time

Learning to combine and save masters and color schemes as templates for consistency and convenience

Determining the difference between design and content templates

Using PowerPoint wizards to help create masters and templates

Learning which information gets saved in a presentation file

Discovering how PowerPoint resolves conflicts in slide designs

This first chapter briefly tells you what PowerPoint is (and is not) and then moves on to a discussion of PowerPoint's underlying design — specifically, the different types of *masters* and *templates* that we'll be working with throughout the book to create cool *presentations.*

What PowerPoint Is — and Isn't

A technical person would probably define PowerPoint as an application program for creating and presenting an *electronic slide show*, or sequence of images. Although that definition is accurate as far as it goes, we prefer to think of PowerPoint as a *communications tool* that you use to inform and persuade others. If you think of PowerPoint in this way, too, you'll automatically create more effective presentations.

A presentation-oriented tool

PowerPoint is, first and foremost, a slide-oriented presentation tool. Whether you use it to create a computer-based presentation for delivery with an LCD panel or projection system (see Chapter 18), 35mm slides, or even just printed graphical handouts that accompany your talk, PowerPoint was designed around the assumption that you'll be delivering a linear presentation to two or more people in a meeting room or auditorium.

Having said that, it's worth noting that the software add-ins to PowerPoint 7, and the new features built into Version 8, enable you to create Internet-compatible versions of your slide shows that you can publish on the World Wide Web or on intranet Web servers. Chapter 22 explores these capabilities in-depth.

Although you can use PowerPoint to create interactive, multimedia computer-based training (CBT) programs, the program was not designed for that purpose. Better CBT tools are available, such as Macromedia's Director and Asymetrix's Toolbook.

A text- and graphics-oriented tool

Microsoft designed PowerPoint around the building blocks of text and graphics. Part III shows how to embed sound and video into your PowerPoint presentations, especially with Versions 7 and 8 — a powerful way of jazzing up your slide shows — that is, if you have the appropriate delivery hardware (good multimedia speakers, for example). PowerPoint works best, however, when most of your content is in textual or still-graphic form, with multimedia accents.

A glue application

Think of PowerPoint as a *glue application* that combines text with the graphics and multimedia clips that you create by using other single-purpose programs. In this respect, PowerPoint is like a desktop publishing program that *glues* text from a word processor together with graphics from a paint or image editing program.

Much of this book discusses how to use other programs to create art that you can integrate into your slide shows with PowerPoint. Although you can use PowerPoint to make drawings and graphical backgrounds, its built-in tools are limited compared with what you have available in programs such as Adobe Photoshop, Metatools's Kai's Power Tools, Adobe Illustrator, and Fractal Design Painter (demos of which are included on the bundled CD-

ROM, among others — see Appendix B for details). You certainly don't have to master all these programs to create cool PowerPoint slide shows, but a casual familiarity with them will be a big help.

PowerPoint strengths

PowerPoint has two main strengths, detailed in the following bullets: It's widely available as part of the Microsoft Office program family, and it makes learning learn how to create simple slide shows easy:

- Microsoft Office, which also contains Word, Excel, Access (in the professional version), and Schedule + (or its successor, Outlook, in Office 97), is, hands-down, the most popular *suite* of office automation programs for the PC. PowerPoint's inclusion in Office means three things: Most people already have it; many menus and commands are similar to other Office programs; and PowerPoint can work (in a limited way) with other Office programs.

Just because Office includes PowerPoint doesn't mean that PowerPoint shares all the customizability features of Excel, Word, and Access. For example, though you can customize the PowerPoint toolbars and set preferences via Tools⇨Options in Versions 4 and 7, you can't write PowerPoint macros, nor can you write program modules in the Visual Basic programming language, until Version 8 (which provides both features). Later, you'll see that these restrictions do not limit you as much as you may think. For example, a PowerPoint slide show is, in many ways, like a giant macro itself. Furthermore, you probably don't have the time or inclination to learn Visual Basic anyway!

- We created our first PowerPoint slide show in one afternoon without ever having seen the program before. True, it was an exceptionally boring slide show, but it looked reasonably sharp. And the fact that we delivered it directly from the computer was enough to wow the audience. (Of course, computer-driven slide shows aren't that unusual today.)

Although it's easy to create a "canned" (boring) slide show in PowerPoint, most users don't go on to learn how to create cool (exciting) slide shows, because the learning curve gets a little steeper. This book flattens that learning curve and shows you, as quickly and painlessly as possible, how to go beyond the basics and create fantastic and cool presentations without having to become a computer graphics genius.

The more adept you are at using PowerPoint, the more effectively you will communicate with it. But before you can go beyond the basics, you must master them — fortunately, that's not an especially tall order. Once you understand masters, templates, and presentations, you're well on your way.

Because this is an intermediate-level book, it doesn't explain all the different parts of the basic PowerPoint screen (toolbars, menus, and so on) or the different views (Slide View, Slide Sorter View, and so on). The PowerPoint help system and user manual does that well, as do half a dozen introductory books. If you're not already familiar with PowerPoint's toolbars and views, we recommend that you spend some time with one or more of these other references before proceeding (the online help is probably all you'll need).

Masters

A *master* is a modifiable default specification for a slide show component (such as — you guessed it — a slide!). PowerPoint uses a master automatically unless the designer overrides it, therefore reducing the amount of redundant work required to build a presentation. For example, if you want your company's name to appear at the bottom of every slide, place it onto the Slide Master (one operation) rather than on each individual slide (many operations). PowerPoint provides the following masters:

- Slide Master
- Title Master (Versions 7 and 8 only)
- Handout Master
- Notes Master
- Outline Master (Version 4 only)

The Slide Master

Of the five master types, the Slide Master is the one you'll probably spend the most time creating and customizing. Any graphics, text, and backgrounds you place on the Slide Master will automatically appear on every slide in the presentation, in the position specified on the Slide Master. You can override any or all of these choices on a per-slide basis.

To work with the Slide Master, follow these techniques:

- Choose View⇨Master⇨Slide Master. You see *placeholders* for the different levels of text titles and bullets (see Figure 1-1). PowerPoint 7 and 8 add placeholders for the date, footer, and slide number.
- To change the style of any text on the Slide Master, select the text with the arrow cursor to highlight it and choose Format⇨Font, and then make your changes from the Font dialog box. You can also use the drop-down font name and size listboxes on the formatting toolbar.

- Add any text or graphic elements you'd like to appear on most slides in the presentation. You can always edit individual slides so that master elements don't appear.
- Once you've defined your Slide Master, new slides that you add with the Insert⇨New Slide command will adhere to the Slide Master design.

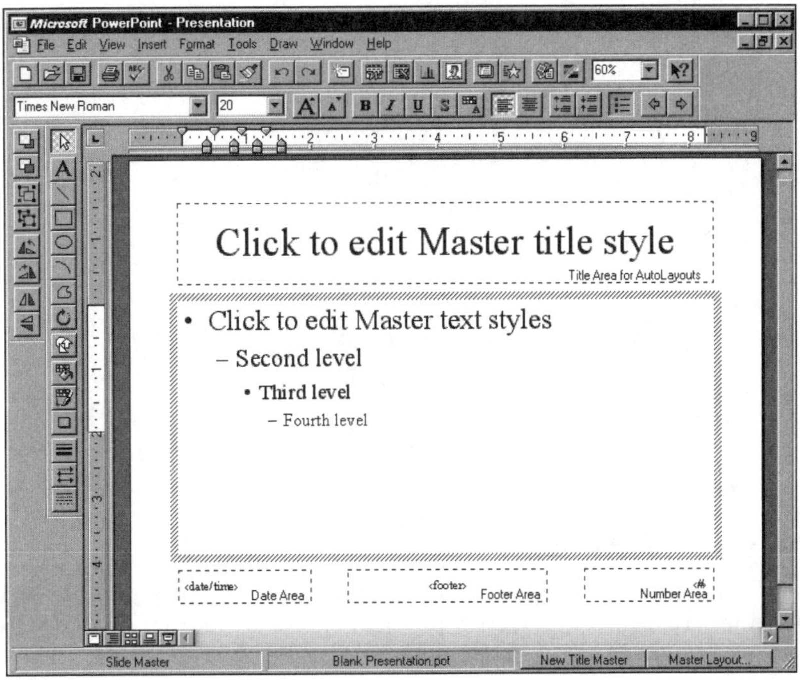

Figure 1-1: The Slide Master in PowerPoint 7, showing placeholders for slide title and body text.

Title Master

versions 7&8

By default, the Title Master has the same settings as the Slide Master, but you can change these settings to specify different ones for title slides. To work with the Title Master, select View⇨Master⇨Title Master.

You can modify the text type, size, and placement just as you did in the Slide Master. You can also insert clip art or bitmap graphics onto the Title Master with the Insert commands.

tip

If the Title Master menu option is grayed out because no Title Master exists yet for a specific presentation, view the Slide Master and click the New Title Master button at the bottom of the screen (Version 7) or select Insert⇨New Title Master (Version 8).

After you modify the Title Master, you can apply its formatting to the slides you want to be title slides, such as the presentation's opening slide and the slides that introduce new sections. The Title Master is handy in that it frees you from having to format each title slide individually, in detail. Select the slide in Slide Show view and specify the Title Slide AutoLayout by clicking Format⇨Slide Layout and choosing the box in the upper-left corner of the window (see Figure 1-2). The Title Master formatting is applied to the slide. (*AutoLayouts* are predefined slide layouts that Microsoft has provided for convenience.)

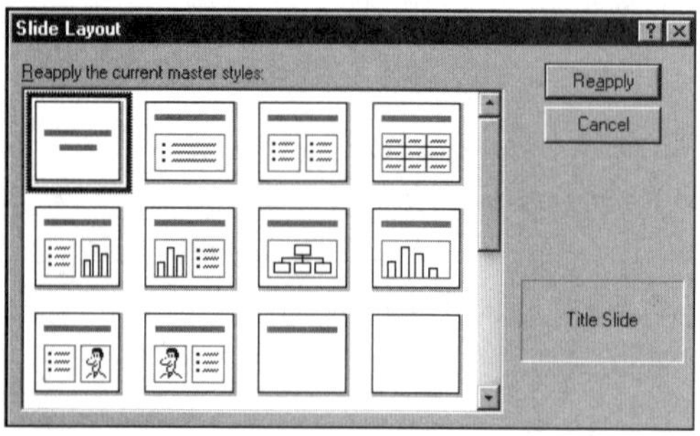

Figure 1-2: Choosing the Title Slide AutoLayout.

Handout Master

versions 4, 7 & 8

Handouts are printouts of your slides; you can use them yourself or pass them out to your audience members so they can follow your presentation and refer to your slides afterward. You can print handouts at two, three, or six slides per page.

You may not need to modify the default "look" of these handouts if they're for your own use, but you may want to jazz them up if you're going to distribute them. You can modify handout appearance by using the Handout Master. To see it, choose View⇨Master⇨Handout Master.

At the Handout Master screen (Figure 1-3), you can insert text (for example, page headers and footers) as well as artwork (such as for borders), as long as the inserted material falls outside the boundaries indicating where the actual slides will print.

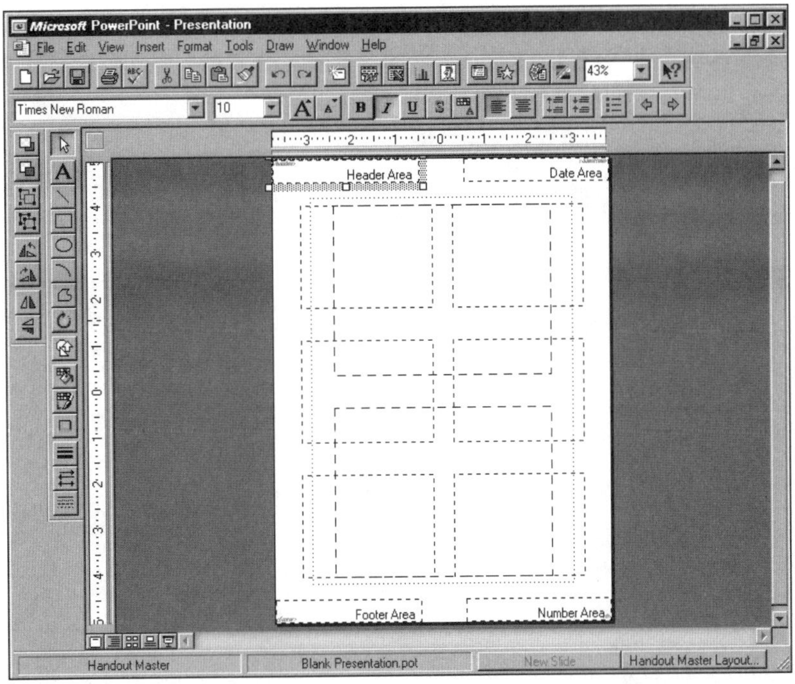

Figure 1-3: PowerPoint 7's Handout Master screen, showing optional headers and footers (dashed lines indicate where slides will print). Version 8's screen adds a toolbar that permits easy selection of two, three, or six slides per page.

version 4

Here are some details on modifying the Handout Master:

- Add the date to your Handout Master by clicking the text tool on the page to create a text box, choosing Insert⇨Date, and then moving the text box to where you want it with the arrow cursor. The symbol for the date is // and will be replaced by the actual date at print time.
- Similarly, add the time with Insert⇨Time. The symbol is : :, which is replaced by the actual time at print time.
- Add the page number with Insert⇨Page Number. The symbol is ##, which, again, is updated at print time.

versions 7&8

- To change the positioning, typeface, and content of the date, time, header, footer, and page number text boxes even though they're all preset on the Handout Master, edit them just as you would any PowerPoint text object.

- To control whether the date is fixed or automatically updated at the time of printing, select View⇨Header and Footer. You'll see the screen shown in Figure 1-4.

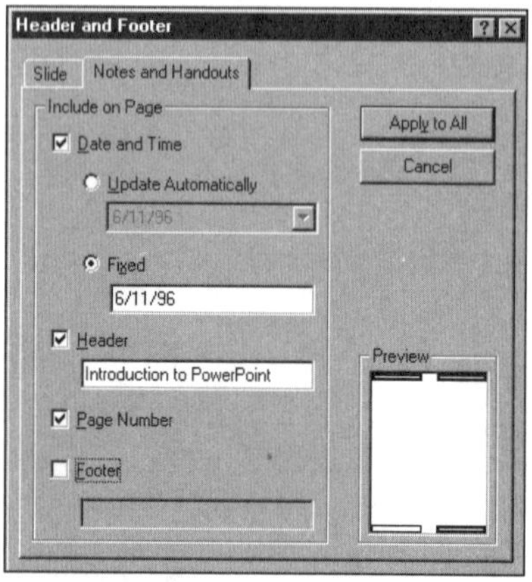

Figure 1-4: Here's where you define the date type and header/footer text for the Handout Master in Versions 7 and 8.

- Add text anywhere outside the slide boundaries by clicking the text tool (the letter *A*, or an *A* in a text box on Version 8's Drawing toolbar) and then clicking on the Handout Master screen.
- To change the style of any text on the Handout Master, click on the text box to highlight it. Choose Format⇨Font and then make your changes from the Font dialog box. You can also use the drop-down font name and size listboxes on the formatting toolbar.
- Print your handouts with File⇨Print; in the Print What field, specify Handouts and the number of slides you'd like per page (two, three, or six). In Versions 7 and 8, you can check the Frame Slides field to print a thin black border around the slides, which is useful if you're using a light-colored background.

If you choose three slides per page, the slides appear on the left of the page and lines for notes appear on the right side — a nifty feature.

Notes Master

Speakers' notes are text attachments to each slide that you can print out; they remind you of key points as you give your presentation. You can create titles, headers and footers, visuals, and page numbers with the Notes

Master just as you can with the Handout Master. Here are a few tips on working with the Notes Master:

- To view the Notes Master, choose View⇨Master⇨Notes Master.
- To modify the font and point size of each indented level, highlight the text line in the notes area and choose Format⇨Font, or use the drop-down font name and size listboxes on the formatting toolbar.
- To change the indent spacing, choose View⇨Ruler, click on the text line you want to change, and move the tab stops as desired (Figure 1-5).
- After you're done configuring the Notes Master, you can create notes while building your presentation. Select View⇨Notes Pages or click on the Notes Pages View button in the toolbar at the lower-left corner of the screen (this button is fourth from the left).

Merely tabbing to indent lines on the Notes Page View won't trigger the typestyle you designed on the Notes Master. You have to use the right-arrow button on the formatting toolbar (the "Demote – Indent More" button).

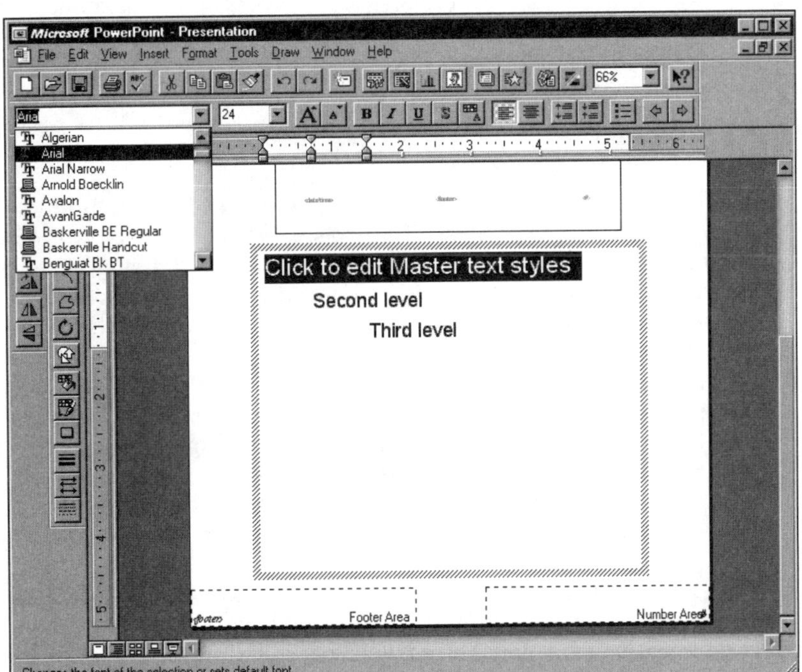

Figure 1-5: Configuring the Notes Master's typeface, size, and tab stops.

When you work with the Notes Master or when you create slide notes, magnify the notes box to make it easier to see by selecting View⇨Zoom or by clicking on the zoom percentage on the standard toolbar. A zoom factor of less than 66 percent is probably too small.

versions 7&8

- Although the date, time, header, footer, and page number are all preset on the PowerPoint 7 and 8 Notes Master, you can change their positioning, typeface, and content just as on the Handout Master.
- Choose View⇨Header and Footer to control whether the date is to be fixed or updated automatically at the time of printing.

Outline Master

version 4

PowerPoint outlines enable you to work with slide titles and body text in a classical outline organizational form. The Outline Master in PowerPoint 4 enables you to add special text (such as headers, footers, page numbers, and so on) that appears when you print your slide show outline. It's pretty minimal — you just get a blank page, with nothing preformatted for you — but otherwise, the Outline Master works the same way as the Handout and Notes Masters. To view the Outline Master, select View⇨Master⇨Outline Master.

versions 7&8

The Outline Master is only available in Version 4. In Versions 7 and 8, the Handout Master format applies to outlines and handouts, which in practice works well. So, if you want headers and footers on your outlines in Version 7 or 8, make the appropriate changes on the Handout Master.

Templates

You can conveniently combine master settings (such as the Slide Master and, in Versions 7 and 8, the Title Master) and a slide show color scheme (eight colors, each for specific slide elements) into a single file to create the basis for a new PowerPoint slide show. PowerPoint provides this capability in the form of *templates*. Templates, therefore, are models for creating new presentations.

Templates are great for standardizing slide shows with a consistent look and feel; they also save time when you're creating several presentations. The temptation is to use only the predefined templates Microsoft provides with the PowerPoint product, but you later see that it's easy to modify them or even make your own templates for a cooler, more customized look.

tip

For no particularly good reason that we can figure out, templates do *not* incorporate the Handout Master, Notes Master, or Outline Master. These master settings are only stored with individual presentation files, which have a *.PPT extension (presumably for PowerPoinT).

Version 4 has only one kind of template; Versions 7 and 8 have two. We first take a look at the kind common to all three versions — design templates.

Design templates

A PowerPoint *design template* defines the look of your slide show and consists of the following items:

- Slide Master elements (fonts, bullet types, background, animations [Version 8], and so on)
- Title Master elements (Versions 7 and 8 only)
- Slide show color scheme

Version 4 calls the design template a *template,* and Versions 7 and 8 call it a *design template.* For consistency, this book uses the term *design template.*

In Version 4, design templates use the same file extension as presentations — that is, *.PPT — and contain a single slide. In Versions 7 and 8, design templates use a different extension — *.POT, presumably for POwerpoint Template — and don't actually contain any slides.

Microsoft provides several "canned" design templates that you can open, edit, and save; in Version 8, some of these templates even include animation effects. The general technique is as follows:

1. Open a design template file (*.PPT in Version 4; *.POT in Versions 7 and 8) with File⇨Open (and make sure that Files of Type is set at *.POT for Versions 7 and 8). PowerPoint 7 and 8 typically store design templates in \MSOffice\Templates\Presentation Designs, and Version 4 stores them in \Powerpnt\Template. You'll see a dialog box such as the one shown in Figure 1-6.
2. Choose the Slide Master View with View⇨Master⇨Slide Master and make any changes you like.
3. Save your changes by choosing File⇨Save in Version 4, or File⇨Save As with the *.POT file type specified in Versions 7 and 8.

Be careful to perform a Save As rather than a Save operation in Version 7 or 8 if you want to preserve the original template!

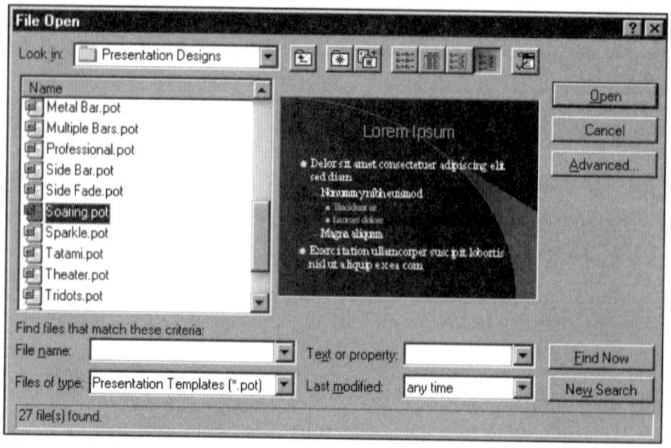

Figure 1-6: Opening a design template in Version 7 or 8. The Version 4 dialog box is similar.

You can apply a design template to a new slide show by choosing File⇨New and clicking the Presentation Designs tab in Version 7 or 8, or by choosing File⇨New⇨Template in Version 4.

To apply a design template to an existing slide show, simply open the slide show and choose Format⇨Apply Design (Version 8), Format⇨Apply Design Template (Version 7), or Format⇨Presentation Template (Version 4). Then select the design template you want from the dialog box. The Slide Master settings and slide show color scheme in the design template will replace the same elements in the original slide show.

In PowerPoint 4, once you apply a design template, you can't remove it — that is, you can't click Edit⇨Undo to reverse the operation. So, be sure to save your work before you apply a design template. Thankfully, this limitation is gone in Version 7.

Also in PowerPoint 4, applying a design template destroys any previous formatting you've made for Handout Masters and Notes Masters. This bug was fixed in Version 7.

The default design template typically resides in the main PowerPoint folder as DEFAULT.PPT. To reset a slide show to the default design, select Format⇨Presentation Template, navigate up to the main PowerPoint folder, and choose DEFAULT.PPT.

The default design template typically resides in \MSOffice\Templates as Blank Presentation.POT. To reset a slide show to the default design, select Format⇨Apply Design (Version 8) or Format⇨Apply Design Template (Version 7), navigate up to \MSOffice\Templates, and choose Blank Presentation.POT.

The Blank Presentation.POT file only contains a Slide Master and does *not* contain a Title Master. It's funny that way — all the other design templates have both Slide and Title Masters.

PowerPoint uses *wizards* to automate common procedures. PowerPoint 4's *Pick-a-Look* wizard, accessible by a button on the standard toolbar, guides you through choosing a design template and specifying masters options (see Figure 1-7). PowerPoint 7 and 8's *AutoContent* wizard duplicates the Pick-a-Look wizard's functionality and takes it a few steps further, as you'll see in the next section on presentation or "content" templates.

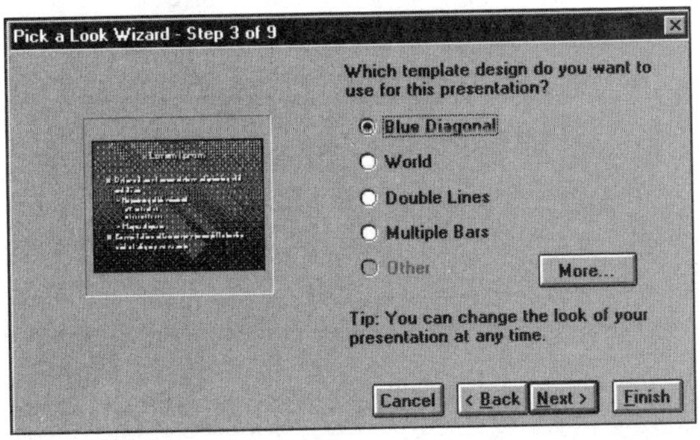

Figure 1-7: Setting design template and masters options with PowerPoint 4's Pick-a-Look wizard.

Content templates

PowerPoint 7 and 8 add a second type of template called a *presentation template* in Version 7 and a *content template* in Version 8 (they're the same thing, and we'll use the newer term henceforth). Content templates contain everything a design template contains, as well as elements that aren't on the Slide or Title Masters but that you want to appear on individual slides. Microsoft calls such elements *boilerplate.*

For example, if you wanted to create a template in which the final slide includes the text *Thank You for Your Attention* and an embedded *"ta-daa"* sound, you'd make a content template, because a design template doesn't contain specific text and sounds.

You may never need to use content templates if your standard slide show designs don't need to contain anything besides the standard master elements. If you move from PowerPoint 4 to Version 7 or 8, however, spend some time with the content templates to see if they can save you some development time.

To apply a content template to a new slide show, select File➪New and click the Presentations tab. Then choose from the existing templates, as shown in Figure 1-8.

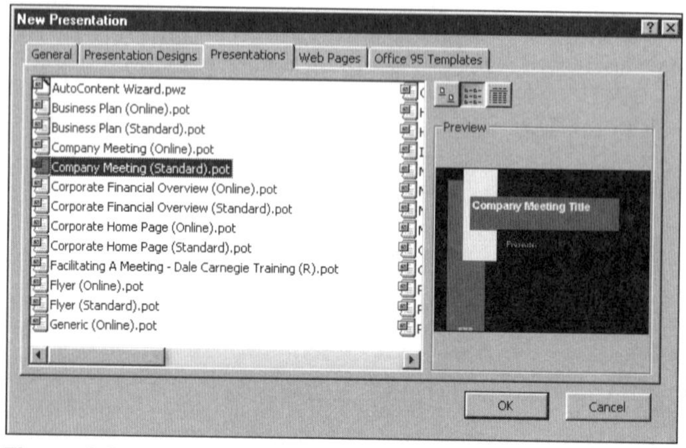

Figure 1-8: Applying a content template to a new slide show in PowerPoint 8.

You wouldn't really want to apply content templates to existing slide shows, because the boilerplate elements won't carry over. Content templates are designed for new slide shows. Nineteen come predefined with PowerPoint 7; none are especially good-looking or use cool graphics, though Company Meeting, Creativity Session, and General aren't too bad. Thirty-eight content templates ship with Version 8, although only 19 designs are really available, each having a variant for Web publishing (see Chapter 22). Business Plan, Corporate Financial Overview, Corporate Home Page, H.R. Information Kiosk, and Marketing Plan have some attractive design features. The templates from Dale Carnegie Training have some fun features, such as graphic elements that bleed off the edge of the slide, but the graphics often interfere with slide titles — a design "don't."

Content templates have the same file type (*.POT) as design templates; you can't tell the difference by looking at the filenames. Which leads us to the following tip.

Keep content templates in a separate directory from design templates:

- Use \MSOffice\Templates\Presentations for content templates
- Use \MSOffice\Templates\Presentation Designs for design templates

Don't be confused — Presentation Designs means the same as Design Templates. This directory name is the only place we've seen where Microsoft uses the Presentation Designs nomenclature. Focus on the word *design,* and you'll be fine.

tip

PowerPoint 7 and 8's AutoContent wizard, which is a somewhat souped-up version of PowerPoint 4's Pick-a-Look wizard, automates the process of building a presentation "look" by using content templates. This wizard offers a better, more flexible option than just selecting one of the predefined content templates. To access the wizard, select File⇨New⇨Presentations⇨AutoContent Wizard. You see the screen shown in Figure 1-9 in Version 7, and the screen in Figure 1-10 in Version 8.

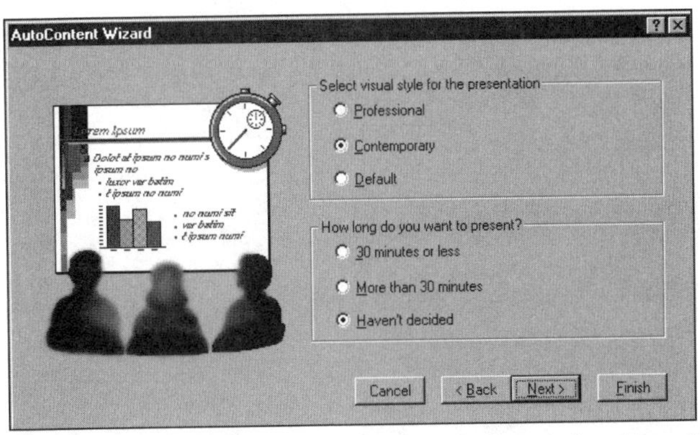

Figure 1-9: Using PowerPoint 7's AutoContent wizard to select and configure a content template.

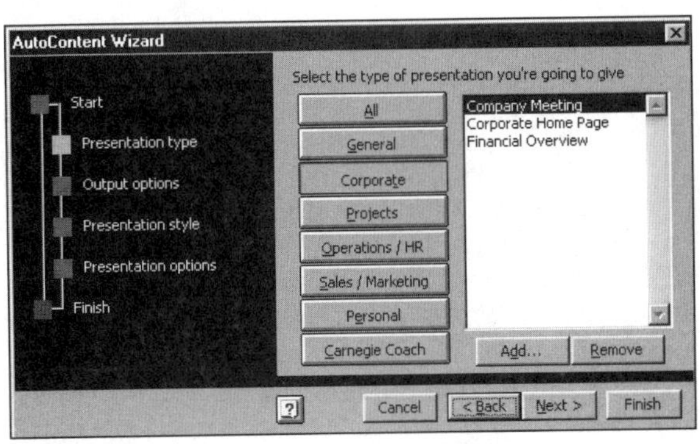

Figure 1-10: PowerPoint 8's AutoContent wizard adds new templates and presents a progress window on the left side of the dialog box.

Presentations

The third part of PowerPoint's architecture, after masters and templates, is the presentation itself. The finished presentation file (format *.PPT) contains the following:

- All "look and feel" formatting in the various masters, whether you created the presentation by using masters alone or from predefined design templates
- All unmodified boilerplates, if you used a content template (Versions 7 and 8 only)
- All text, graphics, and multimedia content added to each slide individually, including variances from the masters for particular slides
- Slide setup and view settings, such as slide sizing, page orientation, and so on — in short, everything you can see with File⇨Slide Setup (Versions 4 and 7) or File⇨Page Setup (Version 8), as shown in Figure 1-11

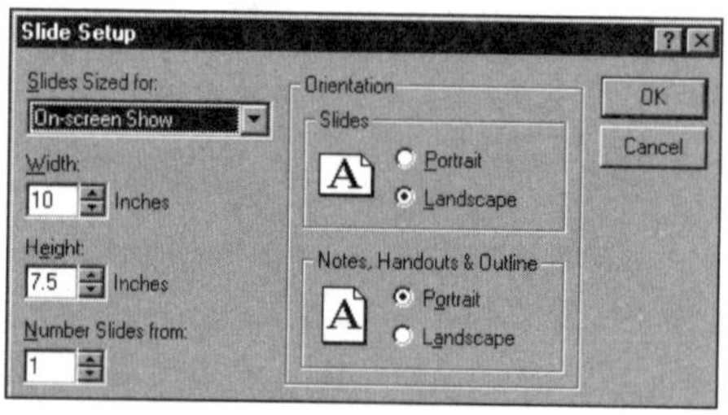

Figure 1-11: *Slide setup preferences are saved with *.PPT files.*

Masters and templates are just ways to create finished *.PPT presentation files conveniently and consistently. The presentation reflects all the design decisions made throughout the process, including specific variances from templates and masters, where appropriate.

warning

If you create a presentation based on a design template and then modify an element of that template, such as the Slide Master, only the *.PPT file is affected — that is, the original design template isn't modified. Similarly, if you use PowerPoint 7 or 8 to create a slide show based on a content template, any changes you make to the boilerplate text and graphics won't normally be saved to the original content template, but will just become part of the *.PPT file.

Conflicts

We've explored several ways to influence the way a given slide looks: Slide Masters, Title Masters, slide AutoLayouts, design templates, content templates, and individual slide settings. Who wins if a conflict occurs between two or more of these influences?

Microsoft put it succinctly in the *Office 95 Resource Kit* by saying "the setting closest to the slide has precedence." Here's the order to determine which design influence prevails in case of a conflict, with the highest priority influence first:

1. Settings made on a specific slide as an exception to the Slide or Title Master
2. A specific slide's AutoLayout (Format⇨Slide Layout in Versions 7 and 8, Format⇨Slide Layout in Version 4)
3. Settings made in the Slide Master or (Versions 7 and 8) Title Master
4. Settings made in the content template (Versions 7 and 8)
5. Settings made in the design template (Versions 4, 7, and 8)

Summary

This chapter has introduced PowerPoint as a communications tool.

PowerPoint is known for its presentation features, not as a CBT authoring tool; it's best for text and graphics content with multimedia accents, and you can create art in other programs that PowerPoint glues together into a slide show.

PowerPoint benefits from being part of the Microsoft Office suite in that it's widely available; the menus and commands are familiar to Word, Excel, and Access users; and PowerPoint has some features that work with other Office programs (such as importing outlines, discussed in Chapter 6).

The program is simple to learn for creating basic slide shows, but you must have a clear understanding of masters, templates, and presentation files to create cool slide shows.

Masters enable you to specify default settings you'd like to use throughout a presentation; templates offer a convenient way to save the Slide and Title Masters in a single file along with the color scheme.

You can use PowerPoint 4's Pick-a-Look wizard, or PowerPoint 7 and 8's AutoContent wizard, to automate the design process or at least create a starting point.

The final look of an individual slide depends on all these design influences, but the settings you make for a particular slide take priority over masters and templates.

If all of the preceding information makes sense to you, pat yourself on the back; you're already more sophisticated than most PowerPoint users, and well on your way to maximizing PowerPoint's capabilities!

Now that we've outlined PowerPoint's "big picture" architecture, the next four chapters fill in the details by examining the primary slide elements of backgrounds, text, clip art, and illustrations.

Backgrounds 2

In This Chapter

Understanding the role of backgrounds in a presentation

Balancing background consistency and variety

Modifying backgrounds for individual slides or slide groups

Using textures and pictures on backgrounds

Choosing background colors

Applying background effects

This chapter discusses how to use PowerPoint's built-in facilities to create cool backgrounds and provides some style pointers you won't find in the manual.

Creating the proper slide backgrounds for your presentation is important, because the backgrounds will set the mood for your entire slide show. Although you may find background creation difficult, it is one area in which your creativity can run wild. PowerPoint provides some cool tools that can miraculously transform you from amateur to pro. The more options you have, however, the easier it is to get carried away; you can work hours spicing up your backgrounds only to end up with way too much spice!

Keep the Background in the Background

Slide backgrounds are important, but only to frame the ideas your foreground elements present. When framing art, you never want to notice the frame first. Instead, the frame should complement the artwork, blending with it to complete the look as a whole. Think of your slide background as a picture frame that must never distract the audience's attention from your graphs, text, and clip art.

When in doubt, therefore, keep it simple. Too much razzle-dazzle in a background always works against you. As we'll show you, PowerPoint provides you with plenty of other, more suitable areas where you can wow the audience.

Keeping backgrounds simple doesn't imply that you shouldn't use sophisticated tools to create your backgrounds. When you have a little time, you can create your own textures and gradients using other applications to give your backgrounds a customized look. Chapter 7 discusses how to use Photoshop, Kai's Power Tools, and KPT Bryce to create cool bitmaps that you can use as slide backgrounds. With the tips Chapter 7 provides, you don't have to be an expert in these programs to produce great results. For now, however, this chapter focuses on the tools you can use within PowerPoint itself.

tip

Create your backgrounds *last*, and focus on completing the main body of your presentation first. When you finish with the text, charts, and so on, you have a better idea of the mood you want to set and the style of your presentation. At that point, you can insert an appropriate background.

We write from experience. Once, we created several beautiful backgrounds as the first task in a presentation project. The backgrounds looked great with the slide blank, but because of the complexity and size of the graphs and flowcharts we dropped in later, the backgrounds were almost completely hidden. We ultimately used a simple, bright background that took much less time to create, so the time spent creating the complex original backgrounds was wasted. Rule of thumb: Reserve multicolor, highly textured, or complicated backgrounds for text slides only.

Consistency or Variety?

Favoring variety over consistency and changing your background with every slide can result in a disjointed, distracting presentation. If you remain consistent throughout the presentation, you enable your audience to focus on what's important, which is why PowerPoint uses the concept of a Slide Master. If you're planning to use the same background for every slide, or at least for most slides, you can create it in the View⇨Master⇨Slide Master screen, so you don't need to change each slide individually.

Remember, the Slide Master differs from the Title Master in that the Title Master elements only apply to slides you've formatted to use the title slide AutoLayout.

Selectively disabling Slide Master graphics

tip You can have individual slides vary from the Slide Master's background, color scheme, and text details by simply making those changes to the slide. For example, choose Format⇨Background (Version 8), Format⇨Custom Background (Version 7), or Format⇨Slide Background (Version 4).

warning You can only disable the graphic images that you place on the Slide Master as a group on a per-slide basis, by choosing Omit Background Graphics from the Master in the Background dialog box (Figure 2-1). That is, you can't selectively show one Slide Master graphic while you hide another one, except by disabling all Slide Master graphics and then re-importing the graphics you want for that particular slide. Moral: Just put the graphics you want on every slide, such as a company logo, onto the Slide Master.

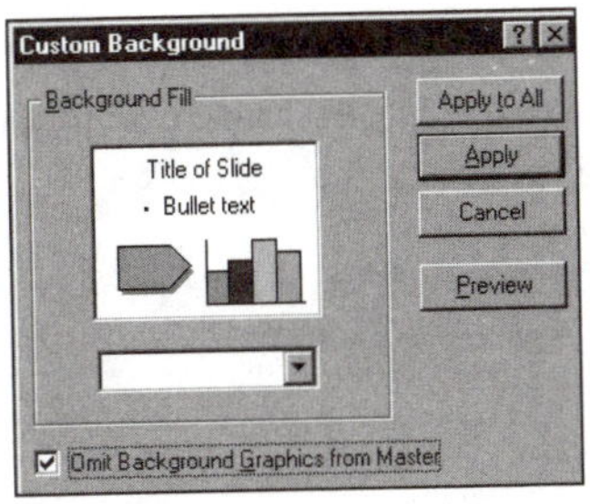

Figure 2-1: Omitting Slide Master background graphics from a particular slide.

Backgrounds as organizers

If your presentation runs long (say, more than 30 minutes), a background color change may help keep it alive. You may want to use a specific color to denote a group of related thoughts or topics.

Example: Suppose that you're presenting a slide show about your project team to a group of managers planning next year's budgets. You organize your show as follows:

1. The first 20 slides cover the project overview — rationale, goals, and team profile — with a blue-to-white gradient background on each slide. (We show you how to create such gradients later in this chapter.)
2. The next 14 slides cover project costs, budgets, and projected revenues; these slides have a green-to-white gradient.

The background color scheme change helps the audience organize the presentation in their minds, and it can even be subtly mnemonic (the green section is the one about money).

warning

It's unfortunate that in situations such as the presentation discussed earlier, PowerPoint doesn't permit you to create multiple slide masters for different sections of a slide show. If you want to vary the background, you must perform the slide formatting manually, though the copy and paste commands make the process a little less burdensome when you work with imported bitmap backgrounds. You can't apply a template to an individual slide, either; the rule is "one slide show, one template." If you use PowerPoint 4, however, see the following cool technique.

The Format Painter

version 4

PowerPoint 4 users can use a little-known shortcut that helps speed the process of duplicating a background over a single slide or a group of slides — the Format Painter. Here's how to use it:

1. Select Slide Sorter View and highlight the slide with the background you want to apply to another slide.
2. Click the Format Painter tool (which looks like a wide paintbrush) on the standard toolbar. Notice that your arrow cursor is now accompanied by a small paintbrush icon that moves with it.
3. Click the slide to which you want to apply the background.

To "paint" multiple slides in this manner, in Step 2, *double-click* the Format Painter instead of single-clicking it. Notice that the button has toggled on and stays depressed. To apply the background, click on as many slides as you like. After you finish, click the Format Painter tool to deselect it.

warning

This convenient use of the Format Painter tool didn't make it into PowerPoint 7 or 8, though the tool can still change text object attributes (pattern, shadow, font, and so on). Format Painter doesn't work with pictures and graphs, either.

Textures and Pictures

If your presentation has an overall theme that lends itself to a visual image, consider pulling your slides together with a background *texture* or *picture*. For example

- A presentation reviewing the marketing strategies for a new line of office chairs might use a background texture that looks like the chair's fabric.

- A training presentation for camp counselors might have a background picture of the sun setting over a lake, as in Figure 2-2.

Figure 2-2: Using a stock photograph from Kai's Power Photos as a topical background.

You can create a textured background by using the *textured fill* effect in PowerPoint 7 or 8, discussed later in this chapter. Or, with Version 4, 7, or 8, you can bring in the texture as a bitmap image that fills the entire slide.

Bringing in a full-screen picture or texture

To create a background image that fills the entire slide, follow these steps:

1. Select View⇨Master⇨Slide Master to display the Slide Master.
2. Select Insert⇨Picture to select the image (which can be in any of the graphics PowerPoint understands). These formats include Windows bitmap (*.BMP), Windows metafile (*.WMF), JPEG (*.JPG), Micrografx Designer/Draw (*.DRW), Macintosh PICT (*.PCT), Corel Draw! (*.CDR), PC Paintbrush (*.PCX), computer graphics metafile (*.CGM), Targa (*.TGA), and Tagged Image File Format (*.TIF). Scale the image, if necessary, to fill the slide.

You can buy stock images from vendors such as PhotoDisc (see Appendix A), use some of the sample files included on this book's CD-ROM or on the Office/PowerPoint CD-ROM, or create your own cool pictures, as we'll demonstrate in Chapters 7 and 8.

3. Select Draw⇨Send to Back to allow other objects to be seen in front of the background.

This method creates an image that is fully selectable and resizable from the Slide Master View.

versions 7 & 8

Although this method also works for PowerPoint 7 and 8, the following method creates a *nonselectable* background, which may be more convenient in that you won't select it by accident when you work with other components on the Slide Master:

1. Select Format⇨Custom Background (Version 7) or Format⇨Background (Version 8).
2. In the Background Fill drop-down list, choose Picture (Version 7) or Fill Effects⇨Picture⇨Select Picture (Version 8), and locate the image you want to use.
3. Click Apply to All to tell PowerPoint that you want this image as part of the Slide Master (Figure 2-3). PowerPoint automatically scales the image to fit the screen.

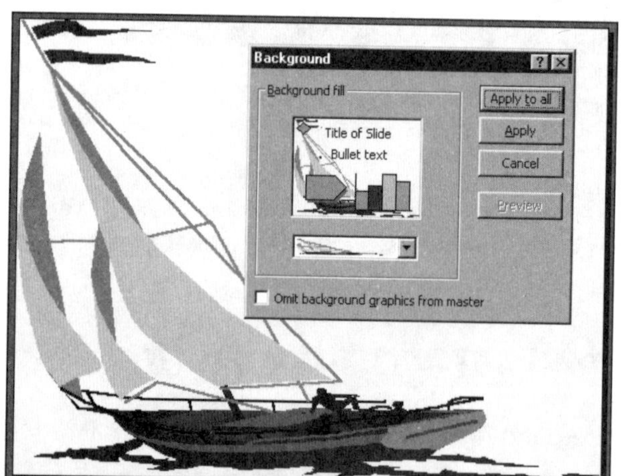

Figure 2-3: Importing a picture as a full-screen, nonselectable background prevents you from accidentally selecting the picture later.

Interestingly, although the image has effectively become part of the Slide Master, you can't select it from the Slide Master View. The only way to change this background image is to repeat the above process with a different picture.

Bringing in a partial-screen picture

You may want to bring in a graphic that doesn't fill the entire slide and make it part of your background. For example, a small company logo in the upper-right corner of the screen could dress up the slide show, as long as it's not so large or prominent that it becomes distracting. You also may want to apply a texture as a *border*, or a picture as an *inset*, if your slides begin to appear cluttered with full-screen background images. Background textures and pictures can be fun, but they can also be fussy and interfere with text and graphs.

Terminology note: Microsoft refers to such graphics as Slide Master objects — not part of the background.

To bring in a picture for a partial-screen background element

1. Select View⇨Master⇨Slide Master to display the Slide Master.
2. Select Insert⇨Picture to select the image, which can be in any of the graphics formats PowerPoint understands. Scale the image to the desired size, and move it to where you want it.
3. Select Draw⇨Send to Back, or Draw⇨Order⇨Send to Back in Version 8, to enable other objects (such as titles) to be seen in front of the picture, if they would be obscured by it otherwise.

Chapter 7 presents detailed tips on creating your own background textures and pictures with other graphics applications.

Background Color

Cooler colors (such as the blue, green, and purple families) have a nice "feel" to them and are pleasing to the eye; these colors make good backgrounds. If you must use hot colors (such as reds, oranges, and yellows), select a less saturated (that is, less intense) hue. Mix in a little black or white to tone down these colors. Don't assault your audience with a glaring orange or brilliant red background; it only distracts them and leaves them squinting. Save hot colors to emphasize an important pie chart segment or an escalating sales-figure line diagram.

PowerPoint 4, 7, and 8 use the concept of *color schemes,* as mentioned in Chapter 1. Each scheme contains eight complementary colors, which correspond to screen elements such as text, shadows, background fills, and so on The schemes available change depending on the design template you use.

If you stay within a slide show's color scheme when choosing a background color or color gradient, and you switch to a different color scheme later, PowerPoint will replace your original background color with one of the colors in the new scheme. On the other hand, if you choose a background color that's *not* in the original color scheme, it will *not* automatically change if you switch to a different color scheme later. You may, therefore, have to change it manually to avoid clashing with the foreground colors in the new scheme.

You can use "other colors" (that is, non-scheme colors) two ways in PowerPoint backgrounds: with the *standard palette* and with the *custom palette*. Although you can also use these palettes for text and graphics elements, we introduce them here in the context of backgrounds, because this is the first place you're likely to encounter them.

The standard palette lets you choose from a wider group of colors than the template color scheme, though you're still limited to 128 choices. To get to the standard palette, do the following:

version 4

- Select Format⇨Slide Background⇨Change Color. You'll see a rectangular choice box.

versions 7&8

- Select Format⇨Custom Background, click the down arrow, and, in the expanded menu, scroll down to Other Color. (Select Format⇨Background and scroll to More Colors in Version 8.) You'll see a hexagonal color picker, as shown in Figure 2-4.

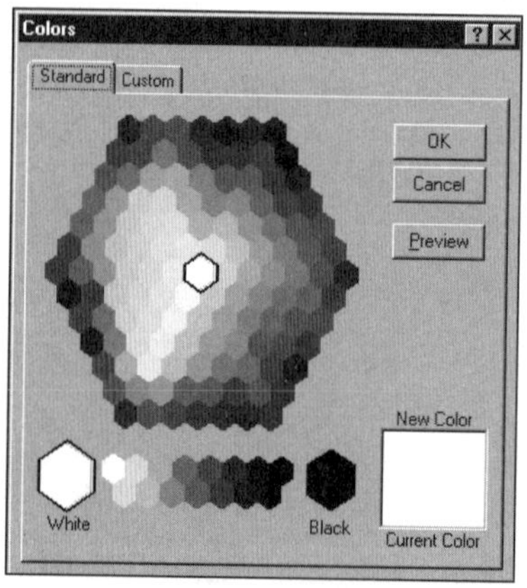

Figure 2-4: PowerPoint 7 and 8's standard palette color picker is quick and convenient.

The custom palette enables you to use a more sophisticated dialog box that permits you to directly key in exact numerical color values, or use a bull's-eye that scoots around the rainbow of colors and works in combination with a slider that controls luminance levels. To get to the custom palette:

version 4

- Select Format⇨Slide Background⇨Change Color⇨More Colors.

versions 7&8

- Select Format⇨Custom Background, click the down arrow, and, in the expanded menu, scroll down to Other Color and click the Custom tab. (Select Format⇨Background and scroll to More Colors in Version 8.) You'll see the hue, saturation, and luminance window, as shown in Figure 2-5. (We'll define these terms in a minute.)

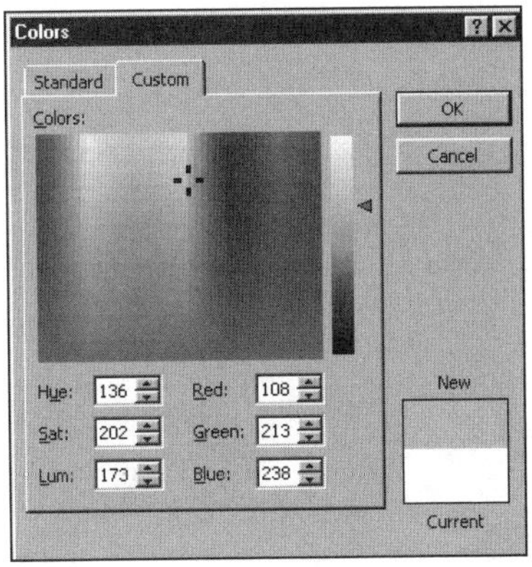

Figure 2-5: PowerPoint 8's custom palette color picker offers greater control than the standard palette color picker. (Version 7 offers the same capability.)

tip

You can use your own non-scheme color (either off the standard palette or the custom palette) for a background, without adding it to the current template's color scheme. Remember, though, that your custom color won't automatically change if you change to a different eight-color scheme later.

versions 4,7&8

The custom palette is oriented around the Hue, Saturation, and Luminance color model (HSL).

After navigating your way to the custom palette, you're now in complete control of the colors you choose. To turn your arrow cursor into a bull's-eye, just click and drag in the palette rectangle.

Here's how you use the bull's-eye cursor in the custom palette:

- To change the hue, move the bull's-eye horizontally and then apply a different color.
- To change the saturation, which affects the intensity or level of gray in the color, move the cursor vertically. Higher saturation values mean more intense colors (less gray).
- Finally, to provide this color space's third dimension, luminance, leave the bull's-eye cursor stationary, but drag the arrow on the slider bar (next to the color rectangle) up or down. Luminance, or luminosity, affects the amount of black and white added to a color.

To match a color precisely, for example, from a Pantone color swatch, type in numeric values using the fields at the bottom of the custom color picker screen. PowerPoint provides both HSL and Red–Green–Blue (RGB) models, so you can use whichever one feels most comfortable. Let's define the RGB model.

In the RGB system (which many third-party paint programs also use), you simply specify the relative amounts of each color (red, green, and blue) up to the maximum of 255. In RGB (also called *additive* color), black corresponds to 0 – 0 – 0 and white corresponds to 255 – 255 – 255 (PowerPoint 7 and 8) or 65535 – 65535 – 65535 (PowerPoint 4).

Artists may be more familiar with HSL, and computer users may be more familiar with RGB. Or, if you're uncomfortable with color models altogether, you can always move the bull's-eye cursor around the custom color picker screen until you find a color you like!

When you've decided on a color, the nearest solid color your video card and monitor can display will appear in the *solid* color box at the lower-left corner of the screen. The *color* box attempts to simulate the color more accurately through *dithering* — that is, a pattern of different-colored dots in close proximity. With a high-color or true-color display, these two boxes appear identical, and the feature is absent in Versions 7 and 8.

Darker backgrounds work best when you're creating 35mm slides. For overhead transparencies, however, use lighter background colors. Another good idea is to use light colored backgrounds if you're planning to deliver a presentation using an LCD panel connected to a computer, so you won't have to dim the room lights quite as much.

Background F/X

In addition to textures, pictures, and colors, PowerPoint offers several special background effects, such as gradients and fills. Versions 7 and 8 go far beyond Version 4 in this area, but PowerPoint 4 does have some one-color gradient shading effects with different geometries that you can use to good effect.

Have you ever seen a movie where the opening scene and the introductory credits were almost the same color value? Reading white text against a snow-covered mountain background is nearly impossible; don't make the same mistake when you design gradient backgrounds.

Effects you can create with PowerPoint 4

To create a single-color gradient background, select Format⇨Slide Background to display the dialog box in Figure 2-6. Select your color by clicking the Change Color button at the lower-left corner of the screen. You can now select from the standard palette, or click the More Colors button for the custom palette. Next, choose the gradient style you want by combining choices from the center box labeled Variants and the Shade Styles box on the left. To vary the gradient fill's spectrum range, move the Dark/Light slider control and watch the change in the Variants boxes. When you're happy with your choices, select Apply to modify the current slide only, or Apply to All to modify the Slide Master.

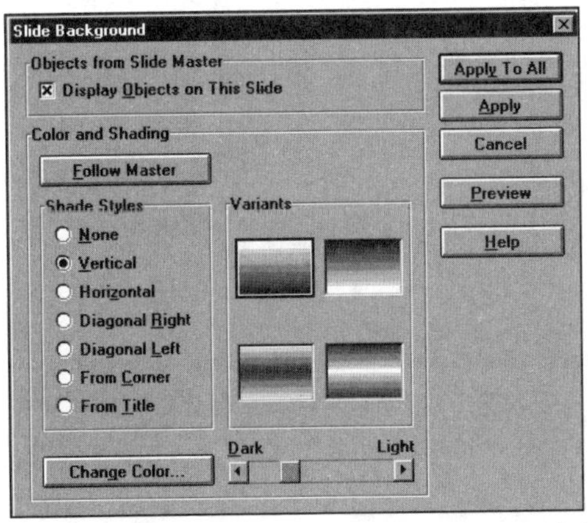

Figure 2-6: PowerPoint 4's Slide Background dialog box lets you choose from several gradient patterns.

tip

To create a gradient that appears to have two colors, for example, purple and pink, move the slider to dead center. You'll notice that the Variants selections are now solid. Now move the slider one or two clicks to the left or right, and you'll have a two-toned effect with the same hue. The effect works better with some colors than others, so spend a little time experimenting.

versions 4, 7&8

After opening the Background dialog box, move it off to the side to see as much of the slide underneath as possible. When you finish creating your background, use the Preview button to see if you like it before returning to slide mode.

versions 4, 7&8

You can achieve a cool, simulated 3-D effect by shading foreground objects with gradients that move in the opposite direction from your background gradient. For example, shade the background dark to light from top to bottom, and shade selected foreground objects light to dark from top to bottom. See this book's color insert for an example of this *opposing gradients* technique, which lends balance to your overall slide design and makes the foreground objects seem to "pop out" in relief.

warning

PowerPoint stores color information internally by using 24-bit data for a palette of 16.7 million colors. If you create a great-looking presentation on a system that has 24-bit color display capability and then present the same show on a computer with a 256-color (8-bit) display, PowerPoint will perform *palette management.* That is, PowerPoint will select the most-used 256 colors out of the 16.7 million in the internal palette and create a new palette — not just for the presentation as a whole, but for each change or slide where the program feels it's necessary to optimize a new palette.

Palette management can be a problem if your slide has numerous gradients or requires more than the maximum 256 colors. You can experience *banding* in the gradient layers, and some colors may just drop out, with or without an error message. Moral: Know your delivery platform's hardware capabilities before going wild with gradient-filled backgrounds and foreground objects.

Effects that require PowerPoint 7 or 8

versions 7&8

To see several background looks, such as Shaded, Patterned, Textured, Picture, and Other Color, select Format➪Custom Background (Version 7) or Format➪Background (Version 8) and click the drop-down list box. Make a selection; then to apply it to the current slide, click Apply; to apply it to all slides, click Apply to All. This section provides more details on the background effects.

Shaded fill

From the drop-down list box, select Shaded (Version 7) or Fill Effects➪Gradient (Version 8). You have three choices under Colors: One Color, Two Color, and Preset Colors.

One Color allows you to create a gradient with one interesting color and black or white. This option is just like PowerPoint 4's gradient option; a slider controls the amount of black or white added. As you move the slider, the change appears in the Shade Style boxes.

Two Color allows a gradient effect between two selected colors and eliminates the Dark/Light slider (Figure 2-7). After creating a look, click OK in Version 7, and a small preview of the custom background appears. In Version 8, the miniature preview is always visible in the Sample box at the lower right. To preview the slide underneath, click the Preview button.

Preset Colors is a group of ready-made backgrounds (such as Fire, Ocean, Rainbow, Gold, and so on). Most of these backgrounds are fairly unattractive and even garish, but Nightfall, Daybreak, Parchment, Mahogany, and Gold aren't bad. To avoid that "canned" feel, stay away from the presets.

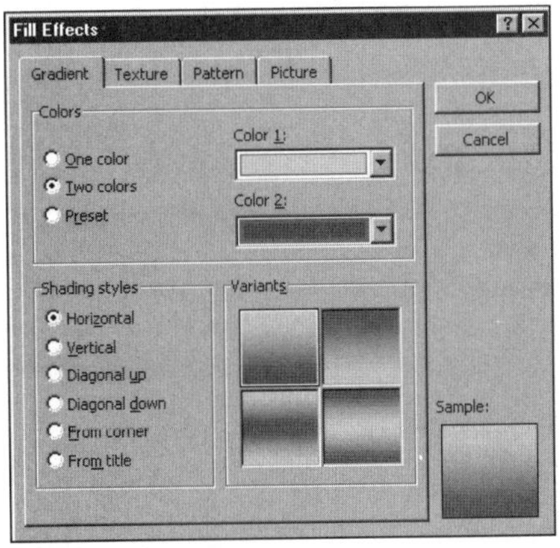

Figure 2-7: PowerPoint 8's two-color gradient fill provides more artistic flexibility than Version 4's one-color gradient. Version 7's dialog box omits the Sample window.

Patterned fill

From the drop-down list box, select Patterned (Version 7) or Fill Effects⇨Pattern (Version 8), and choose a desired preset pattern from the options shown. As you try different foreground and background colors, the Pattern Fill boxes change with your selections. Choose smaller, tighter patterns if you plan to use text in the slide foreground. Choosing similar foreground and background pattern colors produces a richer, subtler, and less fussy texture.

Textured fill

From the list box, select Textured (Version 7) or Fill Effects⇨Texture (Version 8), and choose one of the textures provided. Version 7 offers 12 choices: Oak, Walnut, Medium Wood, Brown Marble, White Marble, Green Marble, Sand, Cork, Granite, Paper, Cloth, and Woven Mat (Figure 2-8). Version 8 doubles that number, although some of the new choices may not be widely applicable (Fish Fossil, Water Droplets). You can also click Other and specify any bitmap image you like. Experiment with the Windows 95 wallpaper bitmaps (*.BMP), which usually reside in the C:\WINDOWS directory.

Picture fill

From the list box, click Picture (Version 7) or Fill Effects⇨Picture (Version 8) and find a filename. (We discussed this option earlier in the chapter.)

Other Color fill

From the list box, click Other Color (Version 7) or More Colors (Version 8), remembering that in PowerPoint lingo, "other color" refers to any color out-

:olor scheme. In the Colors window, you can select a color
: Standard Color tab or the Custom Color tab.

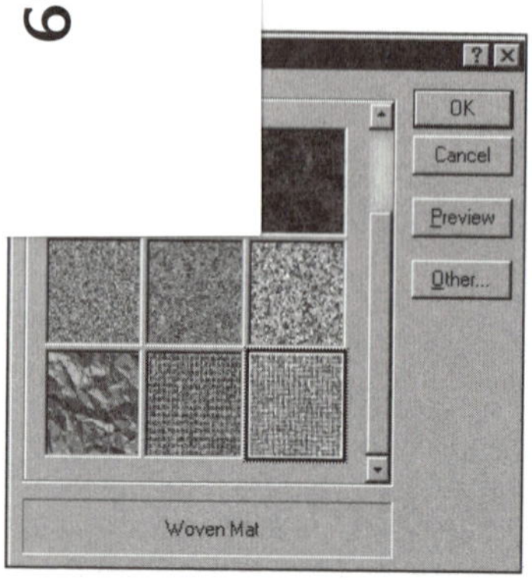

Figure 2-8: PowerPoint 7 and 8's Textured fill offers some attractive background possibilities.

Summary

In this chapter, you've learned that the proper role of the slide background in a presentation is to underscore foreground items and not distract from them.

Consistency is a virtue for all but the longest presentations, in which background changes can help the audience mentally organize the slide show's different sections.

Textures or pictures should match and enhance the presentation's theme, and background colors should generally be *cool* rather than *hot*.

The standard and custom palettes don't automatically change when you select different color schemes, but they offer unlimited color choices.

Background gradients and other special effects can add panache, especially when foreground elements use opposing gradients, but gradients require displays capable of more than 256 colors to look great.

Now that you've learned about slide show structure and how to set the stage with backgrounds, you're ready to focus on that most important of foreground elements — text.

Text

3

In This Chapter

Using TrueType and PostScript fonts

Justifying and aligning text

Creating cool shadow effects

Using embossed text

Using AutoShapes with text

Rotating text

Using AutoCorrect in Versions 7 and 8

Creating special characters and symbols

Chapter 1 discussed PowerPoint's underlying structure and organization, whereas Chapter 2 examined graphics backgrounds. The rest of Part I deals with *foreground* elements: text (the most common and important element), clip art, charts, graphs, and drawings. We start here with text — the slide show's backbone.

Most PowerPoint presentations rely heavily — even exclusively — on text, and Microsoft has provided several tools and options for creating good-looking slide text. Getting the most out of PowerPoint's text tools involves knowing a few tricks, however, which we explore here in a text-basics crash course.

Then in Chapter 10, we expand the topic further and explore using the included WordArt utility to create even cooler text effects that go beyond the basics you learn here.

The Pleasures (and Risks) of Scalable Fonts

Fonts are the building blocks of text. Windows users typically work with *scalable* fonts — that is, fonts that can be scaled up or down to any size. The two types of scalable fonts in Windows are *TrueType*, which is supported "out of the box" by Windows, and *PostScript*, which is supported by a separate program called Adobe Type Manager (ATM for short, see Figure 3-1). A side benefit of using scalable fonts is *device independence;* the look of the fonts remains approximately the same regardless of the output device.

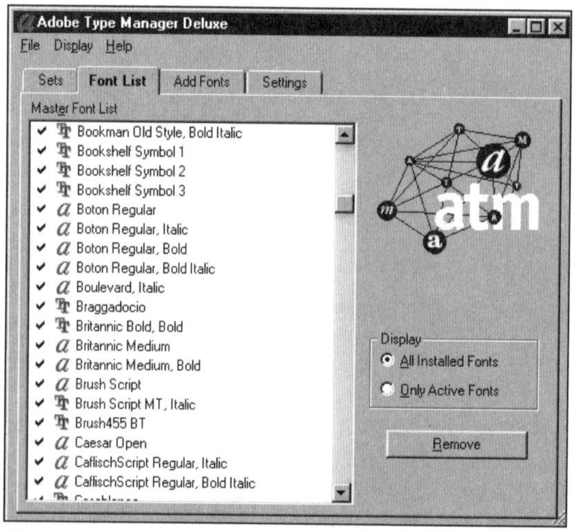

Figure 3-1: Adobe Type Manager's control panel manages PostScript fonts, which don't appear in Windows' Fonts control panel. ATM 4.0, or ATM Deluxe (shown), also manages TrueType fonts now.

You can use either TrueType or PostScript fonts in PowerPoint slides. Life is a little simpler if you stick with TrueType — all Windows PCs support TrueType automatically — but the universe of high-quality fonts available to you increases if you also use PostScript.

Using ATM

If you use ATM with Windows 95, make sure that you have Version 3.02 or later and that you do your PostScript font management (installs, deletes, and so on) from the ATM control panel to ensure that the relevant *.INI files are properly updated. ATM Version 4.0 (ATM Deluxe) for Windows 95 adds convenient features such as font sets and TrueType management, although it still has trouble displaying rotated PostScript fonts correctly in PowerPoint 7.

ATM 3.*x* is incompatible with Windows 95 when the video board's graphics acceleration slider has a setting of None (run the System control panel and select Performance⇨Graphics). Set the slider to any other position, and ATM should work fine. Also, don't install ATM 3.*x* into the Windows\Fonts folder; ironically, ATM won't work from there!

Changing the default font

You can change the font used in the title or main body of your presentation slides by using the Slide Master, as discussed in Chapter 1. You can change the default font used elsewhere on slides in Versions 7 and 8 by making your choices in the Format⇨Font dialog box and clicking Default for new objects. In Version 4, use the following "secret" procedure:

1. Open DEFAULT.PPT.
2. Create a text object on the screen and format it according to the new default setting you want (such as with Format⇨Font).
3. Select the text object (not just the text — look for handles to appear around the object).
4. Select Format⇨Pick Up Object Style. Press Esc to deselect the object.
5. Select Format⇨Apply to Defaults. Delete the text object and save the file using any name you like.

Using font embedding

To make sure that your text displays properly on a different computer, PowerPoint provides a feature called *font embedding* that enables you to include TrueType fonts with your presentation. (Using font embedding will increase the size of your PPT files, though not by a great deal.)

To embed fonts with a particular file, select File⇨Save As and click Embed TrueType in Version 7 or 8, or Embed TrueType Fonts in Version 4.

If you use TrueType embedding and plan to give your presentation with any version of the standalone PowerPoint Viewer utility, your fonts may not display correctly unless they are installed through the Fonts control panel (or Fonts folder in Windows 95) of the delivery machine. Also, you may lose embedding information if you save the file in PowerPoint 4 format from Version 7 or 8. These problems negate the value of TrueType embedding unless you normally present from a PC running the full version of PowerPoint and always use the same version of PowerPoint when developing and delivering your presentations.

Furthermore, some TrueType fonts don't support font embedding, and you get a warning message when you try to save the file with embedding activated. Our advice: Always copy the actual font files to the delivery PC and then, to be on the safe side, install them on the machine, as long as your software license permits you to do so.

Justifying and Aligning Text

In PowerPoint, you can line up text along either the left or right margins, center it, or justify it so that it lines up along both the left and the right margins. Specify your alignment preference by selecting the text, choosing Format⇨Alignment, and then selecting the option you want.

When preparing a slide featuring a table of information, the easiest way to make sure that the columns of data align properly is to create a separate text box for each column and then align that column as an individual unit. Otherwise, if each row of text spans multiple columns, you have to spend a great deal of time adding and removing space characters to get the alignment looking right. (Trust us — we know from experience!)

Another professional touch is to use the same alignment for table headings that you do for the columns that appear below the headings.

If the text object has the Word-wrap Text in Object option deselected (in the Format⇨Text Box⇨Text Box dialog box in Version 8, or in the Format⇨Text Anchor dialog box in Versions 4 and 7), you won't be able to use the Justify alignment option, unless you first draw a text box.

Shadow Effects

One way to add legibility and even drama to slide text is by using shadows. The following sections describe how to create sharp-looking single and double shadows.

Single shadows

Although you may find it more convenient to apply the text shadow effect directly from the toolbar (by clicking the button with the letter *S* on the Formatting toolbar) or from the Font dialog box, you give up color and depth control by relying on the default setting. To regain that control, as well as the capability to choose a shadow direction other than down and to the right, click the Shadow button on Version 8's Drawing toolbar, or select Format⇨Shadow in Versions 4 and 7, instead.

Experiment with different combinations of font styles, shadow colors, and offset settings. Not all combinations are successful. Generally, heavier shadows (higher offset numbers, where offset is the text-to-shadow separation) work best with simpler fonts, whereas shallower shadows (lower offsets) look better with fancier fonts.

For a realistic shadow, set the Up/Down offset two points lower than the Right/Left offset.

For a realistic shadow, set the Up/Down offset two points lower than the Right/Left offset and then, with the Semi-Transparent box checked, select a nice gray as your color and choose a higher offset for deeper shadowing. Note for Version 8 users: From the Drawing toolbar, click the Shadow button and Shadow Settings to display the Shadow toolbar. The "nudge" buttons move your shadow one point at a time, but you can hold down Shift to move six points at a time. It helps to zoom in tight while fine-tuning a shadow. The Semitransparent option is now accessible from the Shadow Color button.

To realize the full impact of the Semi-Transparent setting in PowerPoint 7 and 8, use it with complex backgrounds so that you can see some texture coming through the shadow. When used with a solid background, the Semi-Transparent feature only shows a color change.

Double shadows

Double shadows are cool because they not only call lots of attention to the word but also reflect your imagination. They work best with simpler fonts. You can play with interesting colors in your double shadows and, in Versions 7 and 8, use the Semi-Transparent function. You will typically use double shadowing in informal presentations (Figure 3-2).

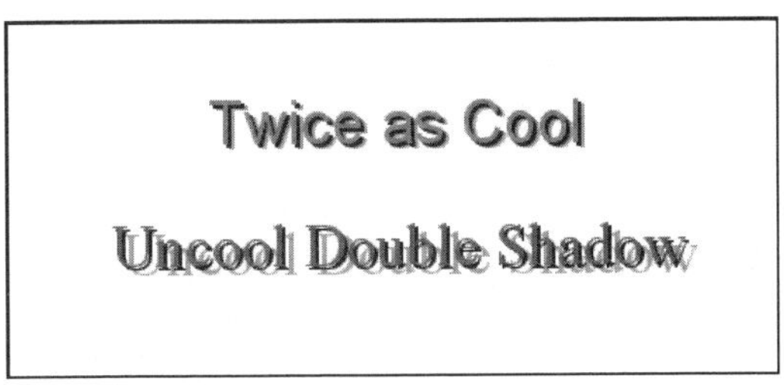

Figure 3-2: Cool and uncool double shadows. The double shadow on the top uses a tight offset and a clean font; the one on the bottom uses a larger offset and a serif font, which make it look busy.

To create a double shadow in PowerPoint 4 and 7, select your text and make sure that the text color is anything but black. Click on the Text Shadow button from the Standard toolbar to create the first shadow. Then, from the main menu, select Format⇨Shadow and set your offsets to Down 4 points and Right 6 points. From the Shadow dialog box, you can experiment with other offsets, colors, and (in Version 7) with the Semi-Transparent effect.

To create a double shadow in PowerPoint 8, select your text and make sure that the text color is anything but black. Click on the Text Shadow button from the Standard toolbar to create the first shadow. Then, from the Drawing toolbar, click the Shadow button and click Shadow Style 14. Click the Shadow button again, activate the Shadow Settings toolbar, and use the nudge buttons to fine-tune the shadow.

Embossing

To emboss text and give it a "raised relief" look, simply select Format⇨Font and check the Emboss check box. Figure 3-3 shows an example.

Figure 3-3: The art of embossing text. The embossing effect produces different effects with different backgrounds and text colors.

You should note a few points when working with embossed text:

- Embossed text takes on the same color as the background when you're using a solid colored background. For example, if the background color is a solid light gray, PowerPoint creates the embossed effect by applying a darker gray shadow down and to the right of the text and a white shadow up and to the left of the text. The text color becomes the same as the background color, a solid light gray.
- When using a Texture, Pattern, or Picture as your background, the text becomes white and PowerPoint applies a dark gray shadow down and to the right of the text.

- When using a gradient background in Version 7 or 8, the text uses Color 1 if you have a two-color gradient and Color if you use a one-color gradient.
- Embossing does not work with a black background.
- With a white background, you only see the dark-gray shadowing down and to the right of the text — a neat effect, but indistinct in smaller point sizes.
- Embossing works best with a heavier font style or with boldface fonts. Try embossing Courier New without boldface and then with boldface activated to see the difference!

My, What Shapely Text You Have

PowerPoint offers a variety of predesigned shapes, called AutoShapes, to create common drawing designs. But did you know that you can fill these shapes with text, and the text will conform to the shape exactly as you tell it? You can even resize the shape, and the text will adjust automatically (Figure 3-4), as long as you use the text anchor option.

Figure 3-4: Anchored text automatically adjusts to fill a resized bubble AutoShape. Note that many AutoShapes have adjustment points that appear as yellow diamonds when the shape is selected.

PowerPoint 8's much-expanded AutoShapes menu has been moved to the Drawing toolbar as a button that displays a submenu of categories: Basic Shapes, Block Arrows, Flowchart, Stars and Banners, Callouts, and so on (Figure 3-5).

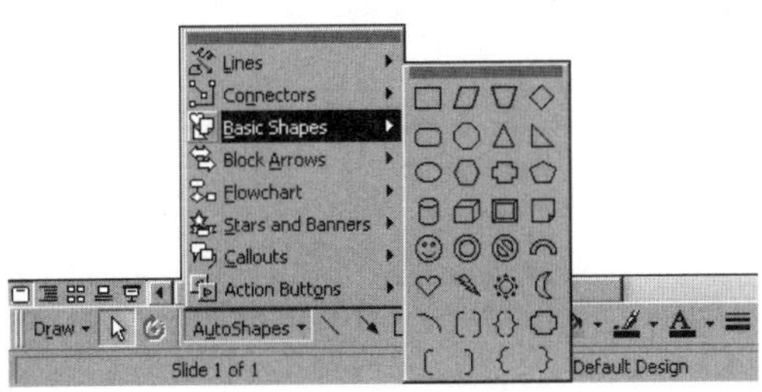

Figure 3-5: Version 8's AutoShapes feature adds new choices, such as Lightning Bolt and Smiley Face, and now categorizes shapes by type.

The AutoShapes toolbar in Versions 4 and 7 offers 24 predesigned shapes to choose from, including stars, arrows, quadrilaterals, and more. (You display the toolbar by selecting View⇨Toolbar⇨AutoShapes.)

To use one of the predesigned shapes and fill it with conformable lines of text, follow these steps:

1. From the AutoShapes toolbar, select a cool shape. Your arrow cursor will turn into a plus sign (+).
2. Click and drag the plus sign to the desired size.
3. With the shape still highlighted, type in your text (but don't select the Text tool!).
4. With the shape still highlighted, in Version 7, select Format⇨Text Anchor to view the Text Anchor dialog box (Figure 3-6). In Version 8, select Format⇨AutoShape⇨Text Box (Figure 3-7).
5. Now you have several decisions to make:
   - Select the appropriate Anchor Point from the extended list.
   - In Version 8, set Internal Margins (you can set up to a 22-inch top/bottom margin and left/right margin). In Versions 4 and 7, set margins in the Box Margins text box (you can set up to a 10-inch top/bottom margin and left/right margin).
   - If you check Resize autoshape to fit text (Version 8) or Adjust Object Size to Fit Text (Versions 4 and 7), the shape contracts or expands to fit snugly around your text. If you select Word wrap text in autoshape (Version 8) or Word-wrap Text in Object (Versions 4 and 7), PowerPoint wraps the text to additional lines, if necessary, so that the text doesn't spill over the shape's left and right boundaries. If you check *both* options, your text word-wraps to honor the shape's left and right boundaries, and the shape's top and bottom margins grow to accommodate the text.
   - In Version 8, if you check Rotate text within autoshape by 90 degrees, the text rotates a quarter turn clockwise. Caveat: You may have problems performing this operation with PostScript fonts.

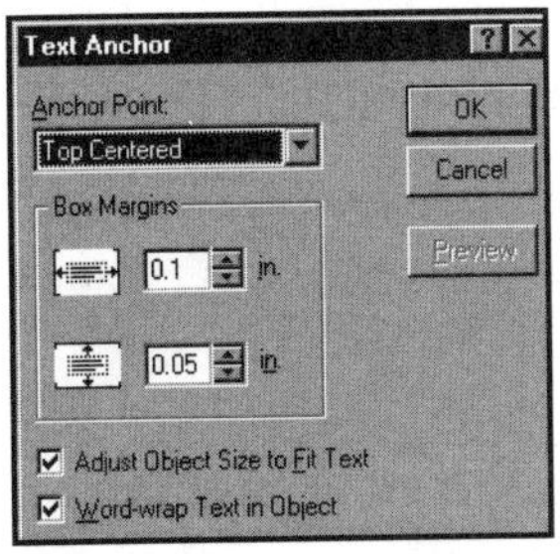

Figure 3-6: Version 7's Text Anchor dialog box lets you define how you want your text to interact with the AutoShape.

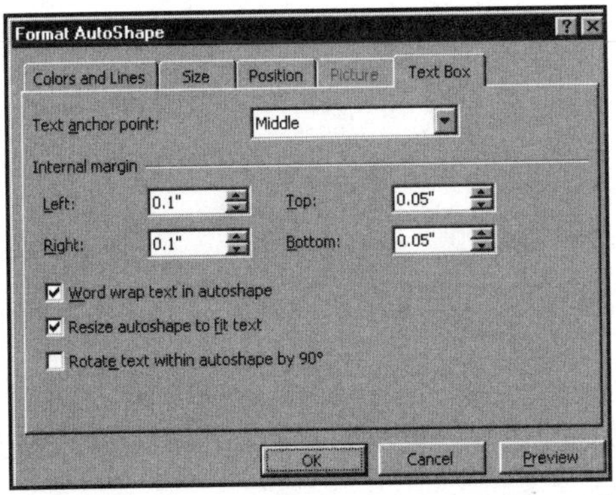

Figure 3-7: Version 8's Format AutoShape dialog box has a Text Box tab that parallels Version 7's Text Anchor dialog box.

tip

A good way to make sure that your changes are being implemented as you intended is to type in your text, open the Format Autoshape (Version 8) or Text Anchor (Versions 4 and 7) dialog box, and play with the different settings, selecting Preview after each change. (You may have to reposition the Text Anchor window to see the results on your slide.)

For exact resizing of a shape, type in the percentage at the Size tab of the Format Autoshape dialog box in Version 8, or select Draw⇨Scale from PowerPoint's main menu in Versions 4 and 7.

To shadow the text only, use the Standard toolbar's Text Shadow button; to shadow the shape only, use the Drawing toolbar's Shadow button in Version 8 and Format⇨Shadow in Versions 4 and 7. You can also apply embossing, superscripting, and subscripting to text within a shape.

tip

If you later decide that you don't like the shape you selected, you can change it with Draw⇨Change Autoshape, and the new shape will take on the characteristics of the old one (fill, line style, shadows, color, and so on).

But beware: If you scale a shape by using the adjustment handles and later decide to change shapes, PowerPoint may not retain the adjustments if the second shape differs much from the first shape.

When using the Text Anchor, the text becomes part of the shape; thus, if you delete the shape, you also delete the text.

Flip Tip

If you group text to an object by selecting both and choosing Draw⇨Group, you can then flip it or rotate the group by using Draw⇨Rotate/Flip and then choosing an option from the expanded menu that appears. Here are two items to keep in mind for this trick:

- When rotating, the text rotates with the object.
- When flipping, the text does *not* flip, so that you can still read it. (Good thinking!)

AutoCorrect

AutoCorrect is a cool new feature in Version 7, and Microsoft has made it even cooler in Version 8. To correct misspellings, capitalization errors, and the common typos you make while you type, turn on AutoCorrect by choosing Tools⇨AutoCorrect⇨Replace text as you type (Figure 3-8).

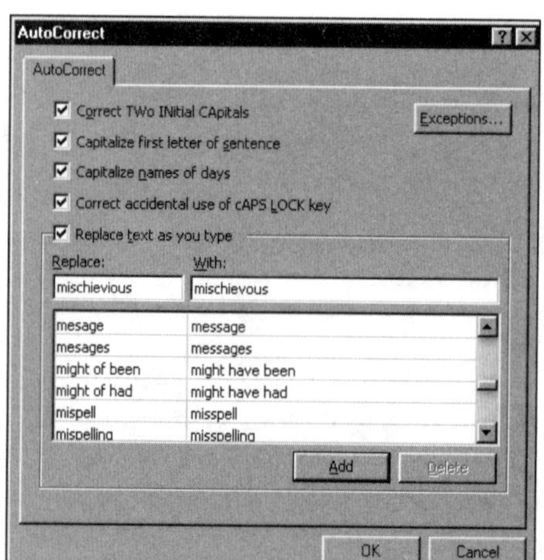

Figure 3-8: AutoCorrect in PowerPoint 8. Version 7 omits the checks for Caps Lock and capitalization at the start of sentences, as well as the Exceptions button.

Here's an example of how AutoCorrect works. Say that you frequently misspell *mischievous* as *mischievious*. In the AutoCorrect dialog box, type **mischievious** in the Replace field and **mischievous** in the With box and then click Add. Now you no longer need to worry about the misspelling or mistyping again.

tip: AutoCorrect's dictionary is part of the Office application suite, so you only need to type in your entries once to use them with other Office programs.

warning: AutoCorrect doesn't work in PowerPoint's Meeting Minder or Mail Routing modes. (Chapter 21 discusses Meeting Minder.)

warning: In Version 8, when you use AutoCorrect to check for capitals at the start of a sentence, PowerPoint takes its cues off all periods — whether or not they're intended to designate the end of a sentence. For example, if your sentence reads "The 260 lb. cow was sold to Bob, who also weighed 260 lbs. at the time," AutoCorrect will change it to "The 260 lb. Cow was sold to Bob, who also weighed 260 lbs. At the time." Use the First Letter tab on the AutoCorrect Exceptions dialog box to fix this problem by adding "lb." and "lbs." to the exceptions list.

Text with Character

The typical PC keyboard doesn't have every possible text character on it (if it did, you'd never fit it on your desk). PowerPoint can generate some of these "special" characters, but the methods for doing so aren't always obvious.

Smart Quotes

If you prefer curly quotation marks, you can use the Smart Quotes feature. This feature also is helpful when you're distinguishing between dimensioning, when you want to use straight quotation marks to represent measurements of feet and inches, and when quoting, when you want to use curly marks (Figure 3-9).

To use the Smart Quotes feature, select Tools⇨Options⇨Edit and either check or clear the Replace Straight Quotes with Smart Quotes check box.

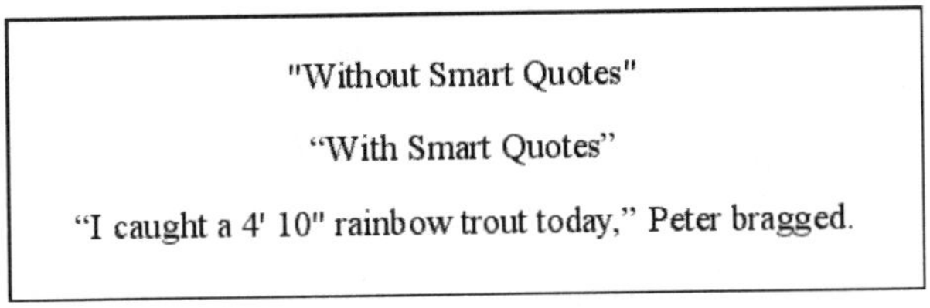

Figure 3-9: The art of Smart Quotes.

warning

You must make your Smart Quotes selection first and *then* type in your text. If you type the text first, highlight it, and then make your choice of curly or straight quotes, PowerPoint won't fix them. Is this a bug? You be the judge.

Accents and more

Have you ever needed to add an accented character, copyright notice, or trademark symbol to a slide? How about use a long "em" dash instead of a double hyphen? Or, maybe just add a cool Wingding symbol for fun?

You can do all this easily in Version 8 with the Insert⇨Symbol command, but with PowerPoint 4 and 7, the feature you need is obscure and buried a bit deep. PowerPoint 4 and 7, unlike many other Windows applications, don't have the Insert⇨Symbol command, and you don't want to have to remember numeric ASCII codes (as was required in the days of text-mode applications such as WordStar). Fortunately, the Windows Character Map applet makes it easy to select special symbols from a window that displays them all. Therefore, what you want to do is customize your toolbar by affixing the Character Map button to it.

To affix the Character Map button to the toolbar and use it to insert special symbols, follow these steps:

1. Select Tools⇨Customize.
2. In the Customize Toolbars dialog box, scroll down and select Tools from the Categories window. From the Buttons window, use the scroll box to the right and drag down to the last screen.
3. Highlight and drag the Character Map Utility button (the last icon on the list) to your toolbar. We like to place it right below the text tool on the Drawing toolbar. Click Close.
4. To open the Character Map dialog box, click on the newly installed button from your toolbar (Figure 3-10).
5. Highlight the symbol or accented character you want to use and click on Select, or simply double-click your choice. Notice that your selection appears under Characters to Copy. You're not limited to making one choice at a time — add as many as you want by continuing to double-click characters.
6. After you have made your choices, click on Copy and then Close.
7. Select Edit⇨Paste. The symbols can now be treated as text characters on your slide.

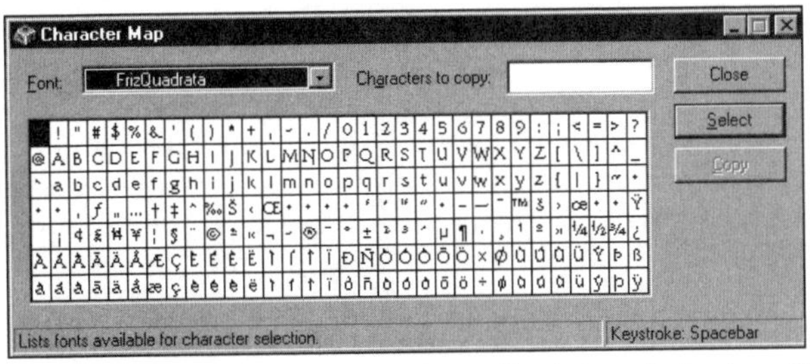

Figure 3-10: The Character Map utility is handy for inserting special characters.

tip To zoom in on the symbol for a closer look, select the character and hold down the left mouse button.

warning If the original Windows installer didn't do a complete installation, the Character Map utility may not be present, because it's an optional component. You can easily reinstall it by using the Windows 3.*x* Setup program or Windows 95's Add/Remove Software wizard.

Summary

Text is your primary vehicle for communicating in PowerPoint, and in order to create cool PowerPoint presentations, you're well advised to master the tools Microsoft provides. The following list summarizes some of the more important points covered in this chapter:

Use TrueType or PostScript fonts for best results, but we recommend that you avoid relying on TrueType's font embedding feature — install the fonts you need onto the delivery PC instead.

You can also change PowerPoint's default text style to match what you use most often.

The built-in alignment options will save you lots of time and avoid that "ragged" look, especially when presenting tabular data.

Shadows add to readability, and double shadows are particularly cool.

Embossed text can convey an impressive "chiseled" look as long as you follow a few design guidelines.

You can use PowerPoint's predefined AutoShapes to place text elements inside a shape, although in Chapter 10 we look at an even more sophisticated way to do this task with WordArt.

You can rotate and flip text for special effects by grouping it with other objects.

Use AutoCorrect in Versions 7 and 8 to ensure good spelling and capitalization and even fix common errors while you type. And use Character Map for those unusual characters, such as accents and symbols, that you need occasionally.

Although good-looking text is very important, presenters with a sense of style do not live by text alone. Clip art is the most convenient way to get graphical images into your slide show and is the subject of the next chapter.

Clip Art

4

In This Chapter

Defining clip art

The difference between vector and bitmap images

Why bitmap files do not make good clip art

Getting acquainted with the ClipArt Gallery

Using PowerPoint 7 and 8's AutoClipArt utility

Discovering style pointers to help you use clip art tastefully

It is often said that a picture is worth a thousand words. To restate that adage for PowerPoint users, a strategically placed, visually pleasing, and informative picture is worth a thousand words.

Clip art provides the easiest way to include pictures in PowerPoint. In Version 8, select Insert⇨Picture⇨Clip Art and pick a graphic from the ClipArt Gallery. In Versions 4 and 7, select Insert⇨ClipArt. Once you place a piece of clip art on your slide, you can move it around, scale it by using the selection handles, or flip and rotate it with PowerPoint's drawing commands and toolbar buttons.

Clip art is cooler than text. It can punch up a presentation, help get your point across, and even help keep a drowsy audience awake. But beware: When used improperly or excessively, clip art can muddle your message instead of enhance it.

(Terminology note: Although Version 8 uses the name *Clip Gallery* — dropping the *Art* because it now also manages sounds and videos — for simplicity, the book will refer to that feature as the *ClipArt Gallery,* as Versions 4 and 7 do. As always, the version icons will clue you in as to which version is being discussed.)

What Exactly Is Clip Art?

In computer graphics, the term *clip art* almost always refers to *vector-based* images, and that definition is the one this book uses. Vector-based images, such as technical and architectural drawings and clip art, use mathematical formulas that specify image appearance: lines, curves, polygons, and other geometrical objects.

For example, a pencil line drawing is vector-based because the pencil strokes have definite start and end points, and you can mathematically define each stroke as a line or a curve.

Vector graphics are *resolution-independent*, which means that you can scale them up or down without losing definition.

tip

The other main kind of computer graphics file is the *bitmap* image, which uses a dot-by-dot internal description instead of formulas. A bitmap image loses clarity when you increase or decrease its size (for example, see Figure 4-1). Clip art usually needs to be enlarged or reduced to fit its intended use. For that reason, it uses vector rather than bitmap technology.

Figure 4-1: A bitmap image that looks good at 100 percent loses clarity when enlarged to 400 percent. PowerPoint 8 scales bitmaps better than Version 7, but does not completely avoid the problem.

warning

PowerPoint enables you to add bitmap images and vector images to its ClipArt Gallery. (In fact, you will find bitmap images in the \MSOffice\Clipart folder after performing a default PowerPoint 7 or 8 installation!) We advise against this practice, though. We already mentioned the scaling problem associated with bitmap images, but there are other problems, too.

You can't rotate or flip bitmap clip art images. In addition, bitmaps won't "float" transparently over your slide; instead, they appear over a white rectangle that delimits the image's outermost boundaries. (PowerPoint 8 provides a new tool to select a single color and make it transparent, called the Set Transparent Color tool, which somewhat alleviates this problem. See Chapter 7 for details.)

Clip art, therefore, is usually vector-based. How does it differ from *illustrations*, which are also vector-based? Clip art images usually are small and do not fill an entire screen or page. Full-size, vector-based images are usually called illustrations, so the only real difference between an illustration and a clip art image is size.

tip

Most clip art images that you'll use with PowerPoint contain several components or pieces. Breaking clip art images apart with Draw⇨Ungroup enables you to work with those individual pieces. We explain how you use this "disassemble" command to create cool clip art effects in Chapter 9.

Clip Art File Formats

Several varieties of vector-based graphics exist on the Windows platform:

- The *Windows Metafile (*.WMF)* format is the one Microsoft uses for most of the PowerPoint clip art supplied with PowerPoint and Office. A WMF file essentially consists of a collection of Windows drawing commands that a programmer might use, making WMF specific to Windows PCs (meaning that you can't read them directly on a Macintosh, for example). These files are small and device-independent, and many Windows programs can read and write them. The WMF format is the best choice for clip art in the Windows environment.
- The *Computer Graphics Metafile (*.CGM)* format originated in the world of minicomputer graphics, so its use is not limited to the Windows world. CGM is also one of the few graphics formats with a formal standard, which was written by the American National Standards Institute (ANSI). The standard is not very rigid, however, and CGM files don't always translate well between computers. These files are larger than WMF files, and not as many Windows programs can read and write them.
- *Encapsulated PostScript* (*.EPS) is primarily a file format for printing vector and bitmap graphics. You may want to use EPS files if you intend to only print your slide show. When importing an EPS file, PowerPoint usually displays only a text box or a low-resolution, bitmap preview image (usually TIFF). EPS, therefore, is not a convenient format to use for clip art, though you may be able to convert EPS files to WMF or CGM with a program such as Quarterdeck's Hijaak.

In addition to the preceding formats, PowerPoint can read some of the vector-based graphic formats that were pioneered by particular graphics programs and later became *de facto* standards with widespread use. These formats include

- The Corel Draw! format, *.CDR
- The Micrografx Designer format, *.DRW
- The AutoCAD format, *.DXF
- AutoCAD plotter files, *.ADI.
- The Hewlett-Packard Graphics Language formats, *.HGL and *.PLT
- WordPerfect Graphics, *.WPG

warning

Vendor-specific file formats such as *.CDR have usually changed several times as a result of the vendors introducing new and improved versions of their graphics programs. Therefore, although PowerPoint comes with graphics *filters* to read these files, you have no guarantee that the filters will work with all versions of the file formats.

PowerPoint can read images in a variety of bitmap formats, but we don't consider them to be "true" clip art. Chapter 7 examines bitmap formats in detail.

Introducing ClipArt Gallery

Microsoft's ClipArt Gallery helps you manage and use clip art images. ClipArt Gallery is really a separate application that PowerPoint and other Office applications can use through Windows' Object Linking and Embedding (OLE) technology (we take an in-depth look at OLE in Chapter 12). You are given the option to install ClipArt Gallery while installing PowerPoint or Office, or you can install it later by running the PowerPoint or Office Setup program.

You can activate ClipArt Gallery in one of the two following ways to see the screen shown in Figure 4-2:

1. Select Insert➪Picture➪Clip Art (Version 8) or Insert➪ClipArt (Versions 4 and 7).
2. Select Insert➪Object and choose Microsoft Clip Gallery (Version 8) or Microsoft ClipArt Gallery (Versions 4 and 7) from the Object Type list.

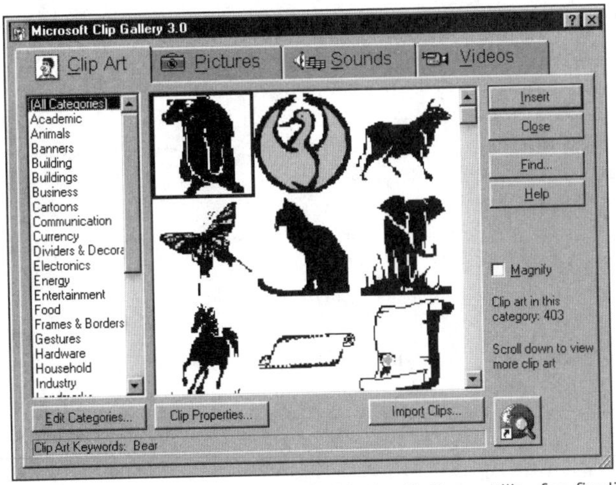

Figure 4-2: Version 3.0 of the ClipArt Gallery utility for finding and inserting images ships with PowerPoint 8 and manages digitized sounds and movies. Now you must click Clip Properties, however, to display the selected image's filename: Two steps forward, one step back!

ClipArt Gallery organizes images into categories, as you can see from the left column in Figure 4-2. It displays *thumbnails*, or miniatures, of the clip art images in the window labeled Pictures. ClipArt Gallery also enables you to describe images with key words that you can search for later (by using the Find button on the ClipArt Gallery's main screen) when hunting for a particular image.

ClipArt Gallery uses its own special file format to store clip art images: the *picture store* file (*.PCS).

You won't be able to access the clip art files in *.PCS files by using the Insert⇨Picture command in PowerPoint. Instead, you have to use the ClipArt Gallery to access them. PCS is a special Microsoft database format designed especially for ClipArt Gallery.

ClipArt Gallery also stores category data, index data, and thumbnails in separate files, depending on which version of the Gallery you're using.

PowerPoint 4 comes with Version 1.0 or 1.1 of ClipArt Gallery, PowerPoint 7 comes with Version 2.0, and PowerPoint 8 with Version 3.0. One difference between the versions is that ClipArt Gallery 1.0 uses the file types *.IDX and *.THM to contain index, category, and thumbnail information, whereas ClipArt Gallery 2.0 and 3.0 use a single file type, *.CAG, for the same purposes. The filename that ClipArt Gallery 2.0 typically uses is ARTGALRY.CAG, and it resides in the \WINDOWS folder.

You may not be able to run ClipArt Gallery Version 1 if Windows is running from the hard drive's root directory. If you try to do so, an error message may appear that says ClipArt Gallery cannot create an index file. If this is the case, download the Microsoft application note GE1031 from any Microsoft online support site and update the ARTGALRY.EXE, CTL3DV2.DLL, and PICSTORE.DLL files.

After a standard installation, ClipArt Gallery's program files reside in the \Program Files\Common Files\Microsoft Shared\Artgalry folder, and the picture store files reside in \MSOffice\Clipart\Pcsfiles.

You can replace any clip art image by double-clicking on it and choosing another image from the ClipArt Gallery. If you have disassembled an image and then decide to replace it, however, double-clicking on the image will no longer bring up the ClipArt Gallery. Instead, you have to delete the ungrouped image and reopen ClipArt Gallery.

If you have the CD-ROM version of PowerPoint, a great deal of extra clip art is available in the Valupack\Clipart folder. Copy all the *.PCS and *.CAG files (25 sets in Version 7) to your hard drive's \MSOffice\Clipart\Pcsfiles folder.

If you have an Internet Web browser installed, you can also connect to Microsoft's Web site to download additional clip art; Microsoft calls this *Clip Gallery Live*. Simply click the globe icon at the ClipArt Gallery's lower-right corner.

AutoClipArt

AutoClipArt automatically suggests specific clip art images (and, in Version 8, sounds and movies) by matching the words in your slide's text with words in the ClipArt Gallery (either file title, category title, or image description). To run AutoClipArt, follow these steps:

1. Select Tools➪AutoClipArt.
2. A list of matching words appears in an expanding list, as in Figure 4-3. You can choose to view the suggestions by word or by slide number.

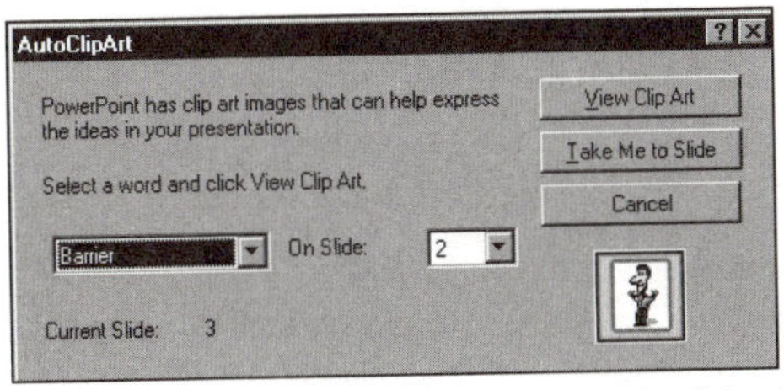

Figure 4-3: AutoClipArt tries to match slide show text with clip art, picture, sound, and video clip keywords.

3. Click View Clip Art. The ClipArt Gallery dialog box appears, and AutoClipArt presents a selected group of images from which you can choose.
4. Highlight the image you want (first choosing the appropriate tab in Version 8) and click Insert or Close.

The manuals won't tell you so, but you have to run ClipArt Gallery and then import the PowerPoint Popular Clip Art package supplied with PowerPoint before AutoClipArt will work.

According to PowerPoint's online help, you can run AutoClipArt in the background while performing other tasks. This feature is not available in Version 7, however (it's a documentation error), so don't waste your time trying to make it work!

Style Points

Here are a few style points to keep in mind when adding clip art to your slides:

- Use clip art sparingly. Not every slide needs a clip art image. Depending on the length of your presentation, experiment with using clip art every third or fifth slide.
- Use clip art at the beginning of a new topic or section.
- If you use several charts and graphs in your presentation, stay away from clip art unless you can combine the two elements tastefully (as you'll see in the next chapter). Clip art de-emphasizes your chart or graph and can cause visual overload.
- As a general rule, use no more than one clip art image per slide. Although a slide may project several points via text elements, select the major point and then add an appropriate clip art image. Attaching a graphic to every text element only causes clutter (just compare Figures 4-4 and 4-5).

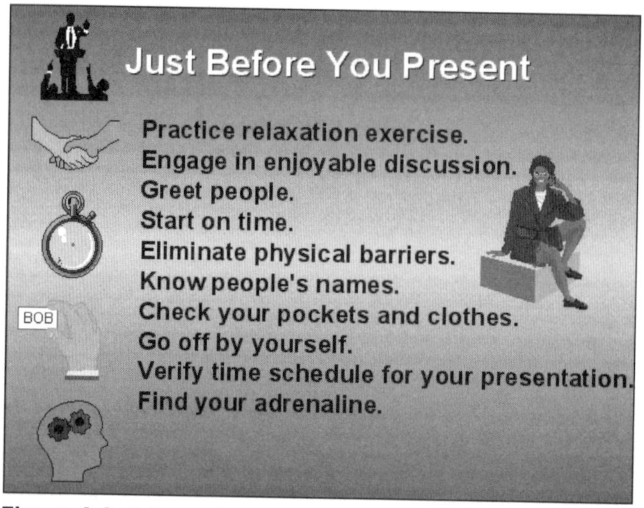

Figure 4-4: A fussy, cluttered slide with too much clip art.

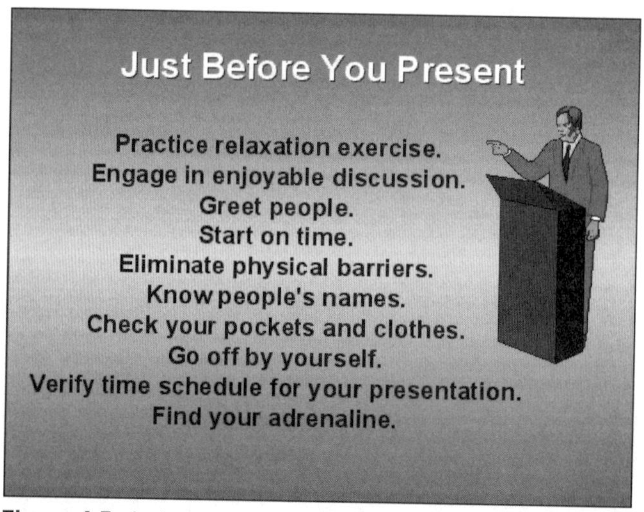

Figure 4-5: A clean, elegant slide with just enough clip art. (How could this slide be improved even further?)

Summary

This chapter presented clip art basics:

You learned what clip art is, which file formats you may encounter, and the fundamentals of ClipArt Gallery.

You discovered how to use Version 7 and 8's AutoClipArt feature.

We presented a few key style pointers to help you use these little graphical accents wisely.

Chapter 9 takes a closer look at using third-party clip art not included with PowerPoint or Office. It also offers tips on managing the ClipArt Gallery, as well as on disassembling and modifying clip art for cool effects.

The final types of slide elements we explore in Part I are the charts and graphs used to present numerical data in a graphical format. These elements are the subject of the next chapter.

Charting, Graphing, and Drawing

5

In This Chapter

Getting started with Microsoft Graph

Selecting the right type of graph for the information you want to convey

Enhancing charts and graphs with custom chart types, superimposed clip art, ungrouping techniques, and graphical builds

Applying PowerPoint's built-in drawing tools with control and precision by using drawing options, gridlines, and guidelines

PowerPoint offers built-in features for creating graphics in ways other than by importing clip art. You can run the Microsoft Graph utility from within PowerPoint to create charts and graphs. This chapter offers some tips on charts and graphs and provides suggestions on how to enhance Microsoft Graph's output with PowerPoint's line and fill tools.

PowerPoint also provides some drawing tools that you can use to create geometric shapes. Although these tools — even with PowerPoint 8's welcome enhancements — don't offer the flexibility and power of dedicated illustration programs, such as those that Chapter 8 examines, you can nevertheless use them to quickly create some appealing effects.

Using Microsoft Graph

versions 4, 7 & 8

The success of periodicals such as *USA Today* attests to the power of charts and graphs in conveying information quickly and powerfully. Former President Bush preferred the briefings he received every morning in the White House to be graphical rather than tabular or textual in nature — he knew he could grasp ideas more quickly from graphs and charts than from tables of figures or paragraphs of prose.

You can create your own charts and graphs with Microsoft Graph — a separate, little OLE server program that you can run from PowerPoint or, in fact, from any Microsoft Office program (Chapter 12 explains the OLE server concept in detail). Both PowerPoint 7 and PowerPoint 4 come with Microsoft Graph Version 5.0, whereas PowerPoint 8 comes with Graph Version 8.0.

This brief overview of Graph includes charting basics, a few tips on the aesthetics and psychology of graphs, and suggestions for increasing the cool quotient of your graphs.

Charting basics

After you fire up Graph with Insert➪Microsoft Graph (or Insert➪Chart in Version 8), the program changes PowerPoint's menus and toolbars to Graph's menus and toolbars. Graph also presents you with a datasheet dialog box, where you can enter the values you want Graph to display in graphical form. The datasheet dialog box (Figure 5-1) enables you to have a practically unlimited number of columns and rows in your charts and graphs.

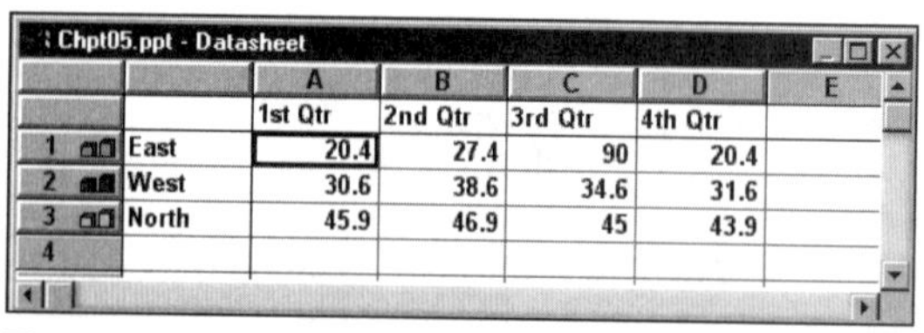
Chpt05.ppt - Datasheet

		A	B	C	D	E
		1st Qtr	2nd Qtr	3rd Qtr	4th Qtr	
1	East	20.4	27.4	90	20.4	
2	West	30.6	38.6	34.6	31.6	
3	North	45.9	46.9	45	43.9	
4						

Figure 5-1: Microsoft Graph's datasheet dialog box looks and works much like any spreadsheet program.

tip

Each row in the datasheet represents a *series* of data, corresponding to a line in a line graph or a set of similarly colored bars in a bar graph, for example. Try to keep the number of series to four (five if you decide not to use a legend) to help avoid clutter.

The quickest way to generate a chart or graph with PowerPoint 4 or 7 is to use the Format➪AutoFormat command and then select a chart type from the Galleries list and a style from the Formats section, shown in Figure 5-2. In PowerPoint 8, select Chart➪Chart Type to bring up a similar dialog box. All in all, you have dozens of options; Graph 8.0 offers a Custom Types tab in the Chart Type dialog box with some cool new designs (Figure 5-3). When you settle on a chart format, click outside of Graph to return to PowerPoint. You can return to Graph from PowerPoint by double-clicking the graph object on the slide.

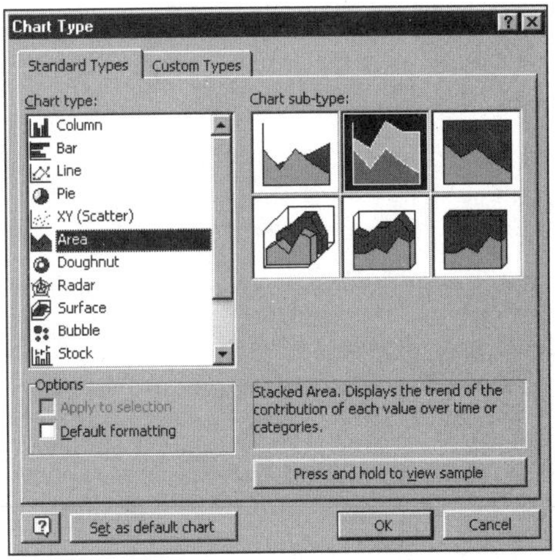

Figure 5-2: Chart types in Graph enable you to easily generate a wide variety of styles. Graph 5.0 calls chart types AutoFormats, but the term is no longer used in Graph 8.0 (shown).

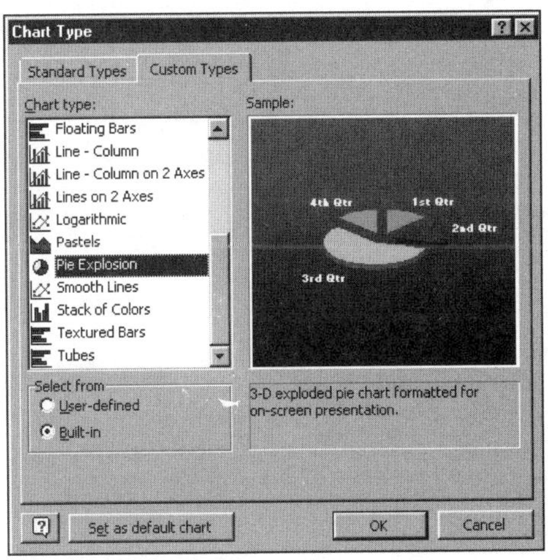

Figure 5-3: Graph 8.0's Custom Types include various new, ready-for-prime-time formats, such as the Pie Explosion.

Cool versus confusing graphs

Accuracy is cool, but graphs and charts can distort information just as effectively as they can illustrate and enlighten it. The PowerPoint designer must understand how humans perceive graphics in order to walk the line between distorting the truth and making one's point with drama and style. Here are a few tips to help you:

- Although the 3-D column chart (in which vertical bars line up on a 3-D coordinate grid) is a very economical way of doing numerical comparisons in terms of presenting a great deal of data in a small amount of space, the chart is hard to read if the bars go deeper than one level.
- Graph 8.0's new cylindrical, pyramid, and cone chart types look interesting, but be aware that the shapes and their 3-D perspectives may make it difficult for your audience to identify values precisely. When using these chart types, consider including the data table beneath the graphic (Select Chart⇨Chart Options⇨Data Table⇨Show data table).
- In a line graph, don't show more than three lines and stick to one method of differentiating the lines: thickness, dots/dashes/solids, or color. Try a simple test: Follow each of the lines from left to right. Do you get frustrated? If you do, so will your audience.
- In scaled charts, it's easy to make small differences appear very large by not starting at (0, 0). This practice isn't really fair to the audience. Similarly, scaled bar charts that contain one or more offscale and "broken" bars also do not present information in a completely honest way. Make sure that you compare quantities that are similar enough to fit in the same scale range without breaking a bar.
- Whenever the X-axis values are numerous or closely spaced — on a timeline scale (Graph 8.0), for example — your audience may have a hard time seeing or reading them. Help your audience by including the X-axis range in your slide title; for example, **3D4U Inc. Stock Prices, January 1995 to December 1997**.
- Pie charts are less effective for conveying precise numerical data but are very good for making a quick point. The problem with pie charts is that you often end up with two or three big slices and four or five tiny ones that you must add captions to in order to identify them. Combine the tiny slices into an Other category for easier readability and, in Graph 8.0, use a "bar of pie" format, as shown in Figure 5-4 (we prefer the "bar of pie" to the "pie of pie" format, for space reasons).
- If you're going to use callouts (a big enough pie won't need them), make sure that you use them for each section of the pie (Graph 8.0 does this automatically). You can use the PowerPoint drawing tools to make custom callout lines that use a contrasting line color when the lines insert into the body of the pie.

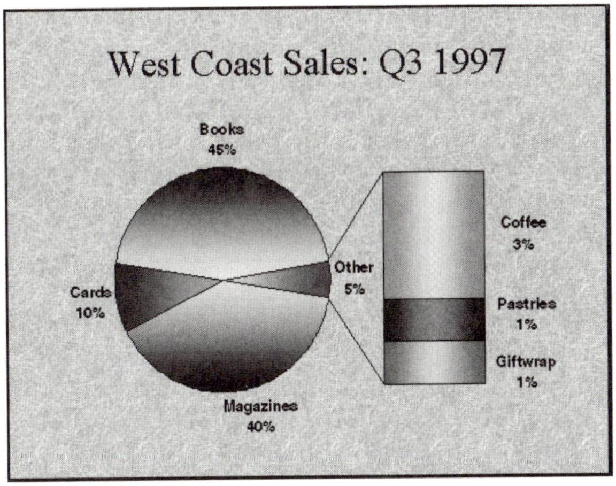

Figure 5-4: Graph 8.0's "bar of pie" shows small quantities more clearly than a pure pie chart can. Gradient fills add a touch of class. If you use Graph 5.0, create a homemade "bar of pie" with two separate charts.

Spiffing up your charts

versions 4, 7 & 8

You may be tempted to create a reasonably good-looking chart or graph with Microsoft Graph, plunk it down onto a PowerPoint slide, and be done. It doesn't take much, however, to move from merely good-looking graphs to really cool ones, so let's explore five ways to enhance those graphs:

- Creating custom 3-D formats
- Superimposing clip art
- Creating gradient fills for graph components
- Putting graph components into motion
- Creating your own axis titles

Creating custom 3-D graphs

Microsoft Graph provides a little-known mechanism, the 3-D View, for creating super-cool, 3-D graphing effects that you can save as custom chart types (or *AutoFormats* in Graph 5.0) to reuse later.

To use the 3-D View, it's important to understand the way PowerPoint defines the X, Y, and Z axes.

Most graphs have two or three axes, though doughnut and pie charts have no axes, and radar charts have their own unique axes. Scatter charts use the X and Y axes only. Bar charts may vary the X axis by placing 0 in the middle of the chart.

In a 3-D chart, a third axis, labeled Z, is the *value* axis, and it gives depth to the chart. The horizontal surface that forms the floor of the chart is the X axis (*category*, or *length*). The vertical axis is the Y axis (*series*, or *height*). In Graph 8.0's new bubble chart, which market researchers and financial analysts will appreciate, the Z value is the bubble diameter.

With that behind us, here's the procedure for using the 3-D View feature:

1. With Graph active, select Chart⇨3-D View (Version 8) or Format⇨3-D View (Versions 4 and 7). The Format 3-D View dialog box appears (Figure 5-5), and the tweaking begins.

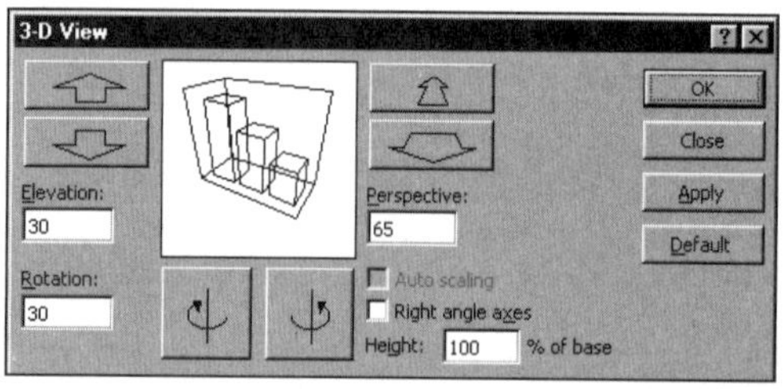

Figure 5-5: Getting ready to create a custom 3-D graph format.

2. The up and down arrows on the left side of the Format 3-D View dialog box control Elevation, which rotates the chart around the X axis. A 90-degree elevation makes the view look directly down on the top of the chart, whereas -90 degrees provides a view from directly below the chart. You can click on the arrows to move in 5-degree increments or type the precise number of degrees you want to move.
3. The Rotation buttons rotate the chart around the Y axis in increments of 10 degrees. Again, you can type an exact number of degrees directly if you prefer.

tip

You can always reset your graph's orientation by selecting Default from the 3-D View dialog box.

4. If you want to experiment with perspective, deselect Right Angle Axes; you will see up and down arrows on the right of the 3-D View dialog box. These arrows simulate the effect of lines converging in the distance. The best advice is to experiment with them, keeping in mind that too much perspective can make your graph harder to read. To eliminate all perspective but not the 3-D effect, check Right Angle Axes.

5. Change Height: % of Base to change the graph's *aspect ratio.* For example, if you specify 400%, then the chart's height becomes four times the length of its base.
6. Finally, use Auto Scaling to more nearly match the original size of a chart that you've changed from 2-D to 3-D. Right Angle Axes must be turned on to perform Auto Scaling.

If you like the result, keep it! Save your new, custom 3-D view for future use as an AutoFormat. Here's how to do it in Version 7:

1. Select Format⇨AutoFormat and click the User-Defined radio button.
2. Select Customize.
3. Select Add from the User-Defined AutoFormat dialog box.
4. Type a Format Name and Description in the Add Custom AutoFormat dialog box and click OK.

Here's how to save your 3-D view in Version 8:

1. Select Chart⇨Chart Type⇨Custom Types and click the User-Defined radio button.
2. Select Add.
3. Type a Name and Description in the Add Custom Chart Type dialog box and click OK.

Superimposing clip art

While you're working in Microsoft Graph, you can't insert clip art the usual way, from the Insert menu. (Graph 8.0 allows you to switch to another application, load a clip art image, copy it, return to Graph, and perform a paste operation, but that process is a little tedious.) You can insert clip art easily, however, after you're back in PowerPoint. For a cool effect, position a clip art image over a nonessential part of the graph and then send it to the bottom drawing layer with Draw⇨Send to Back (Versions 4 and 7) or Draw⇨Order⇨Send to Back (Version 8), so that it appears behind the graph's gridlines. If you want to give the clip art image more emphasis, leave it superimposed over the graph.

Creating gradient fills for bars, pies, and doughnuts

version 8

Graph 8.0 enables you to apply gradients and other custom fill effects to graph elements. To do this, display the drawing toolbar by selecting View⇨Toolbars⇨Drawing, click on the object of interest, and then use the Fill button on the drawing toolbar (it looks like a paint bucket). We explore this toolbar more in the second part of this chapter.

versions 4 & 7

Graph 5.0 won't let you apply a gradient to a pie slice, bar, or doughnut section, but you can work around this problem. When you're absolutely certain you have your chart or graph just the way you want it, disassemble (or ungroup) it in PowerPoint with Draw⇨Ungroup. Disassembling converts your imported graph or chart to a PowerPoint drawing, and you can now select individual parts of the graph and apply gradients for cool effects, as in Figure 5-6.

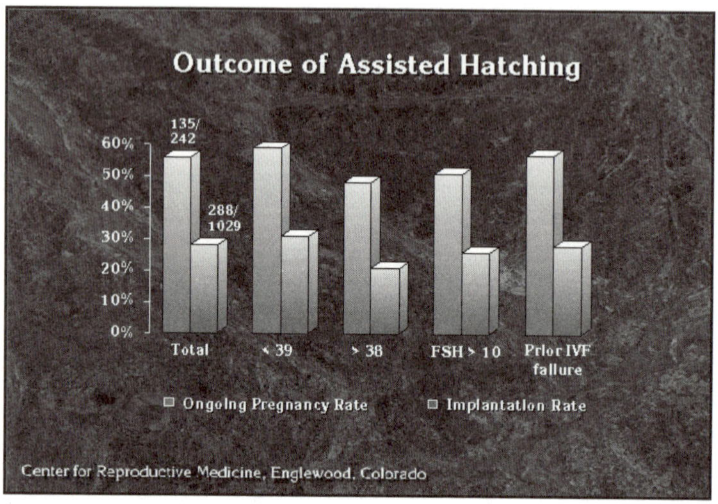

Figure 5-6: Disassembling a graph enables you to apply cool gradients for a sharp-looking bar chart.

warning

Once you disassemble a graph, you can't go back to Microsoft Graph by double-clicking on it. Therefore, you may want to use PowerPoint's Save As command to save your slide show before converting graphs to drawing objects, just in case you discover a numerical error or want to update the graph later.

Putting graphs in motion

version 8

You do not have to disassemble a graph to add motion effects in PowerPoint 8. Simply right-click the graph object, choose Custom Animation, and adjust the settings in the Chart Effects tab (Figure 5-7). Experiment with different options to see which best fit your planned narration. Match the motion effect to the chart type; for example, Wipe Up is a good effect for a vertical bar chart. Animating the grid and legend is usually overkill.

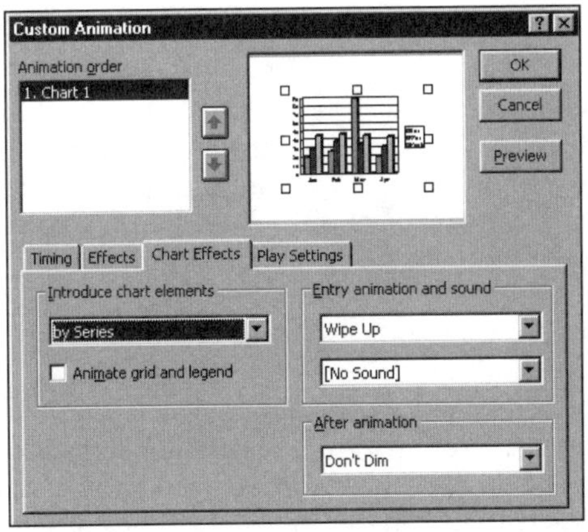

Figure 5-7: PowerPoint 8 provides motion effects for most chart types without requiring disassembly.

Although PowerPoint 7 doesn't offer built-in motion effects as Version 8 does, you can still disassemble a graph as described in the preceding section, select parts of the graph (bars, pie slices, and so on), and assign animated motions to them. For example, you can have all your bars drop down from the top of the slide, in a left-to-right sequence. Chapter 11 presents all the details on creating animated graphic build effects with PowerPoint 7.

Creating your own axis titles

Graph 8.0 enables you to reposition axis titles by clicking and dragging them; you can even disable Graph's axis titles with Chart⇨Chart Options⇨Axes and then use the new WordArt utility to create axis titles (display the toolbar with View⇨Toolbars⇨WordArt). If you use Graph 5.0, don't feel constrained by its fairly limited options for placing titles on X and Y axes. Once you disassemble a graph, you can delete the axis titles that Graph created and make your own title to gain positioning flexibility, as you can see in the examples in this book's color insert.

Note: PowerPoint comes with a utility for creating *organizational charts.* Organization Chart 1.0 ships with PowerPoint 4, and Organization Chart 2.0 ships with PowerPoint 7 and 8. This chapter doesn't address the Organization Chart utility, largely because it's rarely used, but you can apply the preceding techniques to enhance organization chart objects in much the same way that you enhance graphs and charts. If you do spend a great deal of time making org charts, check out ShapeWare's Visio program, which offers even more flexibility than the Microsoft utility.

Creating Simple Drawings

versions 4, 7 & 8

PowerPoint supplies its users with several basic drawing tools that work much like any other drawing program's tools: straight lines, arced lines, freeform shapes, rectangles, and ellipses. Version 8 adds flowcharting symbols, intelligent connectors that grow or shrink when you resize objects, and adjustable curves. All of these tools are available in the Drawing toolbar. PowerPoint also offers *AutoShapes*, preset shapes for quick draws. AutoShapes reside on a separate toolbar in Versions 4 and 7; you find them on the Drawing toolbar in Version 8.

You can modify the objects you create with PowerPoint's drawing tools by changing color fill, line color and style, arrowheads, and so on, either with the Drawing (and Drawing +, in Versions 4 and 7) toolbars or via the Format⇨Colors and Lines command. You can create reasonably good-looking drawings by using these tools, as Figure 5-8 illustrates.

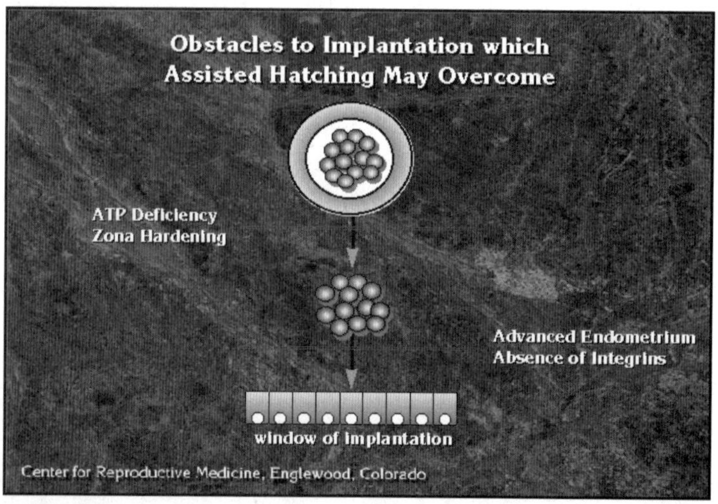

Figure 5-8: A technical illustration created entirely with PowerPoint's built-in drawing tools and enhanced with PowerPoint's fill and line options.

This section offers a few pointers on how to make your PowerPoint drawings look clean and cool while using the built-in drawing tools. The topics include the following:

- Drawing regular, or uniform, shapes
- Drawing objects by using a precise center point
- Drawing exact horizontal, vertical, and angled lines

- Distributing objects evenly on a slide (Version 8)
- Aligning objects by using guides and grids

Drawing regular shapes

Regular, or *uniform*, shapes are symmetrical in every dimension. For example, a regular rectangle is a square, and a regular ellipse is a circle. You can also create regular shapes for all PowerPoint AutoShapes. The key to creating a regular shape is to hold down Shift while dragging the cursor to create the shape. For example, to create a square, follow these steps:

1. Select the Rectangle tool from the Drawing toolbar.
2. Hold down Shift and drag the cursor to draw a perfect square.

tip: After creating the shape, you can always select any of the corner handles to modify it.

Getting centered

If you know the exact location where you need to place a drawing object, you can draw it outward from the precise center location that you specify. You have this capability for all shapes except the Freeform shape. To perform this task, follow these steps:

1. Select the desired shape from the Drawing toolbar, or select an AutoShape.
2. Place the crosshair at the center point for the object you want to draw.
3. Click on that location and hold down Ctrl as you drag the shape into place. Watch how PowerPoint draws the shape symmetrically outward from the center.

tip: If you need to constrain the centered shape to be a *regular* shape (as defined earlier), hold down both Shift and Ctrl while you drag the cursor.

Going straight

When nothing but a perfectly straight horizontal or vertical line will do, you may find the Freehand Line tool to be frustrating, as you repeatedly zoom in to find that your line isn't perfect and then have to try again. To draw an exact horizontal, vertical, or 45-degree line, follow these steps

1. Select the Line tool from the Drawing toolbar.

2. Hold down Shift while you click and drag to create the line. PowerPoint *constrains* the line to one of the three rigid angles, depending on where you move your mouse.

Spreading the wealth

When you've created a handful of drawing objects and you want to space them evenly on the slide, PowerPoint 8 provides a new command, Draw⇨Align or Distribute, that's very convenient. Toggle the Relative to Slide menu choice depending on whether you want to spread out the objects across the entire slide or relative to each other (you have to choose at least three objects in the latter case). Then select the objects (use Shift-click) and select Draw⇨Align or Distribute, followed by Distribute Horizontally or Distribute Vertically. A cool time-saver!

Getting your ducks in a row

Misaligned drawing objects aren't cool, they're sloppy. PowerPoint offers two ways to align objects accurately: Snap to Grid and Guides.

Snap to Grid

Activate the Snap to Grid feature by toggling it on in the Draw menu (Versions 4 and 7) or by selecting Draw⇨Snap⇨To Grid (Version 8). A check mark (or, in Version 8, a depressed button shape) indicates that the feature is on, which is the default setting. The invisible grid forces all objects to "snap" into place horizontally and vertically to the nearest grid-lines, which are fixed at one pica (1/12-inch) apart.

There may be times when you need to place an object more precisely than the grid permits. At such times, you can either toggle off the grid as described earlier or suspend it temporarily for a one-time-only move by holding down Alt while you move the object.

You can align new objects to an edge of an existing object with the new Draw⇨Snap⇨To Shape command. You can also align an object with another object by selecting both objects (use Shift-click), choosing Draw⇨Align or Distribute, and then selecting one of the six alignment options on the menu.

Guides

Think of *guides* as movable, viewable gridlines. When you place an object near a guide, it snaps into place and aligns its edge precisely with the guide. Place an object's center near a guide, and the center point snaps to the guide. Guides work whether Snap to Grid is on or off.

Turn on the default centerline guides with the View⇨Guides command. The guides appear as dotted lines crossing at the exact middle of the slide.

tip

Add guides of your own by holding down Ctrl and dragging a guideline to a new position. As you move the guide, a number with an arrow appears (Figure 5-9). The number indicates exactly how far you are from the center of the slide and the arrow indicates on which side of the slide's center your guideline falls (as if you couldn't tell!). You can delete a guide by dragging it off the slide.

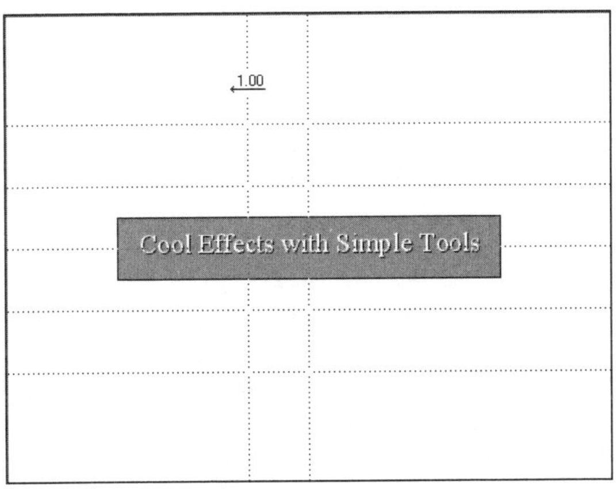

Figure 5-9: Create your own guidelines by holding down Ctrl and dragging from an existing guideline. The number indicates the new guideline's distance from center.

warning

If the Snap to Grid feature is on, you will only be able to place new guides at grid intervals. Disable Snap to Grid to place guides with complete freedom.

tip

You can even use guidelines with objects that have been rotated. In Figure 5-10, some of the stars (created with AutoShapes) have been free-rotated and some have not; all of the stars snap to guidelines, however, either by their center or their edge.

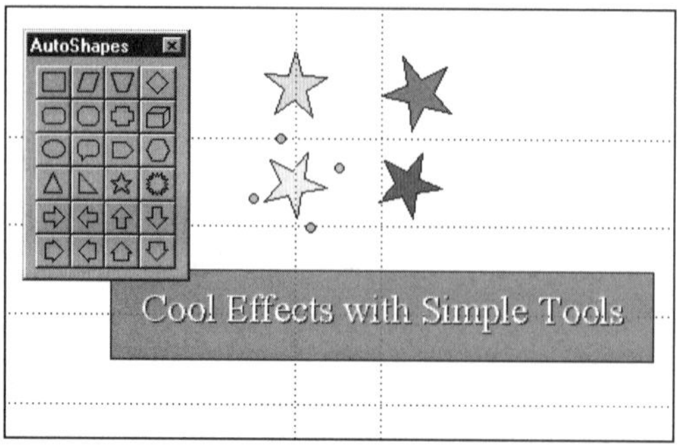

Figure 5-10: You can rotate objects and still use guidelines to align them. You can also snap to guidelines with the object's center point or with object edges.

Summary

This chapter provides several tips and tricks to help you with your charting, drawing, and graphing tasks in PowerPoint. Some tips include the following:

Microsoft Graph is a powerful tool that enables you to create a wide variety of graphs and charts easily and quickly.

Don't make the common mistake of trying to convey too much data in a single graph — and take care to choose graph types that are easy to read and understand.

You can spiff up your graphs by creating your own 3-D chart types, disassembling graphs, adding interesting fills to key graph components, creating your own axis titles and legends, and even adding motion — whether with PowerPoint 8's built-in chart animation settings or with PowerPoint 7's graphics build feature.

For non-numerical graphics, PowerPoint's drawing tools, though simple, can create cool effects.

You can add precision to your PowerPoint drawings with regular (constrained) shapes, exact line angles, and grid or guidelines for performing exact alignments.

The next part of this book, Part II, takes you beyond the basics and shows you how to further customize your slide shows by using third-party software and some of PowerPoint's lesser-known built-in tricks and tools. Chapter 6 begins Part II by presenting a set of guidelines for laying out PowerPoint slides.

PART II

BEYOND BASICS: CUSTOMIZING PRESENTATIONS

Part I presented PowerPoint's building blocks: templates, backgrounds, text, clip art, charts, graphs, and drawings. Most slide show designers stop there, but not in this book! In Part II, we're going to do two things: learn how to *combine* those building blocks in a visually sophisticated way and discover how you can *jazz up* the basic elements with the help of third-party software.

The result will be customized presentations that break away from the canned feel of so many boilerplate PowerPoint slide shows. The topics to be covered include customizing your presentations' screen layouts, bitmaps, illustrations, clip art, special text effects, and builds and transitions.

Screen Layout Guidelines

6

In This Chapter

Identifying presentation goals and sequencing methods

Creating a presentation outline within PowerPoint

Importing a presentation outline created outside of PowerPoint

Placing text on your slides

Placing graphics on your slides

Exploring color backgrounds and applications

Using PowerPoint 7 and 8's Style Checker

This chapter presents ideas for creating a presentation outline and examines ways to customize the slide show's look through the visual layout of slide elements.

This chapter addresses ways to combine PowerPoint's building blocks — templates, backgrounds, and text — effectively and harmoniously. You learn about some PowerPoint features that can help shape your ideas into coherent, multi-slide presentation layouts. You also learn some tips about the visual layout of your individual slides, with special emphases on text, graphics, and color.

If your slide show doesn't have a logical flow, and if your slides don't have good visual balance, no amount of fancy graphics or multimedia clips will make up for those shortcomings. If, however, your slides flow smoothly and adhere to aesthetically sound design guidelines from the start, the cool enhancements we explore in later chapters will make your message even stronger and more memorable.

So, put your PowerPoint user manual away; you're about to leave it behind (along with your amateur status). It's time to get professional and begin exploring how to design great slide shows instead of merely good ones.

Creating a Great Outline

In this section, you learn how to create a strong outline that will make sense to your audience and how to lay out your ideas across multiple slides. Before you begin your slide show outline, zero in on your message and what you need to accomplish:

- *Persuasion* (bringing your audience around to your point of view). In this type of presentation, your outline should raise and meet the most obvious objections or challenges to your position.
- *Education* (getting across facts, statistics, and so on). In an informative slide show, your outline should divide the subject matter into convenient "chunks" that your audience can assimilate easily. Plan to use images for better retention.

> **tip** In either case, sprinkle some questions for the audience throughout your slide show. You want to get them involved and engaged, so make them respond to you from time to time.

The second decision is how you're going to *sequence* your presentation. Two options are as follows:

- Build up to, and end with, the main message. A variation on this approach is to present a question at the beginning, then present the relevant facts and arguments, and end with your conclusion. This sequence often works better with technical audiences (scientists, engineers, and so on) because it parallels the scientific method.
- Start with the main message and supply supporting facts and arguments. This approach often works better with business audiences who want to know your point up front.

You may find that the key to a successful, long slide show is combining these two sequencing techniques. That is, tell your audience what you're going to tell them, then tell them, and then tell them what you told them.

> **tip** As you develop your outline, be aware of *parallel structure*. For example, don't use past tense in one place and present tense in another similar place in the outline (unless, of course, it's necessary to support your meaning). If your primary headings start with a gerund (creating, delivering, finalizing, selling), start them all this way.

After you've chosen your presentation's goals and sequencing, it's time to make your outline. You can do so in two ways: from scratch within PowerPoint or by importing a pre-existing outline.

Building an outline from scratch

You create a slide show outline in Outline View. Follow these steps:

1. Open a new slide show with File⇨New⇨Blank Presentation. (Although we won't use any canned presentation templates discussed in Chapter 1, you should explore them if you haven't done so already.)
2. Click View⇨Outline, or click the Outline View icon on the toolbar at the bottom of the screen. The slide number and a slide icon appear to the left.
3. Type in your first title or topic and then press Enter. A second slide icon appears on the left.
4. Wait a minute — you weren't ready for the second slide! If you want to add bullet items for Slide 1, click the Demote (Indent More) button on the formatting toolbar along the screen's left edge (it's the button with a right arrow). The slide icon goes away.
5. You're now at your first bullet for Slide 1. Enter the text for this slide's first point.
6. For more bullets, press Enter. To create various indentation levels at any time, click the right arrow button, Demote (Indent More), or the left arrow button, Promote (Indent Less).
7. When you're happy with Slide 1, press Ctrl+Enter to move to the next slide.
8. Repeat these steps until your outline is complete.

PowerPoint 8 has a helpful new feature called Slide Miniature. While you're working in Outline View, PowerPoint displays a tiny replica of the slide on which you're working, so that you can easily see when the slide is full and, therefore, that it's time to create a new one. No more switching between views — a great time saver.

The further you indent and add layers of bullets, the smaller the font size becomes (Figure 6-1). You may need to go back later and selectively change your font sizes. We suggest you stay with two levels of headings (main and sub) to make it easier for the audience to follow (Figure 6-2).

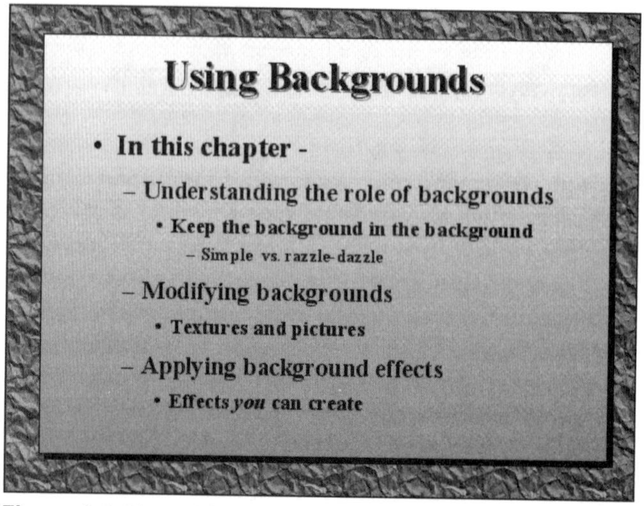

Figure 6-1: Too many levels of text create clutter and are hard to read.

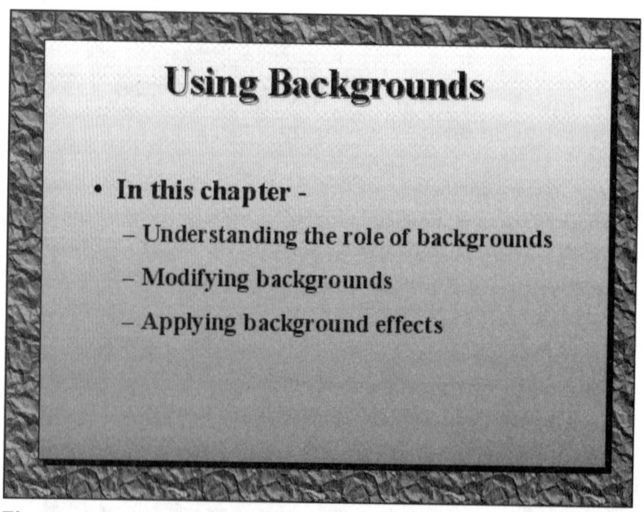

Figure 6-2: A more readable slide, with details to follow on later slides.

Importing a pre-existing outline

In some cases, you may prefer to use a word processor or text editor to create your slide show outline. As long as that document uses a format that PowerPoint understands (RTF and TXT in Version 4, as well as DOC and WPD in Version 7, and HTM in Version 8), it can create a slide show outline directly from the document, saving you valuable time (Figures 6-3 and 6-4).

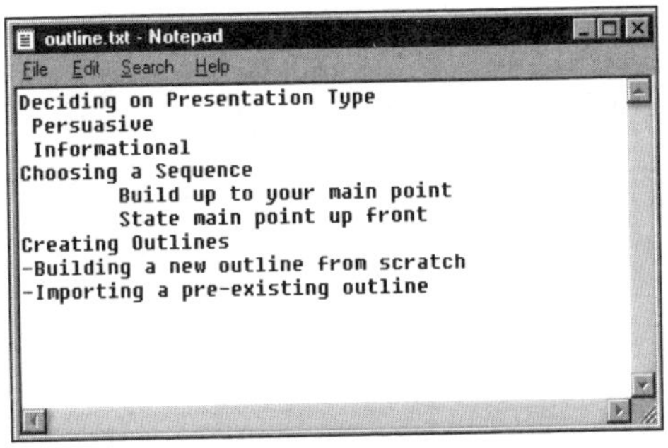

Figure 6-3: The original outline as a text file.

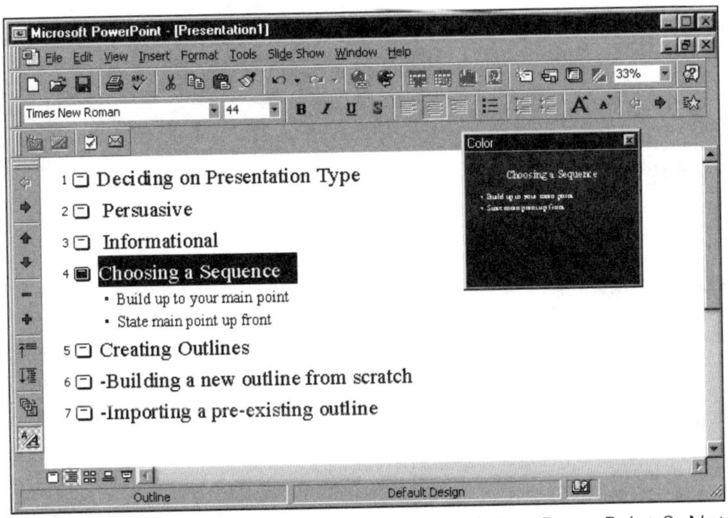

Figure 6-4: The same outline after importing it into PowerPoint 8. Note the convenient thumbnail window at the upper-right corner of the window.

Here's a "gotcha" that you're not likely to see documented elsewhere. Whatever its format, your original document must use *tabs* to indicate slide bullets. If you just use spaces or hyphens to indent subsidiary points, for example, PowerPoint puts each point on its own slide. (Take another look at Figures 6-3 and 6-4.)

To import a pre-existing outline, follow these steps:

1. Select File⇨New⇨Blank Presentation to open a new slide show.
2. Click View⇨Outline, or click the Outline View icon on the toolbar at the bottom of the screen. The slide number and a slide icon appear to the left.

3. Select File➪Open and navigate to the directory that contains your outline document by changing the Look in: field (Versions 7 and 8) or the Directories and Drives fields (Version 4).
4. Select All Outlines (Versions 7 and 8) in the Files of Type field or select Outlines (Version 4) in the List Files of Type. If your file doesn't appear, you may not have used the proper filename extension; try displaying All Files to find your document.
5. Double-click the file to select it for importing. You can also click Open in Versions 7 and 8 or OK in Version 4.

tip

If you get an error message that blocks you from opening a file that is to be imported, you may need to go back to the application that created the file and save it in one of the compatible formats listed there.

To refine your outline, go back to Outline View at any time and review and organize your thoughts. If you prefer to work with one slide at a time, use Slide View and enter text directly onto the slide. You'll normally bounce back and forth between Slide View and Outline View as you zero in on the final outline.

Placing Text

Now we change our focus from multislide outlining issues to single-slide layout, starting with the text element. The text placement "dos and don'ts" in this section (which all apply equally to Versions 4, 7, and 8) fall into the following categories:

- Typeface consistency
- Slide titles
- Text size
- Text color
- Bullets and numbering
- Text quantity

Typeface consistency

Don't clutter your slides with an array of typefaces. Try to stick with no more than two complementary styles (Table 6-1 lists some complementary and non-complementary typefaces); one style is preferable. You can always accent your typeface with bold, italic, and underline styles (as well as with color and size changes) by using Format➪Font.

Table 6-1: Complementary and Non-Complementary Typefaces

Complementary	Non-Complementary
Arial, Century Gothic	Arial, Book Antiqua
Bookman Old Style, Times New Roman	Bookman Old Style, Tahoma
Impact, Haettenschweiler	Impact, Algerian
Century Gothic, Desdemona	Century Gothic, Kino MT

Readable, simple fonts are best, especially to present directly from a computer. You don't have to completely dismiss ornate fonts; you may, however, want to limit them to headings and slide titles in which the larger point size will help readability.

Slide titles

As a rule, each slide should have a title. Titles help the audience follow your presentation's logical flow (for an example, see Figures 6-6 and 6-7 later in this chapter). Think of the title as an announcement or opening for each slide or set of related slides.

Here are a few titling tips:

- When you break out ideas over multiple slides, number your titles so the audience knows that more are coming. For example: *Troubleshooting Tips (1 of 4)* or, if you have less room, *Troubleshooting Tips (1)*. Version 8's automatic Expand Slide feature uses a different approach: Each top-level bullet becomes a new slide's title. Decide which method best suits your needs.
- Limit titles to two lines of text; any more than this and you lose the meaning of *title!* You also have less space for the main slide information if the title is top-heavy.
- Unless you're working against a specific design element, center titles horizontally on the slide.
- To accent the title, use boldface and add a slight drop-shadow. For fancier effects, ungroup your text and apply a gradient. These techniques are especially useful if you don't have enough slide "real estate" to make the title lines a larger point size (see the section that follows). See Chapters 3 and 10 for more on creating text shadows and gradients.

Text size

Regardless of the presentation mode (35mm slides, computer projection, and so on), try to use text sizes of 18 points or greater. With most typefaces, text sizes below 18 points make the audience members strain to read your slides; if you make them work too hard, they'll subconsciously resist your message. If you lay out your presentation to videotape, or print handouts with three or more slides per page, small text sizes work against you even more.

Choose a larger font size for your slide titles (such as 32 or 36 points). Then set the text in the body of your presentation at 20 or 24. Good general-purpose combinations are 32 and 20 or 36 and 24.

Text color

Establish enough contrast between text and background colors so that reading is easy. Remember from Chapter 2 that darker backgrounds work best for 35mm slides, and lighter colors work best for overhead transparencies and LCD panel presentations. Therefore, use lighter text colors for 35mm work and darker text colors for overheads and computer projections.

When you read about backgrounds in Chapter 2, you learned not to use "hot" colors that can distract your audience from the foreground message. For text, however, if you have a particularly important point to emphasize, use some of those hotter colors. Just don't get too obnoxious with them; bright red text on a yellow background may stand out, but it smacks of cheesy sensationalism.

Bullets and numbering

Bullets are great for organizing text; however, they're also easy to overuse. Either use bullets on your main heading or on subheadings; don't use both. When you use bullets in only one indentation level, you further distinguish your two levels of organization and clarify your outline.

Modifying the line spacing attribute and adding more room between bullets can sometimes improve the overall balance and ease of reading when you use bulleted lists. Select the slide text, choose Format⇨Line Spacing, and reset the value to 1.25 or 1.50. (Select Preview before you commit yourself.)

Resize your bullets and add a dash of color to make them cooler. To make your bullets larger or smaller, select the slide text, choose Format⇨Bullets, and change the % of Text value in the Size field. To change bullet color, select the pop-up color menu, from which you can either pick a scheme color you like, or click Other Color (More Colors in Version 8) to gain access to the two PowerPoint color palettes. (As always, click Preview before you commit.) When you choose a bullet color that's lighter than the background but in the same color family, you produce bullets that look much cooler than plain white and are also easier on the eyes. Use moderation, of course; you don't want your bullets so large and colorful that they overshadow the text.

You can easily forget about the old, reliable, numbered-list system because of the variety of cool bullet styles that PowerPoint makes available. Mixing numbered lists with your presentation adds variety and makes sense whenever you have a prescribed linear sequence to get across. If the sequence doesn't matter, use bullets; if it does, use numbers. (To learn when to use numbers versus bullets, look at the lists in this book.)

Text quantity

Your slides may not always be large enough to get all your relevant ideas onto a single screen. The amateur uses smaller point sizes and interline spacing to cram everything onto the slide (Figure 6-5), but the professional (you) breaks the points across multiple slides (Figures 6-6 and 6-7). When you do, use the same background, title, and slide layout for the connected slides.

version 8

As mentioned earlier, Version 8 offers an automatic Expand Slide feature that creates a new slide from each top-level bullet point. To use it, from Outline or Slide Sorter View, highlight the cluttered slide and select Tools⇨Expand Slide.

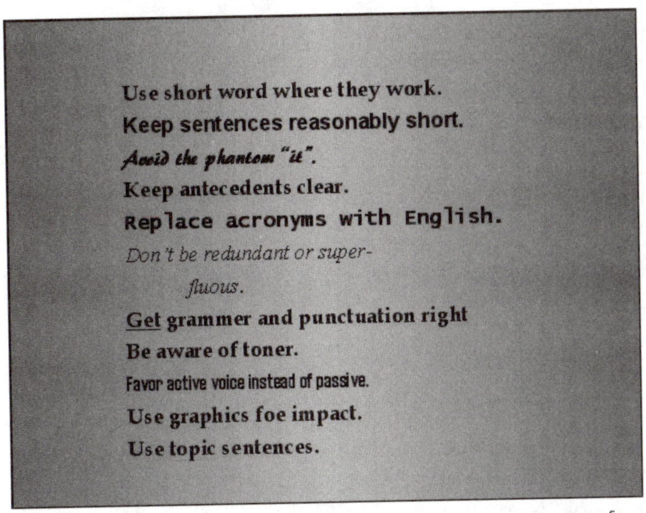

Figure 6-5: An untitled, cluttered slide with too many typefaces (and a few typos).

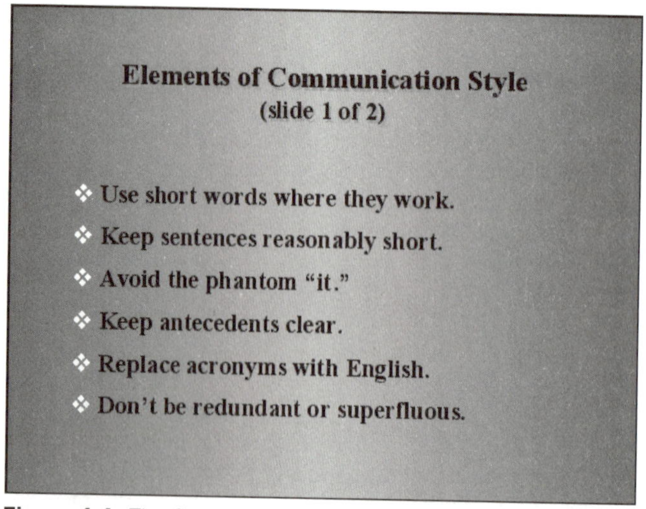

Figure 6-6: The first of two slides with a proper title, consistent fonts, and less clutter.

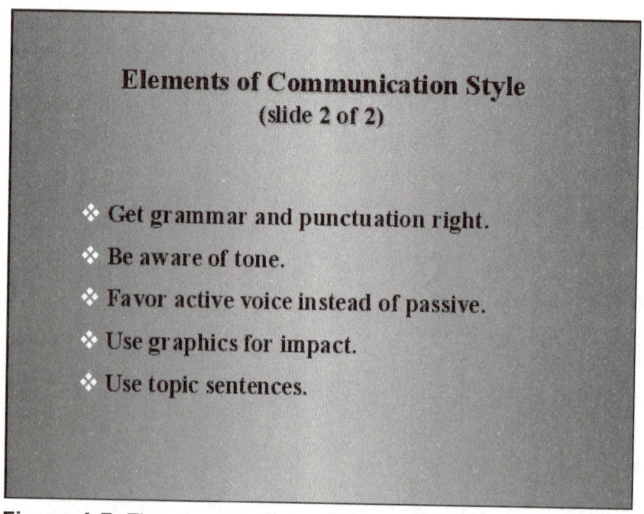

Figure 6-7: The second of two slides with a proper title, consistent fonts, and less clutter.

Microsoft suggests a *6 x 6 rule* — no more than 6 lines (not sentences!) per slide and 6 words per line. This rule may be a bit too constraining, but not by much. It helps keep your words short; for example, substitute *use* for *utilize*, *now* for *immediately*, and so on. Also, avoid widows and orphans — single lines at the top or bottom of a slide that continue to or from another slide. And don't put important text near the bottom of the slide; audience members in the back row may not be able to see it!

tip

To help avoid text clutter, avoid hyphenation — that is, if you can do so without upsetting the balance of your slides.

warning

Here's one more reason to avoid jamming too much text onto a slide. When you videotape a PowerPoint presentation, 25 pixels' worth (pixel = screen dot) of space on all four sides may drop off the screen during the recording session (or during audience viewing of the videotape later). Video professionals refer to this area as the *safe area,* or *safety.* If you think that you may record your show to videotape, leave a margin of at least 25 dots at each edge where no text appears.

tip

Drama is an important communications tool that your audience will appreciate. To emphasize one major point, nothing beats creating a dramatic slide with only one bullet item. (Flip through any magazine and look at how the advertising professionals use white space — it's the same concept.) A single-bullet slide stands out even more if you precede the slide with a string of multiple-bullet slides.

Placing Graphics

Although having a lot of text is normal for most presentations, one and a half zillion studies confirm that people remember graphical images more easily than text. So, whenever possible, use charts, tables, pictures, and clip art to express key points (Figures 6-8 through 6-11).

Chapter 5 presented the basics of PowerPoint's charting, graphing, and drawing capabilities. Here are a couple of tips on how to lay out these graphical elements on the slide.

tip

If you've ever looked carefully at a professionally framed painting or photograph, you may have noticed that the framer left more space at the bottom than at the top. If the distance from the top of the picture (or mat) to the top of the frame is equal to the distance from the bottom of the picture (or mat) to the bottom of the frame, the spacing throws off your visual sense and doesn't look right. To counteract this effect, professional framers add an extra ¼ inch to ½ inch to the bottom margin. Use the same technique for your slides.

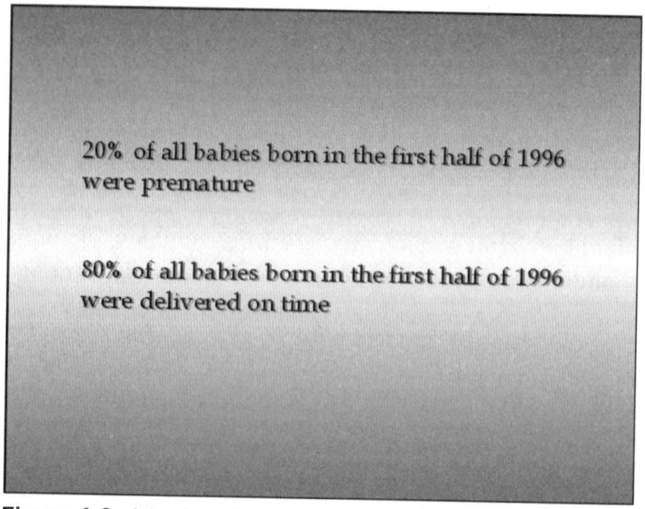

Figure 6-8: A boring slide that no one will remember.

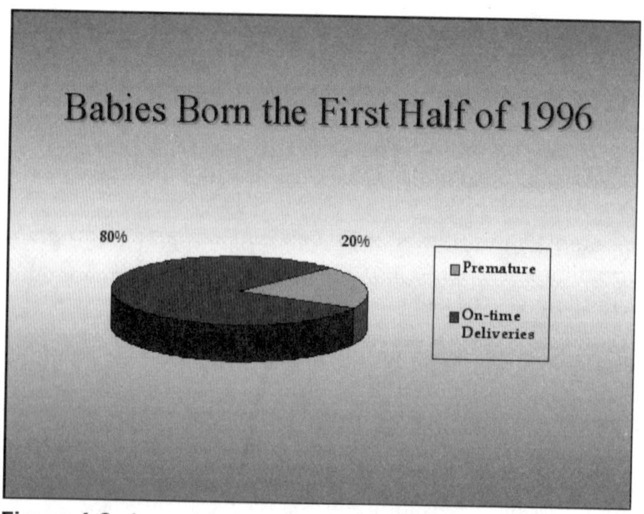

Figure 6-9: A graphical slide expressing the same data.

When you use charts, be consistent; that is, stick with horizontal bar charts instead of mixing horizontal and vertical charts. If you're using pie charts, keep them the same size throughout the slide show. Consistency helps avoid a cobbled-together feel.

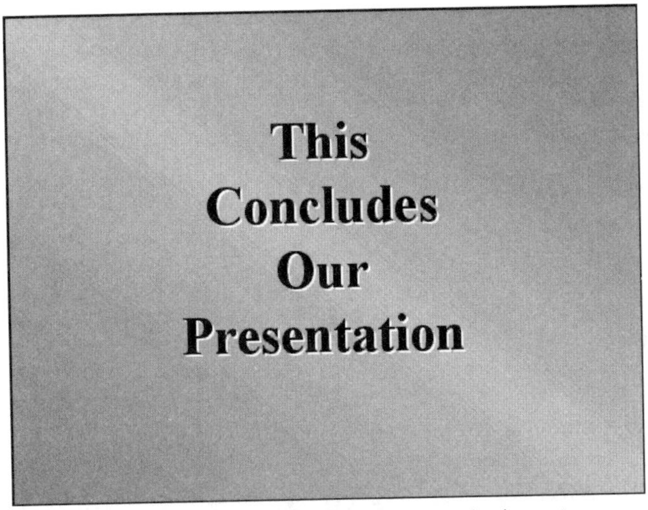

Figure 6-10: A simple text slide without much character.

Figure 6-11: A graphical way of saying the same thing.

tip Normally, you should center your graphical elements horizontally on the slide, like the text slide titles. If you want to introduce an element of drama, however, create a *build* in which the bars of a horizontal bar chart appear sequentially and the last bar to appear protrudes far to the right, throwing the chart off balance for effect. (See Chapter 11 for a detailed discussion of builds.)

In Versions 7 and 8, you're no longer limited to placing graphics within slide boundaries. In Version 8, simply move the graphic partly off the slide; in Version 7, move the graphic while holding down Alt. For a cool effect, try placing the appropriate graphic half off the slide; the effect can be quite charming in Slide Show View (see Figure 6-12, which is in Slide View).

Figure 6-12: Expand your presentation's virtual world by placing graphics partly off the slide in Versions 7 and 8.

warning

The same caveat discussed in the text section about the *safe area* of videotaped presentations applies to placing graphical elements.

Using Color

Color is a very effective presentation tool when you use it properly. As mentioned in Chapter 2, color sets the mood for the entire presentation. Color can also help discriminate between degrees of importance, emphasize a particular text item or graphic element, associate the presentation with a company, group, or department, or simply add "cool." On the downside, you can distract your audience and even foil the delivery of your message with improper use of color.

A quick lesson in color

Color is one of the hardest presentation concepts to grasp. Color is called a "concept" because people see color differently.

In the physical sense, color is an attribute of light energy — specifically, the frequency of the light wave that reaches the eye. (You can also consider light to be particles, but that concept is more technical than necessary for this book.) Reds are longer light waves with lower frequencies; blues are shorter waves with higher frequencies. The eye's retina consists of different kinds of cells called *cones* and *rods*. Cones sense color; rods sense brightness (the intensity, or amplitude, of the light wave).

Every person is created differently and, therefore, interprets color differently. For example, some people don't perceive red and green because they have an imbalance of the retina, with blue being dominant. (Can you see how this common imbalance affects the colors you choose for your slide show?) And, of course, many individuals don't distinguish colors at all. (You should always check PowerPoint's Black and White View to simulate how such an individual can see your show.)

Understanding the RGB and CMYK color models is worthwhile, because PowerPoint and many other graphics programs enable you to specify colors by using one model or the other, or both. We were all taught in school that the primary colors are red, yellow, and blue, and that the secondary colors are orange, green, and purple. In the world of computers and printing, however, we must re-adjust our thinking. The computer *primary* colors of red, green, and blue (RGB) produce white when you project them onto a screen in equal amounts, so RGB is called *additive* color. In printing, the *secondary* colors of cyan, magenta, and yellow (CMY) produce black when you add them onto a printed page in equal amounts; but a complete absence of the secondary colors corresponds to white (just as a page is white if it has no ink on it), so CMY is called *subtractive* color. If you've seen the acronym *CMYK*, you're probably wondering why *K* is missing. The *K* is short for *blacK*, because printer's inks aren't pure; therefore, you need a separate ink for the common black color.

Although the physical explanation of color is scientific and objective, subjective facets of color perception do exist (such as psychological and cultural). Individuals associate colors with different feelings or ideas based on their own experience and psychology. To a skier, green on white may signify *simple*, and black on white may signify *difficult*; to a hiker, green may signify the great outdoors, whereas to a financier, green may signify wealth. Different cultures have their own color associations. The Chinese, for example, identify red with prosperity and good fortune.

Color mixes can be bad and good. Cool colors such as blues, purples, and greens are pleasant colors that cause feelings of tranquillity and peacefulness. On the other hand, hot colors such as orange, yellow, and red evoke lively feelings (such as excitement and action). Color combinations that create tension are considered complementary colors. They are opposite of each other on the color wheel: red and green, blue and orange, purple and yellow. When you separate complementary colors, they seem less intense than when they are side-by-side.

Color dos and don'ts

Building on your new knowledge, here are some specific color tips for PowerPoint shows:

- If you must use complementary colors, break the tension by lowering the saturation (intensity) of each color, avoiding large area fills, and perhaps adding a neutral border (such as gray or beige) between them.
- Instead of always changing font style or size to stress a point, try changing color.
- Avoid red and green combinations; many individuals can't easily distinguish between them.
- If you must make a presentation to a group from a different culture from your own, consult with someone from that same culture to identify colors that may have positive or negative connotations.
- If you plan to capture your slides to videotape, avoid colors that vibrate on playback; bright red and lime green are notorious, for example. Also, certain colors don't make their way to videotape at all — for example, rich blues are significantly dulled. Avoid saturated colors of all hues; they often bleed and create ghosting or blurred edges.
- If you plan to turn an electronic slide show into 35mm slides, remove all pattern fills. Closely spaced patterns tend to come across on 35mm slides as a solid color rather than as patterns. Use gradient fills for the best color impact.
- If you plan to print your slides onto color pages (for example, in a book or in an annual report), be aware that what looks great on your (RGB) computer screen may not look great on the (CMYK) printed page. Very bright blues, for example, don't translate well. If you're working with a graphics service bureau to translate your PowerPoint slides into printed images, start with a typical sample slide to see if you're using an unacceptable color shift with the backgrounds and colors. You can also grab a screen (using PrtScr) and paste it into a high-end image editing program (such as Adobe Photoshop). Change the image mode from RGB to CMYK for a quick preview.

tip

To change the color scheme of multiple slides, use the Slide Sorter View, which permits you to select and modify several slides at once

warning

If you import a cool background or other object, and the color seems uneven or "off," you may be viewing the object in Slide View or Slide Sorter View. Change to Slide Show View; it gives you a truer reading of how your colors will look during the actual presentation.

Style Checker

PowerPoint 7 and 8 provide a new tool, called the *Style Checker*, that runs a check on spelling, visual clarity, and case and end punctuation (Figure 6-13). To access it, open your presentation and select Tools⇨Style Checker.

Figure 6-13: PowerPoint 7 and 8's Style Checker verifies spelling, visual clarity, and punctuation.

Style Checker is a consistency check for text and graphics. To display the dialog box shown in Figure 6-14, click the Options button and the Case and End Punctuation tab. In this dialog box, you can enforce the same case options (for example, UPPERCASE, Title Case) for all slide titles and slide body text. You can also enforce consistent end punctuation for the same categories. If you want all your slide titles to end "up in the air" without a period, for example, you can enforce that rule here.

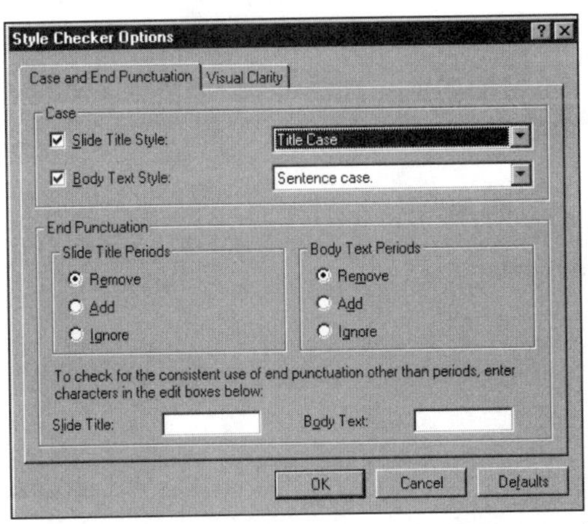

Figure 6-14: Specifying Case and End Punctuation options in Style Checker.

To display the dialog box shown in Figure 6-15, click the Options button and the Visual Clarity tab. In this dialog box, you can have Style Checker warn you if the displayed quantities exceed the limits you specify. One warning: The Check for Title and Placeholder Text Off Slide option does *not* include the safe area for laying presentations off to videotape.

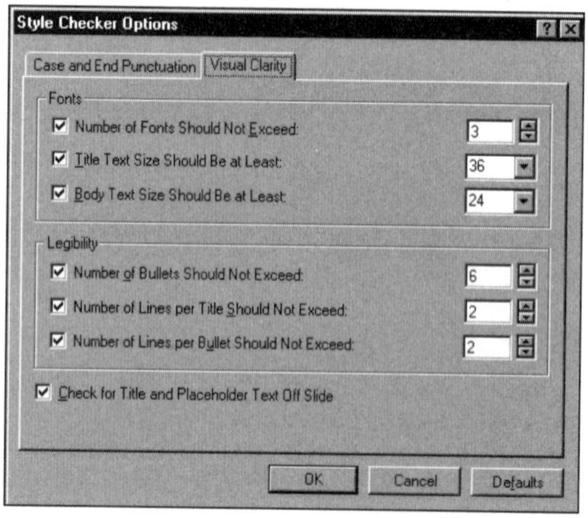

Figure 6-15: Specifying Visual Clarity options in Style Checker.

Summary

In this chapter, we started to pull together presentation elements to create something a little more special than a typical, canned presentation.

Outlining techniques can make your slide show flow logically.

You can create an outline from scratch within PowerPoint or use the outline import feature to pull in an outline created in a text editor or word processor.

Focusing on the layout of individual slides, you now have some tips for laying out text and graphics elements, and for using color to your advantage.

PowerPoint 7 and 8's Style Checker is a useful tool for ensuring the consistency and proper placement of slide punctuation, text, and bullet elements.

Now that our slide show has a skeleton, and we've started to consider ways to assemble a good-looking slide, we can move on. In Chapter 7, you learn how to create cool bitmap graphics that go beyond the standard backgrounds and gradients that PowerPoint's built-in tools can create.

Creating Cool Bitmaps

7

In This Chapter

Discovering the pros and cons of bitmap images

Understanding bitmap file types and which to use in favor of others

Learning where to find ready-made bitmap images

Distinguishing the three main categories of bitmap programs: image editors, filters, and special-purpose tools

Using third-party bitmap tools by preparing a cool slide background from scratch

Discovering the pros and cons of PowerPoint 8's new Set Transparent Color tool

Finding out the basics of scanning bitmaps for use in PowerPoint

Learning undocumented tricks to import bitmaps onto PowerPoint slides flawlessly

Perhaps the most breathtaking PowerPoint slides use beautiful bitmap images created outside of PowerPoint. Unlike clip art or other vector-based images, which store information as curves and formulas, bitmap images store information as a collection or series of arranged dots, or *pixels*. When you zoom in to a bitmap image with a paint program, you can see each pixel; but at normal size, the image can exhibit the detail and immediacy of a color photograph or a fine work of art.

This chapter looks at the pros and cons of bitmap images and presents the common file types you'll encounter. It then presents some options for finding and using existing bitmap images. To be really cool, though, you'll want to create some of your own bitmap graphics. To help you do that, we explain the main categories of bitmap software, take you through an example that uses such software to create a gorgeous PowerPoint slide, and suggest how to use a color scanner to quickly create custom images for your presentations. Finally, we show you how to bring your cool bitmaps into PowerPoint without a hitch.

Bitmap Pros and Cons

With the right software, you have total control over a bitmap image's appearance, because you can modify it down to the individual pixel. This total control over every detail constitutes the power of bitmap graphics.

For example, one aspect of this control is the capability to trick the eye into seeing more colors than are really there. Put a red pixel right next to a yellow one, and the eye will see orange. Each pixel represents a single color in the overall picture, much like a tile in a mosaic. Bitmap images, therefore, can appear to have many more colors than PowerPoint actually permits.

Graphics software can take advantage of such optical illusions to perform many great effects. For example, *anti-aliased* text will appear to have smooth, rather than jagged, diagonals, because the bitmap software drops in some edge pixels that blur the diagonal by averaging the text color and the background color. The eye sees a smoother line than it would otherwise (Figure 7-1).

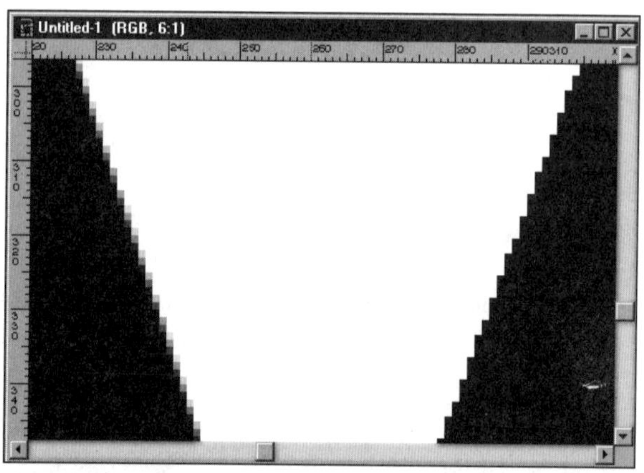

Figure 7-1: The anti-aliasing bitmap technique smooths out jagged edges on the letter to the left by dropping in gray pixels to trick the eye.

The sharpness and quality of bitmap graphics depend on how many pixels there are to manipulate. PowerPoint users don't have much choice here; you'll usually be presenting on a PC that can display either 640 horizontal by 480 vertical dots or 800 horizontal by 600 vertical dots.

tip

If you use bitmap graphics, develop your slide show on a PC that has the same display resolution as the PC you'll use to present. A bitmap that looks great at 640 x 480 may not look as great at 800 x 600.

Aside from resolution, *color depth* (the amount of color information a single pixel displays) determines how good your bitmaps will look. Typical PC display color depths are as follows:

- 4-bit color (16 colors at a time, or *VGA* color)
- 8-bit color (256 colors at a time)
- 15-bit or 16-bit color (thousands of colors at a time, or *high* color)
- 24-bit color (16.7 million colors at a time, or *true* color)

tip

The best method is to use the maximum color depth possible for all your bitmap files until just before you import them into PowerPoint. Then, if necessary, reduce the color depth with image editing software to match what your delivery PC can support. PowerPoint can perform color-depth reduction (Microsoft calls it *palette management*), but you can't expect it to do as nice a job as a good image editing program will do.

If bitmap graphics offer so much control, why not use bitmaps all the time? You may remember from Chapter 4 that bitmap images don't scale well, either up or down, so they're best suited for fixed-size, full-screen images. Bitmaps are, therefore, a natural choice for slide show backgrounds. They're also a good choice when you know for certain what screen resolution you'll be using to present.

Another potential drawback is that bitmaps don't come in irregular shapes: they're always rectangular. The following tip may help, though, if you have to use a bitmap and you want it to look like a clip art image.

tip

If you use bitmap graphics that are not full-screen size, and you want an irregular foreground image to appear to "float," in Version 4 or 7, you can surround it with pixels the same color as your solid PowerPoint background. In PowerPoint 8, use the new Set Transparent Color tool to eliminate the background color, as explained a little later in this chapter. Neither trick works on complex or gradient backgrounds, though.

Bitmap File Types

Dozens of different bitmap file formats exist in the PC world. The following list includes many of the more common ones, roughly in order of attractiveness for PowerPoint users:

- *PC Paintbrush* (*.PCX) was developed by ZSoft and is the granddaddy of PC graphics file formats. No less than five varieties have been in common use, varying primarily in color depth. PCX files use a simple form of compression called RLE (Run-Length Encoding). They're more compact than uncompressed formats, but not as small as other formats, such as compressed TIFF or GIF. They save and load quickly.

- *TIFF files* (Tagged Image File Format, *.TIF) were originally specified by Aldus Corporation and can be any size, resolution, or color depth. They can be compressed or uncompressed, and they can store lots of information about the image or just the bare-bones pixel data. The PowerPoint TIFF reader handles most file format variants with aplomb, and compressed TIFF is our favorite format for PowerPoint use.
- *Windows BitMap* (*.BMP) is an uncompressed format designed more for speed of loading and saving than for economy of disk space. Because of the large file sizes, you want to avoid this format when you have a choice.
- In Windows, the *RLE* (Run-Length Encoding) format is a simple compressed version of the BMP format. RLE compression looks for repeated pixels and counts them. Files with a high percentage of solid areas will compress more under RLE than files with a more varied distribution of colors and values, so RLE compression doesn't do much for complex, photo-realistic bitmaps.
- *Graphics Interchange Format* (*.GIF, pronounced "jif") files use a structure developed by CompuServe. GIF files are about as small as you can get and may contain up to 256 colors from a 24-bit palette. The nicest thing about GIF files other than their small size is their high degree of standardization. They take a long time to display.
- *Targa files* (*.TGA) are either 8-, 16-, 24- (most commonly), or 32-bit color or gray-scale files. AT&T developed this format for its TrueVision video board line, and the format is fairly free of frustrating variants. Targa files are usually very large and don't compress well.
- *JPEG* (*.JPG) stands for Joint Photographic Expert Group and is the most widely used graphic file compression technology. Its primary benefit is designating *specific areas* for higher or lower quality compression. In this way, focus points or highlights may be compressed less than the rest of the image, for an overall higher quality result. JPEG files are popular on the Internet because of their small size, but compressing can involve a loss of quality, so we prefer to not use JPEG for PowerPoint slides.

Proprietary file types also exist, such as Photoshop's *.PSD format, but they usually don't offer any dramatic advantage over *.PCX or *.TIF. The most popular graphic file type on the Macintosh side is PICT, but take care: PICT files can be either bitmap or vector, so if you can't open a PICT file in a bitmap program such as Photoshop, it's probably the vector variety. PowerPoint can read most PICT files.

Finding Cool Bitmaps

The quickest way to get cool bitmaps into your slide shows is by buying them. Tens of thousands of background textures, stock photographs, and computer-generated images are available from companies such as

MetaTools and PhotoDisc (see Appendix A). Some companies, such as Publishers Depot, offer stock images over the Internet.

If you have PowerPoint or Office on CD-ROM, you can view some sample stock photos in the \ValuPack\PPPhotos directory; some photos in JPEG format are also available in \ValuPack\Photos. PowerPoint 8's Connect to Web for Additional Clips button (on the lower right of the Clip Gallery's Pictures window) provides access to thousands of pictures via the Internet, so go surfing. And don't forget about the samples on this book's CD-ROM — you can add them to the new Clip Gallery for easy access from the Pictures tab.

Much digitized photography is sold for use by print professionals, and, therefore, the files have a much higher resolution than you need for PowerPoint slide shows. Plan to invest in a solid image editing program, such as Picture Publisher or Photoshop, that can reduce the size of these images and still maintain most of their clarity and beauty.

Before using stock digital images in any product that you may offer for sale, double-check the license agreement. The good news is that almost all stock photography can be used in PowerPoint slide shows without the user having to pay a royalty.

Customizing Bitmaps 1: Paint Software

Programs that can create or edit bitmap images are known generically as *paint* programs. PowerPoint has some drawing capabilities for vector images but includes no painting tools, for the simple reason that both Windows 3.*x* and Windows 95 come with a little paint utility (PBRUSH.EXE for 3.*x*, MSPAINT.EXE for 95).

Windows Paint

For fixing an errant pixel here or there or for cropping an image down to size, Windows Paint is an adequate tool; it loads fairly quickly and certainly is not difficult to use. It's not the only tool you want for working with bitmap graphics, however, if you plan to create cool PowerPoint slides. Windows Paint only works with BMP and (in Windows 95) PCX formats; its resizing capabilities are minimal, its tool set is very small, and, most importantly, it doesn't offer any special effects beyond airbrushing.

So, if Windows Paint won't cut it, what do you need?

- Mainly, you need a competent program for general bitmap manipulation, enhancement, and special effects.

- Next, you need some cool filters to generate even more effects.
- Finally, you need special-purpose paint programs that can perform tricks the general-purpose programs can't.

Here are some notes on each item, with a few specific recommendations.

Image editing software

The two "heavy hitters" in bitmap graphics on the PC are Adobe's Photoshop and Micrografx's Picture Publisher. These programs are so sophisticated that the market no longer calls them paint programs; rather, they're called *image editing* programs.

version 8

PowerPoint 8 offers some basic bitmap manipulation tools via the Picture toolbar, which this chapter discusses later in the context of scanning. Further, Office 97 comes with a little image editing program called Photo Editor, based on Media Cybernetics' Halo Desktop Imager (Figure 7-2). Although it's not an "industrial-strength" program, if you deal with bitmap images only occasionally, you may find that Photo Editor meets your needs.

Figure 7-2: The Photo Editor applet ships with Office 97 and can scan original images or modify existing ones. It offers a handful of special effects; for example, Despeckle is useful for cleaning up grainy photographs.

warning

The more powerful image editing programs are known for their memory appetite, and you wouldn't want to try running Photoshop or Picture Publisher on anything less than an 8MB PC. (Painter for Windows 95 requires 12MB!) Fortunately, working with screen images is much less demanding than creating images for print media, as the computer screen's resolution is much lower than the printed page.

Photoshop and Picture Publisher can handle just about every type of bitmap image available, and both offer incredibly flexible tools for manipulating pixels. Such tools include the *magic wand,* which can pluck an irregular shape out from a different-colored background, and *layering,* which enables you to build a composite image as though you were layering transparencies one on top of another. These programs also do a great job of resizing bitmap images so that they look good at different sizes — no easy task. Versions of both programs are available for Windows 3.*x* and Windows 95.

Most importantly for our purposes, both programs can produce a variety of very cool special effects through mini-programs called *filters* (also known as *plug-ins*).

Filters

Filters are mini-programs that other graphics programs, such as Photoshop, can "call" to perform particular effects to the selected image or image portion. Sometimes a filter just does what its name implies, without giving you any options (the *blur* filter). Other filters let you specify variables that control filter options, such as intensity, direction, and so on.

Several companies offer excellent filters for Photoshop, Picture Publisher, and Painter. They include Adobe (Gallery Effects) and MetaTools (Kai's Power Tools).

Specialized paint programs

Finally, we should mention specialized paint programs, which offer some special features that are not found in general-purpose, image editing software. One famous example is Fractal Design's Painter, a program that simulates traditional artists' tools, such as chalk, charcoal, watercolor, felt-tip pen, and so on. Painter does what it does so well that it's far and away the market leader in natural-media effects. Versions are available for both Windows 3.*x* and Windows 95.

Another specialized program that imaging aficionados have been using for years is MetaTools' KPT Bryce, a 3-D modeling and rendering program that enables you to create natural and supernatural landscapes, seascapes, and terrains with remarkable ease (Figures 7-3 and 7-4). We used the Mac version of KPT Bryce to create the "cyberscapes" in this book's color plates, but the Windows version is now available.

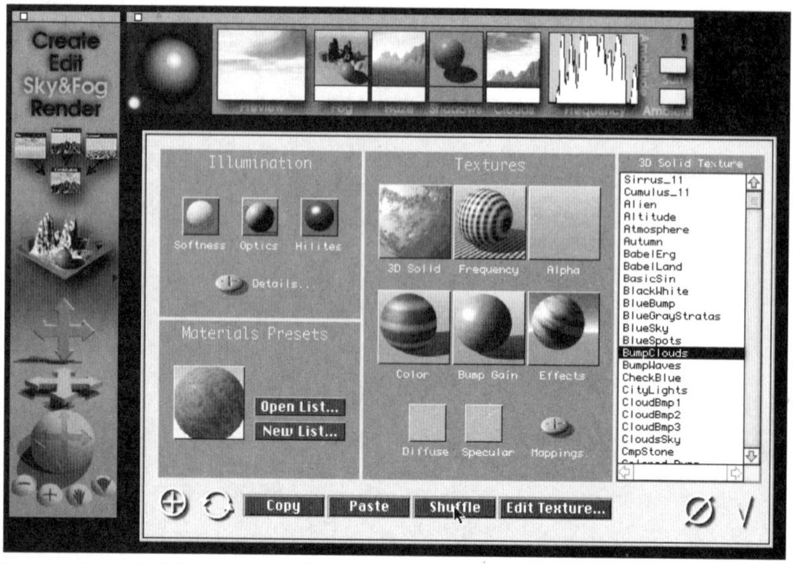

Figure 7-3: KPT Bryce's Sky & Fog Palette (top) enables you to manipulate various lighting effects for your cyberscapes. The Materials Editor (center) is where you create the "skin" for each of your terrains and objects.

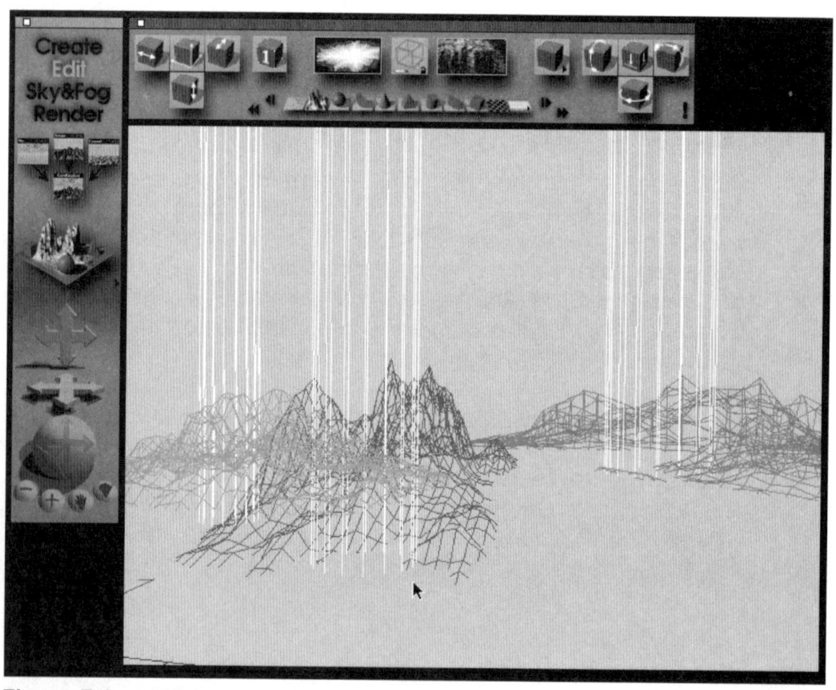

Figure 7-4: A KPT Bryce scene in "wireframe" view, before rendering. The Edit Palette (top) uses pictograms rather than words.

KPT Bryce is so popular because it's easy to learn and use, unlike most 3-D programs, which have such steep learning curves that it's scary. You have total control of all the elements of nature, such as cloud type, fog, haze, turbulence, weather, terrain, light source, and more. Also, your efforts are rewarded with astonishingly high quality output through the use of a graphics technique called *ray tracing*, which is discussed further in the next chapter.

Customizing Bitmaps 2: An Elaborate Example

Stock images often look gorgeous and win easily on the heads-turned-per-hours-invested scale, but there will be times when you can't find the exact stock image you want. Although we wouldn't have said so six or seven years ago, making your own beautiful bitmap images can be easy with the programs currently available.

The following example demonstrates how we created a very sophisticated background for a slide show on pollution, using many of the bitmap graphics tools mentioned earlier: Photoshop, Kai's Power Photos, Kai's Power Tools, Gallery Effects, and Painter. It doesn't matter whether you have all these tools or fully understand every step of the example. The point is that if you spend a little time learning the basics of a few powerful graphics programs, you can create fine art images for PowerPoint in short order. The entire example that follows took us about two hours. (You can see the final, full-color image in this book's color insert and on the enclosed CD-ROM.)

Scenario: You've been asked to give a talk titled "World Pollution — A Dirty Subject." You want a cool-looking thematic title slide, perhaps one you can also use as a background. You look at all the backgrounds PowerPoint has to offer, and nothing is suitable. So, you decide to create a little junkyard magic yourself!

Here's how you do it (Note: All the filters in this example use the default settings):

1. Start with a stock photograph of urban graffiti on a smooth wall. Run Photoshop and open the KPT Power Photos file 0030062.TIF on the Volume 3, Disk 2 CD-ROM ("Urban Textures and Backgrounds"). Use the high-res version; it's a large file and takes a minute to open.
2. Use Photoshop's cropping tool to crop the black edge by dragging the tool to form a dotted rectangle over the "good" area of the photo.
3. Reduce the image size to appropriate dimensions for a PowerPoint screen (approximately 641 x 481 — we explain the extra pixel later

in the chapter). Select Image➪Image Size and keep the Constrain Proportions box checked to avoid distortion when resizing. Set the scaling unit to pixels and type **481** as the height; the width will auto-scale to 720 or so (Figure 7-5).

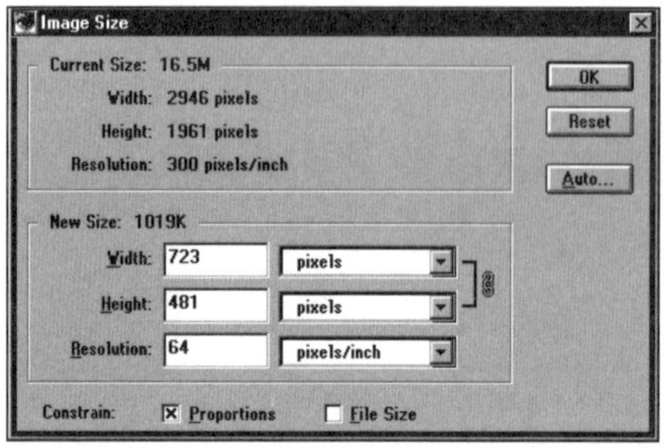

Figure 7-5: The first step in downsizing an image in Photoshop is to scale it proportionally so that the width is at least 640 and the height is at least 480.

4. Next, we fix the width dimension by cropping part of the image. Choose Image➪Canvas Size and type **641** pixels for the width. Highlight the center square on the placement grid to tell Photoshop to crop the image in equal amounts from the left and right edges. You now have a layer called *Background* on the floating layers palette, which should be turned on throughout this exercise.

5. Now apply a cool filter. To make the graffiti image look as if it were spray-painted onto a brick wall, select Filters➪Adobe Gallery Effects: Classic Art 2➪Texturizer. Click Texture Controls, select Brick, and then click Apply (Figure 7-6).

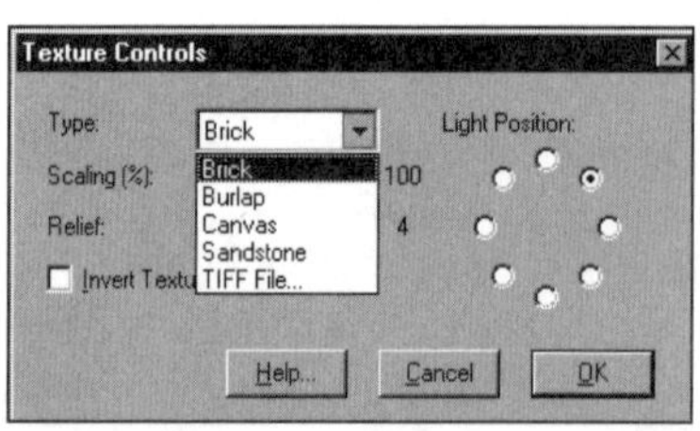

Figure 7-6: Applying a Gallery Effects "brick wall" filter to the scaled-down image. Note the other textures available; many filters provide such variations on a theme.

6. Use the Image⇨Adjust⇨Brightness and Contrast⇨Contrast command to lower the contrast to -50. We don't want this image to be too bold. It now looks like Figure 7-7.

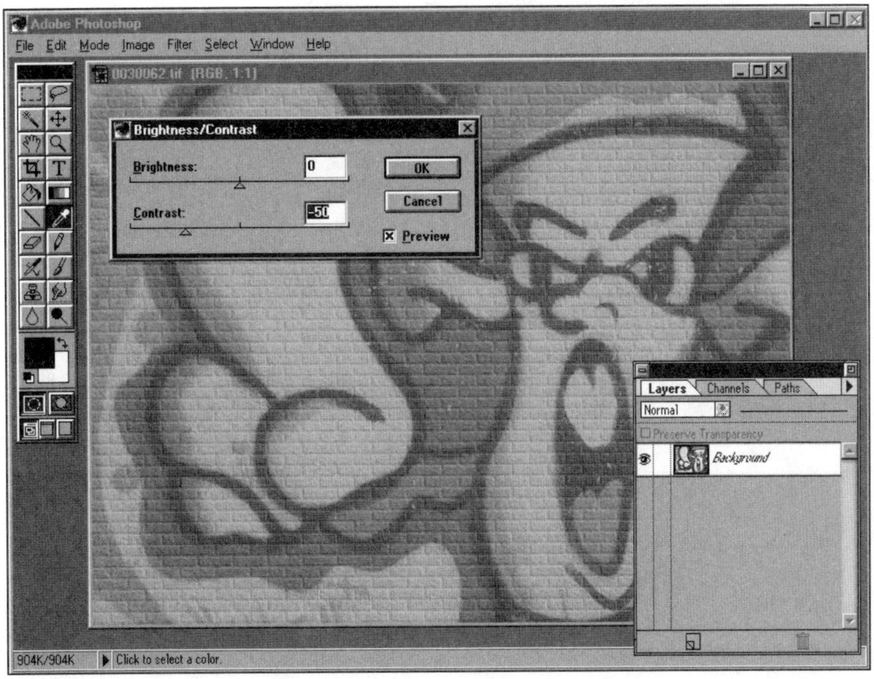

Figure 7-7: The brick wall graffiti image, at reduced contrast. Note the Layers window to the lower right.

7. Next, apply a subtle gradient using Kai's Power Tools. Choose Filter⇨KPT 3.0⇨KPT Gradient Designer to see the unusual dialog box shown in Figure 7-8. Click in the bar under the curly bracket at the left edge, drag down to the checkerboard at the bottom of the screen, and choose a semi-transparent black (alpha = 175, R = 0, G = 0, B = 0). Do the same at the right edge, but choose transparent (alpha = 0). You've just created a linear monochrome gradient that will help images along the left edge stand out.

Figure 7-8: Kai's Power Tools' filters are known for their idiosyncratic dialog boxes; this one can produce any gradient you can imagine.

8. Now say that you want to illustrate noise pollution with a barking dog. To manipulate the dog image separately from everything else, create a new layer for it. Open the Layers dialog box, if it isn't open already, with Window⇨Palettes⇨Show Layers. Click the right arrow, select New Layer, and call the new layer "dog" (Figure 7-9).

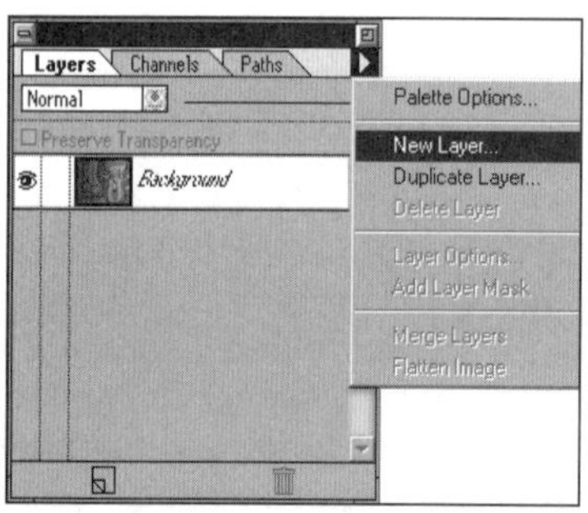

Figure 7-9: Create a new layer for any image you may want to manipulate separately. Layering was the key new feature in Photoshop Version 3.

9. With the "dog" layer still selected, load a suitable dog photograph (KPT Power Photos file 0130070.TIF on the Volume 13 CD-ROM, "Junkyards").

10. Scale the dog photo to 200 x 287 pixels at 64 resolution. Now say you want to cut out the dog figure and paste it into your main image. Double-click the magic wand tool from the Photoshop toolbar and set the tolerance to 1. Click the dog photo's white background to select it and then choose Select⇨Inverse to select the dog. The dog will have an irregular dotted line around it, as in Figure 7-10.

Figure 7-10: The magic wand tool plucks an irregularly shaped image from a different-colored background by finding outlines and edges.

11. Copy the dog with Edit⇨Copy, close the window, return to your main image, and click Edit⇨Paste. Note that the dog "floats" over the brick wall; that's the magic of the magic wand tool. Move the dog to the lower-left corner.
12. Give the dog a motion effect with Filter⇨Blur⇨Motion Blur, using the default settings.
13. Now let's add some garbage: wrecked automobiles. Create a new layer titled "cars." Open the photo 0130050.TIF on the "Junkyards" CD-ROM. Resize the image to 200 x 300, choose Select⇨All, and then choose Edit⇨Copy.
14. Close the cars window, return to the main image, select Edit⇨Paste, and move the cars to the lower-right corner. The picture doesn't reach the top of the screen, so stretch it with Image⇨Effects⇨Scale and then drag the upper-left corner handle. Click inside the image to finalize the stretch and set the opacity slider to 50% in the Layers box to make the cars image semi-transparent. The image now looks something like Figure 7-11.

Figure 7-11: The polluted world begins to take shape.

15. In a similar manner, add some signs (0130061.TIF on "Junkyards") modified with the Gallery Effects film grain filter and copied with the magic wand. Also add a factory image (0030097.TIF on "Urban Textures and Backgrounds") in its own layer, at 50% opaque.
16. All these layers are getting a little out of sequence. Click and drag the Factory layer so that it's seated between Dog and Background — you want the dog to be in the foreground (top layer).
17. Save the file as a Photoshop image to preserve all those layers for future editing, then *flatten* it for export to TIFF by using the Layers window's Flatten Image command. If you think of layers as individual acetate transparency sheets, think of flattening as laminating all those transparencies together into a single entity. Save the flattened image as a TIFF file.
18. Finally, you want to lay in a cool "bark" for the mean junkyard dog. Fire up Fractal Design's Painter for Windows and open the flattened TIFF file. From the Brushes window, select the Airbrush tool and the Thin Stroke variant. In the Controls menu, set the opacity slider to 50%, the grain slider to 60%, and click the Freehand radio button as shown in Figure 7-12. Choose Window⇨Color Set, select a fierce red, and draw in your bark.

Figure 7-12: Painter's artistic tools are perfect for adding cool freehand effects.

19. Save the file, open PowerPoint, and select Insert⇨Picture. Lay in some text announcing the title of your talk; we used Century Gothic, 44 points, white text with both bold and shadow turned on.

Great work! The final image (see this book's color insert) is very cool for an opening slide but too cluttered to use throughout the presentation. You need to create a toned-down version for that. Here's how:

1. Open Photoshop and the TIFF file containing the opening slide image.
2. Change the foreground color to black. Create a new layer and fill it with Edit⇨Fill (specify settings of foreground color, 100% opacity, and normal mode).
3. From the floating Layers window, set the opacity to 80% or so. Flatten the image and save it under a new name.

Can you approximate the darkening effect using PowerPoint's built-in tools? (Hint: create a box with no outline, black fill, and semi-transparency for a 50% black.) Why is the Photoshop technique better? Would you rather PowerPoint apply a fixed percentage of transparency, or specify the percentage yourself?

Here's another way to tone down an image for use as a background: Click the Image Control button in the Picture toolbar (displayed with View⇨Toolbars⇨Picture) and choose Watermark. To take this idea one step further, first convert the image to Grayscale and then to a Watermark!

You could stop at this point and be very satisfied with yourself, but there's a way to make this presentation even cooler. To unify the show graphically, use *parts* of the opening image in section title slides, such as the one in Figure 7-13. Can you figure out how we did it? (Hint: thank goodness for layers.)

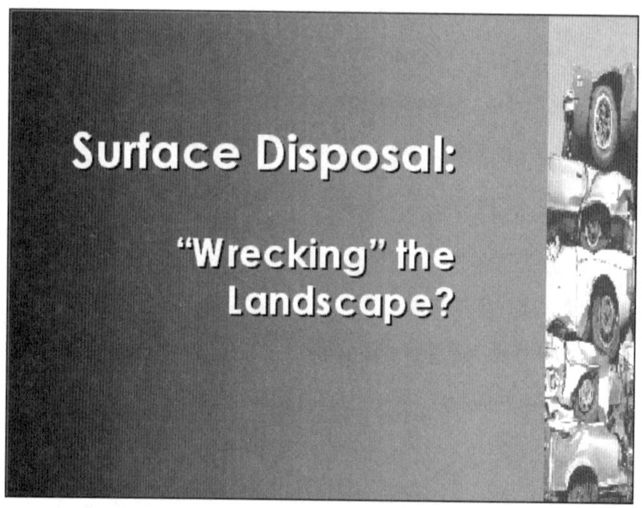

Figure 7-13: Using pieces of the opening slide as section titles provides a graphical unity to the entire presentation.

Customizing Bitmaps 3: Scanning

Have no time to learn your way around cool paint software but still want to customize your show? Another great way to wow your audience is to scan an image, such as a full-color photograph, into your PC and tune it up for inclusion on a PowerPoint slide. For example, you may be trying to land a lucrative advertising contract, and you want to introduce your company's creative talent to the potential customer with slides such as Figure 7-14.

Not everyone has access to a color scanner, but for a few hundred dollars, it may be worth it to you. Flatbed units with at least 600 dpi resolution and 24-bit color capability are the best choices. Another option is to have a graphics service bureau perform scanning for you on a per-job fee.

Figure 7-14: Using scanned photographs in a slide show adds impact.

If you do buy a scanner to connect to your PC — for example, via the parallel port or a SCSI port — you can usually install software drivers that will work with your image editing software. The relevant standard is called *TWAIN*, and most good scanners come with TWAIN drivers (in Windows 95, use *TWAIN_32* drivers). Scanning becomes as simple as running your favorite image editing program, selecting File⇨Acquire⇨TWAIN, and setting your scan parameters in a dialog box such as shown in Figure 7-15. With PowerPoint 8, you can scan directly from PowerPoint by selecting Insert⇨Picture⇨From Scanner, which activates the Photo Editor program that ships with Office 97.

tip

Set the scan resolution to produce an image as close as possible to the ultimate size you'll want. The less resizing you have to do after scanning, the better your image will look.

tip

Cameras, film, and PC scanners all introduce color errors into a scanned photograph, altering the original image's contrast, brightness, and color balance (relative amounts of red, green, and blue). Some image editing software enables you to correct most of these quickly and simply. For example, Photoshop offers the command Image⇨Adjust⇨Levels⇨Auto, which does a great job correcting color balance inaccuracies on most photographs as long as they contain some white and some black.

Figure 7-15: With a correctly installed TWAIN scanner, you can bring photographs into your favorite image editing program, or into PowerPoint 8, via the Photo Editor applet.

Microsoft has added a few image editing tools to PowerPoint 8's Picture toolbar (Figure 7-16). You can't control an image's color balance from PowerPoint; you still need a program like Photoshop for that. You can control contrast and brightness a click at a time, however (each click equals 3 percent); you can crop the image and apply a border to it, or even convert it to grayscale, black and white, or a watermark. (The Recolor button doesn't apply to bitmaps.) The Format Picture button displays a dialog box that gives you even more precise control over these settings.

If you're unhappy with the final outcome, use the Reset Picture button to take the picture back to its original state at the time of placement, or use the Standard toolbar's Undo button if you only want to reverse your actions back to a certain point.

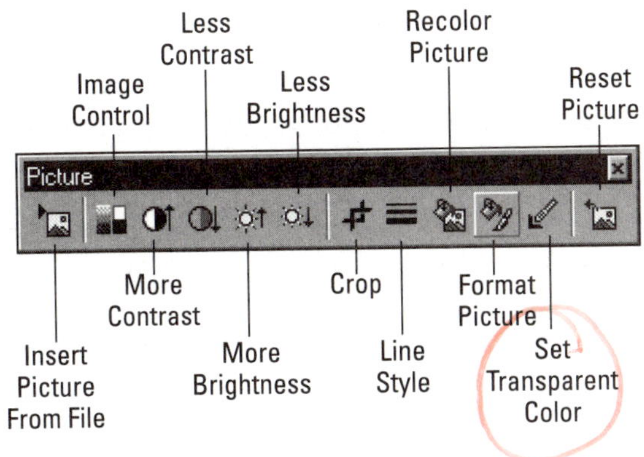

Figure 7-16: Picture toolbar buttons.

Bitmaps and PowerPoint

Now that you've created some cool bitmap images, it's time to bring them into your PowerPoint slide show and place them so they look just the way you want.

Getting bitmaps into PowerPoint

The quickest way to import a bitmap graphic into PowerPoint 8 is to click the Insert Picture from File button on the Picture toolbar, which you can display with View⇨Toolbars⇨Picture.

The usual mechanism for importing a bitmap graphic into PowerPoint is Insert⇨Picture, which brings up a dialog box that you can use to find the file you want. The Files of type list box shows the types of images PowerPoint is configured to import. If a particular file type isn't listed, run the PowerPoint or Office setup program to install all the graphics filters.

Sizing bitmaps

The number-one problem when importing bitmaps into PowerPoint is getting them to come in at the correct size. For example, you may have a 640 x 480 graphic that should fill an entire PowerPoint slide, but instead it only fills part of the slide. You could just use the selection handles to scale the image to fill the slide, but you're likely to distort the picture in the process.

The key to fixing this annoying sizing problem is to set the image resolution (in dots per inch, or dpi) to one-tenth the display width. That is, if you use a 640 x 480 display, set the image dpi to 64. If you use an 800 x 600 display, set the dpi to 80. You set the image resolution in your image editing program; for example, in Photoshop, you'd select Image➪Image Size➪Resolution. Photoshop stores the resolution number as part of the image file itself. We don't know exactly why PowerPoint works this way, but it does! And you'll never find this trick documented in a manual or a help file.

If you're using Version 8, the image resolution rule we just explained doesn't seem to work, but you can usually achieve good results by choosing Format➪Picture➪Size, Best scale for slide show, and the appropriate Resolution value. PowerPoint 8 does a nicer job of scaling bitmap images than 4 or 7, so you'll see less distortion if you're forced to resize using the picture's selection handles.

We're not out of the woods yet. The second most common problem is that even with the file resolution set properly, PowerPoint 4 and 7 often import bitmap graphics at a 99% scaling factor instead of 100%. Sometimes it's 99.9%; sometimes 99.8%. The result is that when displaying a full-size bitmap in Slide Show view, a white or gray line appears at the bottom or right edge of the screen. Most uncool.

Fortunately, we've got you covered here also. Change the image scale to 100% with the Draw➪Scale command. Or, create your bitmap to be 1 pixel wider and 1 pixel taller than the screen resolution (for example, 641 x 481 for a standard VGA size screen), and leave the scaling factor alone. Which method you choose is a matter of taste.

Fixing color problems

The third bitmap tip has to do with color problems. Occasionally, a graphic looks horrible when imported into PowerPoint, though it looks great in Photoshop: all the colors are wrong, often unrecognizable. The solution is to reduce the color depth in your image editing program, rather than allow PowerPoint to perform palette management. For example, if your presentation PC has a 256-color display, reduce the bitmap's color depth to 8 bits (this is often called *indexed color*) in Photoshop or Picture Publisher and then import it. The imported graphic should look almost as good as the original.

If you have access to a Macintosh, get a copy of DeBabelizer, from Equilibrium Technologies. It does the best job of color depth reduction we've seen — even better than Photoshop.

Using the Set Transparent Color tool

The new Set Transparent Color tool eliminates one particular color, allowing you to see through to the background. This tool is used mainly for bitmap images such as photographs, but it also works with some clip art. Choose the tool from the Picture toolbar; your cursor turns into an eraser-like icon. Click on the part of the image that has the color you want eliminated, and it erases the color area.

You can only exclude one color at a time; therefore, the tool doesn't work well with photographs, which usually have multicolored backgrounds. To work around this problem, follow these steps:

1. Open the image in Photoshop.
2. Select the area you want to exclude by using the Magic Wand tool. Play with various Tolerance settings to capture everything you need, and remember, for multiple selections hold down Shift. You can also use the Lasso tool for selection.

Make sure that you have selected everything you want to eliminate, because extra pixels that can cause ragged borders or float about the image are a pesky problem. Avoid laying images down against a solid black background, because the problem becomes most evident in that scenario.

3. Choose Select➪Inverse so that the area you want to include is now selected.
4. Select Edit➪Copy to put the image on the Windows clipboard.
5. Return to PowerPoint and select Edit➪Paste. Your image comes in with a solid white background that the Set Transparent Color tool can easily handle.

Summary

Beautiful bitmap graphics add a large dash of cool to any PowerPoint presentation:

You can buy stock images for maximum effect in minimum time.

To create your own graphics, equip yourself with a good image editor, some cool filters, and one or two special-effects paint programs.

Scanning graphics is a cool way to add realism to a slide show, especially if you don't have to scale your scans afterwards. Use your image editor's automatic correction commands to quickly compensate for the inevitable color errors.

Use this chapter's importing tips to overcome a few PowerPoint quirks, and you'll be a bitmap guru!

Bitmaps won't be suitable for every graphic need the PowerPoint designer may encounter. When scalability is important — for example, when you're not sure what resolution display you'll be using to present a slideshow — you'll want to use vector-based illustrations. Another very cool trick is to drop 3-D images onto your slides, again a job for illustration tools. Creating cool illustrations is the subject of the next chapter.

Creating Cool Illustrations

8

In This Chapter

Overcoming PowerPoint's draw tool limitations with third-party, 2-D illustration software

Learning how Bézier curves give you more control over curve shapes

Converting bitmap images to vector images with tracing technology

Avoiding problems with EPS illustration files in PowerPoint

Learning the differences between 3-D illustration and 2-D illustration

Understanding different ways to model 3-D objects

Achieving photorealistic effects with shaders and rendering techniques

Bringing your 3-D graphics onto PowerPoint slides for surprising effects

The last chapter hinted at some of the amazingly cool things you can do with pixel-oriented bitmap images. Bitmaps have some important drawbacks, however, that prevent them from meeting all of the PowerPoint user's graphics needs. One of the biggest drawbacks is that you can't scale bitmaps up or down without losing image quality. Although that fact may not seem terribly important, consider this: Do you think you'll still be presenting at 640 x 480 resolution five or ten years from now? Another drawback is that bitmaps always come into PowerPoint as rectangles, limiting your ability to "float" images over backgrounds unless you have PowerPoint 8 and your bitmaps have perfectly solid backgrounds.

Spend a few hours with PowerPoint's built-in vector graphics, which create lines, curves, and shapes, and you'll realize that although PowerPoint provides the basic 2-D drawing tools, it is not a full-fledged *illustration* program by any means:

- For 2-D illustration, PowerPoint 4 and 7 don't offer flexible *Bézier curve* drawing, discussed later in this chapter (although Version 8 does — hurrah!). In all versions, you can't specify precise line widths; object fills are limited; text handling is limited, even with the WordArt utility; you can't control the spacing of the Snap to Grid feature; you can't turn a bitmap image into an illustration; and so on.
- As for 3-D illustration, in Versions 4 and 7, it's simply absent. In the help system, Microsoft suggests that you can simulate 3-D objects with 2-D ones, such as making a cylinder out of two ellipses and two lines, but that's far too uncool for us! Version 8 introduces some welcome 3-D tools that we explore in Chapter 9 on third-party clip art, but they, too, have significant limitations. For example, no free-form modeler is available, lighting is uniform and does not fall off with distance, shadows are uniform, you can only rotate 3-D objects around 2 axes, and no camera facility is available.

PowerPoint's vector graphics limitations are good news, in a sense, for the slide show designer committed to cool, because when you use the advanced 2-D and 3-D illustration features of third-party software to create gorgeous vector images for your presentation, they definitely won't look "canned."

2-D Illustration

All 2-D illustration programs manipulate lines, curves, and objects in a two-dimensional space. That's not to say that these programs can't create the illusion of 3-D effects, but you can't manipulate objects in a 3-D space as you can with 3-D illustration software. For example, you can't move your viewpoint (or camera) in three dimensions to take different snapshots of the same scene.

Despite their two-dimensional design, these programs can generate beautiful illustrations for PowerPoint slides, and they give you more artistic control than PowerPoint's drawing tools. As an added bonus, these programs can also create unique bitmaps through the use of special fills and gradients.

Among the more popular Windows 2-D illustration tools are Micrografx Designer, Adobe Illustrator, and CorelDraw!. Designer has always been strong for technical illustrations but has evolved into a strong, general-purpose illustrating tool. Its combination with Picture Publisher and ABC Flowcharter in the ABC Graphics Suite is an attractive one, and its speed under Windows 95 is impressive. Illustrator built up a loyal following on the Macintosh platform, where its current version is perhaps the best overall 2-D illustration tool on small computers; the Windows version is, as of this writing, two major releases behind the Mac version, however. Draw! began life with an elegant and uncluttered design that won over many PC users, but even after six releases, it's plagued by more than its share of bugs.

Although none of these three programs is perfect, any of them can create cool graphics with their sophisticated, vector-based tools. Pick one, therefore, and get to know it! To whet your appetite, the following sections describe some of the benefits that these programs provide: Bézier curves, precise line and fill control, and bitmap tracing.

Bézier curves

PowerPoint 4 and 7 offer the arc tool, which you can reshape by using the selection handles, but you can't easily create complex, sinuous curves that way. To make curvilinear shapes that you can control completely, you need *Bézier curves* and *node editing*, features provided by full-fledged, 2-D illustration programs (and now by PowerPoint 8).

The Bézier curve is a flexible, complex type of curve whose shape is mathematically determined by two control points. Unlike arcs, Bézier curves can have varying radius lengths and can change direction from one end to the other.

The start and end of a Bézier curve are called *nodes*. Each node has a *control point* associated with it. The distance between a control point and a node determines the curve's depth or height at that point. The angle of the control point determines the slope of the curve at that point.

Trust us on this one point: Bézier curves are much easier to work with than they are to explain! Figure 8-1 shows how you can use curve control points to reshape the base of a lightbulb illustration in Adobe Illustrator.

When using Bézier curves, limiting the number of nodes will make redrawing and printing faster, keep file sizes down, and make the drawing easier to edit later.

In PowerPoint 8, click on an ungrouped curve and choose Draw⇨Edit Points, then right-click a node (PowerPoint calls it a *vertex*) and select Smooth Point or Straight Point to edit it as a Bézier curve. (The Smooth Point option forces both control points to be the same distance from the vertex — see Figure 8-2.)

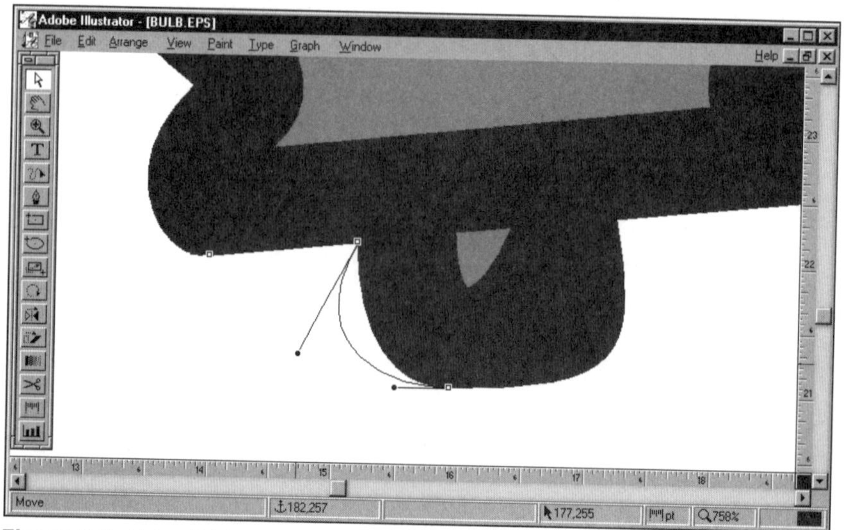

Figure 8-1: Using Bézier curves in Adobe Illustrator, you can reshape the bottom contact of a lightbulb precisely and easily.

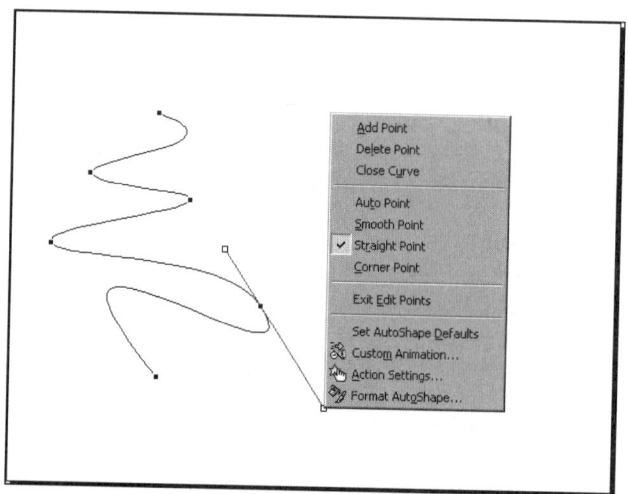

Figure 8-2: Bézier curves in PowerPoint 8 are most useful for curves you create within PowerPoint. Smooth Points enforce symmetrical control points, whereas Straight Points (shown) can be asymmetrical.

You may want to experiment with editing the same image in PowerPoint 8 versus Adobe Illustrator. PowerPoint tends to use a large number of non-Bézier vertexes for imported clip art in WMF format, whereas Illustrator uses a small number of Bézier nodes in the EPS format (which PowerPoint cannot read directly) for an image that's much easier to edit. Moral: If you can obtain illustrations in EPS format, use a tool such as Illustrator to do your Bézier editing, and use PowerPoint 8's Bézier feature for curves you create within PowerPoint using the Curve AutoShape tool.

Line and fill control

Two-dimensional illustration programs let you specify precisely how thick you want your lines to be, whereas PowerPoint 4 and 7 limit you to a few preset line widths. With a good 2-D program, you can typically choose from a wide variety of dotted and dashed line types and a similarly wide variety of line terminators (arrowheads, circles, boxes, and so on). PowerPoint 8 rivals some illustration packages in the variety of line styles it offers, and it gives you total control over line thickness via Format⇨Colors and Lines.

Illustration programs also offer many cool bitmap effects for filling objects. Figure 8-3 shows how to design a complex and beautiful CorelDraw! fractal texture fill, and Figure 8-4 shows how to create an offset square gradient in Micrografx Designer. Such versatile object fill control opens the door to some very effective slide backgrounds for PowerPoint use.

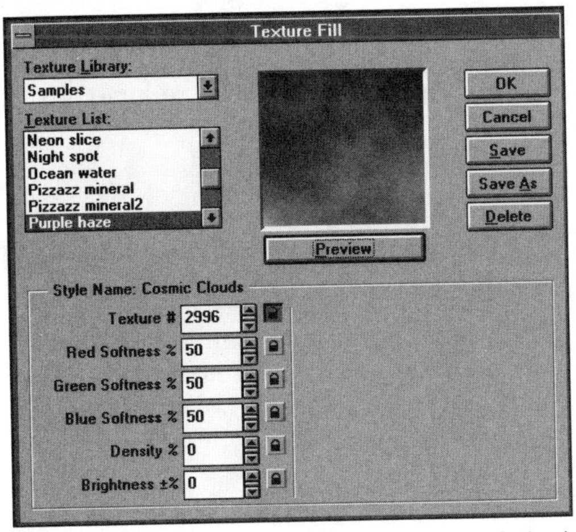

Figure 8-3: CorelDraw! offers a nearly unlimited number of complex object fills with its texture fill settings and variants.

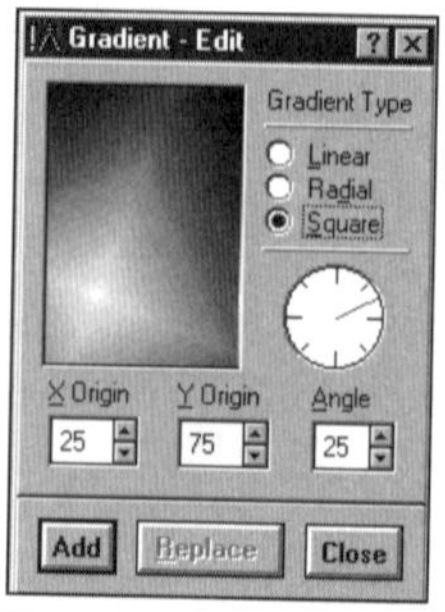

Figure 8-4: Micrografx Designer can create offset gradients whose center you can place anywhere inside an object by using the X and Y displacement options.

Tracing

You'll occasionally have a bitmap image that you want to convert to a vector image to enable easier scaling, to use fancy fill effects, or to distort and warp the image outlines. The procedure for finding the outlines in a bitmap picture and converting them to curves you can manipulate with illustration tools is called *tracing.*

PowerPoint doesn't offer tracing, but Illustrator, Designer, and Draw! do; standalone utilities such as Adobe Streamline are even available that specialize in tracing bitmaps.

tip

The best candidates for tracing are bitmap images with high edge contrasts. Subtle pastel bitmap graphics won't trace well. Monochrome (black-and-white) bitmaps trace the best, with grayscale next, and color last. Converting a color image to grayscale, or, at least, reducing its color depth, will produce better results.

Bringing 2-D illustrations into PowerPoint

We mentioned in Chapter 4 that the Windows Metafile (WMF) format is best for importing clip art into PowerPoint, and the same is true for 2-D illustrations. Designer and Draw! can save files in WMF format.

warning

Adobe Illustrator can only save files in PostScript format (*.AI or *.EPS). A great deal of clip art comes in EPS format as well, including the Image Club samples on this book's CD-ROM. Although you can often load EPS artwork into PowerPoint with Insert⇨Picture, what you see on the screen isn't the actual vector illustration; it's the preview bitmap part of the EPS file. Scaling an EPS bitmap produces the same ragged edges you get from scaling any bitmap.

Fortunately, you can use your illustration program to load an AI or EPS file and then export it as a Windows Metafile (Figure 8-5).

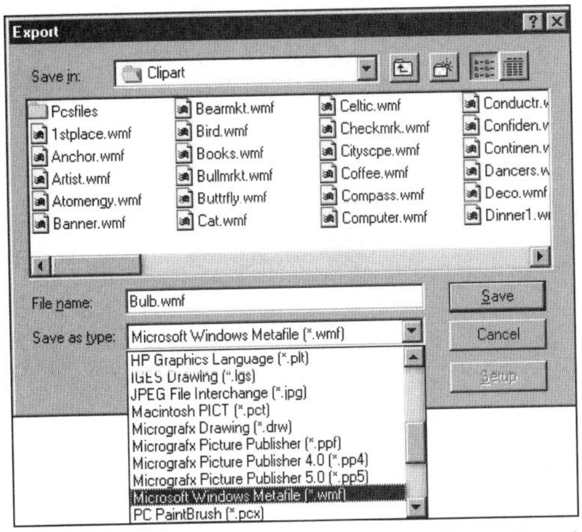

Figure 8-5: Micrografx Designer makes a handy "Swiss Army Knife" for converting EPS or AI files to WMF format.

Figure 8-6 shows a PowerPoint slide with two images based on the same file. The image on the left is an EPS preview bitmap, the result of using Insert⇨Picture to retrieve the file BULB.EPS in the Image Club directory on your CD-ROM. You can see that its edges are jagged after rescaling to a large size, and it doesn't float above the colored slide background as a true vector image should. The image on the right is a true WMF file, created by reading BULB.EPS into Designer, exporting it as BULB.WMF, and performing Insert⇨Picture with BULB.WMF instead of BULB.EPS. Notice how much cleaner the image on the right looks when rescaled to fill the slide, and how it floats properly above the slide background.

3-D Illustration

Simulating 3-D effects with drop shadows, PowerPoint 8's extrusion and lighting tools on the 3-D Effects toolbar, or by arranging objects one in front of another is fine, but these effects aren't nearly as high on the "cool" scale as true 3-D illustration effects. With true 3-D, you generate a computer model in three dimensions through a process called *modeling*. Next, you apply surface characteristics such as color and texture, which appear when your 3-D illustration program *renders* the object. You can move, rotate, flip, scale, and otherwise manipulate the model, and it looks "real" on-screen: All the angles, shadows, and surfaces are visually correct. You can then take a snapshot of the 3-D scene to create a bitmap image for importing into PowerPoint. Later, you can reposition your camera anywhere in the 3-D space and change the scene's lighting, to take a different snapshot for a different effect.

Figure 8-6: The lightbulb on the left is an EPS file bitmap preview and doesn't scale well. The lightbulb on the right was converted to a WMF file in Designer before importation into PowerPoint and, as a vector file format, scales up nicely.

tip

Three-dimensional software uses vector tools to model objects, so we categorize it as illustration software. The final output after you take a snapshot of a scene, however, is in the form of a bitmap (PCX, BMP, TIF, and so on).

warning

Don't make the mistake of trying to export your scene in a 3-D vector format such as DXF; this format doesn't support image data such as textures, lighting, or cameras, so all you get is the geometrical shapes — what you'd see in *wireframe* mode.

As you may suspect, 3-D illustration requires some fairly sophisticated software and powerful processing capability, due to all the extra information that a 3-D illustration contains. Not long ago, you couldn't touch a good 3-D illustration program for less than $5,000. Today, products such as Ray Dream Designer, Trispectives, and Caligari TrueSpace cost much less and do a great job.

Modeling

Modeling is the process of designing the 3-D object's structure and surface properties; think of it as computer-based sculpting. You normally perform initial geometrical modeling in a *wireframe* view to make life easier on the computer and to speed up redraws.

tip: The more flexible 3-D illustration programs enable you to import 2-D files you created in Illustrator, Draw!, or Designer, and use those files as cross sections or lathe patterns to create true 3-D objects. In this way, one tool builds on another!

You can either use graphics *primitives*, such as cubes, spheres, and cones, or you can get fancy and create your own models with the freeform modeling tools in your 3-D program. Freeform modeling usually works by taking a 2-D object and *extruding* it — that is, giving it depth — or by taking that object and *lathing* it — that is, spinning it to create a 3-D object, just as you would spin a piece of wood on a lathe. Most 3-D programs today allow you to *deform* your freeform models by stretching, squeezing, or twisting them, too.

If you're in a real hurry, of course, you can use 3-D clip art; the better 3-D illustration programs come with dozens or even hundreds of images that you can manipulate, and you can buy more from third-party vendors such as ViewPoint or Acuris.

When you're finished designing the wireframe, you have to choose what sort of surface color, texture, graininess, reflectivity, and so on you want to assign to your object. This process is called *shading*. PowerPoint 8 offers basic shading options on the 3-D toolbar, such as metal and plastic, but these are very limited. Simpler modeling software offers a convenient set of predefined combinations that approximate real-world materials such as marble, wood, and metal. More advanced software gives you total control over the tiniest variables, such as how tight you want the wood grain on your mahogany desktop!

Rendering

Rendering is the last step in creating a 3-D image. The illustration program considers all the settings you've made — lighting position and type, camera position, object colors and textures, and so on — and takes a snapshot of the scene for saving to disk as a bitmap image. You can then use that bitmap image in PowerPoint as you would any stock photograph or other still graphic.

You'll have several options for rendering your 3-D illustration; each represents a trade-off between image quality and speed. In all cases, however, the more complex the scene, the longer it will take to render:

- *Ray tracing* produces great-looking images and also takes the longest. It's so computationally intensive that some 3-D illustration programs don't even support it. The program actually traces hypothetical light rays as they leave your scene's light sources and bounce off scene objects, creating reflections, shadows, and transparency effects, depending on the object materials you choose.

- *Phong shading* is much faster than ray tracing, but it doesn't catch reflections. It does produce good-looking, anti-aliased (smoothed) results for scenes that don't have reflective objects.
- *Gouraud shading* is faster still but may not look quite as good as phong shading.

In addition to the preceding options, many 3-D programs have their own proprietary rendering techniques. Experimentation is the key to understanding the level of rendering quality that you need for a specific image.

Example: creating a cool, floating plaque

In this example, we use Ray Dream Designer to create a photorealistic, burl elm plaque that you might use on PowerPoint title slides for a surprising and elegant effect. We even float some 3-D text in front of it and use a spotlight to create realistic highlights and shadows:

1. First, model the plaque. The technique is to drag the freehand modeling tool into the perspective window and then use the pen tool to draw a cross section with a beveled top and bottom, as in Figure 8-7. (FYI: Setting Snap to Grid is a good idea for simple modeling.)

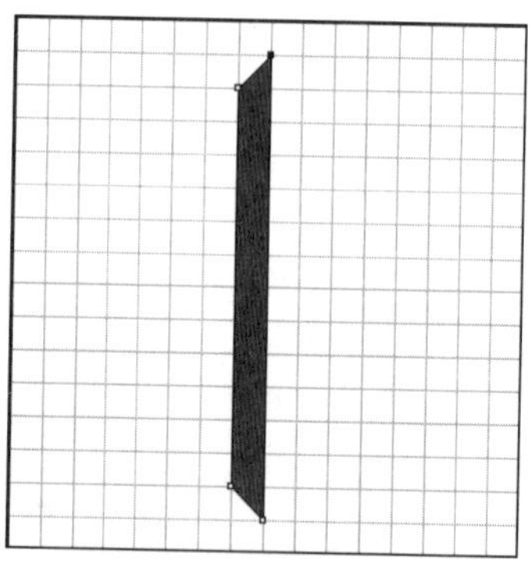

Figure 8-7: Begin modeling a plaque by defining a cross section in Ray Dream Designer's drawing plane.

2. Switch to Perspective view (View⇨Preset position⇨Reference) and extrude the plaque to give it some length. Figure 8-8 shows the results of a simple extrude operation.

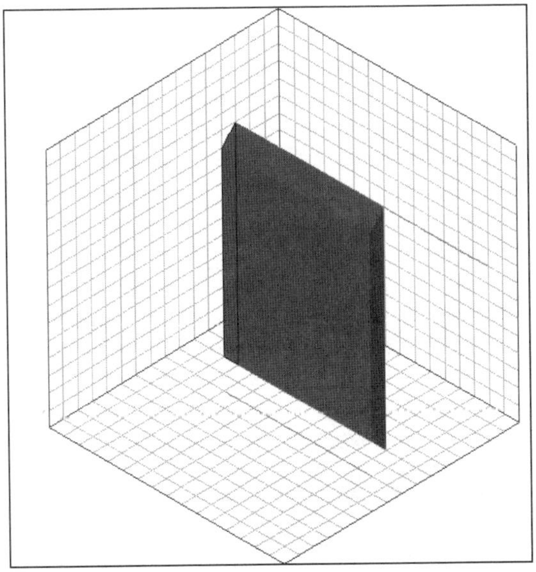

Figure 8-8: Extruding converts the 2-D cross section into a 3-D object.

3. Choose Windows⇨Shaders Browser to display the Shaders dialog box (Figure 8-9). Select an attractive wood (we used burl elm) and then drag and drop the shader sphere onto the plaque.

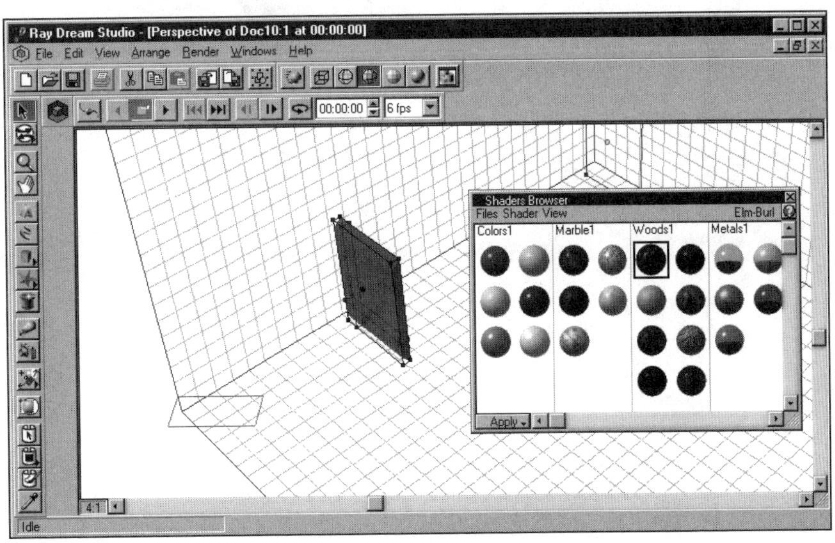

Figure 8-9: Assign a predefined shader, which gives the extruded plaque a characteristic woodgrain texture, color, highlight, and shininess.

4. Put text in front of your plaque by using Ray Dream Designer's text tool (both TrueType and PostScript fonts work here). Apply a straight bevel to the front face of the text and then scale it with the selection handles. Ray Dream's virtual trackball tool lets you rotate the text into position in front of the plaque. Assign a light wood shader to the text object.

5. A light already appears in the scene by default, so select it and move it into position in front of the plaque with your arrow cursor. Most 3-D illustration tools have a "point at" command, and Ray Dream Designer is no exception. Click the light, Shift-click the plaque, and choose Arrange⇨Point At to point the spotlight toward the plaque. Figure 8-10 shows the perspective view of the plaque, text, and light.

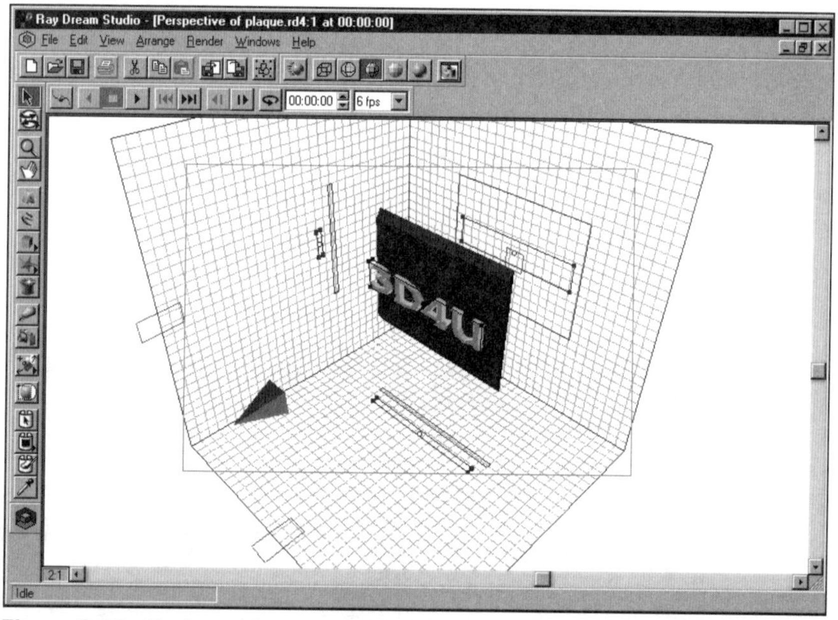

Figure 8-10: Moving objects around in 3-D space takes a little practice with tools such as the virtual trackball. Here's our plaque with some floating text and a spotlight all in position.

6. Time to render! Render⇨Settings brings up the dialog box in Figure 8-11, where you choose your rendering method and set detailed options.

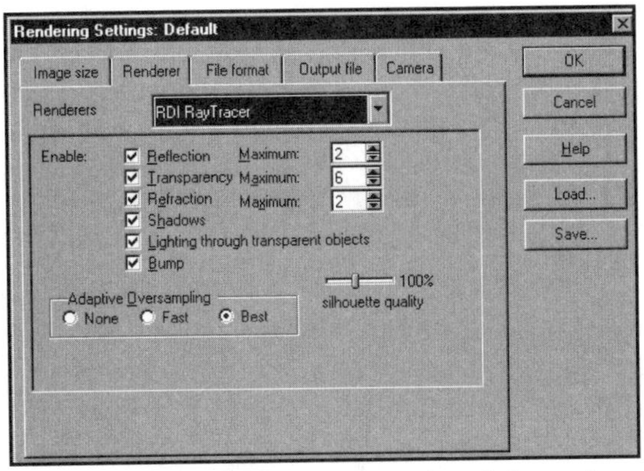

Figure 8-11: Specify ray tracing with all the options enabled for maximum render quality. The high setting for adaptive oversampling produces an image free of random flecks and jagged edges that might otherwise creep in.

7. Select a view that shows the plaque dead-on with View⇨Preset position⇨Left and then initiate rendering with Render⇨Render⇨Multimedia Illustration, which defaults to 640 x 480 and millions of colors. The finished product, which you can save as a BMP or other bitmap format, appears in this book's color insert. Note how realistic it looks: The shadows are non-uniform, the light is brighter in the center and diffuse toward the edges, and the beveled edges of the plaque are a little darker than the plaque's front face.

If you think *that's* impressive, we haven't even told you about *texture mapping*, a technique in which you wrap a 2-D graphic around a 3-D object like a decal. (Well, we have to leave a few features for you to discover on your own!)

Suffice it to say that 3-D illustration is about as cool as it gets in the realm of still computer graphics. Tools such as Ray Dream Designer and TrueSpace 2 aren't the easiest products to learn, but give yourself two or three days, and you'll be creating 3-D images that make PowerPoint's built-in graphics look hopelessly pale by comparison.

Bringing 3-D illustrations into PowerPoint

You use the same techniques for importing 3-D illustrations into PowerPoint that you used in Chapter 7. Remember, 3-D illustration programs use vector tools, but the finished product takes the form of a 2-D graphic file. One special technique that you should know about, however, is *compositing*, that is, layering separate graphical elements to form a single unified image.

You may run into a situation in which you need to drop a 3-D object — be it a wooden cube, a metallic sphere, or a 3-D text logo — onto a 2-D bitmap graphic that you already have. If your 3-D illustration program supports *masking*, you can "composite" a 3-D object onto a 2-D graphic. Compositing is an advanced graphics technique, but conceptually it's not hard to understand. The key is to have your 3-D program draw an outline around your 3-D objects and then save that outline with the rendered file, so that later you can select the objects separately from the background.

The procedure typically goes something like this:

1. Set a solid background color before rendering your 3-D object and tell your 3-D illustration program to create a *mask*, or *alpha channel*. The mask is just a fourth data channel, after the red, green, and blue color channels. It contains the outline of your 3-D object's boundaries, preferably anti-aliased for better blending.
2. Render the image and save it in a file format that supports alpha channels.
3. Open the image in Photoshop, copy the selection defined by the alpha channel, open your background image, and paste the 3-D object or objects down. They'll float over the background image as if they were vector graphics.

Summary

Think of 2-D illustrations as full-sized clip art: vector graphics that you can scale up or down without any loss of quality, that float above your PowerPoint slide backgrounds, and that won't take up much disk space. Here are some points to keep in mind when using illustration programs:

Use a good illustration program for those situations when simple circles and squares won't do.

2-D illustration software can also create cool bitmap effects with flexible gradients and fractal texture fills.

If you really want to wow your audience, give them some 3-D graphics with photorealistic object textures, lifelike shadows, even reflections and transparency.

Make your own 3-D objects or use 3-D clip art, but learn to position lights and cameras to get just the effect you want, and then render your 3-D scenes into 2-D bitmap graphics files for importing onto PowerPoint slides.

> Illustration software takes time to learn, but once you do, you'll find it to be a great tool for creating cool.

There will be times when timetables and deadlines prevent you from using the remarkable tools of full-fledged 2-D and 3-D illustration programs. When time isn't available for Bézier curves or 3-D modeling, third-party clip art can fill the bill. With the tricks in the next chapter, you can successfully manage a large clip art library and enhance clip art images by disassembling them and working with their component parts.

Using Third-Party Clip Art

9

In This Chapter

Adding, deleting, and moving clip art images within the ClipArt Gallery database

Understanding ClipArt Gallery's update command and when to use it

Turning flat, 2-D clip art into exciting, 3-D images

Enhancing your presentations with advanced clip art style tips from the pros

PowerPoint ships with hundreds of clip art images, but you likely have other software programs that contain hundreds more. Paint, illustration, desktop publishing, and even word processing programs for Windows often come with their own clip art libraries. (For example, the ABC Graphics Suite from Micrografx comes with more than 30,000 images!) Cool slide shows use images that audiences aren't likely to have seen before, so you may even want to buy clip art libraries from sources such as Image Club (see Appendix A). Before you know it, you will have thousands of images on your PC.

Merely having all those cool images doesn't do you much good, however, if you can't easily keep track of them and find the right image when you need it. Therefore, this chapter begins by providing tips on using the ClipArt Gallery utility to add images to, delete images from, categorize, and update your clip art database. It then takes you further by showing you how to customize and dramatize your clip art by disassembling, modifying, and reassembling it. The chapter closes with a few advanced clip art style points that help you apply clip art successfully.

Note: As in Chapter 4, *ClipArt Gallery* is used here to refer to all versions of the utility, including PowerPoint 8's *Clip Gallery*.

Managing the ClipArt Gallery

versions 4, 7 & 8

Chapter 4 introduced the Microsoft ClipArt Gallery, a convenient tool for viewing and finding clip art images. Once you begin working with clip art from sources other than Microsoft, you need to know more about how to use ClipArt Gallery's other key functions: adding, deleting, moving, and updating clip art files.

The rest of this chapter assumes that you use ClipArt Gallery 1 with PowerPoint 4, ClipArt Gallery 2 with PowerPoint 7, and Clip Gallery 3 with PowerPoint 8 — the typical situations. We should mention, however, that if you run PowerPoint 4 under Windows 95, it does work with ClipArt Gallery 2 or 3, if present.

Before we dig in to the details, we should note that Microsoft's ClipArt Gallery isn't the only game in town. For example, if you have the Micrografx ABC Graphics Suite, you have a utility named Media Manager that duplicates much of ClipArt Gallery's functionality. Which product you decide to use is a matter of preference. You may find that some third-party clip art managers can support file formats that ClipArt Gallery doesn't.

Adding images

versions 7 & 8

You can add a new clip art image to the ClipArt Gallery as follows:

1. Select Insert⇨Picture⇨Clip Art (Version 8) or Insert⇨Clip Art (Version 7), or click on the Insert Clip Art button on the standard toolbar.
2. In Version 8, select Import Clips to open the Add clip art to Clip Gallery dialog box. In Version 7, select Organize to open the Organize Clip Art dialog box, then select Add Pictures to open a standard file open dialog box.
3. In the Look in: field, select the folder that contains the picture or pictures that you want to add. In the Files of type: field, specify All Pictures, unless you want to restrict viewing to one particular file type.

tip

Chapter 4 lists the file types typically used for clip art: the broadly supported formats *.WMF, *.CGM, *.EPS, and the vendor-specific formats *.CDR, *.DRW, *.DXF, *.ADI, *.HGL, *.PLT, and *.WPG. In Versions 7 and 8, you can also specify predefined ClipArt Gallery Packages (*.CAG), if supplied by the clip art vendor, to merge an entire third-party clip art database with your main ARTGALRY.CAG file.

warning Remember that incorporating bitmap file types, such as BMP, GIF, or PCX, into clip art libraries may prove frustrating later because of their many limitations compared to vector-based clip art.

4. Click on the file you want in the File window and then select Open, or simply double-click on the file. A graphics filter automatically reads the picture and prepares it for copying into the Gallery.

tip Adding more than one image at a time is easy. To select multiple consecutive file names, hold down Shift and highlight them. To select non-consecutive files, hold down Ctrl while selecting files. PowerPoint walks you through adding each file, prompting you to select a category or okay the preset category. You can also select more files than you think you will need, and thumbnail previews will appear one at a time in the Clip Properties (Version 8) or Picture Properties (Version 7) dialog box. If you want to omit one of the selected images, click Skip this picture.

warning If you're adding images from a CD-ROM, ClipArt Gallery will always look to the CD-ROM drive in the future when retrieving those images. The same goes for adding images from a network drive. ClipArt Gallery does not automatically install such images onto your hard drive. If you want to guarantee future availability, copy the desired files to your hard drive before adding them to ClipArt Gallery. Also, be aware that although clip art images can reside on network drives or CD-ROMs, the index files (*.IDX and *.THM in Version 4, *.CAG in Versions 7 and 8) must reside on the local hard drive.

5. In the Clip Properties (Version 8) or Picture Properties (Version 7) dialog box (Figure 9-1), specify keywords to describe the newly added image so that you can locate it more easily later. You also have the choice of placing your image into one or more preset categories or creating a new one with the New Category button.

tip You can place images into more than one category. For example, if you're adding an image of a dancing couple, you may want to place it into both the Entertainment and People categories.

tip Here's an advanced tip that almost no one knows. The description you add in the Picture Properties dialog box won't work with PowerPoint 7 and 8's AutoClipArt feature (see Chapter 4) unless you specify *concept keywords*, with spaces around them, as part of the description. Find the list of keywords in the file AutoClipArt Concepts.TXT, in the \Documentation\ PowerPoint folder on the Office Resource Kit CD-ROM. You can use as many concept keywords as you like.

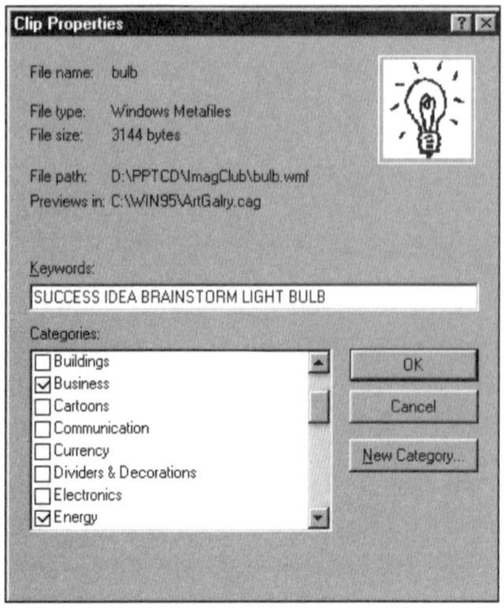

Figure 9-1: Specify image keywords and one or more categories in Version 8's Clip Properties dialog box to make finding the image easier. Version 7's Picture Properties dialog box is similar.

Your image now has a thumbnail, category, and description like all the other clip art images in the Gallery. If you created a new category, it now appears in the Gallery's category list.

version 4 The procedure for adding clip art in Version 4 is very similar to the one for Version 7, except that you click on Options➪Add at the ClipArt Gallery main dialog box, which is shown in Figure 9-2.

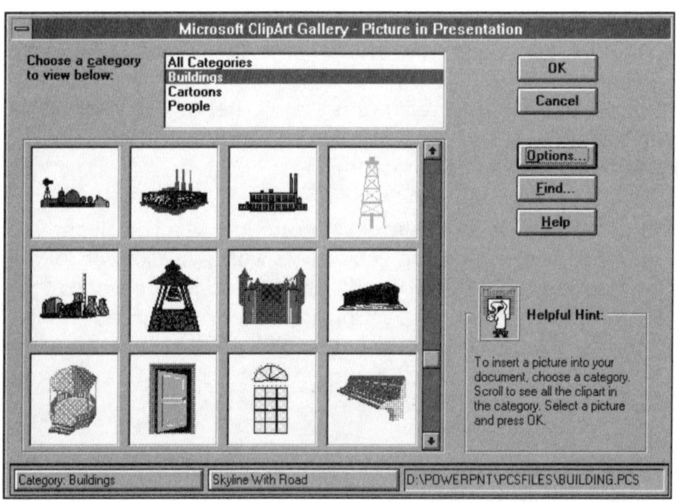

Figure 9-2: Most ClipArt Gallery functions in PowerPoint 4 are available via the main dialog box's Options button.

Deleting images

You've just made a presentation, and several audience members have chided you about the ugliness of some of your clip art images. (It happens — a great deal of second-rate clip art is circulating out there!) You decide to remove them from the Gallery so that they won't embarrass you again. To delete a single image, follow these steps:

1. From PowerPoint, select Insert⇨Clip Art (Version 7) or Insert⇨Picture⇨Clip Art (Version 8) to run the ClipArt Gallery.
2. Find the image, click on it, and then press Del. (In Versions 7 and 8, you can also right-click the image and select Delete Picture from the menu that appears.)
3. Click on Yes in the dialog box to confirm the deletion. The thumbnail and description will vanish from the ClipArt Gallery, though PowerPoint does not delete the image file itself.

To delete an entire image category, follow these steps:

1. From PowerPoint, run the ClipArt Gallery.
2. Depending on which version of PowerPoint you have, do one of the following:
   - Find the category, click on it, and then press Del. You can also right-click the category and select Delete Category from the menu that appears. All images that appear only in the deleted category will be removed from the database.
   - Select Options⇨Change a Category⇨Delete a Category and specify the Category to Delete. The images will still be accessible from the All Categories choice on the Gallery's main dialog box, but the category will be gone.
3. Click Yes in the dialog box to confirm the deletion. Remember, the category may disappear, but the image files are still there.

You can always re-add a deleted image or category by following the steps provided earlier in the "Adding Images" section.

Moving images between categories

Changing the ClipArt Gallery category or categories in which a particular image resides is easy. Just follow these steps in Versions 7 and 8:

1. Right-click on the image in the ClipArt Gallery's main window and select Clip Properties (Version 8) or Picture Properties (Version 7).
2. A check mark indicates the category or categories to which the image currently belongs. Uncheck the boxes you don't want and check the box or boxes you do want. You can also create a new category with the New Category button.

Moving an image to another category in Version 4 is a bit different:

1. Click on the image in the ClipArt Gallery's main window and then click Options⇨Edit Picture Information.
2. Specify the new category in the New: field.

Updating the Gallery

The Update feature instructs ClipArt Gallery to search local or network and removable drives to match its database entries against the image files that are actually present. If a clip art file listed in the Gallery is no longer present on the computer, or if the file has been moved to a different location, you see the dialog box in Figure 9-3. You can Browse (Update Location in Version 8) to find the file in its new location, Remove the file's database entry from the Gallery, or Skip it if you don't want to make a decision right away.

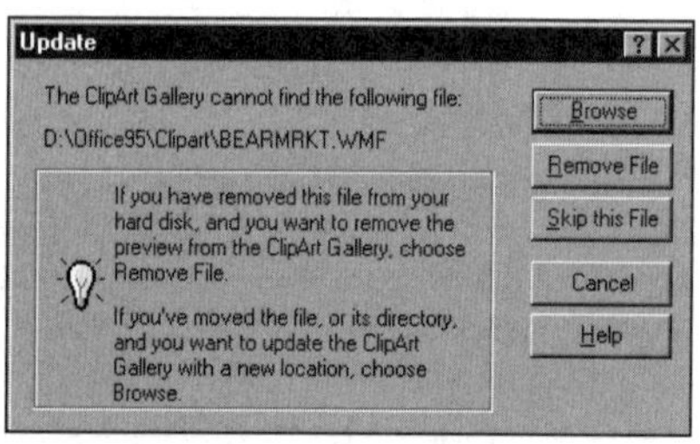

Figure 9-3: The Update feature in ClipArt Gallery 2.0 and 3.0 finds moved or deleted images.

To run the Update feature in Versions 7 and 8, follow these steps:

1. In Version 7, click on Organize⇨Update Pictures from the ClipArt Gallery's main dialog box. In Version 8, right-click any image and choose Update Clip Previews.
2. Toggle on the Check network drives and Check removable drives options if you want to search these places as well as the local hard drive(s).
3. Click the Update All (Version 8) or Update (Version 7) button.

The Update function in Version 4 works in a similar way, but the function is called Refresh instead of Update. Click Options to see the screen in Figure 9-4 and then click Refresh.

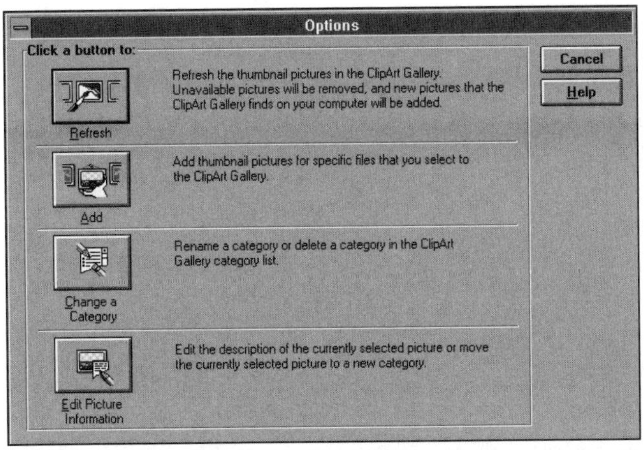

Figure 9-4: PowerPoint 4's ClipArt Gallery Options screen offers the Refresh feature, which is similar to the Update feature in Version 7.

A new feature in Clip Gallery 3.0 is the Connect to Web for additional clips button in the lower-right corner. If you have a Web browser and Internet access, this button connects you to Clip Gallery Live — a Web site that has additional clip art, bitmaps, sounds, music, and videos that you can download. You can also reach Clip Gallery Live by running the PowerPoint Central presentation (Tools⇨PowerPoint Central).

Disassembling and Enhancing Clip Art

Much of the available third-party clip art in PowerPoint 4 and 7 is flat and two-dimensional. Version 8 adds much clip art with a 3-D feel; however, the images can still be improved. In this section, we load you up with tips for adding cool 3-D effects.

In PowerPoint 4, 7, and 8, you can disassemble, or *ungroup*, a clip art image after inserting it into your presentation. Once disassembled, you can deal with the individual pieces of the image separately and enjoy greater control over the image's final appearance. Disassembling clip art also enables you to create a 3-D look.

In the following exercises, we manipulate images supplied in the clip art libraries. By breaking them down, changing solid colors to gradient colors, applying textures and patterns, and finally, adding shadows, we can create a cool 3-D look — and spark your creativity for future projects.

Just follow these steps:

1. Open a blank presentation and select Insert➪Clip Art.
2. Choose the Buildings category, select the arched window (called Window in Version 4 and Window of Opportunity in Version 7) and then click on Insert (Version 7) or OK (Version 4).
3. Place the image and, if you like, resize it by dragging the handles. You can also resize the image by selecting Draw➪Scale and entering a percentage in the Scale To box.

By holding down Shift while dragging any corner handle, you maintain the image's proportions, or *aspect ratio*, during resizing. Using Shift in this manner is called *constraining* the resize operation.

4. With the window image selected, select the Ungroup tool from the Drawing + toolbar. (The tooltip reads *Ungroup* in Version 4, and *Disassemble Picture* in Version 7.) You can also use the menu commands Draw➪Ungroup.

As usual, you can use Tools➪Customize➪Categories➪Arrange to put the Group and Ungroup buttons wherever you want them.

5. You will see the warning message shown in Figure 9-5. Click OK to convert the imported clip art object to a PowerPoint drawing and activate the first ungrouping step. (This conversion does not affect the original clip art.) PowerPoint breaks the arched window into two pieces.

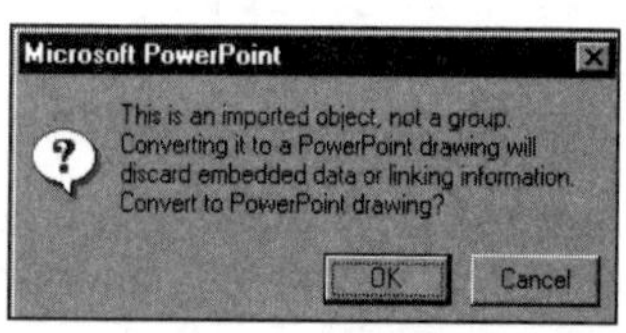

Figure 9-5: PowerPoint's warning that ungrouping a clip art image will break its automatic link to ClipArt Gallery.

6. Continue selecting pieces and clicking on the Ungroup tool until the image is completely disassembled.
7. Focusing on the bottom, square part of the window first, select a pane of glass. (Notice that the square has a handle on each corner and each side.) Hold down Shift and select the remaining square panes of glass.

8. Select Format➪Colors and Lines➪Fill➪Shaded.

The remaining steps vary a little depending on your version of PowerPoint, as indicated.

9. **Version 7:** In the Shaded Fill dialog box's Colors area, turn on the Two Color radio button. Select a light blue for Color 1 and a darker blue for Color 2. Turn on Diagonal Up under Shade Styles and then make the upper-right selection in the Variants area. Click OK. Notice that the Fill bar in the Colors and Lines dialog box has changed to your selection. Click OK again.

   Version 4: Turn on Diagonal Right under Shade Styles and then make the upper-left selection in the Variants area. Select blue for your Color. Move the Dark/Light slider all the way to the right and click OK. Notice that the Fill bar in the Colors and Lines dialog box has changed to your selection. Click OK again.

10. **Version 7:** Focus on the top, arched part of the window. Select the lower-left pane of glass and choose Format➪Colors and Lines➪Fill➪Shaded. Turn on the Two Color button, change Color 1 to the previously selected dark blue, and then change Color 2 to the previously selected light blue. Turn on Vertical under Shade Styles and then make the upper-left selection in the Variants area. Click twice on OK.

    Version 4: Focus on the top, arched part of the window. Select the lower-left pane of glass from the arch and choose Format➪Colors and Lines➪Fill➪Shaded. Turn on Horizontal under Shade Styles and then make the upper-right selection in the Variants area. Select blue for your Color. Move the Dark/Light slider all the way to the right and click twice on OK.

11. For both versions, select the lower-right pane of glass from the arch and repeat Step 10 with one exception: Select the upper-left selection under Variants. Then click twice on OK.

12. While holding down Shift, select the remaining middle panes of glass from the arch. Repeat Step 10 with one small change: In Version 7, select Horizontal under Shade Styles and make the upper-left selection under Variants. Then click twice on OK. In Version 4, select Vertical under Shade Styles and make the upper-left selection under Variants. Then click twice on OK.

13. **Version 7:** While holding down Shift, select the upper and lower window frames. Select Format➪Colors and Lines➪Fill➪Textured. You can now choose a nice wood grain look from the Textures gallery in the Textured Fill dialog box. Click twice on OK.

    Version 4: While holding down Shift, select the upper and lower window frames. Select Format➪Colors and Lines➪Fill➪Pattern. In the Pattern Fill dialog box, click on Foreground➪Other Color and choose a nice brown. Click OK and Background➪Other Color to choose a lighter brown. Click OK and select a pattern that looks the most like a wood grain to you. Click twice on OK.

14. The final step for both versions is to select the wood grain window frame, click Format⇨Shadow, and apply any desired shadow. In Version 7, you can use the Semi-Transparent option to enable other objects to show through the shadow.

If you're a perfectionist, you can go one step further and fill in the window latch with solid black. Figure 9-6 shows the before and after clip art. What a difference it makes!

Figure 9-6: Ungrouping clip art and applying gradients, textures, patterns, and shadows to the components makes your images come alive.

version 8

Using the new PowerPoint 8 features, we take a boring, flat, black-and-white image, disassemble it, and add textures, extrusions, and lighting to create a stunning 3-D image. Let the cool begin:

1. Open a blank presentation and select Insert⇨Picture ⇨Clip Art.
2. Choose the Dividers & Decorations category, select the "A" with artist's palette (Labeled A under Clip Properties) and then click Insert.
3. Place the image and, if you like, resize it by dragging the handles. You can also resize the image by selecting Format⇨Picture⇨Size and entering a percentage in the Height and Width boxes.
4. With the "A" image selected, select Draw⇨Ungroup. Answer Yes to the warning message.

5. Select and delete the various black lines that surround the artist's palette until you are left with just the gray palette. Select it and choose Format⇨Colors and Lines. From the Colors and Lines tab, select Fill Color⇨Fill Effects. From the Texture tab, select Oak and click OK twice.

6. From the Drawing toolbar, click on the 3-D button and choose 3-D Style 2 (see Figure 9-7). Turn on the 3-D Settings toolbar, click the 3-D Color button and select a dark brown, using More 3-D Colors if necessary.

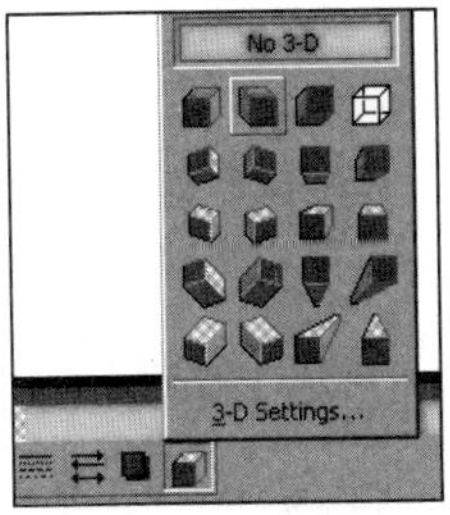

Figure 9-7: Hold the cursor over a 3-D style, and PowerPoint 8 will display its style number. Activate the 3-D toolbar by selecting 3-D Settings.

7. Select the "A" and notice that it is broken into two parts. Select both parts and regroup them with Draw⇨Group. Then nudge the "A" to the left three nudges. With the "A" still selected, select Format⇨Colors and Lines. From the Colors and Lines tab, select Fill Color⇨Fill Effects. From the Gradient tab, select Two colors. Choose a dark green for color 1 and a light green for color 2, accessing More Colors if necessary. Now set your Shading styles to Vertical, select the lower-left gradient, and click OK twice. From the Drawing toolbar, click on the 3-D button and choose 3-D Style 2.

8. To deal with the paint spots, Zoom in 100% (View⇨Zoom⇨100%), select the inner circles, and delete them as far as the outermost circle. With the outermost circle selected, choose Format⇨Colors and Lines. From the Colors and Lines tab, select Fill Color⇨Fill Effects. From the Gradient tab, select Two colors. Choose a darker color for color 1 and a lighter color for color 2, accessing More Colors if necessary (we chose purple, blue, and yellow). Now set your Shading styles to From Center, select the left gradient, and click OK twice.

9. Finally, select all the pieces and regroup the entire image. Choose Lighting from the 3-D Settings toolbar (Figure 9-8) and apply a directional lighting; we chose middle right, but pick one you like.

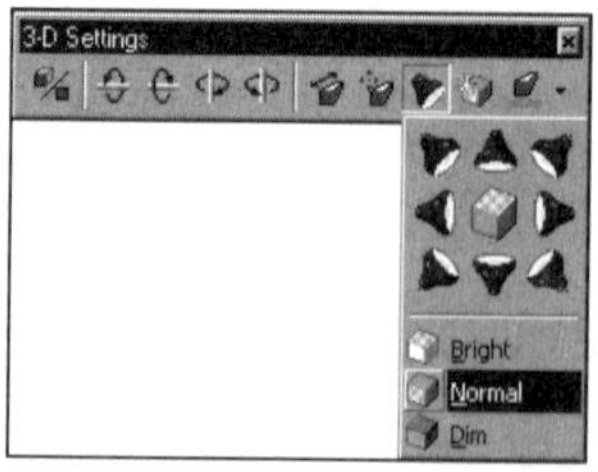

Figure 9-8: PowerPoint 8's 3-D toolbar enables you to change the lighting direction and intensity.

10. Zoom out and view a much cooler 3-D image! To see what it should look like, check out this book's color insert.

Advanced Clip Art Style Points

Here are some advanced style tips for adding third-party clip art to your slides:

- Be consistent with style. When selecting clip art images for your presentation, place them all on one slide and make sure that they flow together harmoniously. In Figure 9-9, the three images on the left — from the categories of music, entertainment, and food — don't go well together, but the three images on the right flow nicely. This tip is doubly important if you're using graphics from more than one vendor.

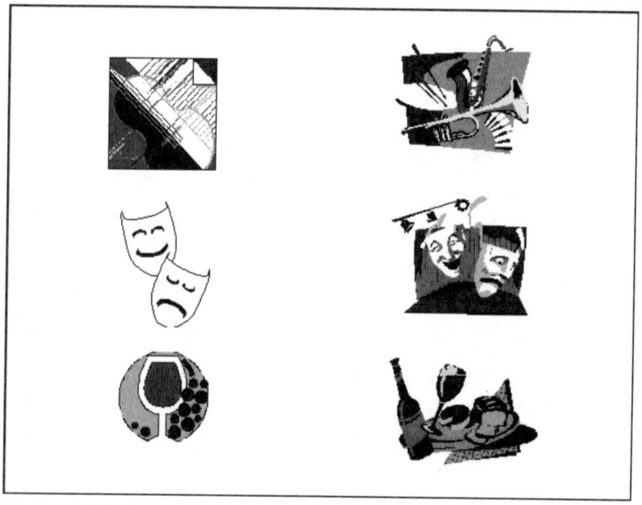

Figure 9-9: You can detect inconsistent clip art styles (left) from consistent styles (right) by placing images onto a single slide.

- A great deal of third-party clip art is very informal and even a little corny. Take care to match the clip art style to the type of meeting and to the image you want to project. If the graphics are too cartoonish, will your audience take you seriously? Conversely, if the images are too sober, will your audience think you're a stiff?
- Cool clip art helps the audience visualize your point, makes your objective easier to understand, amuses or entertains your audience, and is interesting to look at. If a clip art image doesn't fit one of these categories, don't use it.
- When presenting, don't rely on clip art to speak for you — you still need to add comments to your visuals. The audience came primarily to hear you; slide graphics are just icing on the cake. There's just no substitute for a polished delivery.

Summary

Extending your clip art library increases the likelihood that you will find just the image you want, as well as the probability that your audience hasn't already seen it a hundred times. Some of the more important highlights of this chapter include the following:

Organize third-party clip art with Microsoft's convenient ClipArt Gallery applet.

Don't feel bound to the predefined categories; create your own and move images between categories.

Use descriptions to help you find clip art and, in Versions 7 and 8, use concept keywords to enhance the AutoClipArt utility.

Use the Update or Refresh command to keep the Gallery's database consistent with the image files to which it refers.

Collect cool clip art from Clip Gallery Live on the Internet.

Make those clip art images pop into relief by taking them apart and jazzing up the component parts with PowerPoint 4 and 7's fill and shadow tools, and add major cool through extrusions and lighting in Version 8.

So far in Part II, we've discussed how to design cool bitmap and vector images and how to manage and enhance third-party clip art for dramatic effects. The next chapter examines the types of customizations you can perform with text elements, using the built-in but little-known WordArt utility.

Text Effects and WordArt

10

In This Chapter

Fitting text to a path

Warping text inside a distortion envelope

Controlling justification and spacing

Slanting, rotating, and shading text

Using WordArt to enhance the meaning of a word or phrase

Ungrouping WordArt objects for precise control in PowerPoint

Creating text shadowing and mirroring effects

Creating 3-D extrusions and controlling lighting with WordArt 2.5

This chapter demonstrates how to use the WordArt companion program to enhance and manipulate text for some cool effects. Two versions of WordArt exist: 2.0, for use with PowerPoint 4 and 7, and 2.5, for use with PowerPoint 8.

WordArt 2.0 is an applet that comes free with PowerPoint, though many slide show creators don't know it exists. WordArt 2.0 can enhance text with color, colored patterns, and the outlining of individual letters — all of which make your presentations easier and more interesting to read. WordArt manipulates text by stretching, rotating, and applying various distortion paths that control a text object's shape; it can also add 3-D effects with shadowing.

Unlike WordArt 2.0, WordArt 2.5 is not an applet that other Office programs can share; Microsoft has implemented it as a tool on PowerPoint's drawing toolbar. WordArt 2.5 does not write over WordArt 2.0, so you still have access to 2.0 if you used an earlier version of PowerPoint. With the new and improved WordArt 2.5, you can now extrude text for a cool 3-D look, add more complex shadowing (controlling shadow depth and perspective), control lighting, and even fill text with bitmapped pictures.

When you use WordArt skillfully, you can make boring text exciting. WordArt is convenient, too — you can use it without ever leaving your PowerPoint presentation screen.

warning Although WordArt is fun to use, overdoing the special effects is a common trap, especially with the new Version 2.5.

Getting Started with WordArt

WordArt 2.0 and 2.5 are very different, so we introduce them separately.

WordArt 2.0 for PowerPoint 4 and 7

Follow these steps to get started with WordArt 2.0:

1. At a new or existing slide, select Insert⇨Object from PowerPoint's main menu and then choose Microsoft WordArt 2.0 from the Object Type list. The program loads, and you see the screen in Figure 10-1.

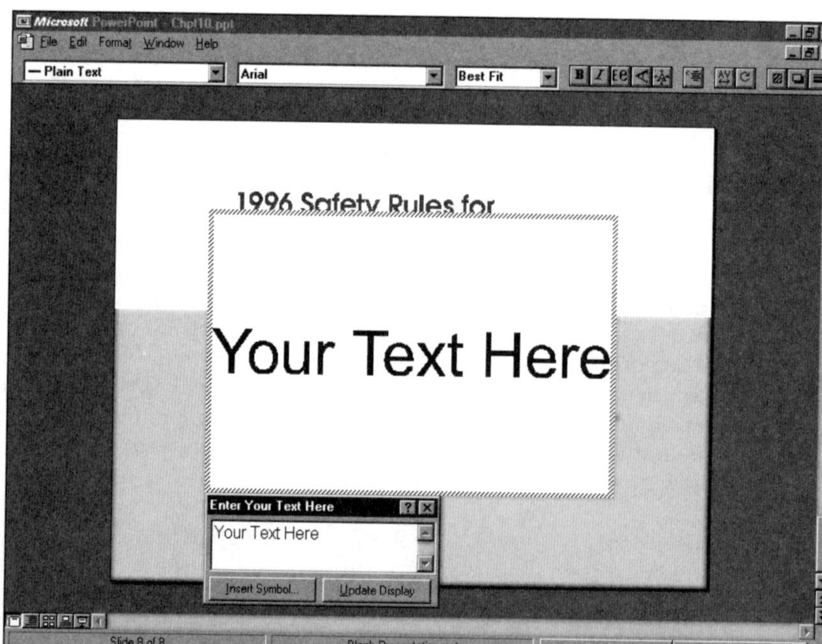

Figure 10-1: WordArt's main screen, which changes PowerPoint menus to WordArt menus.

2. Type your text in the Enter Your Text Here window and click the Update Display button. All WordArt effects start in the Enter Your Text Here window; you can't select previously created plain PowerPoint text and apply WordArt effects to it.

WordArt 2.0's toolbar appears along the top of the screen; it replaces the standard PowerPoint toolbar when you're running WordArt. The toolbar consists of 3 pull-down lists and 11 buttons.

WordArt can apply predefined tools to fit your text to a shape, or *distortion envelope* (curve, slant, 3-D perspective, wave, fade up, fade down, and so on). To see these tools, click the down arrow in the Shape list box at the far left of the toolbar (Figure 10-2).

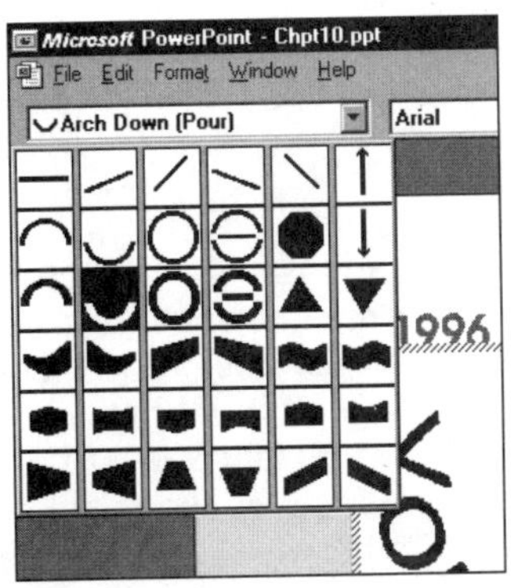

Figure 10-2: Predefined text shapes appear in a WordArt 2.0 drop-down list box.

In Version 2.0, you can find the font-style and point-size lists to the right of the shape list. Note that even if you have Adobe Type Manager installed, and PostScript fonts appear in the PowerPoint menu font list, they won't appear in WordArt's font list. WordArt 2.0 only works with TrueType fonts.

tip If you must use PostScript fonts and you want some of the effects that WordArt can generate, either upgrade to PowerPoint 8 or use Adobe's TypeAlign product. You can purchase it as a separate product; it also comes bundled with Illustrator 4.1 for Windows and Windows 95.

On the right side of WordArt 2.0's toolbar are the following 11 buttons:

B The Bold button toggles boldface on or off.

I The Italic button toggles italics on or off.

Ee The Even Text Height button enlarges lowercase text to match uppercase text, so all characters are at even height.

warning

The Even Text Height button won't work with the Arch Up (Curve), Arch Down (Curve), Circle (Curve), and Button (Curve) distortion tools from the leftmost pull-down menu. Instead, you can substitute with these tools: Arch Up (Pour), Arch Down (Pour), Circle (Pour), and Button (Pour).

The Flip button rotates individual characters 90 degrees.

The Stretch button stretches text to the limits of its frame — that is, the border outlined around the text.

The Alignment button justifies text. When you click this button, you reveal a pull-down menu with the following choices: Center, Left, Right, Stretch Justify, Letter Justify, and Word Justify. Center, Left, and Right do just as you would think, justifying text by using the frame as the guide. Stretch Justify lengthens the letters to fill the space between the left and right margins, but it distorts the text in the process. Letter Justify adds space between letters, and Word Justify adds space between words.

The Character Spacing button adds to or subtracts from the spacing between letters. PowerPoint refers to this action as *tracking;* you can choose manual or custom tracking from the Spacing Between Characters dialog box. Whatever spacing options you choose, leave Automatically Kern Character Pairs checked for better-looking text; it varies the spacing between certain characters that would otherwise look too cramped or too far apart.

The Slider and Rotation button modifies the slant or arc and can also rotate text. For uncurved text, the slider produces a slant effect (similar to italics) from 0 percent to 100 percent, where 50 percent equals no slant. For curved text, you can change the arc, but you cannot control the slant. Rotation spins text from -360 degrees (clockwise) to +360 degrees (counterclockwise).

The Shading button fills text with one of 21 different patterns. You can select two colors (one each for the foreground and background) for many cool effects.

The Drop Shadow button drop-shadows text. Choose from 8 different drop shadows and 16 different color selections on the list.

The Character Outline button outlines text. Choose from 7 line weights, ranging from None to Extra Wide, and from 16 color options. Note that the color applies to the outline only; the text color remains the same.

When you're finished creating WordArt text in Version 2.0, simply click outside the text area to return to your PowerPoint slide.

WordArt 2.5 for PowerPoint 8

Because WordArt 2.5 is a PowerPoint tool, you can run it by simply clicking a button. Follow these steps to get started with WordArt 2.5:

1. Select the WordArt command button (the dancing "A") from the Drawing toolbar to open WordArt. (If you prefer, add WordArt as a toolbar by right-clicking on any toolbar and checking WordArt.) The WordArt Gallery appears (Figure 10-3).
2. Select from a variety of text styles, including cool 3-D choices, and click OK. (You can change the style later from the toolbar if you want.)
3. Next, enter your text at the Edit WordArt Text box, applying the desired font, size, and style. Click OK to see the results of your selections.
4. Use the WordArt toolbar, which appears automatically if it wasn't already on-screen, to make further changes to your text. For example, clicking the Format WordArt button with your text selected brings up a dialog box that enables you to control Colors and Lines, Size, Position, Picture, and Text Box. Overall, WordArt 2.5 offers more layers and more choices than 2.0.

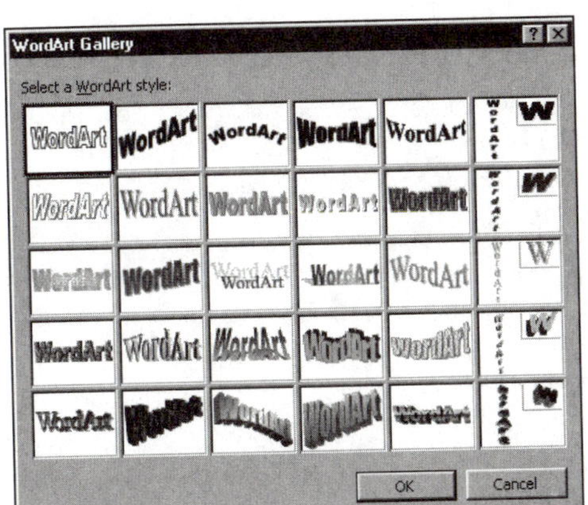

Figure 10-3: Make your initial style selection in the WordArt 2.5 Gallery. You can modify the style later with the WordArt toolbar.

Once you're in WordArt 2.5, the toolbar (Figure 10-4) gives you the same options as WordArt 2.0, plus many more.

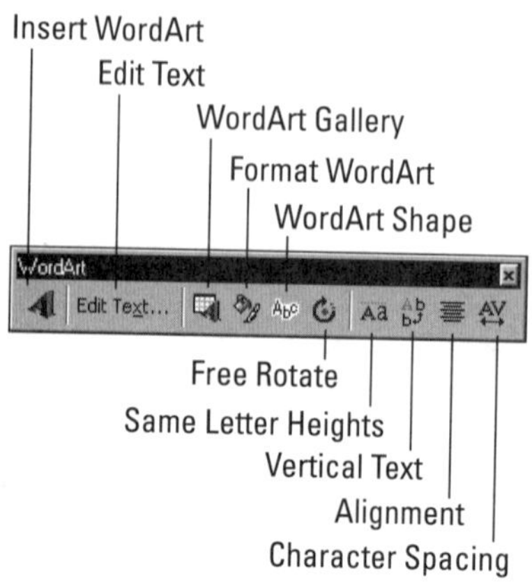

Figure 10-4: The WordArt 2.5 toolbar.

A quick review of the buttons follows:

- The Edit Text button takes you to a dialog box where you can control the font, font size, and font style.
- The WordArt Gallery button opens up a map of preset text styles, mainly 3-D.
- The Format WordArt button takes you to a dialog box with five tabs, as follows:
    - The Colors and Lines tab provides options for color fills (solid, gradient, and semitransparent), texture fills (with new textures added), pattern fills, and picture (bitmap) fills; line color, line weight (you now have complete control here), line style, dashes, and connectors; and arrowheads.
    - The Size tab provides options for rotating text and for resizing text height and width by a certain percentage or to a specific dimension — either independently or while keeping the object's aspect ratio (height to width) locked.
    - The Position tab allows precise placement of an object on the slide, measured from the top-left corner or from the slide's center.
    - The Picture and Text Box tabs aren't used within WordArt.
- The WordArt Shapes button expands the shapes map for fitting text to a shape. Select the shape you want, and WordArt applies the warping immediately. Note the new shapes "ring inside" and "ring outside" apply cool 3-D effects with little effort; these are best used with fewer words and a large font.

- The Free Rotate button enables you to rotate WordArt text to any angle.
- The WordArt Same Letter Heights button forces all the letters, regardless of case, to become the same height.
- The WordArt Vertical Text button throws the text into a crossword-style stacked vertical alignment.
- The WordArt Alignment button works like WordArt 2.0's alignment button, discussed earlier.
- The WordArt Character Spacing button also works like it did in WordArt 2.0.

WordArt notes

When you are in the WordArt 2.0 program, click only in the area provided for text editing. If you click outside this area, you leave WordArt and go back to your presentation. To return to WordArt, choose the WordArt object and then select Edit⇨WordArt 2.0 Object⇨Edit. For a shortcut, double-click the WordArt object.

From the Enter Your Text Here window in WordArt 2.0, you can also add symbols (such as the copyright or trademark characters). Just click the Insert Symbol button and choose a symbol from the chart that appears. This feature is absent from WordArt 2.5.

You can't combine symbols and text in the same string; you must deal with these characters separately. For example, you can't type the snowflake symbol at the same time you type **Snowy Mountain Ski Resort.**

You can't undo changes in WordArt 2.0. You can, however, toggle many features; most of the buttons in WordArt 2.0 are toggles (On – highlighted, Off – not highlighted). Because WordArt 2.5 is a tool, you can undo as many times as needed, thanks to the new multiple undo feature. Select Tools⇨Options⇨Edit and type the amount of undos you prefer, but beware — it only goes as high as 150 (grin)!

In either version of WordArt, text is always an object, so it cannot be spell-checked. However, there is a difference between WordArt object types. WordArt 2.0 objects can be ungrouped within PowerPoint to turn them into drawing objects; WordArt 2.5 objects are already drawing objects and therefore can't be ungrouped.

Play around with WordArt to familiarize yourself with it. Explore all the settings, not just text distortion and WordArt Gallery; you will have more control over your text for future presentations. In Version 2.0, don't be discouraged by the occasional Windows General Protection Fault or Illegal Operation error; do save your work often, though, when using WordArt. The rest of this chapter provides some examples of WordArt in action.

Cool WordArt Exercises

When you work with words, you can do more than select a font size and style. After you select a word or phrase, ask yourself the following questions:

- What does this word or phrase mean?
- Can I attach a color, gradient, or pattern?
- What kind of texture can I apply?
- Can I apply an action to it?
- Does it bring to mind a certain shape?
- Can I fill the text with a cool bitmapped image that embellishes the meaning?

To get your creative brain cells firing, try the following exercises. Have fun!

Express yourself with expressive words

In this section, you learn to give your words action and meaning with WordArt.

Take your audience on a journey to the center of the earth by creatively using the words *center* (for location) and *earth* (for shape):

1. Start WordArt 2.0. Type **Journey to** and press Enter; type **the Center** and press Enter; and then type **of the Earth** and click Update Display. For the special effect to work here, you must break your phrase into three lines.
2. Select a font style (such as Book Antiqua, shown later in Figure 10-7), and then specify 64 as the font size. Toggle on the Bold button. A message appears asking whether to `Resize WordArt Object?`. Click Yes; WordArt automatically resizes the frame to fit your text.
3. From the Shapes map, select Bottom (Curve).
4. Click the Shading button and select Olive as the foreground color and Silver as the background color. From the Style selections, choose a pattern that most reminds you of *terra firma*. After you view your choice in the Sample preview, click OK. If you get the Resize warning message here, click Yes.
5. Return to your presentation; place and resize as necessary. You should see something similar to Figure 10-5.

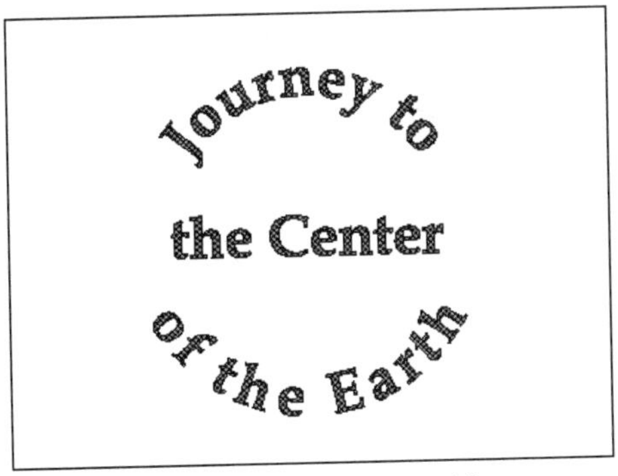

Figure 10-5: Curved WordArt objects suggest the planet Earth.

Make your audience feel as if they are on the ocean by adding a cool color and some motion to your words:

1. Click the WordArt button to open. From the WordArt Gallery, select the style that is located in the fourth row down — fourth row over (blue wave) and click OK.
2. Type **Ocean Front Property** in the Edit WordArt Text dialog box, leaving the Font setting on Impact and changing the font Size to 32 and bold.
3. Now you need to make several adjustments to the dictated style. First, select WordArt Character Spacing from the WordArt toolbar and check Loose. Second, select the Shadow button from the Drawing toolbar and select No Shadow. Third, to create a very wavy wave, move the yellow diamond (located to the left of your text) to the downmost position.
4. From the Format menu, select Colors and Lines. Choose No Line from the Color box under Line. From the Fill area, select Color⇨Fill Effects and click the Picture tab. Choose Select Picture and select BEACH.TIF from the CD-ROM that comes with this book (it's under \Book\Tutorial\V7&8). Click OK. Note that the picture now fills the Color box under Fill. Click OK. (For a shortcut, if you only want to fill an object and don't need to modify lines, use the Drawing toolbar's Fill tool.)

Two caveats regarding Picture fills: Don't ever use the High-Res version offered on many CD photo packages (these take forever to open and redraw); instead, select Low-Res. Also, you have no control over how the picture is placed onto your text or object.

5. To create a continuous wave effect, choose the Ocean Front Property object and then select Edit⇨Duplicate (or press Ctrl-D).
6. Align the duplicate to the left or right of the original. Repeat as necessary until you achieve the desired motion effect (Figure 10-6).

We thought it would be cool to have the beach scene run across both sets of text instead of just duplicating the same scene on the individual sets. So, we duplicated Ocean Front Property, grouped them together, and then filled the grouped image with the beach scene. Unfortunately, PowerPoint still handled the text separately and did not apply it across the grouped text. Therefore, to achieve this effect, type **Ocean Front Property** twice at the Edit WordArt Text screen. You now must manually resize your text. For our completed image, we applied 3-D style #1 and selected Parallel from the Direction map and 36 pt. from the Depth map.

Figure 10-6: WordArt can create a wavy effect for "Ocean Front Property."

One step further

Now you can take these two ideas one step further by adding gradients, patterned color, shadows, 3-D effects, and lighting.

versions 4 & 7

To begin handling the WordArt 2.0 image, "Journey to the Center of the Earth," you must first ungroup or disassemble the text in PowerPoint (use Draw⇨Ungroup, or click the Ungroup button on the Drawing + toolbar). If the text is not ungrouped, PowerPoint works with the background of the selected image and not the individual letters.

When you group an image (that is, when it is still a WordArt object), the selection handles surround the entire image. When you ungroup an image, the handles surround individual letters.

warning

Don't disassemble a WordArt object if you've outlined the text. PowerPoint sees an ungrouped WordArt object as a drawing object, *not* as text. Therefore, PowerPoint outlines the object (much as the pencil tool would) by connecting the dots; this outlining creates a "cobweb" effect on certain letters (Figure 10-7). Moral: If you use text outlines, you can't ungroup and manipulate the text later as drawing objects in PowerPoint.

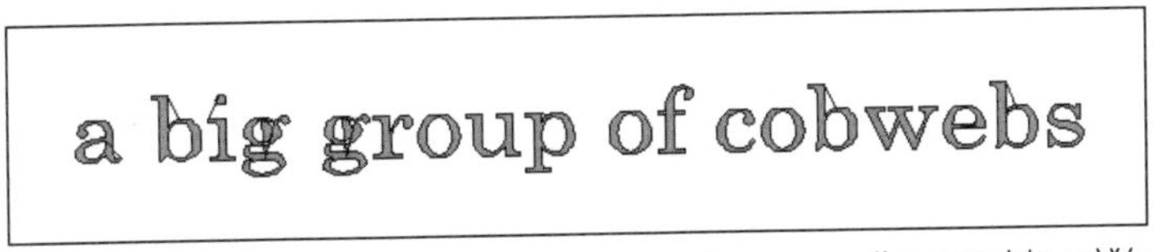

Figure 10-7: The cobweb effect occurs when you disassemble a WordArt object that has outlined text.

You can't ungroup the text you created in Presentation mode with the Text tool. PowerPoint can ungroup the text you created in WordArt (with Draw⇨Ungroup), however, because it views the text as an object. Therefore, to fill individual letters with a color, pattern, or gradient, you *must* create the text in WordArt and then ungroup it in PowerPoint. (Creating text in PowerPoint and then filling it fills the background but not the text!)

Now that those caveats are behind us, we can take this "Journey" one step further. Because the procedures vary between PowerPoint 4 and 7, the following section provides steps for both versions.

This example is involved; you must treat three separate groups of letters independently. Ready? Here are the steps to make the center of the Earth a more pleasant place:

1. In Presentation mode, select "Journey to the Center of the Earth" and then ungroup the text by using the Ungroup tool (or Draw⇨Ungroup). Click OK in response to the warning message.
2. Select "Journey to" by dragging a rectangular box around the words with the selection arrow.
3. Select Format⇨Color and Lines and then choose Shaded as your fill style.
4. In the Shaded Fill dialog box, select Vertical (located under Shade Styles). Select Other (in the Color menu) and then choose brown.
5. From the Variants selection, choose the upper-right gradient.
6. Slide the Dark/Light slider from the far left to approximately one-quarter of the way to the right and then click OK.
7. Select "the Center."
8. Select Format⇨Color and Lines and choose Shaded as your fill style.
9. In the Shaded Fill dialog box, select Other (in the Color menu) and then choose a reddish brown.
10. From the Variants selection, choose the lower-left gradient; leave the slider in place, and then click OK.
11. Select "of the Earth."

12. Select Format⇨Color and Lines and then choose Shaded as your fill style.
13. In the Shaded Fill dialog box, select Other (in the Color menu) and then choose brown.
14. From the Variants selection, choose the upper-left gradient and then click OK.
15. Finally, add a shadow with Format⇨Shadow. Choose light gray as the shadow color. Turn on the Down radio button with a setting of 3 and then turn on the Right button with a setting of 4. Click OK. The result is similar to Figure 10-8.

Figure 10-8: After some artistic interpretation, the Earth is a cooler place.

1. In Presentation mode, select "Journey to the Center of the Earth" and then ungroup the text by using the Ungroup tool (or Draw⇨Ungroup). Click OK in response to the warning message.
2. Select "Journey to" by dragging a rectangular box around the words with the selection arrow.
3. Select Format⇨Color and Lines and then choose Shaded as your fill style.
4. From the Shaded Fill dialog box, turn on the Two Color radio button and then choose Color 1 as a medium gray and Color 2 as a brown.
5. From the Variants selection, choose the upper-right gradient.
6. Select "the Center."
7. Select Format⇨Color and Lines and then choose Shaded as your fill style.
8. From the Shaded Fill dialog box, turn on the Two Color radio button and then choose red as Color 1 and a reddish-brown as Color 2.

9. From the Variants selection, choose the lower-left gradient and then click OK.
10. Select “of the Earth.”
11. Select Format⇨Color and Lines and then choose Shaded as your fill style.
12. From the Shaded Fill dialog box, turn on the Two Color radio button and then choose a medium gray for Color 1 and a brown for Color 2.
13. From the Variants selection, choose the upper-left gradient and then click OK.
14. Finally, add a shadow with Format⇨Shadow. Choose light gray as the shadow color. Turn on the Down radio button with a setting of 3 and then turn on the Right button with a setting of 4. Click OK. The result is similar to Figure 10-8.

After you ungroup, object redraw becomes very slow; it remains slow even after you apply your effects and then regroup the objects. Here as elsewhere in PowerPoint, a trade-off exists between speed and “coolness.”

Now let’s enhance the value of our ocean front property:

1. Select Ocean Front Property, and from the Drawing toolbar, select the 3-D tool. From the 3-D map, choose a setting you like; we chose 3-D Style #7. Note how PowerPoint handles the perspective as you read from right to left.
2. Now change the lighting for a more dramatic effect. From the Drawing toolbar, click the 3-D button and select 3-D Settings. From the 3-D Settings toolbar, activate the lighting menu and select up-lighting (bottom, center) with a Bright setting. The result should be similar to Figure 10-9.

Figure 10-9: The ocean waves have more character with 3-D extrusion and lighting effects.

tip

For lighting that needs to shine directly on and in front of an object or text, select the cube that floats in the middle of the lights.

warning

Lighting can only be applied to 3-D objects. If you apply lighting to a 2-D object, PowerPoint automatically turns it into a 3-D object.

PowerPoint 8's 3-D toolbar has many cool functions. To change the extrusion color, select the 3-D Color button. The Surface button lets you change the object's look, with choices of Wire Frame, Matte, Plastic, and Metal. You can also change the following:

- The direction of the extrusion with the Perspective and Parallel options
- The extrusion's Depth with the Custom setting or a really cool Infinity selection
- The object's orientation in the 3-D world with Tilt Right, Left, Up, or Down
- Whether the 3-D effects are on or off (toggling this button stores your 3-D settings, in case you decide to turn them on again later)

Two Last Tricks

This chapter concludes by describing two more handy WordArt tricks: Text shadowing and mirroring.

Shadowing text in WordArt

versions 4 & 7

WordArt 2.0 can create eight cool shadow effects (such as perspective shadowing). These effects can fall either in front of or behind the lettering. You can also use shadowing as a crude form of *anti-aliasing,* which makes angles appear smoother on-screen. The following steps show you how:

1. Select Insert⇨Object and then choose Microsoft WordArt 2.0 from the list.
2. Type your text in the Enter Your Text Here window and then click Update Display.
3. Choose a font style and size.
4. From the toolbar on the upper-right corner of the screen, select the Drop Shadow tool. Various effects appear in the selection window (another place to experiment with different shadow colors).

tip

WordArt 2.0 severely limits the shadow colors from which you can choose. Fortunately, you have a cool workaround! Remember that once you create your drop-shadow, you can go to the PowerPoint presentation window, ungroup the WordArt objects, and then fill the shadow characters with whatever color you like. Use a slightly darker version of the text foreground color for a good-looking shadow that complements rather than clashes. Applying shadow colors letter-by-letter is a tedious operation, so use the Shift-Click technique to select all the shadow characters at once and save time.

version 8

WordArt 2.5 has tremendously improved your capability to shadow text and objects. Located on the Drawing toolbar is the new Shadow button, which offers 20 preset effects. Once applied, you can alter these effects further from the Shadow Settings toolbar — you can nudge your shadow up, down, left, and right, you can apply any color (by using the Standard or Custom palettes), and you can even make the color semitransparent. Have fun!

Creating mirrored text effects

Mirrored text effects are great for water-related phrases such as *Emily's Dive Shop* or *King Crab Population Data*. For example, you can float straight text above a body of water, with a mirrored reflection of the text below the water. You may think of other cool uses, too. To create this mirrored text effect in WordArt 2.0, follow these steps:

1. Create your phrase in WordArt (use the techniques discussed in this chapter).
2. Bring the WordArt object into PowerPoint by clicking outside the WordArt text frame, ungroup it to turn it into a drawing object, and then regroup it.
3. Select Edit⇨Duplicate (or press Ctrl-D) to create the duplicate you want mirrored.
4. Choose the duplicate, and then select Draw⇨Rotate/Flip.

To create this mirrored text effect in WordArt 2.5, follow these steps:

1. Create your phrase in WordArt.
2. With your text highlighted, select Plain Text from the WordArt Shapes map.
3. Select Edit⇨Duplicate (or press Ctrl-D) to create the duplicate you want mirrored.
4. Choose the duplicate and then select Draw⇨Rotate/Flip.

This technique was used to create the slide shown in Figure 10-10. We used a few other tricks to get the look we wanted, but you can figure out those on your own, through a little experimentation!

Figure 10-10: Mirrored text is a nice effect for water-related topics.

Summary

This chapter introduced the cool text capabilities of the WordArt 2.0 utility and the WordArt 2.5 tool:

It showed you how to fit text into a variety of paths and distortion envelopes, rotate and stretch text objects, modify justification and spacing variables; it also showed you how to slant, rotate, and shade your text.

You learned how to apply colors (gradients and shadows) to individual letters or groups of letters by breaking apart WordArt 2.0 objects in PowerPoint's presentation window and how to apply a bitmapped photograph in Version 2.5.

This chapter also pointed out that WordArt 2.0 uses TrueType fonts only while WordArt 2.5 can also use PostScript fonts, and that in WordArt 2.0, outlined text can produce unwanted "cobwebs" when you ungroup it.

Finally, you learned how to create better shadows than WordArt 2.0 permits and how to use the cool new extrusion and lighting effects in 2.5. We also reflected on a cool mirroring tip.

In the next chapter (on builds and transitions), you learn how to take your distinctive graphics and text objects and give them even more life by adding the element of motion.

Transitions and Builds

11

In This Chapter

The difference between a transition effect and a build effect

Built-in transitions that work well and those to avoid

Applying transitions creatively to match slide content

Creating text-build effects in PowerPoint 4, 7, and 8

Using dimmed-build effects to help the audience follow your presentation

Using PowerPoint 7 and 8's graphics build capability to create cool animations without special software

Tricking PowerPoint 4 into simulating graphics builds by using slide transitions

In this chapter, we talk about adding motion to your slide shows through the build and transition effects that PowerPoint provides. Thus far in Part II, we have gone beyond the basics in several PowerPoint areas to achieve cool effects, but all of those effects have been *static*. In this chapter, we introduce the concept of motion by using PowerPoint's built-in *builds* and *transitions*. Later in Part III, we take the motion concept further by bringing in computer-based animations and digital video.

But first things first. Builds and transitions can add cool motions to your presentations and have the distinct virtue of not requiring any extra software to do so. PowerPoint 7 and 8 have more sophisticated motion capabilities, especially with builds, but you can pull a few rabbits out of the hat with Version 4 to create some nice effects. Version 8 introduces the convenient Custom Animation dialog box, which cures the headaches previous versions sometimes induced.

Transitions

The default behavior for PowerPoint when advancing a slide is to redraw the entire screen instantaneously, so that the new slide suddenly (and, sometimes, jarringly) snaps into place. *Transitions* add detectable motion or action to the process of changing slides from one to the next. That is, transitions provide basic *interslide* motion effects, such as fades or wipes.

The general technique for assigning a transition to a slide is to select Slide Sorter View, click on the slide you want (or Shift-click on several slides), and select Tools➪Transitions (Version 4), Tools➪Slide Transitions (Version 7), or Slide Show➪Slide Transitions (Version 8). The transition you select from the Slide Transition dialog box takes place when PowerPoint moves *to* that particular slide (or slides).

When you click on a transition from the drop-down list box, you see a preview of the transition effect in the preview window of the Slide Transition dialog box, which alternates between displaying a drawing of a weird-looking mutt (reminiscent of the Macintosh "cowdog") and a picture of a key (Figure 11-1).

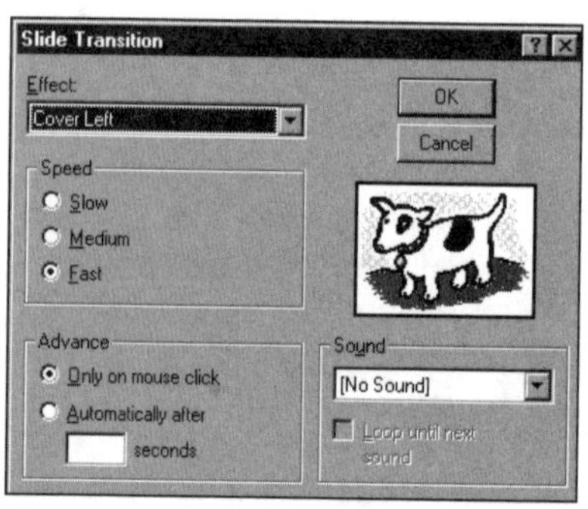

Figure 11-1: PowerPoint 7 and 8's Slide Transition window lets you preview transition effects before you apply them.

Once you become familiar with the various transitions, the easiest way to select them is from the drop-down transition effects list box on the Slide Sorter toolbar (visible only in Slide Sorter View).

tip

You can set transition effects in Slide View or in any other view for that matter, but Slide Sorter View usually is more convenient for two reasons: (1) You can click on any slide and see the assigned transition in the transition effects window on the Slide Sorter toolbar, and (2) you can look below the slide to see if the small square-and-arrow icon is present to indicate that a transition has been assigned for that slide (Figure 11-2).

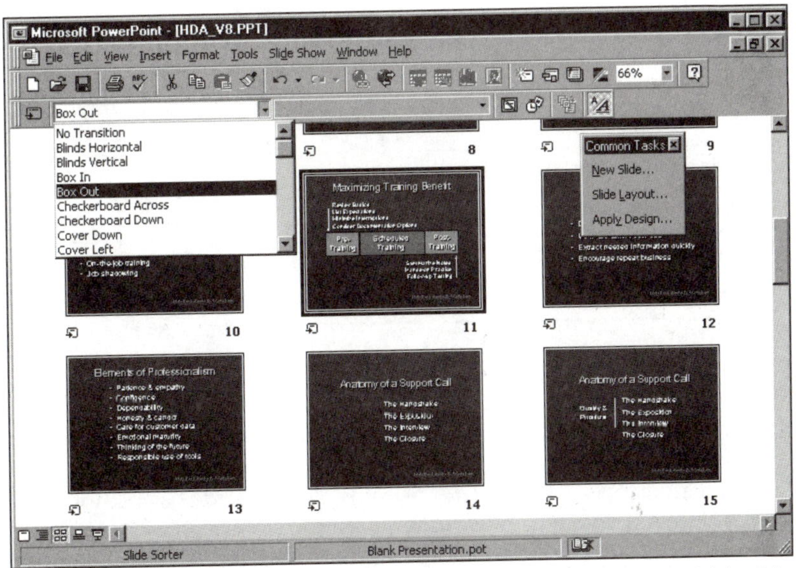

Figure 11-2: Viewing transitions in Slide Sorter View lets you see which slides have transitions and which transitions they use.

Table 11-1 lists the built-in transitions available in PowerPoint (the same options are available in Versions 4, 7, and 8) along with our comments about each one, based on how the transitions work on an 83 MHz Pentium with accelerated graphics. Remember, just because Microsoft includes a transition effect doesn't mean you have to use it. We tend to stay away from any transition that isn't smooth. Jerky motion isn't cool.

Table 11-1: PowerPoint Transitions with Editorial Comments

Transition	Editorial Comment
Blinds (vertical, horizontal)	Good
Box (out, in)	Good
Checkerboard (across, down)	Busy, can be slow
Cover (left, right, up, down, diagonal)	Usually too jerky
Cut	Same as "None"
Cut through Black	Typically flickers annoyingly
Dissolve	Can be busy and slow
Fade through Black	Usually not smooth
Random Bars (horizontal, vertical)	Okay
Split Horizontal (out, in)	Good

(continued)

Table 11-1: PowerPoint Transitions... (continued)

Transition	Editorial Comment
Split Vertical (out, in)	Good
Strips Down/Up (left, right)	Good
Strips Left/Right (down, up)	Good
Uncover (left, right, up, down, diagonal)	Usually too jerky
Wipe (left, right, up, down)	Good

tip

Transitions should complement your presentation, not distract from it. Therefore, you should typically set the transition speed to *Fast* — this setting gives your slide show a snappier feel and pace. To set the transition speed, select Tools⇨Transition⇨Fast (Version 4), Tools⇨Slide Transition⇨Fast (Version 7), or Slide Show⇨Slide Transition⇨Fast (Version 8). Here's a shortcut that works in all three versions: Go to Slide Sorter View, click the Slide Transition button to the left of the Slide Transition Effects field, and select Fast.

tip

Be creative when choosing a transition. For example

- If you're building a little suspense and want to create a "curtain rising" sensation before a particularly important slide, try the Split Vertical Out or the Uncover Up transition. Also try using a slower speed for a little drama (as long as the playback is smooth).
- If an upcoming slide's focal point is in the center, the Box In and Box Out transitions may be good choices.

Above all, don't use every transition that Microsoft provides just because they're there. The more elaborate transitions will seem cooler to your audience if you use them occasionally rather than for every slide. We use a simple wipe transition for most slides and apply a few special transitions here and there for effect or emphasis.

versions 7 & 8

PowerPoint 7 and 8 enable you to associate a sound file with a slide transition, a feature which we discuss in more detail in Chapter 13. For now, though, you should just watch out for uncool looping. Checking the box labeled Loop Until Next Sound makes the sound play continually until the next action in your presentation is executed. You pretty much want to avoid using this option, a fact you will truly appreciate if you've ever gone on the "It's A Small World, After All" ride at Disneyland.

Learn how to create and bring 3-D graphics onto PowerPoint slides for dramatic effects. Here, true 3-D illustration software produces realistic lighting and shadows. The plaque and letters in this slide were modeled and rendered in Ray Dream Designer as described in Chapter 8, cropped in Photoshop, and inserted onto a PowerPoint slide having a complementary gradient background. This book's CD-ROM contains a tryout version of Photoshop, plus demos and trial versions of 3-D illustration programs.

After spending a little time learning the basics of a few powerful graphics programs, you can quickly create cool PowerPoint images. Here's the slide from the example in Chapter 7. Stock photographs were brought into Photoshop, resized, cropped, filtered, and placed into separate, semi-transparent layers. A Gallery Effects filter transformed the graffiti image into a brick wall. Painter was used to apply the airbrush-style dog barks. The final image was brought into PowerPoint where the text was added. The CD-ROM contains stock photo samples, tryout versions of Photoshop and graphics filters, and a demo version of Painter.

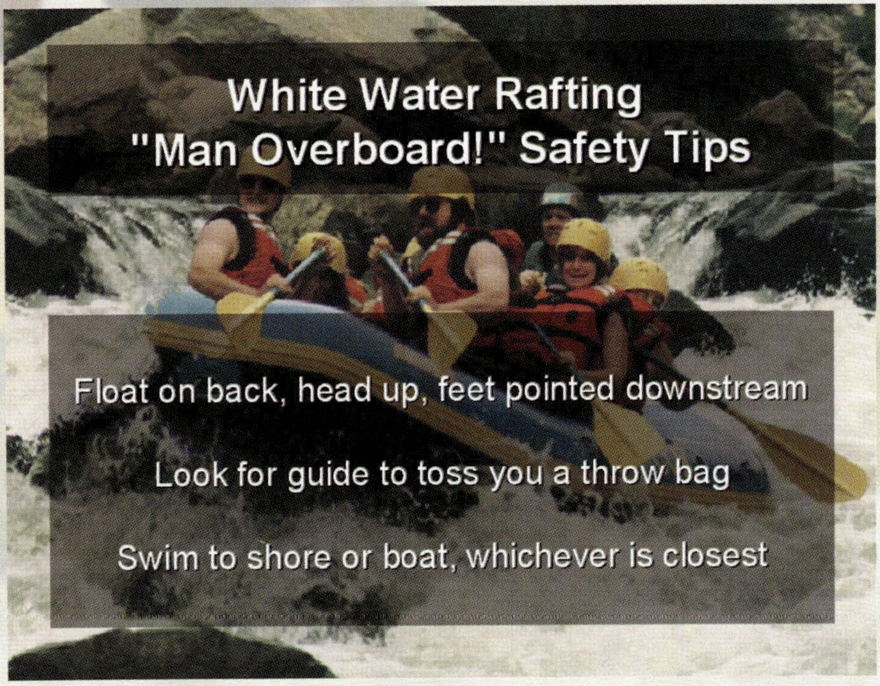

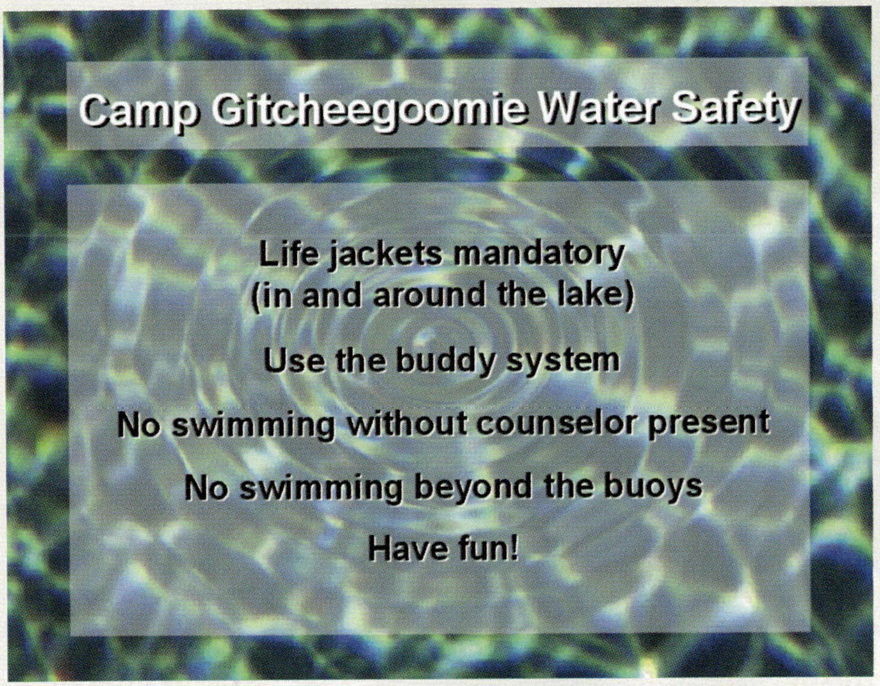

Photographs can make effective backgrounds, and not just for title slides. The top slide was scanned from a color print; the dark transparent rectangles were added in Photoshop. The bottom slide used the ZigZag Photoshop filter to create the pond ripple effect, and light transparent rectangles frame the text. See Chapter 2 for more ideas on creating cool slide backgrounds. The CD-ROM includes stock photo samples from PhotoDisc and MetaTools.

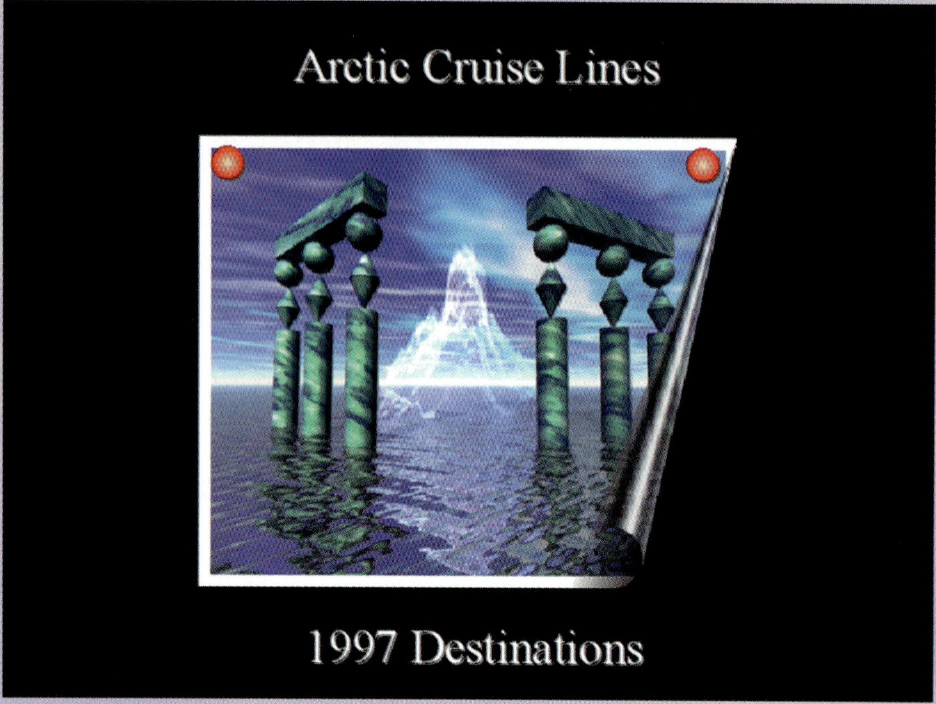

To create other-worldly 3-D scenes with remarkable ease, use KPT Bryce together with PowerPoint as described in Chapter 7. The top slide uses a cropped picture of an ethereal gateway, with a page curl filter applied in Photoshop and thumbtacks applied in PowerPoint.

The bottom slide is a full-screen Bryce image that demonstrates the beautiful reflections ray-tracing (also explained in Chapter 7) can create.

Two more KPT Bryce images illustrate the program's versatility for making your PowerPoint presentations memorable. The top slide uses ungrouped PowerPoint text to permit shading of individual letters. The images match the subject matter.

Opposing gradients, extrusions, and lighting can add a 3-D effect to 2-D clip art. The clip art image at top was brought into a PowerPoint slide and ungrouped, and individual pieces were filled with gradients running counter to the slide background. The text was created in WordArt and treated similarly. The image and text seem to jump out from the background. See Chapters 2 and 9 for more information.

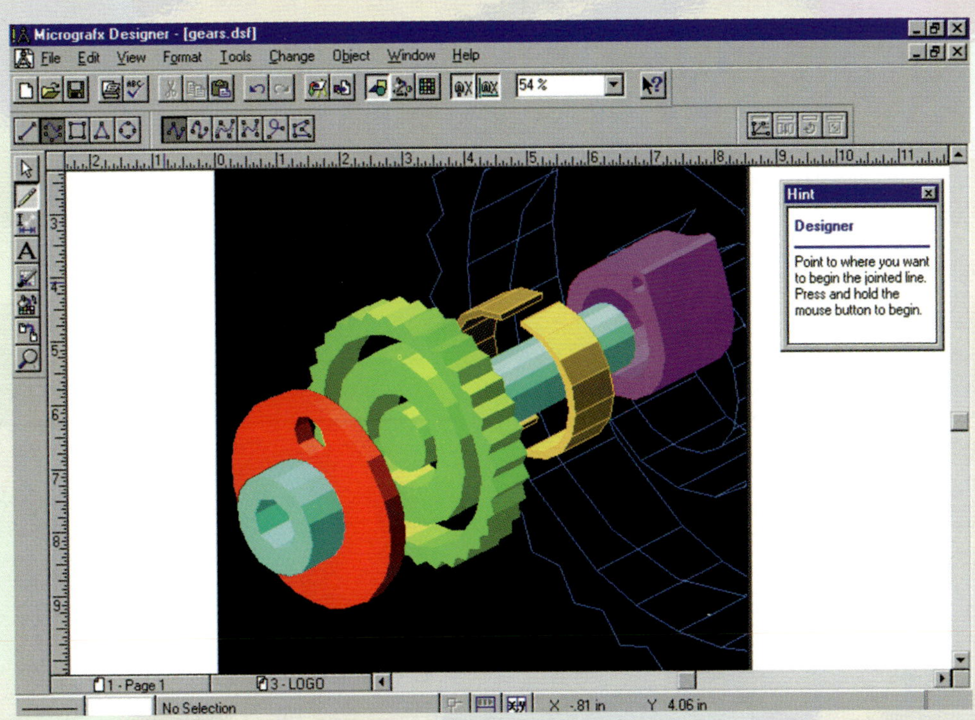

For PowerPoint slides that pop, create 2-D illustrations that have a 3-D look with programs such as Micrografx Designer. The illustration in the top screen was saved as a WMF file, brought into PowerPoint with Insert➪Picture, and scaled to fit the PowerPoint slide at bottom. Chapter 8 provides further details on this technique.

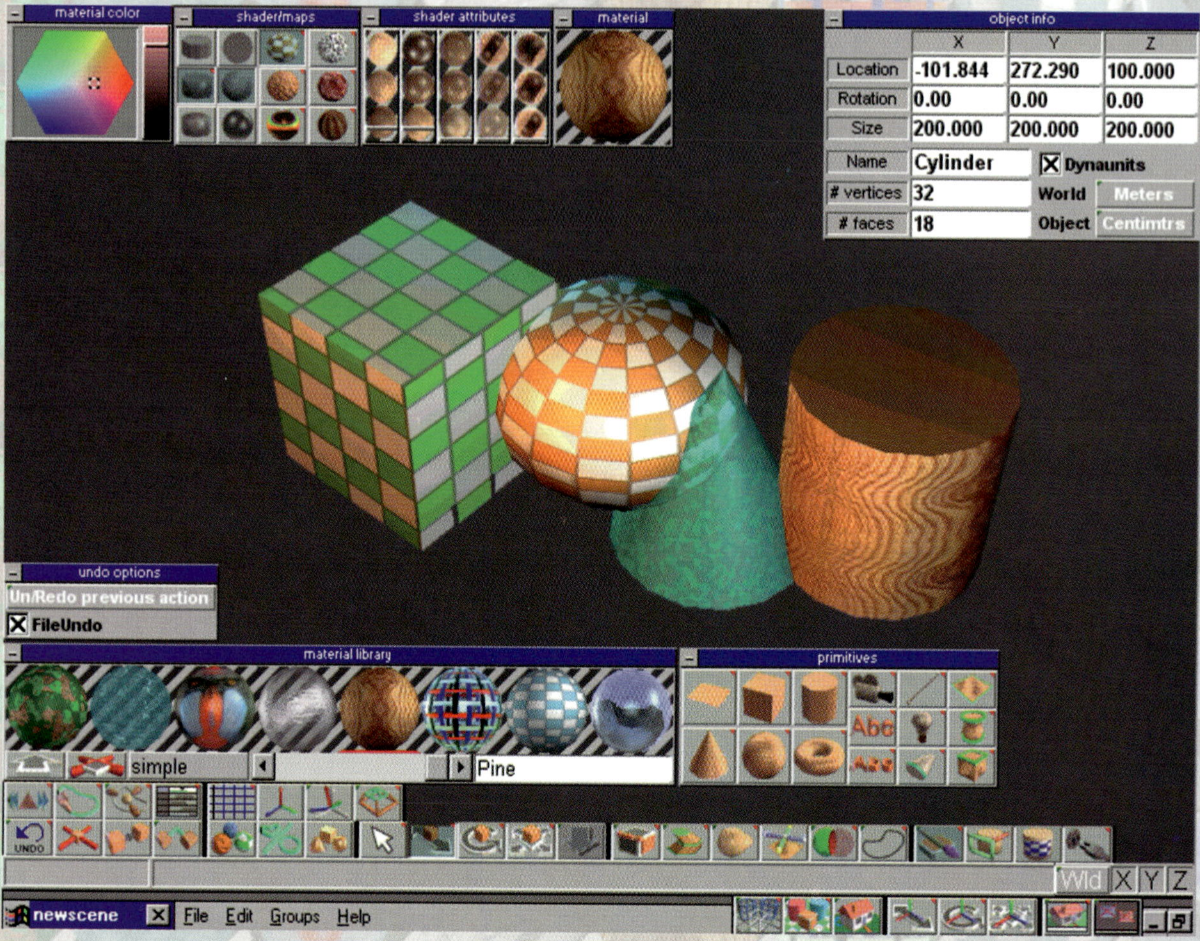

For interesting PowerPoint slide effects, Caligari's powerful TrueSpace 3-D illustration tool can quickly create 3-D "primitives," such as the geometric shapes above, and paint them with unusual surfaces. TrueSpace also creates AVI animations. See Chapters 8 and 14 for discussions of 3-D illustration and computer animation. The CD-ROM includes a trial version of TrueSpace.

These two slides depict how you can enhance clip art as discussed in Chapter 9. The top slide shows that disassembling clip art enables you to treat individual elements separately; for example, to assign a wood texture to the window frame. The bottom slide illustrates new features offered in PowerPoint 8, such as extruding 2-D objects so they look three-dimensional.

Compelling PowerPoint slides can start with effects created through Photoshop's powerful bitmap filters, which work with Picture Publisher, Painter, and Ray Dream Designer as well. The top row shows Diffuse, Pointillize, and Wave. The middle row shows Tiles (square), ZigZag (out from center), and Wind (right). The bottom row shows Pinch, Crystallize, and Radial Blur (zoom). Chapters 7 and 8 discuss using filters in detail.

No need to be an artist when adding unique touches to PowerPoint presentations! The Gallery Effects filters, mentioned in Chapter 7, provide artistic effects. The top row shows Watercolor, Sprayed Strokes, and Dry Brush. The middle row shows Film Grain, the original unfiltered image, and Craquelure. The bottom row shows Sponge, Spatter, and Texturize (canvas).

For more versatility in PowerPoint slide creation, add to your filter library with Kai's Power Tools. The top row shows Grime Layer, Blur-Gaussian Electrify, and Glass Lens Soft. The middle row shows Blur-Gaussian Weave, Vortex Tiling, and Blur-Gaussian Glow. The bottom row shows Scatter Horizontal, Fade Contrast, and Pixel Wind.

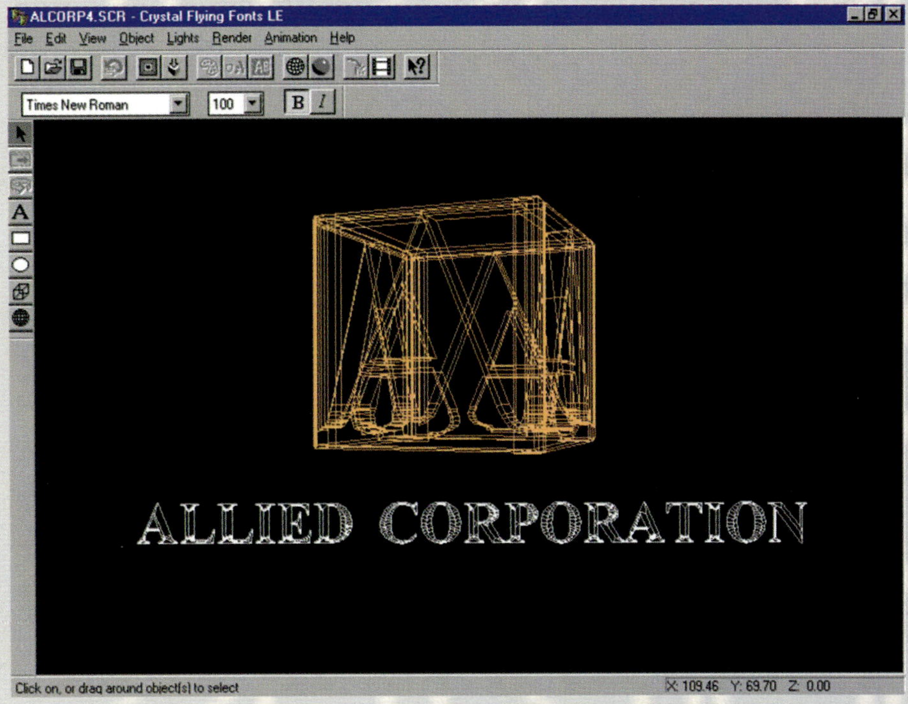

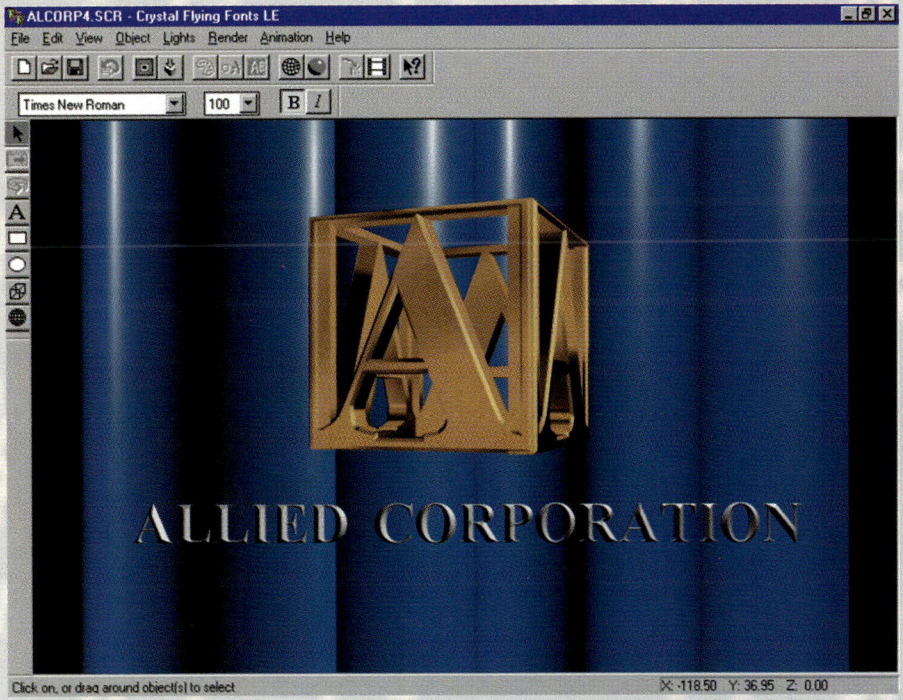

As Chapter 14 explains, you can use animation programs to add impact to your PowerPoint presentations. Here, Crystal Graphics' Flying Fonts is used to model a logo and text element in wireframe mode (top) and then to render the 3-D scene for a title slide (bottom). Flying Fonts can produce 3-D animations that you can link to PowerPoint with Media Player in Versions 4 and 7; PowerPoint 8 can store and play AVI files natively. A demo of Flying Fonts is on the CD-ROM.

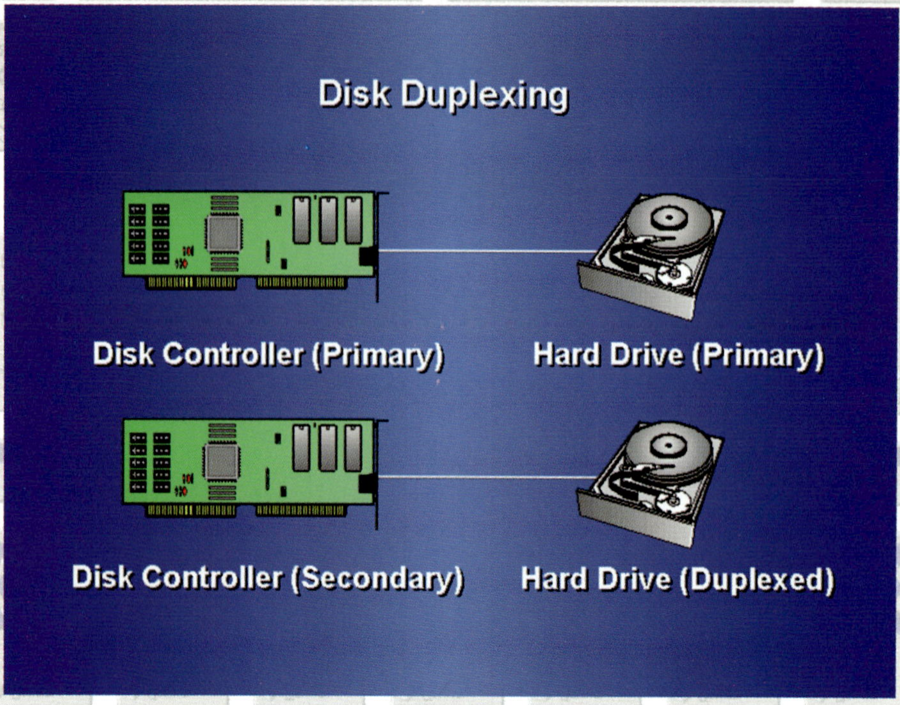

The above slide with clip art would be suitable for a 35mm slide but not a computer-based presentation; PowerPoint takes a long time to draw the intricate circuit boards.

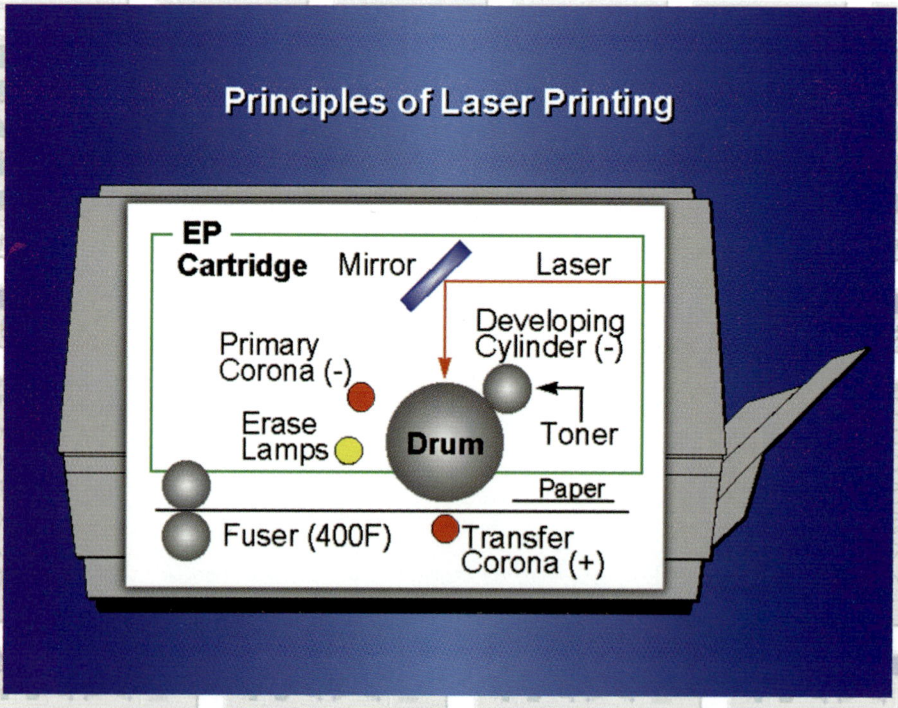

Here's a creative use of a clip art laser printer image: scale it up and cut a rectangular hole in it to demonstrate the machine's inner workings. See Chapter 9 for more ideas.

A good illustration program can help you create cool effects with simple clip art images.

Step 1. Import BULB.EPS into Micrografx Designer and draw two overlapping rectangles over it.

Step 2. Highlight all three objects and select Change➪Combine➪Connect Closed.

Step 3. Draw color-filled shapes to cover the "holes" (or areas of negative space).

Step 4. Highlight the colored shapes and select Change➪Order➪Send to Back.

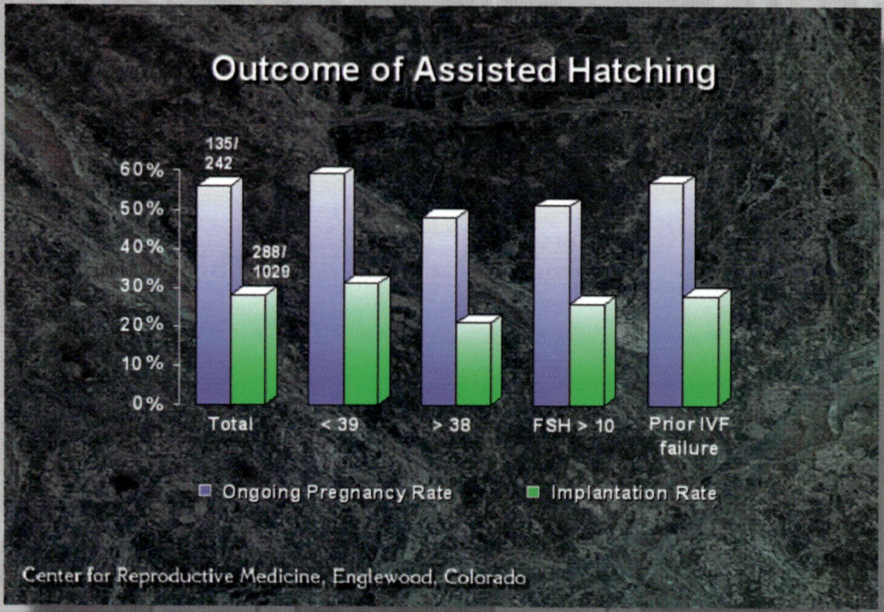

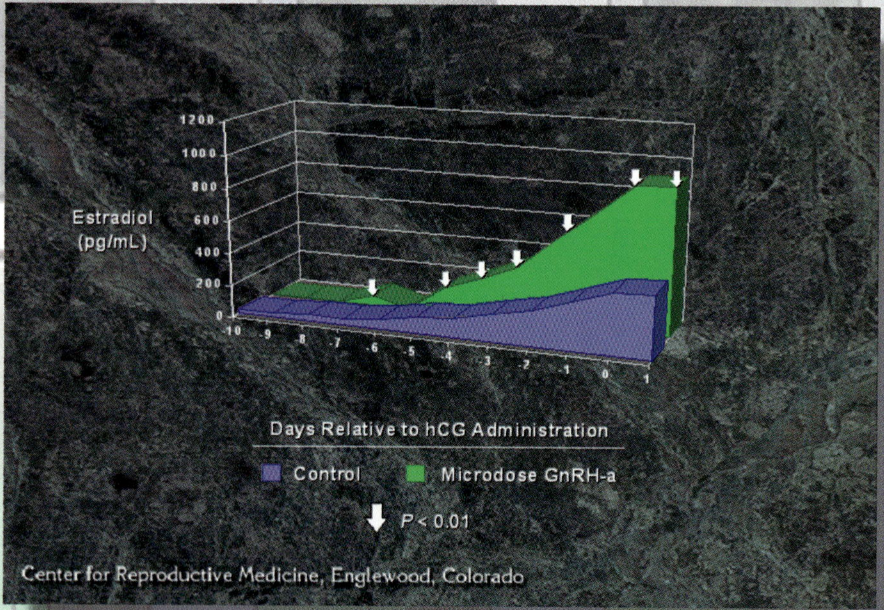

Microsoft Graph was the starting point for these slides. After the basic graphs were created, they were ungrouped in PowerPoint 7, so that custom axis labels, legends, and graphics effects could be added by using PowerPoint's text and fill tools. The new Graph program shipped with PowerPoint 8 can perform many of these enhancements without ungrouping. These slides appear wide because they are sized for 35mm output. See Chapter 5 for more on using graphs in your presentations.

Builds

Builds add motion within a single slide by progressively adding moving elements to a slide. Builds provide *intraslide* motion effects.

Text builds

In college, several of our professors used overhead transparencies and would place a sheet of paper or cardboard over the foil, moving it down little by little to reveal each successive point as the professor reached it in the discussion. This technique was a Stone Age version of a *build*: Revealing points as you want to discuss them, maintaining a little suspense in the process, and helping the audience focus on the topic at hand.

In PowerPoint, the most basic, common type of build shows successive text elements (such as bullet items) one item at a time as the presenter clicks the mouse. The usual technique for implementing this kind of build is to create a new slide with one of the various predefined layouts and then select Tools⇨Build (Version 4), Tools⇨Build Slide Text (Version 7), or, in Version 8, select the text and choose either Slide Show⇨Preset Animation (for canned builds with sound effects) or Slide Show⇨Custom Animation (for custom builds). You can also perform text builds in Versions 7 and 8 with nonbullet items; each text object moves as a unit and stays on the screen after the build effect.

The PowerPoint 4 Build dialog box is shown in Figure 11-3. As you can see, this dialog box is pretty limited: You can choose from several motion effects, but you can't control the speed with which they appear once the effect starts — that is, whether a line of text flies in from the left edge with a rapid motion or a slow one. Many of the motion effects will be familiar because they are the same as the transition effects. Choosing No build effect causes text bullet items to appear instantaneously.

You can also choose the Dim Previous Points option to de-emphasize items that you have moved past. Typically, this option works by changing the item's color to one that more closely matches the background. This feature is helpful for audiences because it enables them to see where you've already been and to know at a glance which point you're currently discussing.

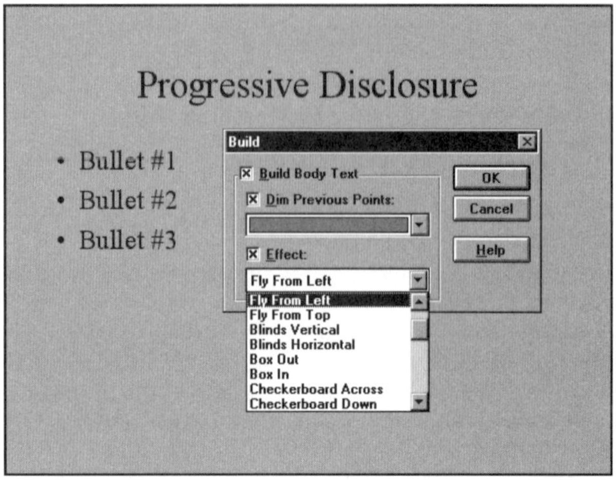

Figure 11-3: PowerPoint 4 doesn't offer a great deal of control or flexibility for creating text-build effects.

The dim feature is a bit limited in scope for PowerPoint 4 if you want to completely hide the previous points: It won't work with gradient backgrounds because you can only make the preceding text points a solid color.

PowerPoint 7 significantly refines the text-build feature. To use it, select Tools⇨Build Slide Text⇨Other to get to the Animation Settings dialog box shown in Figure 11-4.

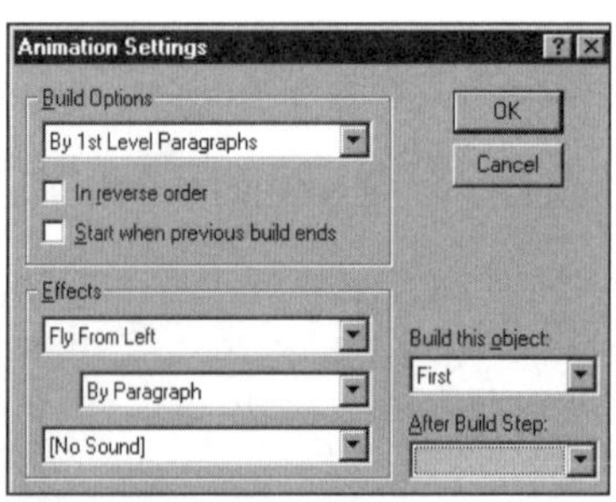

Figure 11-4: PowerPoint 7 enables you to create more sophisticated text build effects.

The Animation Settings dialog box provides several build capabilities:

- The Build Options area enables you to perform builds by any level of paragraph indentation, in reverse order, and automatically, without requiring a mouse click.

- The Effects area offers motion effects, but here you can apply them to paragraphs, words, or even letters. You also can assign sounds to accompany each paragraph, word, or letter. (Note that you will rarely select motion effects by letter — the effect is too distracting!)
- The After Build Step field provides a handy new option, Hide, that makes the previous text element disappear (even on a gradient background!).

version 8

PowerPoint 8 vastly improved its animation dialog box, which is now much easier to use (Figure 11-5). The tabbed dialog box offers more options, adds a preview thumbnail that saves you scads of time, and completely fixes the animation order problem seen in previous versions. Microsoft even tossed in a few really wild effects, such as Spiral. To get to the Custom Animation dialog box, select Slide Show⇨Custom Animation, or right-click a text box and select Custom Animation. (You can also use Preset Animations for text builds, but Custom Animations give you more control.)

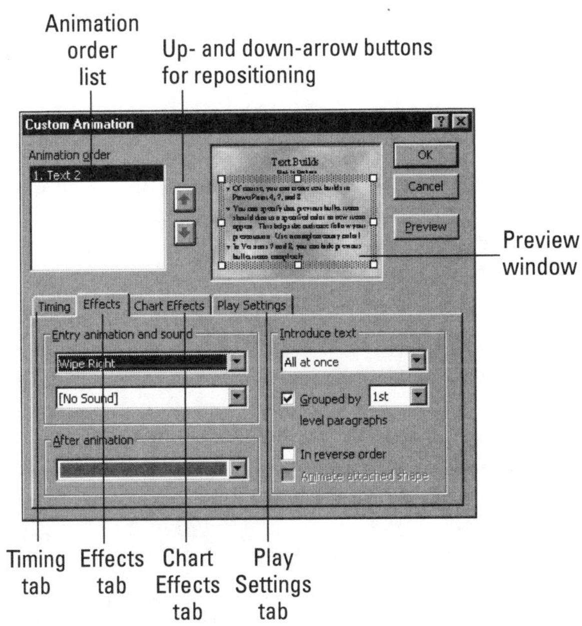

Figure 11-5: PowerPoint 8's Custom Animation dialog box is the new nerve center for both text and graphics builds.

Here are some of the features of Version 8's Custom Animation Box:

- In the Animation order text box, PowerPoint assigns to objects descriptive names and a number that correlates with their creation; then PowerPoint places them in order of animation. A bulleted list is treated as a single object.

- The handy up- and down-arrow buttons enable you to move an object to a different time slot by simply highlighting the object and using the buttons to reposition it.
- The Preview window shows a mini-movie of your work for fast editing — cool for long, complicated animations.
- The Timing tab alerts you of any slide objects without an animation setting. It also controls start time, delay time, and animation execution.
- The Effects tab, which controls build effects and sound, has most of the settings you need for text builds, including bulleted list builds. The options are essentially the same as in Version 7. The new Spiral and Swivel effects are cool additions. Text builds don't require the Chart Effects or Play Settings tabs.
- The Chart Effects tab lets you add any of the Fly effects to the elements of a chart created in Microsoft Graph (see Chapter 5).
- The Play Settings tab enables you to play sounds or music automatically during an animation sequence (see Chapter 13).

Graphics builds

Text builds are great, and you will use them often (preferably without the annoying sound effects!). With graphics builds, though, things really get fun because you can create cool and surprising effects — even some simulated animation. The best way to illustrate the possibilities is to present some examples that you can try yourself, so here goes.

The talking head

In this example, we bring to life the Talking Head image from the ClipArt Gallery. (You may want to review the clip art material in Chapters 4 and 9, because this example builds on that information.)

1. Open a blank presentation and insert a new, blank slide.
2. Select Insert⇨Clip Art, select Communication from the Categories list, and highlight the Talking Head (its description reads "Information Communication"). Click Insert.
3. With the image selected, click the Disassemble Picture button on the Drawing+ toolbar or select Draw⇨Ungroup. Click OK in response to the confirmation message. The image is now broken into two pieces: the head and the voice waves.
4. First, we need to jazz up this boring clip art image. With the head selected, choose Format⇨Color and Lines⇨Fill and Shaded.
5. At the Shaded Fill dialog, click on the Two Color radio button. For color 1, select Other Color from the pull-down menu and choose a

dark peach shade from the lower-left section of the standard color wheel. For color 2, use the same commands to choose a very light peach shade from the middle to lower-left part of the wheel.

6. In the Shade Styles area, toggle on the From Center radio button and highlight the right-hand selection in the Variants area. Click on OK.
7. In the Line area, select black as the Color and, from the Style menu, select the first (top) line weight. Click on OK.
8. Now select the voice wave group. Select Format⇨Color and Lines⇨Fill and Shaded.
9. At the Shaded Fill dialog, click on the Two Color radio button. For color 1, select Other Color from the pull-down menu and choose a navy blue from the upper half of the standard color wheel. For color 2, use the same commands to choose a very light blue (almost white) from the upper half of the wheel.
10. In the Shade Styles area, toggle on the Horizontal radio button and highlight the lower-left selection in the Variants area. Click on OK.
11. In the Line area, select Color⇨No Line. Click on OK.
12. Now that we have great colors and a good-looking gradient, let's animate the voice waves. You could leave the waves as one object and apply a single animation effect to it, but if you click on the Ungroup Objects button (or Draw⇨Ungroup), you get more control over the effect. For example, you can apply a different effect to each wave if you like, and each effect will animate fully before the next one begins; the timing is also better, and you can control the order of the build elements to denote direction of motion.
13. Highlight the first voice wave, closest to the mouth.
14. Display the Animation Effects toolbar with View⇨Toolbar⇨Animation Effects. Click the button labeled Animation Settings (which typically is the rightmost button on the toolbar).
15. In the Build Options area, select Build and Start when previous build ends to make the graphics build take place automatically.
16. In the Effects area, select Wipe Right from the list of effects.
17. Note the order listed in the Build this object field. When you select and assign a build effect to each object, you specify the build sequence number here.

warning: The build sequence number usually does not respond automatically as you would expect it to. If you chose an object that you intended to be number seven in the build order, but the Build this object field shows Second, you have to scroll down and manually choose Seven.

18. In the After Build Step field, select Don't Dim. Click on OK.

tip

You have three choices under After Build Step. Don't Dim returns the image or text to its original state after PowerPoint completes the build step. Hide causes the image or text to vanish after the build. Other Color changes the object's color to one you select after the build, as we saw earlier with text builds.

19. Repeat Steps 13 through 18 until all nine voice waves have the animated builds assigned to them (Figure 11-6).

20. If you like, add a title by using WordArt as discussed in Chapter 10. Now play your slide show — once the head appears, click once to start your animation.

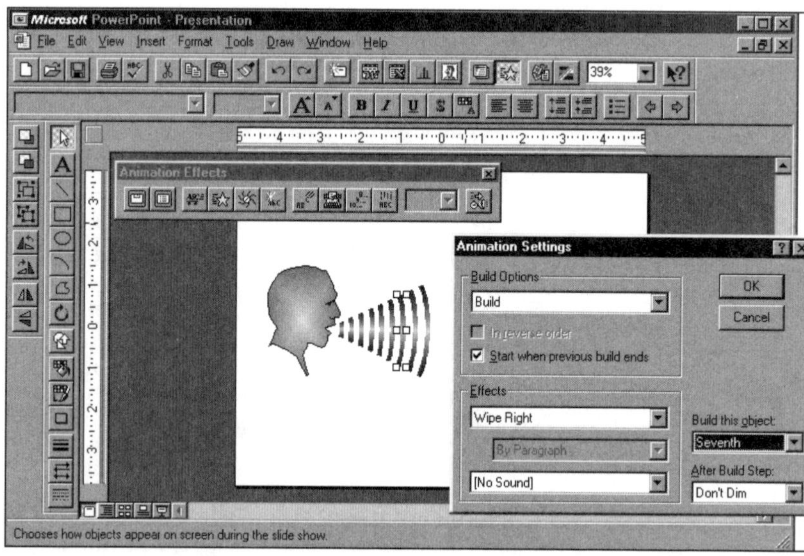

Figure 11-6: Graphics builds can create an animated effect.

One step further

version 7

You can't loop animations or builds, but you can repeat an effect. Here's an example that shows you how and illustrates the Flash effect as well.

1. Perform Steps 1 through 20 from the preceding example.
2. Select all the voice waves by drawing a box around them, click the Animation Settings button, and then select Flash Once, Slow from the Effects list.
3. With the voice waves still selected, select Edit⇨Duplicate and move the duplicated set of waves to a different part of the screen (anywhere is fine).

4. Do a few spot checks by clicking on the individual waves and viewing their Animation Settings. You should notice here that PowerPoint has automatically set the sequence numbers starting with 10 and going up to 18. Make sure that each wave has the settings Flash Once, Slow; Start when previous build ends; and Don't Dim — these should be the default settings.

5. Select all the voice waves in the second set and place them directly on top of the first set. The Zoom tool helps you place them exactly.

Time travel

You can make a shark swim across the bottom of your presentation screen (Figure 11-7) with a caption that reads "Don't Be Eaten Alive by the Competition," or have an airplane fly by pulling a banner with your company logo and the caption "We're Flying High."

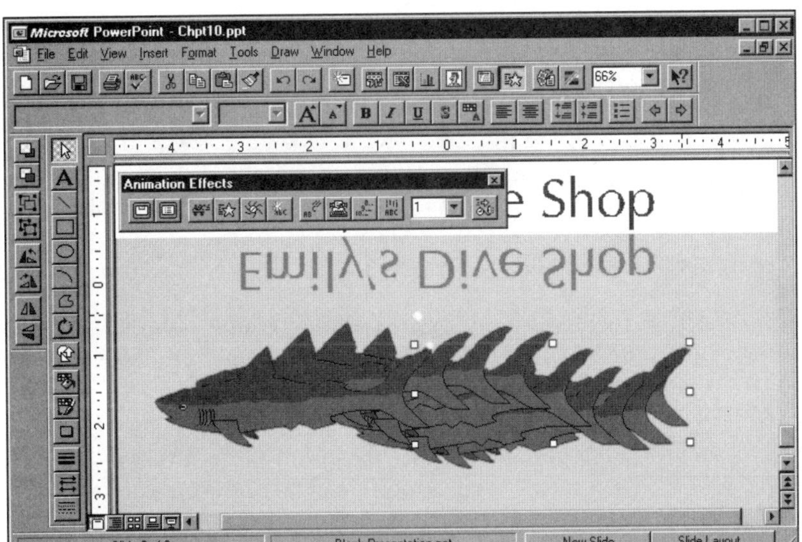

Figure 11-7: Make a shark swim across your display.

How can you perform such simple animations? Here's the technique for Version 7:

1. Time travel is easy in PowerPoint — simply decide on a starting point (A) and an ending point (B) for your graphic object.

2. Place your image at point A and then duplicate it as many times as needed until you've reached point B.

Both PowerPoint 7 and 8 enable you to place an image off the slide boundaries. In Version 7, there's a trick: You must hold down Alt when moving the object off the slide, and you may only be able to move it a little at a time.

3. Once your images are in place, highlight all of them with the arrow tool, click the Animation Settings button on the Animation Effects toolbar, and select Build, Start when previous build ends, and Flash Once, Slow (or whatever speed you like).

4. Set the sequence numbers as desired for each individual object as we did in the previous example. Set the build effect for the final image to No build effect so that it stays on the screen, and then play the show.

The more you repeat the image and the closer together you place your duplicate images, the cooler the effect will be and the longer the animation will run, giving the viewer a chance to adjust to the movement and understand what he or she is seeing.

When animating time travel, using one of the three Flash effects works best because each image automatically disappears immediately after the next image begins to animate. To use any of the other effects and have the objects disappear in this way, you must uncheck the Start when previous build ends option and select Hide under After build step. Then you must manually click through the animation to activate each build.

Time travel is effortless in Version 8:

1. Place your image (for example, the figure holding a helium balloon, labeled Amjoy in the Screen Beans clip art category) at the top and off the slide area.

2. With the image selected, open the Custom Animation dialog box's Effects tab and select Crawl from Bottom under Entry animation. (Fly from Bottom is too fast — the new crawl effects are great for animations.)

3. Move to the Timing tab and select your sequencing preference, either Automatically or On mouse click.

4. Click Preview and watch the little guy float onto the screen and then off again.

You can use one of PowerPoint 8's cool new animation effects to juggle a heavy workload:

1. Open a blank presentation and specify the blank slide AutoLayout.

2. Select Insert⇨Picture⇨Clip Art, choose Screen Beans from the Categories list, and highlight the juggling Screen Bean (labeled Amorgani). Click Insert.

3. With the image selected, choose Draw⇨Ungroup and click Yes. Resize if desired.
4. Hold down Shift and select the calendar, phone receiver, and envelopes. Select Draw⇨Group.
5. Right-click the new group and select Custom Animation. Select Swivel from the Effects tab under Entry animation and sound, and select Automatically or On mouse click, as you prefer, from the Timing tab.
6. Watch a minimovie of the animation in the Preview window.

Putting the pieces together

The next graphical build example illustrates a very effective technique: Bringing in pieces of a graphic from different directions of the screen to make a complete graphic by the last build. Here's how you do it:

1. Insert the 3-D puzzle clip art object (labeled Strategy in the Shapes category in Version 7, labeled Puzzle in Version 8) onto a blank slide.
2. Disassemble, recolor, and resize the object if desired.
3. Highlight any piece you want to start with. In Version 7, from the Animation Settings dialog box, select Build, Start when previous build ends, select Don't Dim, make sure that First appears in the Build this object field, and select one of the eight effects beginning with the word "Fly." In Version 8, from the Custom Animation dialog box, click Timing and Animate Automatically; then select each puzzle piece from the object list and apply a "Fly" effect.
4. Repeat Steps 3 and 4 for each puzzle piece, choosing different directions for the Fly effects until the puzzle is complete. Don't forget to check your build sequence in Version 7!

How about trying this technique with a 3-D pie chart created using Microsoft Graph, as discussed in Chapter 5? Adding motion to pie charts is fun and effective, and even though the pie slices won't look complete when broken apart, no one will really care.

PowerPoint 4 only supports text builds, not graphics builds, which no doubt leaves you Version 4 users feeling a little left out at this point. Don't! You can get around this limitation with a little creativity. Create a series of similar slides by adding a selected object to each slide in the series. You can then use transitions between these multiple slides to create an effect that makes the objects appear as though they're building on a single slide.

In effect, we're using transitions to "fake" a graphics build. Here's the general procedure:

1. Start by creating a slide that looks the way you want it to before the action happens — that is, before the build. We call this Slide #1.
2. From Slide Sorter View, select Slide #1 and Edit⇨Copy.
3. Click the blinking insertion-point cursor to the right of Slide #1 and select Edit⇨Paste. You have now created a copy of Slide #1.
4. Switch to Slide View by clicking on the toolbar button or selecting View⇨Slides. Select Slide #2, making it active.
5. Now create the build effect. Select Insert and either Picture or Clip Art, find the graphic you want for your first build element, and place that image onto Slide #2.
6. Select Tools⇨Transition and choose a cool effect.

warning Select any transition effect other than Cover, Uncover, and Fade. These three won't work.

7. Repeat as desired. When you play the slides, PowerPoint won't redraw text or images that remain the same from slide to slide, and it looks as though you've created a graphics build.

Summary

Transitions add movement from slide to slide, and *builds* add movement from object to object on the same slide. This chapter explored how to use transitions and builds to add motion to your presentations.

Typically, you apply transitions in Slide Sorter View, but you won't want to use all the Microsoft supplies: Some of them just don't work well on average PCs.

The usual type of build is a successive display of text elements, such as bullet items or a numbered list. PowerPoint 4, 7, and 8 provide for text builds with motion effects.

Although Versions 7 and 8 give you more control over the process, you can dim preceding items with both versions, which is a considerate thing to do for your audience.

PowerPoint 7 and 8 can perform builds for graphic elements, permitting you to create simple animations and assign motion to clip art objects. In Version 8, the crawl effects introduce new animation possibilities. Ungrouping clip art objects and animating the pieces individually for your graphics builds opens the door to many cool effects.

> Although PowerPoint 4 doesn't support graphic builds directly, you can simulate the effect by using slide-to-slide transitions, and your audience will never know the difference.

Today's hot computer buzzword is multimedia, and in Part III, we show you how to add sound, animation, and even digital video clips to a PowerPoint slide show. The underlying Windows technology that makes it all possible is called *OLE* (Object Linking and Embedding), which we explore in the next chapter.

PART III

MAXIMUM COOL: INTEGRATING MULTIMEDIA

In Part II, we explored the tools necessary to customize your presentations' screen layouts, bitmaps, illustrations, clip art, special text effects, and builds and transitions. Although we offered dozens of cool tricks and introduced some sophisticated third-party software, most of what Part II covered is well within what PowerPoint's designers had in mind: that is, displaying still graphics.

In Part III, however, we sail adventurously away from the shore and into the uncharted waters of integrating multimedia (sound, animation, and digital video) into PowerPoint slide shows, using Windows' OLE (object linking and embedding) technology.

OLE and Multimedia

12

In This Chapter

Understanding the goals and benefits of OLE technology

Learning how OLE works with PowerPoint to provide multimedia capabilities

Distinguishing *link* operations from *embedding* operations

Discovering the difference between OLE clients and OLE servers

Seeing how OLE associates multimedia files with the appropriate playback programs

Learning the two standard ways of creating OLE connections

Understanding the Media Control Interface

This chapter presents you with the groundwork for integrating multimedia documents into PowerPoint by explaining Microsoft's Object Linking and Embedding (OLE) technology.

The PowerPoint documentation for Versions 4 and 7 says little about multimedia integration, and the online help system in those versions doesn't offer much advice, either. PowerPoint's original creators didn't write it with multimedia in mind, as PCs couldn't handle multimedia playback at the time. Version 8 is the only version that considers multimedia capabilities to be an integral part of the program's design.

In fact, in Versions 4 and 7, PowerPoint doesn't offer multimedia features itself — we can "do" multimedia with those versions of PowerPoint only in association with other Windows programs that *are* multimedia-capable. That association is made possible by a core Windows technology called *Object Linking and Embedding*, or *OLE* (pronounced *oh-LAY*).

OLE isn't a separate product; it's built into both Windows 3.*x* and Windows 95. For example, in Windows 3.*x*, you can see the files OLECLI.DLL, OLESVR.DLL, and SHELL.DLL; these files provide OLE features to

Windows and Windows programs. You need a minimum of 8MB of RAM for Windows 3.*x* and 12MB for Windows 95 to use OLE successfully; having more memory is even better.

Many Windows users never learned about OLE; they didn't have to in order to use their favorite applications. If you want to incorporate multimedia clips into PowerPoint 4 or 7, however, you may not have a choice. Fortunately, OLE isn't too hard to understand, and you'll appreciate its power even when you're not using PowerPoint.

This chapter, then, introduces you to OLE and provides a compass to help you navigate the sometimes choppy seas of multimedia integration. Subsequent chapters in Part III demonstrate how to put OLE to work with sound, animation, and digital video clips. We suggest that you read through this chapter once, then come back to it after you've had a little practice pasting sound and video clips into PowerPoint.

Life has become a little simpler for PowerPoint 8 users: You no longer have to use OLE to incorporate multimedia files. PowerPoint 8 includes *native* (that is, built-in) support for all types of multimedia, including AVI, MOV, WAV, and MIDI files. PowerPoint 8 still uses OLE in conjunction with the bundled Graph, Organizational Chart, Equation Editor, and Photo Editor programs, as well as other Windows application programs, such as Excel.

What Is OLE About?

OLE, along with the other, earlier Windows technologies it supplements (such as the Clipboard and Dynamic Data Exchange, or DDE), is all about providing the following four benefits:

- Reusable, consistent, and specialized programs to perform common functions
- More flexible documents that contain multiple data types (such as slide shows with both "still" graphics and video or sound clips)
- Easy editing of multiple data types from one document
- Not having to update data several times if it's used in more than one place

Reusable, consistent, specialized programs

All PC software used to be self-contained and *monolithic* — that is, if a developer wanted to provide a feature, the programmers would write the code and make it an integral part of the program. It became clear over the years that this approach wastes a great deal of effort and creates gargantuan programs.

Consider how silly it is to have four spell checkers on the same PC — one each for word processing, e-mail, desktop publishing, and spreadsheet programs — each with their own different menus, commands, and custom dictionaries. Yet this is just how it was during personal computing's first several years. There was no such thing as a "reusable" spell checker that always looked and acted the same wherever you were using it.

Furthermore, because software vendors had to provide their own spell checkers, they looked at such a chore as a necessary evil, providing only the minimum features necessary so they could say that they had a spell checker. Users didn't get one killer spell checker; they got many mediocre ones.

A big part of the idea behind OLE technology is to provide the spell check capability as a single, separate, building-block program — one that the user can bring into Quattro Pro, PowerPoint, or Word as needed; one that always looks and works the same, regardless of which host program invokes it. (The idea of program building blocks that users can combine any way they want is the driving force behind many of today's more exciting software development projects.)

You saw an example of OLE at work in Chapter 5, which looked at Microsoft Graph — a program that's also used from within Word for Windows or other Windows applications. When it comes to multimedia, the relevant building blocks for PowerPoint 4 and 7 are the Windows Media Player and Sound Recorder. You also have other, non-Microsoft building block programs from which to choose, such as the Autodesk Animation Player.

More flexible documents

The second benefit that OLE delivers is the capability to have different kinds of information in the same document, which then becomes a so-called *compound document* or *OLE document*. The earliest need for this capability arose when business PC users wanted to include spreadsheet tables or charts in their word processing documents, and this is still the most common use for OLE. For us, the "document" is a PowerPoint slide show, and the different types of data we need are still graphics, text, sound, animation, and digital video.

tip

A chunk of data of a given type in an OLE compound document is called an *object*. An object could be a sound clip, a graph, or a video clip, for example. The *host* program (in our case, PowerPoint) doesn't understand, or need to understand, an object's data type. The host program will rely on another program, such as Sound Recorder, to interpret that object and play it back or edit it. The host program communicates with the other program through OLE commands.

Easier editing

We could create compound documents with earlier technologies; specifically, the Clipboard and Dynamic Data Exchange (DDE). What we *couldn't* do with those tools was easily edit a chunk of data in a compound document without going to Program Manager and running the application that created the chunk of data.

With OLE, just click on the object and use the Edit menu to automatically start the application that created it — assuming that the application is still available on the computer! What happens next depends on what version of OLE is running:

- In OLE Version 1.0 (which Windows 3.1 applications typically use), editing the object opens a new *child* window that looks nearly the same as the originating program (Sound Recorder, Media Player, and so on). You can edit the data, close the child window, and select Update (if so prompted). Then you return to your main program.
- In OLE Version 2.0 (which Windows for Workgroups 3.11 and Windows 95 applications typically use), editing the object won't open a new child window, but it will change the options on the menu bar to reflect the originating program's commands. You can edit the data and then just click outside the data's display window to get back to your main program.

You can't edit all the data you paste into PowerPoint with OLE, because some formats — for example, bitmap graphics — are *converted* during a paste operation, rather than linked or embedded. PowerPoint understands bitmap graphics and doesn't need a separate OLE server program to "play them back." One of OLE's functions is to help an application decide whether to try to convert a pasted data object into a format that the application can deal with itself, or alternatively, to create an OLE container for it and activate a server program to play it back or edit it.

Convenient updating

Consider the following situation. You use OLE to bring a sound clip of your department head talking about next year's budget into a PowerPoint slide show. A week before you're due to give your talk, you get a cool, new sound-editing program (such as Sonic Foundry's Sound Forge) that can clean up the background noise in that sound clip. Then, however, you have to bring the new, edited clip into the PowerPoint file again.

One way OLE can minimize this inconvenience is by pasting the sound file into your slide show as a *link* rather than as an *embedded*, or grafted, data object. The link is nothing more than a pointer to the sound file, which may be stored in a different subdirectory on your disk. When you clean up the sound file's background noise, PowerPoint will automatically run that cleaned-up file when it finds the link on the specific slide on which you've placed it.

Now you begin to see why it's called Object Linking and Embedding! You often have the flexibility to do either one (linking or embedding) when you copy and paste a multimedia clip onto a PowerPoint slide. (See the tip that follows, however, for an important restriction.) When you use links, you only have to maintain the *master copy* of the multimedia clip, wherever it may be. PowerPoint (or any other OLE program into which you've pasted the same link) then automatically uses that master copy, even if it has been modified or updated since the link was originally created.

Of course, if you think the multimedia clip will never be modified, you can *embed* it onto your slide. PowerPoint makes a copy of the original file and incorporates it into the PPT file. With embedded files, no link to a master data file exists; the transfer is just a static, one-time, Clipboard cut-and-paste operation. You still need to have the server application available on the computer, however, to play back the embedded object when you run your slide show or to edit the embedded object using the Edit menu.

If you use Media Player as the server and PowerPoint as the client, you may discover that you don't have the option of embedding the file. Microsoft designed PowerPoint to *link* Media Player clips, never to *embed* them. One reason is that Media Player clips are usually very large; another is that they may consist of nondigital data, such as a VCR tape clip.

When you use links, you must remember to copy the linked files along with the PPT file when you transport your slide show (for example, from a desktop to a notebook PC). PowerPoint 7 and 8's Pack-and-Go wizard gives you this option when you use it to create a portable slide show file.

Links aren't perfect. Move the original sound clip to a different directory, for example, and PowerPoint 4 gets all confused. Windows 3.1 doesn't have any tracking mechanism for monitoring the location of a file that's linked into another program, though Windows 95 can often find the file. If you have to tell PowerPoint where the file has moved to, use the Edit⇨Links command (Figure 12-1). If PowerPoint can't find a linked object during slide show playback, it will ask you to find it yourself (Figure 12-2). Avoid the embarrassment of having to hunt for linked files by testing your links before the show!

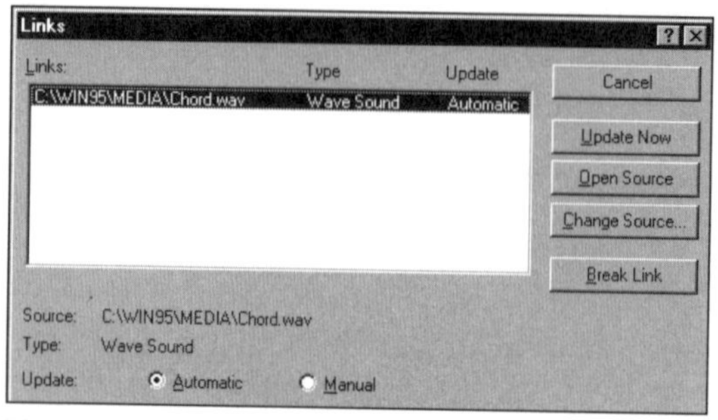

Figure 12-1: Edit an OLE link and respecify the file's full pathname if its location has changed since you created the link.

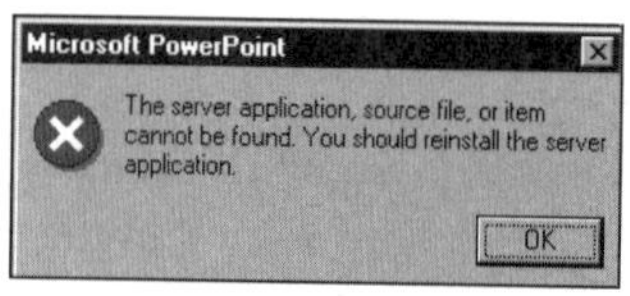

Figure 12-2: Playing back a slide show in which a linked file has been moved produces an embarrassing interruption.

Why Do We Care?

As you can see, OLE does some cool things. You're probably wondering, though, why you need to know about OLE in a book about PowerPoint. When you begin integrating multimedia into PowerPoint 4 and 7 slide shows, OLE assumes a central role. Because PowerPoint can act as an OLE *client*, it can incorporate multimedia through other OLE *servers* — such as Media Player and Sound Recorder. In PowerPoint 8, you don't need Media Player or Sound Recorder anymore (hurray!), but you still use OLE to link or embed documents from Graph, Organizational Chart, Photo Editor, Excel, and other Windows programs.

tip

A *client* document, or program, is one that contains objects (data chunks) managed by another program, the OLE *server*. When you paste a sound clip onto a PowerPoint slide, PowerPoint is acting as the client and either Sound Recorder or Media Player is acting as the server. Some Windows programs (such as PowerPoint and Excel) can act both as OLE clients and as OLE servers; other Windows programs (such as the server-only utilities WordArt and Graph) are limited to one role or the other.

The truth is that if you use multimedia in PowerPoint 4 or 7, you use OLE. Although you don't need to master all the technical details, understanding OLE will help you integrate multimedia into your slide shows with less muss and fuss.

File Types and Associations

When you create an OLE connection, Windows must have some way of determining which program your multimedia clip is associated with — that is, which application to run to play the clip when you run your slide show. The Macintosh includes a code that identifies the creating program in the data file's header. Windows manages this association one of two ways:

- You make the association yourself when you create the multimedia file from within PowerPoint by using the Insert command.
- PowerPoint uses OLE to figure out the association when you use an already created multimedia file that has a particular file extension, or suffix.

Windows maintains a list of file extensions and the applications with which they associate. In Windows 3.*x*, this list appears in two places: the Registration Database (REG.DAT), and the [Embedding] section of the WIN.INI text file. In Windows 95, this list only occurs one place: the Registry — specifically, the HKEY_CLASSES_ROOT subtree. Happily, you can see the file types and associations without running the rather scary Registry Editor utility (REGEDIT.EXE); just open My Computer and select View⇨Options⇨File Types (Figure 12-3).

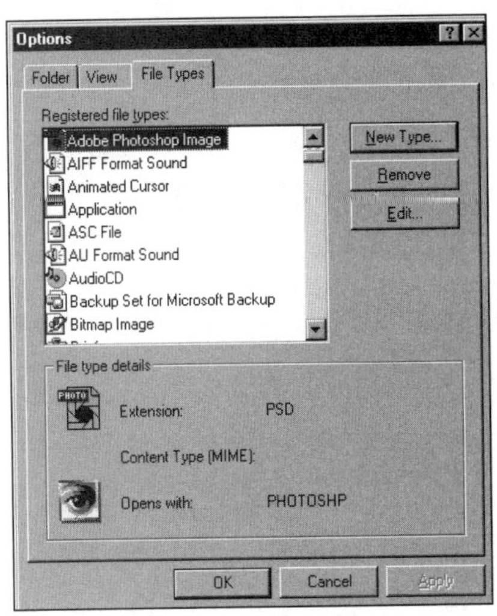

Figure 12-3: Viewing file types and associations in Windows 95 indicates which program will run when you double-click a file with a particular suffix.

You shouldn't have to worry about file types and associations because the Windows installation program sets up your system to use the right ones. For example, *.WAV sound files are associated with Sound Recorder, and AVI digital video clips are associated with Media Player. If you *do* need to change these types and associations, you can do it through the Windows

3.*x* File Manager (the Associate command) or through the File Types tab in Windows 95. Table 12-1 lists typical file types and associations.

Table 12-1 Typical Windows Multimedia File Types and Filename Extensions

File Type	Extension
Waveform Sound	*.WAV
MIDI Sound	*.MID, *.RMI
Video for Windows	*.AVI
QuickTime for Windows	*.MOV
Microsoft Multimedia Movie	*.MMM
AutoDesk Animation	*.FLI, *.FLC
AutoDesk Animation (Windows Player)	*.AAS

Creating OLE Connections

New standards aren't implemented precisely the same way by every software developer, and this fact was painfully obvious with OLE 1.0, though it's less of a factor with OLE 2.0 and Windows 95. The result is that some applications create OLE connections a little differently than others do. With PowerPoint, fortunately, the procedures follow Microsoft's standard model fairly closely.

Generally, you can create OLE connections in two directions: starting with the client, and starting with the server. Which direction is more convenient depends solely on where you're working at the time.

Client-side procedure

Follow these steps to create an OLE connection starting with the client:

1. Position the cursor where you want the object inserted. In PowerPoint, this means selecting the appropriate slide in Slide View.
2. Select Insert⇨Object. You may have other choices for specific file types that you're likely to use often, such as Insert⇨Sound in PowerPoint.
3. Decide whether you want to insert an existing file, or create a new one. If you create a new one, select Create New and pick a file type

from the dialog box. OLE starts the appropriate server application. Otherwise, select Create from File and locate the specific file.

4. Select File⇨Update for a Windows 3.*x* program to create the object. For a Windows 95 program, just click outside the object's display window.

tip The preceding method generally creates an embedded object rather than a linked object.

Server-side procedure

Follow these steps to create an OLE connection in the other direction, starting with the server application:

1. Run the server application (for example, Sound Recorder —), and either create (with File⇨New) or load (with File⇨Open) the multimedia clip you want.
2. Select Edit⇨Copy to put the multimedia clip on the Windows Clipboard and then close the server application. Switch over to the client application (PowerPoint) if it's running, or run it if it's not.
3. Position the cursor where you want the object inserted. In PowerPoint, select the appropriate slide in Slide View.
4. If you want to embed the object, select Edit⇨Paste. If you want to link it, select Edit⇨Paste Special, and then click the Paste Link option.

The following chapters (on sound, animation, and digital video objects) provide more specific details on creating particular kinds of OLE connections, but the preceding procedures provide the standard methods.

The Media Control Interface (MCI)

Applications such as PowerPoint can play back OLE objects for a variety of multimedia hardware, if Windows has Media Control Interface (MCI) drivers for those hardware devices (such as CD players, VCRs, and videodisc players). Later chapters elaborate on the topic of configuring MCI drivers, but here we just want to introduce the MCI concept.

MCI drivers provide many of the same controls regardless of the device being used. For example, *play*, *pause*, and *stop* are typically commands that function approximately the same way on any multimedia hardware device (Figure 12-4). These commands appear, usually as VCR-type buttons, on the playback window when PowerPoint runs the slide show and encounters an MCI-type data file object.

Figure 12-4: Playing a CD audio track in PowerPoint 7 by using Media Player with an MCI driver permits the use of standard controls for play, pause, and stop. Note that with PowerPoint 8, you no longer need Media Player to play CD audio.

Usually, you obtain MCI drivers from the vendor of the multimedia device, though Microsoft provides some drivers with the standard Windows software kit.

Now you can probably see why Microsoft chose to require Media Player objects to be linked, rather than embedded, into PowerPoint slides. If Media Player is to be able to play back from an MCI-compatible videodisc player, for example, it can't possibly embed all the videodisc data into the PPT file; the videodisc contains far too much data. Instead, PowerPoint has to read that data off the videodisc itself, through the OLE link.

tip

Want to know more about OLE? Download a copy of Microsoft Application Note WW0532, "Object Linking and Embedding," from any of the usual Microsoft online sources. Microsoft wrote this document for Windows 3.1, but most of the concepts are the same. If you're a Windows 95 programmer, see Application Note WT1229, "Getting Started Controlling Microsoft PowerPoint for Windows 95 through OLE Automation."

Summary

PowerPoint's multimedia capabilities do exist, but only by proxy in Versions 4 and 7, through links to other programs. The linking technology, collectively known as Object Linking and Embedding, or OLE, has been present in the Windows environment for several years but has only become stable and reliable with Version 2.0.

PowerPoint 8 includes native support for multimedia files and doesn't need Media Player or Sound Recorder anymore, but it still uses OLE for communication with other programs, such as Graph and Excel.

You can place OLE server documents into an OLE client, creating a compound document that now has data in it that is associated with two or more different programs.

On playback, PowerPoint calls the multimedia server programs to handle the multimedia data files. PowerPoint acts as the *glue* application to bring different kinds of information together into a slide show.

OLE permits two kinds of connections: link operations, which create pointers to data stored in a different file, and embedding operations, which make the multimedia data part of the slide show file itself. You can usually create these connections in either direction, starting with the server or starting with the client.

The Media Control Interface provides standard buttons for playing back clips from a variety of multimedia hardware devices.

Now that you understand OLE, clients and servers, linking and embedding, and compound documents, you're ready to apply this knowledge. By using OLE to connect PowerPoint 4 or 7 with Sound Recorder, Media Player, and third-party OLE servers, you can add the dimension of sound to PowerPoint slide shows — the subject of the next chapter, which explores PowerPoint 8's new built-in sound capabilities.

Sound: WAV and MIDI

13

In This Chapter

Understanding and choosing sound cards

Setting up your PC with proper sound drivers (regular and MCI-compatible)

Learning different sound file formats and subformats

Compressing sound files to save disk space

Finding *canned* sound files and customizing them to meet your needs

Creating your own WAV and MIDI files for a unique presentation

Linking and embedding sound files into PowerPoint slides

Customizing sound file play settings and hiding sound file object icons

Setting WAV and MIDI sounds to play across multiple slides

Learning some design tips for effective use of sounds in slide shows

Finding out about several bugs and *gotchas* to avoid when working with sounds

This chapter introduces Windows sound technologies and lays out steps for adding cool sounds to your PowerPoint presentation. Sound can be a very cool way to add multimedia panache to a PowerPoint presentation, partly because almost no one uses it! Because PowerPoint is an OLE client, as discussed in the preceding chapter, it can incorporate sounds on slides. Typically, the OLE server, in this case, is either Sound Recorder or Media Player, both Windows utilities. PowerPoint 8 supports sounds natively and doesn't need a separate OLE server anymore.

The evolution of *Wintel* (Windows/Intel) sound technology has gone through several steps over the last few years. From the Windows 3.0 Multimedia Extensions (1991) to Windows 95's DirectSound (1996), many improvements and changes have been made. Although Windows sound technology can be complex and a little intimidating, we're going to keep it as simple as we can. Thankfully, you don't have to become a sound engineer or a virtuoso musician to incorporate great sounds into your PowerPoint files!

This chapter begins by presenting sound basics: the required hardware and software drivers to make it work, the file formats Windows uses, and the Windows utilities you need. Next, it shows you where you can find off-the-shelf sound files and how you can customize them to your needs. The chapter also gives you a few tips for making your own sound files. Finally, it focuses on the specifics of adding sounds to PowerPoint and controlling their playback behavior.

A "Sound" Foundation

Before you can start working with sounds in PowerPoint, you need an understanding of the hardware and software necessary to implement sound on a Windows PC. Here are the four components introduced in this section:

- Sound cards
- Windows sound drivers
- Windows sound file data formats
- Windows applets for working with sound files

Sound cards

Unlike the Macintosh, the typical IBM-compatible PC doesn't include sound circuitry on the computer's system board; you have to add it as a plug-in adapter, or *sound card*. Because nearly every PC sound card today is Windows-compatible, your choice of a particular make and model comes down to features, bundled software, and price. (Reliability is almost a non-issue; today's sound cards rarely malfunction.)

Some of the features you may want to look for in a sound card include the following:

- 16-bit versus 8-bit sample size capability (how many bits you can use in a single sound sample — 8-bit sound is inherently noisier than 16-bit sound)
- Plug-and-Play compatibility on Windows 95 systems for easier installation and setup

- Basic Musical Instrument Digital Interface (MIDI, described later in this chapter) support to enable playing digital MIDI files (Windows 95 supports the *General MIDI* specification, which assigns the same ID number to the same instrument on all General MIDI hardware)
- Advanced MIDI features (polymessage or *streamed* MIDI, 16-voice polyphony) for faster performance and more flexible sounds
- Sampled MIDI sound versus mathematical wavetable synthesis or *FM synthesis*, for better MIDI sound quality
- The capability to use several different system interrupts and DMA channels for maximum configuration flexibility, as the sound card must not conflict with any other interrupts or DMA channels

warning

If you don't have a sound card, you can use Microsoft's PC Speaker driver (under both Windows 3.*x* and Windows 95) to play sounds through your PC's built-in speaker. (Get the self-extracting, self-documenting file, SPEAK.EXE, from any Microsoft online source.) Using the PC Speaker driver is only a temporary solution; the quality is poor and you're limited in what you can do (no MIDI or AVI file support, no Media Player WAV playback under Windows 95, no working Volume Control under Windows 95, and so on). The moral is that using sound in PowerPoint requires at least a basic sound card. Fortunately, sound cards are inexpensive — you can get a serviceable one with a pair of multimedia speakers for around $150.

tip

Keep in mind that although you can equip your development PC with a terrific sound system, you can end up presenting with a different computer that has different capabilities. Notebook machines, in particular, do not always support high-quality sound. Chapter 18 explores this issue further.

MCI and sound drivers

The low-level software that you need to permit applications to communicate with a sound card comes in two flavors in the Windows environment: audio drivers and MCI audio drivers. Sound Recorder works with regular audio drivers, whereas Media Player requires MCI drivers that adhere to the Media Control Interface (discussed in the preceding chapter).

version 4

With PowerPoint 4 and Windows 3.*x*, you typically install the sound card drivers either during Windows SETUP or in a setup routine supplied by the card manufacturer. If the setup routine gives you the option to choose the drivers you want to install, install all of them to make sure that you can use Media Player (as well as Sound Recorder) with your sound files.

versions 7 & 8

Windows 95 usually autodetects your sound card during installation. If you install the sound card later, you can run the Add New Hardware wizard or, if it's a Plug-and-Play sound card, just let Windows 95 automatically configure it. To double-check that all the appropriate drivers are installed, run the

Multimedia control panel, click on the Advanced tab, and then look for the following (Figure 13-1):

- An entry under Audio Devices
- An entry under MIDI Devices and Instruments
- An entry labeled Wave Audio Device (Media Control) under Media Control Devices
- An entry labeled MIDI Sequencer Device (Media Control) under Media Control Devices

You may have to click the Properties button for each of these devices to make sure that they're enabled.

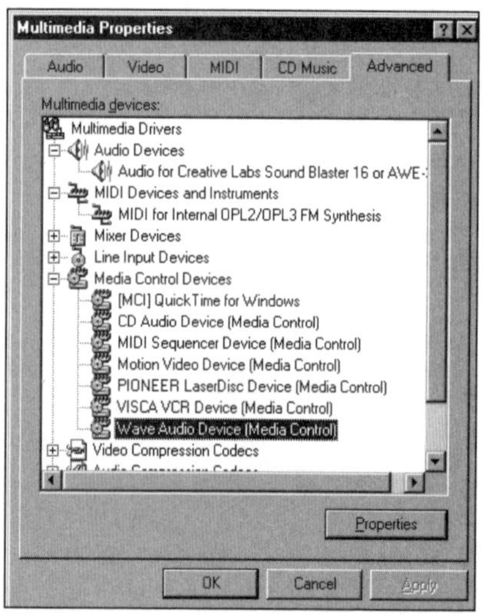

Figure 13-1: *View sound card drivers in Windows 95 with the Multimedia control panel to ensure a correct and complete configuration.*

Sound file formats

WAV and MIDI are the two general sound file formats that Windows 3.*x* and Windows 95 support. Each has many subformats, but here are the differences in a nutshell:

- WAV files (also called *waveform audio* files) are large and well suited for voice recording and analog music sources. WAV files store the actual analog waveform that describes the sound in all its detail. These files typically have the extension .WAV.

- MIDI files are much smaller than WAV files, and they are well suited for synthesized digital music. MIDI files don't store analog waveforms; instead, they store a sequence of codes that trigger the sound card's MIDI synthesizer, which then generates the actual sounds with on-board chips. Then the sound card *interprets* the MIDI file much as a musician interprets sheet music to create an actual performance. These files typically have the extension .MID or .RMI.

Because WAV files are so large, several technologies have evolved to compress them so that they take up much less disk space but retain most of the original file's quality. (Audio compression is analogous to the graphics compression techniques discussed in the context of PCX, GIF, JPEG, and other graphics file formats.) *Codecs* are the software components that manage WAV **co**mpression and **dec**ompression (hence the derivation of the word). You choose compression options when creating a new sound file or editing an existing one; during playback, Windows handles decompression automatically.

versions 7&8

Windows 95 comes with high-performing, 32-bit versions of the following codecs:

- Adaptive Delta Pulse Code Modulation (ADPCM), which can achieve a 4:1 compression ratio
- Interactive Media Association (IMA) ADPCM, which can achieve a 4:1 compression ratio and is faster than regular ADPCM
- Groupe Special Mobile (GSM) 6.10, which can only achieve a 2:1 compression ratio but supports more sampling rates than ADPCM and is best suited for compressing voice clips
- CCITT G.711 A-Law and u-Law, which can only achieve a 2:1 compression ratio but support Microsoft's Telephony Application Program Interface (TAPI)
- Digital Signal Processing (DSP) TrueSpeech, which generally achieves the highest compression ratios of the bunch with voice files

warning

You can't tell a compressed WAV file from an uncompressed one by looking at the file extension; it remains WAV even after compression. Fortunately, you can load the file into Sound Recorder and click File⇨Properties to see format details, including compression. PCM (Pulse Code Modulation) is the typical *uncompressed* Windows sound file format.

Along with WAV file compression options, you have *sampling* options as well. (You may be familiar with sampling rates if you've shopped for a home audio CD player lately.) Higher sampling rates use more data per second to describe the sound; they eat up more disk space but provide greater fidelity. 8 KHz, 11 KHz, 22 KHz, and 44 KHz are the sampling options typically supported by Windows programs. Finally, you can save files as mono or stereo, and with sample sizes of 8 bits or 16 bits.

What should you use? Usually 11 KHz and mono are fine for voice files, but you'll probably want to use 22 KHz or 44 KHz and stereo for music files. We generally save our sound files in the 16-bit format, though some compression options limit you to 8 bits. We suggest you save all your original files in the highest possible quality format, as multimedia professionals do. Store those monster files on a large hard drive or removable drive (such as an Iomega ZIP drive) and then compress the originals as needed for specific uses. This way, if you need to increase the quality down the road, you don't have to re-create the sound file.

Sound Recorder and Media Player

The two bundled *applets* (or accessories) that come with Windows 3.*x* and Windows 95 for working with sound files are Sound Recorder and Media Player. Sound Recorder is just for working with WAV format sound files, whereas Media Player can also play back MIDI files and digital video (AVI) files. You can use Sound Recorder to record and save WAV files as well as play them back.

Under Windows 3.*x*, Sound Recorder can play back in stereo but it can't record in stereo. Also, you can't use Media Player if you're using the PC Speaker driver instead of a sound card.

Between these two utilities, use Sound Recorder rather than Media Player to work with your WAV sound files. Sound Recorder has many more options, as you're about to see. It also works better with PowerPoint 4 and 7, in that you can't *embed* a clip from Media Player into PowerPoint so that it becomes an integral part of your slide show — you can only *link* Media Player clips.

Another tip: Always play back a sound file in one or the other of these utilities before trying to paste it into PowerPoint. In this way, you can be sure that the file is OK and sounds the way you want it to sound.

Finding and Customizing Sounds

Now that you understand about sound cards and sound file formats, the next logical question is, where can you get some premade sound files to use in your slide shows? You have many sources; some right under your nose!

- If you have Windows 95, look in the Windows folder called *Media*. You will probably see both WAV and MIDI files for you to explore.
- The Plus! add-on CD-ROM for Windows 95 includes many sound files.

- If you installed PowerPoint as part of Microsoft Office, look for the Sounds directory under the Office directory.
- Versions 7 and 8 include several sounds as part of the Animation Effects toolbar, although most of these can be annoying.
- The Office 95 and Office 97 CD-ROMs also contain some extra sounds in the *ValuePack* folder. If you bought PowerPoint separately, look for the sample sounds on the PowerPoint Multimedia CD.
- Microsoft's Web site (http://www.microsoft.com/powerpnt) has additional sounds you can download. Connect directly to it in Version 8 with Tools⇨PowerPoint Central or with Help⇨Microsoft on the Web.
- You probably received several sample files on diskette with your sound card or sound editing program.
- CompuServe and America Online have zillions of sound files scattered in different forums. Look for forums having to do with multimedia. You can also use CompuServe's File Finder (GO IBMFF) and specify WAV or MIDI as a keyword.
- You can buy collections of sound clips from third-party sources. Appendix A lists some of these companies.

Before using any *canned* sounds in your PowerPoint show, take a couple of minutes to review the licensing agreement from the sound clip vendor. You can often use sound clips without paying a royalty, as long as you don't package your presentation for sale (especially if the sound clip collection is advertised as being *royalty-free*). It's worth double-checking, however, so that you don't find yourself in violation of any copyright agreements.

When you find some sounds you want to work with, they may not suit your needs precisely. You may want to perform one or more customization steps, such as the following:

- Compressing the files so they're smaller and easier to transport
- Changing the file format or subformat
- Cropping the files to edit out unwanted portions
- Reducing background noise
- Standardizing volume levels with other sound files
- Adding special effects (such as echo or reverse playback)
- Combining certain sound files with others (*mixing*)
- Changing playback duration to better fit your slide show

The provided Sound Recorder applet has some limited capabilities for editing sound files.

For example, you can add or change the compression, sampling, mono/stereo, and bit settings; simply open the file, choose File⇨Save As⇨Change, and then modify the Format and Attributes fields (Figure 13-2).

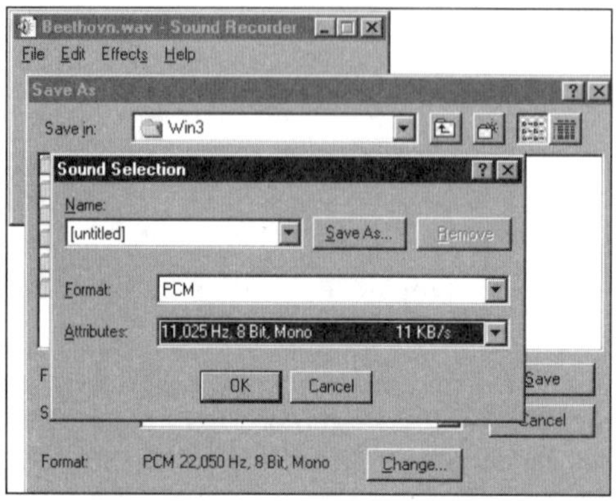

Figure 13-2: Changing sound file format options is easy in Windows 95's Sound Recorder.

Audio professionals know that you can't improve an existing sound file's quality by simply saving it with a different compression format. Your goal in changing formats is to keep as much of the original file's quality as you need, while reducing the disk space requirements to a reasonable level.

Sound Recorder can also change a file's duration, but in doing so, it will change the pitch. More sophisticated tools can change duration *without* changing pitch. Sound Recorder's other effects include adding echo, reversing a file, and mixing two sound files together (Figure 13-3).

Figure 13-3: Sound Recorder's limited Effects menu.

You can have fun experimenting with some sample files to get an idea of what Sound Recorder can do, but you will also encounter Sound Recorder's limitations after just a few minutes. If you work with a fairly large number of files, or if you'd like to perform some of the cooler tricks that Sound Recorder just won't do, you have two choices:

- Get familiar with the software bundled with your sound card. All the major sound card manufacturers throw in a smorgasbord of sound utilities, including a sound editor. Usually, the sound editor isn't limited to working with a single sound card.
- Look into a third-party sound editing utility. One of our favorites is Sonic Foundry's Sound Forge (Figure 13-4), which can perform many editing chores as well as format conversions. Sound Forge is extendable by adding *plug-in* software modules for specific features. Although these features can be expensive, they're hard to beat in terms of quality. For more on Sound Forge, see Appendix A.

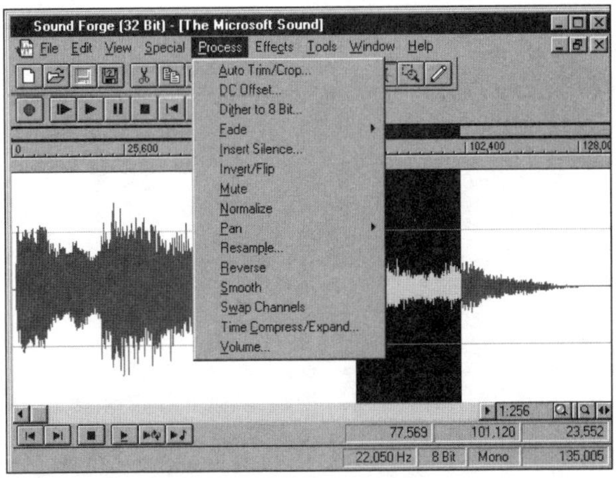

Figure 13-4: Sound Forge for Windows.

Making Your Own Sounds

You can make your own sounds in a few different ways.

Recording WAV files

Recording your own sounds is definitely cool. The most likely application is creating WAV files containing voice-overs, interviews, sound bites, and so on. For example, if you present a slide show to inform company managers about the status of a specific project, you can record brief interviews with team members responsible for different aspects of the project, and play those voice clips back while displaying the relevant slides.

version 8

You can create your own voice recordings from within PowerPoint 8 by using Insert➪Movies and Sounds➪Record Sound. We prefer Sound Recorder, though, in most circumstances. PowerPoint gives you no control over recording or compression options, and you can't edit the sounds later — they're PowerPoint objects, rather than separate WAV files.

PowerPoint 8's sound recording capability is more useful when you want to save a digital record of your verbal presentation with the command Slide Show➪Record Narration (see Figure 13-5). With this tool, you can "record" your live presentation, and PowerPoint will save it with the slide show, so that others can play it back later and hear your narration while the slides advance automatically.

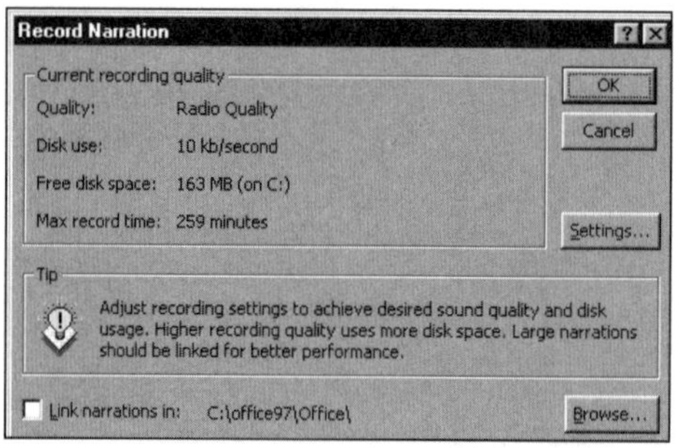

Figure 13-5: PowerPoint 8's Record Narration feature lets you record your presentation to disk with different quality options. Click the Link checkbox to create a separate, editable WAV file.

Recording a voice-over in WAV format by using Sound Recorder is simple — that is, if you can get the interviewee to come over to your office:

1. Plug the microphone that came with your sound card into the microphone jack at the back of the sound card. If you want higher-quality recordings, you can invest in a better microphone, but the supplied mikes usually work fine for voice recording.
2. Move the microphone as far away from any noise sources (including the PC) as you can, unplug your phone, silence your beeper, and politely ask your colleagues in adjacent cubicles to be quiet. (It may be easier to record sound files at lunch, or after business hours, to reduce background noise.)
3. Run Sound Recorder.
4. (Windows 95 only) Set the preferred quality with Edit➪Audio Properties➪Customize. Note that you may have limited options here; you can only use real-mode compressors. We suggest you specify the uncompressed PCM format and a high sampling rate and sample size. Then try different compression options later (after you save the file).

5. Select File➪New and then click the Record button (a red circle in Windows 95, a microphone icon in Windows 3.*x*) to begin recording. Click the Stop button (a black square) to stop recording.

6. Select File➪Save As, specify file format information and the filename, and then write the WAV file to disk.

If you have an interview (or other desired sound) on cassette tape, you can still capture it onto a WAV file. Connect the *line out* jack (of your tape recorder) to the *line in* jack (of your sound card) and run Sound Recorder or an equivalent utility while you play back from the tape recorder. This technique is much better than just holding the sound card microphone up to the tape recorder's built-in speaker; it reduces the amount of noise that can creep in. If you don't have the right cable, your friendly neighborhood Radio Shack can supply it for a few dollars.

You may have to try this a couple of times to get the levels right. Adjust the tape recorder's output level up or down to get a good volume level; you'll usually want to keep it no higher than two-thirds of the maximum to avoid distortion. You can also adjust the mixer at the PC side to control the volume level; for example, pop up Windows 95's built-in multimedia mixer by double-clicking the speaker icon on the Taskbar (see Figure 13-6).

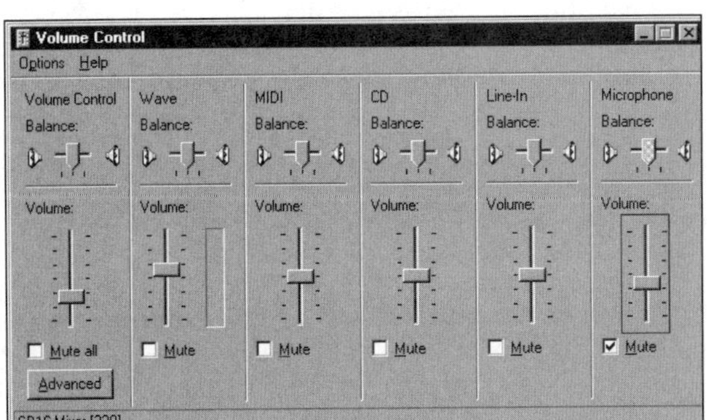

Figure 13-6: Adjusting recording volume with the Windows 95 Volume Control mixer.

Here's a cool tip to increase Sound Recorder's maximum recording time from the default of 60 seconds. (This tip works with Windows 3.*x* as well as Windows 95.) Record a blank WAV file for 60 seconds and then save it with a name such as MINUTE.WAV. Then choose Edit➪Insert File and specify MINUTE.WAV. Repeat as necessary. Then you can record a new file that's as many minutes long as the number of times you inserted MINUTE.WAV.

warning

Sound Recorder in Windows 3.*x* doesn't automatically save files with the proper .WAV file extension, so you have to remember to supply it yourself. (Yes, it's a bug.)

Recording MIDI files

You can also create your own MIDI files if you have a MIDI-capable sound card and a MIDI-compatible musical instrument (such as a synthesizer keyboard). For example, Yamaha makes several reasonably priced MIDI keyboards. Connect the keyboard to your sound card with a MIDI cable (available from the sound card vendor or at most professional music stores) and record the session using the sound card's supplied utility or a third-party MIDI recording program.

You'll probably also want a MIDI *sequencer* (a software utility for laying out MIDI tracks); it fine-tunes the musical score and adds tracks for a multitrack clip. Windows 95 supports up to 16 simultaneous tracks (called *multitrack polyphony*).

Of course, you need access to someone with some musical talent to compose and play the music clips! The nice thing about producing your own MIDI files, if you have the time and talent available, is that you don't have to worry about royalties or licensing. Another benefit is that you can customize your slide show, with music that no one has ever heard anywhere else.

Adding Sound to PowerPoint

By now, you've found or created the WAV and MIDI files you want to include in your slide show, and you've edited and compressed the files so they sound great and don't take up exorbitant amounts of disk space. You also may have collected the files into one subdirectory for easy access. Now it's time to *glue* these files into your PowerPoint presentation by using OLE commands.

Bringing your sound files into PowerPoint is usually the easiest part of the whole exercise. There are, however, several nuances and *gotchas* that you should know about, and that's really the purpose of this last section.

Importing sound files

versions 4, 7 & 8

With OLE operations, you can either start with the OLE client (in this case, PowerPoint) and perform an Insert operation, or you can start with the OLE server (Sound Recorder or Media Player) and perform a Copy operation.

If you want to start with the OLE client (PowerPoint) in Version 8, here's the procedure:

1. Load your presentation, select View⇨Slides to get into Slide View, and then move to the slide where you want the sound to play.
2. Select Insert⇨Object⇨Wave Sound for Windows to use Sound Recorder as the OLE server for a WAV file. Select Insert⇨Object ⇨MIDI Sequence for Windows to use Media Player as the OLE server for a MIDI file (Figure 13-7).

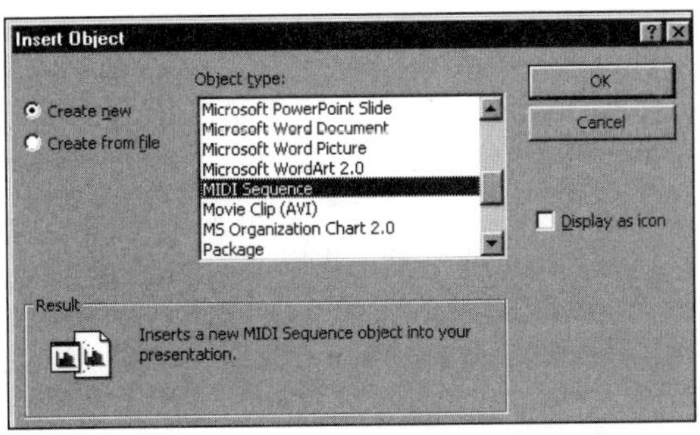

Figure 13-7: Inserting a MIDI file in PowerPoint 8's Insert Object dialog box.

In the Insert Object dialog box, you can select the Link check box to create an OLE link or leave it cleared to embed the WAV file. (MIDI files are always linked, regardless of the check box setting.)

PowerPoint 8 provides a new method of importing WAV sounds: You can import them as *PowerPoint objects*, using the command Insert⇨Movies and Sounds. You can import a specific file or choose the Clip Gallery, which now permits browsing of sound files as well as graphics.

How is this method different? It's easier (fewer menu commands) and it imposes less of a delay when playing the WAV file, because it's not necessary to load Sound Recorder — PowerPoint 8 contains the necessary program code to play the sound. The drawback is that you can't edit the sound after you import it, as you can with a linked or embedded WAV file. So, the trade-off is speed versus flexibility.

You can also import MIDI files as PowerPoint objects, but because MIDI files are always linked, doing so has little benefit.

To start with the OLE client (PowerPoint) in Version 7, follow these steps:

1. Load your presentation, select View⇨Slides to get into Slide View, and then move to the slide where you want the sound to play.

2. Select Insert⇨Sound, find the desired sound file in the dialog box, and then click OK. Windows automatically uses Sound Recorder as the OLE server for WAV files, and Media Player for MIDI files. The sound is *embedded* into your slide in the case of WAV files, and linked in the case of MIDI files.

The procedure for loading sound files starting with the PowerPoint 4 client is very similar to that for PowerPoint 8, with the difference that you don't have the option to load sound files as PowerPoint objects. You'll also need to specify Media Clip instead of MIDI Sequence to load a MIDI file.

You can also start with the OLE server application. (If you want to link a sound file into your Version 7 slide show rather than embed it, you *must* use this method.) The following steps work the same in PowerPoint 4, 7, and 8:

1. To start from Sound Recorder, load the desired sound file and select Edit⇨Copy. Close Sound Recorder with File⇨Exit.
2. Run (or switch to) PowerPoint, select View⇨Slides to get into Slide View, and then move to the slide where you want the sound to play.
3. Select Edit⇨Paste to embed the sound file, or Edit⇨Paste Special⇨Paste Link to link the file (Figure 13-8).

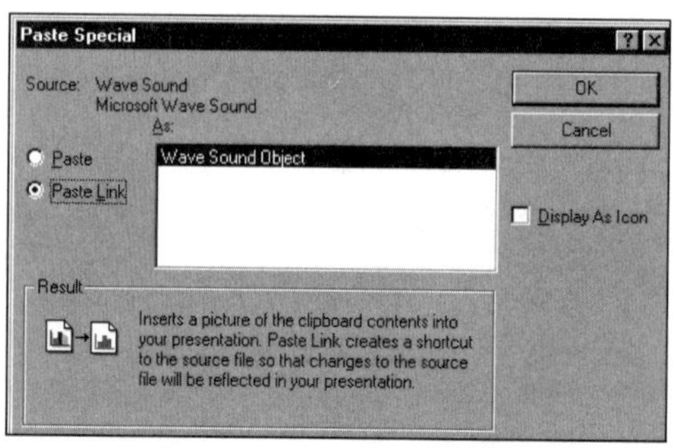

Figure 13-8: Linking a sound file to a PowerPoint 7 slide requires that you start with the OLE server.

After you either embed or link the sound file into your slide, you need to specify precisely how you want the sound to play (the subject of the next section).

Specifying play settings

If you want the sound to play when you click its icon or even merely move the mouse over the icon, right-click the sound icon and choose Action Settings. Using either the Mouse Click or Mouse Over tab, select Play under Object Action.

If you want the sound to play automatically, whether alone or in a sequence, or if you want the icon to fly into the screen with an animated motion (see also Chapter 11), right-click the sound icon and choose Custom Animation. Click Animate on the Timing tab and set other options on the Play Settings tab (Figure 13-9).

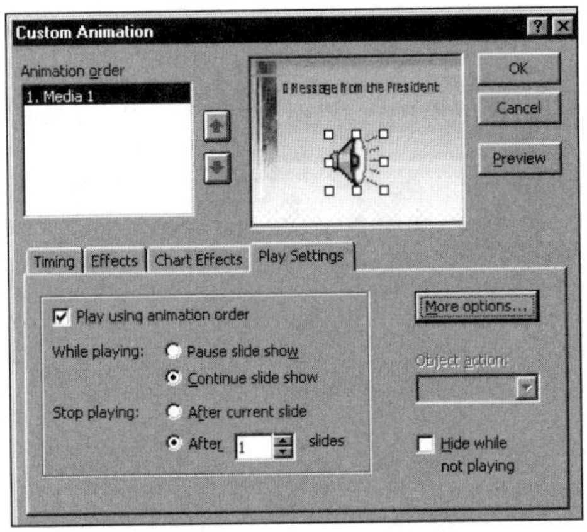

Figure 13-9: Set up automatic playback for a sound in PowerPoint 8 by using the Custom Animation dialog box.

If you click the linked or embedded sound object and select Tools⇨Animation Settings (Version 7) or Tools⇨Play Settings (Version 4), you can provide PowerPoint with the details it needs to determine whether to play the sound when the object is clicked, or after a preset delay.

These two versions of PowerPoint differ only in nuances. Figure 13-10 shows the Version 7 dialog box.

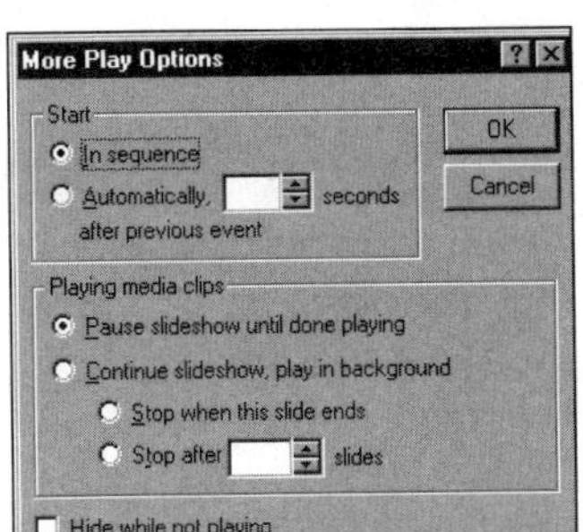

Figure 13-10: Setting Animation Settings in PowerPoint 7.

In all versions, the Hide While Not Playing option is nearly useless. It does nothing to hide the icon when it's not playing — which, coincidentally, brings us to the next section.

Hiding the evidence

Although the object icons for sound files are essential for working with sounds in Slide View, you'll usually prefer not to display them during the slide show. Thus, in this section we present techniques for hiding both Sound Recorder and Media Player object icons.

First, let's look at Sound Recorder (WAV) objects. When you link or embed a WAV sound file onto a slide, an icon appears that also shows up when you run the slide show. This display is so you can click the icon to play the sound during the presentation. You may want to present your slide show this way, for example, if you have a voice-over that you'd like to play only when you're ready for it; or, if you have multiple voice-overs on the same slide, and you'd like to select them one by one.

It's much cooler to create your own custom "button," either by using the PowerPoint drawing tools or by importing a bitmap or illustration from another program. Position that button object over the sound icon. You can resize the sound icon so it fits beneath the button. (Use the standard *bring forward* or *send backward* positioning commands on the drawing toolbar or the Draw menu.)

What if you want the sound to play automatically, however, when you move to the slide on which it's located, without any icon cluttering up your screen?

You could resize the sound icon so that it's barely visible, or tuck it under another object on the screen, and set it to play automatically as described in the preceding section.

Versions 7 and 8 offer an easier and cooler way: Just associate the sound with the slide's transition. Here's how:

1. Don't link or embed the sound file onto the slide. Instead, move to the desired slide in Slide View and select Tools⇨Slide Transition (Version 7) or Slide Show⇨Slide Transition (Version 8).
2. In the Sound field, scroll down to Other Sound (Figure 13-11).
3. Navigate to the WAV file you want and then click OK.

Now when you run the slide show, the sound plays as the slide appears, but without the sound object icon appearing on the screen.

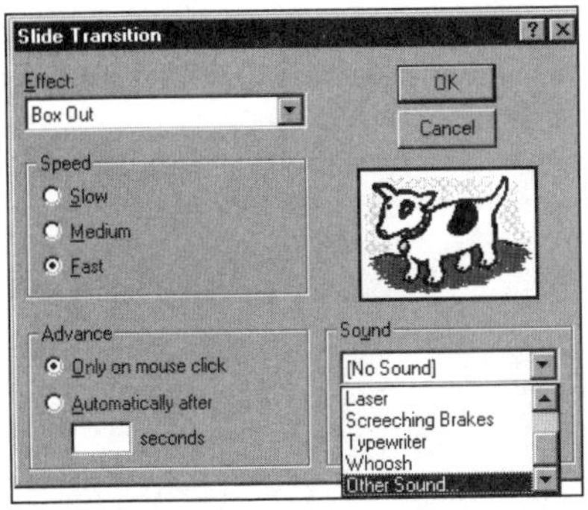

Figure 13-11: Associating a WAV file with a slide transition to inhibit the sound icon.

If you use Media Player as the OLE server for a sound clip (for example, a MIDI clip), you'll see a grayed-out dialog box on the screen when the selection is playing from within PowerPoint, as shown in the slide show fragment in Figure 13-12. This gray box appears when the MIDI clip is playing, even if you've hidden it at all other times with Play Settings (Version 4) or Animation Settings (Versions 7 and 8). You may want it if you think you'll need to pause the clip, but most of the time, this odd gray box is an unwanted intruder.

Figure 13-12: Media Player's odd gray playback box.

Perhaps you can at least obscure this playback window by putting it behind a drawing object (such as a filled rectangle). Good idea, but Media Player still *floats* to the top when the clip plays. The reason is that Media Player is really designed to play digital video clips, and therefore it always makes itself visible during playback, even if you're only using it for a MIDI clip. (A video clip is fairly useless if you can't see it.) Media Player has no option setting that changes this behavior.

versions 7&8

The cool tip for dealing with this problem in PowerPoint 7 and 8 is to drag the sound clip icon off the slide, where you can't see it. Normal clicking-and-dragging works in Version 8 but doesn't work in Version 7; however, if you hold down the Alt key while you click and drag, you can move the MIDI clip out of the field of view. You can still get to it in Slide View, but it won't show up during playback.

You can also hide the playback window in PowerPoint 4, but the procedure is completely different. In Media Player, load the MIDI file and select Edit⇨Options (see Figure 13-13). Deselect the checkboxes labeled Caption, Border around object, and Control Bar on playback. Select Edit⇨Copy Object, go to PowerPoint, and then select Edit⇨Paste. Hide the icon behind a drawing object to complete the operation.

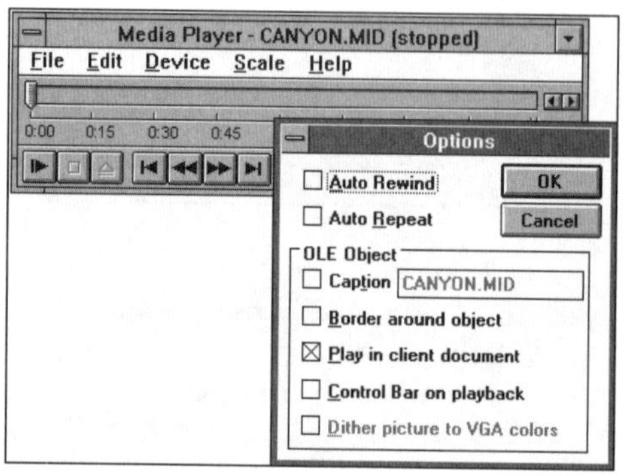

Figure 13-13: Instructing Media Player to disable the playback window in Windows 3.*x*.

Using sounds with build effects in PowerPoint 7

In PowerPoint 4, build effects are associated with body text objects only. In Versions 7 and 8, you can associate build effects with just about any OLE object, including WAV and MIDI files. (See Chapter 11 for details.)

Playing sounds across multiple slides

PowerPoint's default behavior is to stop playing a long sound file when you click past the slide that contains it. There may be times, however, when you'd like a sound to span multiple slides. You can achieve this effect two ways: by associating the sound (which must be in WAV format) with a transition and by inserting the sound as a Media Player object configured to play in the background as you move through your slides.

You learned how to associate a sound with a slide transition in the "Hiding the Evidence" section earlier. You don't have to do anything else; the WAV file will continue to play, even if you advance to other slides.

That approach won't work for a MIDI file, however (life's never that simple), so you have to use a different technique. For example, in Version 7, follow these steps:

1. Insert the MIDI file in the usual way.
2. Choose the MIDI clip and then select Tools➪Animation Settings.
3. Under Play Options, click Play and More.
4. In the Start area, click Automatically, *n* seconds after previous event, and set *n* to whatever delay you want, with zero meaning *as little delay as possible.* (There will always be some delay while PowerPoint loads Media Player behind the scenes.)
5. In the Playing Media Clips area, click Continue slide show, play in background.
6. Set the Stop After *n* Slides field to the number of slides you want the sound to continue playing over. To ensure the clip finishes, set *n* to the number of slides remaining in your show.
7. Click OK twice, and you're done!

The procedure is very similar in Version 8, but you'll use the Custom Animation dialog box shown in Figure 13-9; specifically, the Timing and Play Settings tabs.

You only have one option in PowerPoint 4, and that's to use Media Player. The secret trick to getting sound files to play across multiple files is to manually edit the POWERPNT.INI file (which usually resides in the main Windows directory). In the section labeled

[OLE Play Options]

change the line

MPlayer=Movie,1,1

to

MPlayer=Movie,1

and restart PowerPoint. Then, insert a Media Player object with your MIDI file in the usual way; it will play across multiple slides. (You can't control how many slides, though.)

That's fine for MIDI files, but what about WAV? A cool, little-known fact is that you can use the Windows 3.*x* Media Player to play WAV files as long as you have Media Player Version 1.1E or above, which you may need to download from Microsoft's online sources.

Playing CD-audio tracks in PowerPoint 7 and 8

Both Windows 95 versions of PowerPoint can play CD-audio tracks during a slide show, assuming that the presentation PC has a properly installed CD-ROM drive:

- In Version 7, insert a linked Media Clip object just as you would for a MIDI file, but choose Insert Clip⇨CD Audio and select the audio tracks and timings under Edit⇨Selection.
- In Version 8, you don't need Media Player. Just select Insert⇨Movies and Sounds⇨Play CD Audio Track and choose the tracks or timings in the Play Options dialog box.

With either version, set the sound file to play across multiple slides if you want, using the techniques in the previous section.

Cool tips for sounds

To get your creative brain cells firing, here are a few ideas you may want to consider when you use sounds in your PowerPoint slide shows:

- A relatively long music clip may be pleasant to play during the introduction slide when everyone is getting seated or arriving at the meeting room. The clip should be upbeat, though not obnoxious. (If it's too peaceful, your audience will be asleep before you begin.)
- Long music clips are also a nice touch for breaks (or intermissions) in longer presentations. MIDI files are a better choice than WAV files for this purpose, because they're so much smaller.
- Space out sound files so they break up the slide show and help refocus audience attention. You'll seldom want to use sound files on two or three successive slides.
- Consider using sounds to introduce new sections of your slide show (for example, on title slides). The sounds can help the audience organize the show mentally.
- Voice-over interviews are great, but always rehearse if you're using automatic play settings so that you don't start talking at the same time your PC does!
- You should usually introduce voice-overs so that the audience knows who's speaking before the voice-over starts playing back.
- When rehearsing your slide show, pay attention to sound clip volume levels. If they vary too much, edit or rerecord them. During a presentation, you want to set the PC's volume control once and then forget it — you'll have enough other things on your mind!

- Use audio in moderation. Sound is effective in PowerPoint when it's used for a change of pace, to underline a point, to personalize a presentation (with voice-over interviews), or to indicate section breaks. Using sounds on *every* slide, however, is likely to come off as intrusive, gimmicky, and amateurish — similar to USING CAPITAL LETTERS ALL THE TIME FOR EMPHASIZING TEXT.

"Gotchas"

Watch out for the following situations when working with sound files.

For Version 4

version 4

You can copy sound files from one PowerPoint slide show to another. If, however, you have more than one sound file per slide and you copy them in a group (or copy the entire slide), the sound clips will all play back the same sound when you run the destination slide show. To avoid this bug when copying sound files between presentations, copy them one at a time.

Some larger WAV files just won't play back after you graft them into a PowerPoint slide show. This is another bug, though it's erratic. To work around it, use Sound Recorder to save the WAV file with a different compression format, then reimport it into PowerPoint.

For Versions 4, 7, and 8

versions 4, 7 & 8

If you don't close Sound Recorder before you run a PowerPoint slide show, your linked or embedded WAV files may not play.

Be careful if you perform your OLE linking operations using programs other than Sound Recorder. Although Sound Recorder is a standard part of most Windows installations, your Creative Labs or Turtle Beach sound editor may not be. On the delivery PC, Windows may become confused because it can't find those third-party programs anymore (or at least their relevant entries in the Registry or Registration Database), in which case Windows won't play your sound files.

If you create OLE links for sound files instead of embedding them, remember to include those files (with your PPT file) when you transport your presentation. Windows will try to find them in the same location on the delivery machine that they occupied on the development machine, so you may need to create a new directory on the delivery PC in addition to copying the sound files.

Summary

In this chapter, you stepped into the cool world of multimedia PC sound. To get set up for sound, you need a sound card and the proper Windows drivers to control that card, as well as a set of multimedia speakers.

The two primary types of sound files in the Windows world are WAV (for voice and analog sounds) and MIDI (for synthesized digital music).

WAV files are large, and you can choose from several compression and sampling options to reduce file size without compromising too much quality.

Although Microsoft has provided the basic utilities you need in the form of Sound Recorder and Media Player, your sound card will come with more capable programs. You will also find more sophisticated professional tools readily available on the market.

You can use sounds already on your PC, download new ones from online sources, or buy sound clips from third-party vendors. You can also create your own sounds with nothing more than your sound card's microphone (which is useful for voice-overs, interviews, and so on).

Add sounds to PowerPoint slides by using standard OLE commands, and customize how they'll play back by modifying play settings. For fastest playback in PowerPoint 8, import WAV files as PowerPoint objects.

Embedded sounds become part of your slide show, whereas linked sounds pull from the original WAV or MIDI files.

You can hide the sound file icons during playback.

You can tell PowerPoint to play your sounds across multiple slides, an especially useful feature if you're playing CD-audio tracks.

Don't overuse sound effects, but apply them here and there to add a little spice, underline a point, or *wake up* your audience from time to time. Remember that the end result depends heavily on the multimedia setup of the delivery PC.

In the next chapter, we'll look at how you can use the same OLE techniques used here with sound files to bring in computer animations and add a degree of on-screen motion far beyond what PowerPoint's built-in builds and transitions offer.

Animation

14

In This Chapter

Learning the basic steps of creating an animation

Understanding the differences between animation file formats such as FLC, AVI, and MOV

Creating your own cool, flying-text animation in ten easy steps

Installing the AutoDesk Animation Player for Windows

Creating FLC scripts for greater control

Pulling your animations into PowerPoint and controlling playback

The PowerPoint manuals talk about animation in the sense of animated builds and transitions, but *real* computer animation means much more than these useful but limited effects. With a little help from the right third-party software, you can create true, computer-generated animations that play in a window on a PowerPoint slide.

Though full-fledged computer animation is a sophisticated art that takes years to master, today's third-party tools make it fairly easy for you to create effects such as flying logos, object morphs, and animated lighting effects that add drama and impact to your presentations. This chapter gives you an idea of what you can achieve by using today's popular animation tools and describes how to bring your animations into PowerPoint.

Animation Basics

You need special software to create computer animations; nothing that comes with PowerPoint or Windows is up to this task. Animation software comes in 2-D and 3-D varieties. For years, the most popular 2-D animation programs were AutoDesk's Animator, Animator Pro, and Animator Studio, but nowadays most animation software can handle both 3-D and 2-D animation. Some programs, such as Topas Professional, Trispectives, and TrueSpace, offer animation capabilities as an integral part of the product, along with modeling and rendering capabilities as discussed in Chapter 8. Other programs, such as Ray Dream Designer, offer animation as an add-on module.

Most animation programs enable you to create computer-generated movies by taking the following steps:

1. Create your *objects* — that is, everything that you want to appear in the animation scene — including lights and cameras, if you want to vary from the presets. You can use predefined models, such as those that come with 3-D illustration software, or you can create your own.
2. Figure out how you want the objects to move: where they should start, where they should end up, and what sort of paths they should take. With more sophisticated software, you can animate cameras and spotlights just as a movie director does — for example, you can pan a scene or zoom in for a close-up. You may be able to animate parts of an object, such as the arm of a 3-D human model, rather than entire objects.
3. Position your objects at the start of the animation and take a snapshot (this task is called defining a *key frame*). Move them a little with the software's positioning tools and take another snapshot.
4. Repeat Step 3 until you've reached the endpoint of your animation.

tip: Some animation packages spare you part of this effort by enabling you to just specify starting and ending positions and the sort of motion you want to take place in between (bounce, fly, and so on).

5. Ask the animation program to fill in all the gaps for you and specify how many frames you want to end up with for the finished animation. The program then uses *tweening* (short for "in-betweening") to generate intervening frames, or cells, between the key frames you specified — the computer equivalent of what traditional cel animators have been doing for decades at places like Disney.

tip: The more cells you can design in a given animation sequence, the higher the ultimate quality will be. (If you don't specify enough cells, you get the jerky sort of animation seen on some cheaply made Saturday morning cartoons.) The trade-off is a larger file size.

Key-frame animation is more sophisticated than the earlier, popular type of 2-D animation called *sprite animation*. Sprite animation defines a small object (the sprite) that can be moved around the screen, either opaquely or transparently. Key-frame animation, on the other hand, permits the movement of any object in the scene, whatever its size.

File Formats

The most common PC animation file formats in use today are AVI, QuickTime, and FLC.

AVI and *QuickTime* (*.MOV) are digital video formats that offer a number of compression options, some lossless and some lossy. They also offer audio track capability. Both formats are capable of displaying millions of colors.

FLC (pronounced "flick") is the format developed by AutoDesk, Inc., for its Animator Pro program. FLC is a more flexible and competent version of an older format, FLI, which isn't used anymore. FLC files offer several advantages as an animation format:

- They store computer animations with 100 percent accuracy (that is, without losing any image quality)
- They can be almost any size and dimension
- They can play back at variable speeds
- They support 256 colors with a variable palette

FLC files are supported by many applications, including Premiere, 3D Studio, Crystal Topas, Crystal Flying Fonts, Animator Studio, and Corel Photo-Paint 6. FLC files have no provision for an audio soundtrack, however.

Many computer graphics professionals look down their noses at the FLC format in the trade press because of its color depth limitation and its inability to include audio. We find FLC to be the secret weapon of the PowerPoint presenter, however, in those situations where you don't need a synchronized audio track.

There are three reasons: speed, speed, and speed. FLC files are much smaller, simpler, and more efficient for animation playback than AVI files, and they're somewhat smaller and faster than QuickTime files. So, who cares if FLC files are not in fashion with the graphics gurus?

tip

What if you have a file in AVI or QuickTime format, but you'd like to be able to play it back faster by using the FLC format? No problem — use a digital video editing program, such as Adobe Premiere, to read the AVI or QuickTime file and then export it to the FLC format.

warning

You can use AVI or QuickTime for computer-generated animations that require a synchronized audio track, or if you can't tolerate the title bar that appears during FLC playback in a window. Just remember that if you compress these files, you need to use a compressor that is compatible with animations, such as Microsoft RLE and QuickTime Animation. (The QuickTime

Animation compressor wasn't available until the advent of recent versions of QuickTime for Windows, such as 2.10, and for animators, it's a very welcome addition.) The next chapter on digital video examines the AVI and QuickTime formats and compression options in much more detail.

warning

Some programmers have attempted to extend the basic FLC file architecture to support more colors. For example, the *.FLH format used by the shareware program Dave's Targa Animator supports 16K simultaneous colors. Although you can experiment with such formats, commercial application software does not support high-color and true-color variations on the FLC format. You're probably better off using AVI or MOV.

Creating Your Own Animations

The example that follows uses the very popular animation program from Crystal Graphics, called Flying Fonts. Flying Fonts is a reasonably priced, scaled-down Windows version of the Crystal Graphics long-respected DOS modeling, rendering, and animation program, Crystal Topas, which we've used for years to create gorgeous computer animations. The nice thing about Flying Fonts is its relatively short learning curve compared to Topas.

Of course, many other excellent animation programs are available. You'll want to check out Ray Dream Studio, for example, another inexpensive tool that comes with many preassembled 3-D models. If you have a little more time to invest and want to create even fancier animations, take a look at the more expensive but very powerful Windows programs TrueSpace and (for Windows 95 only) Trispectives.

In this example, we create an opening animation for a PowerPoint slide show called, appropriately enough, "Creating Cool Presentations." Even if you don't have Flying Fonts, you can study the steps and screen snapshots that follow to get a feel for how basic animation programs work. The first five steps borrow from the 3-D illustration techniques introduced in Chapter 8, and the final five steps add the element of motion.

1. Select a typeface (Figure 14-1 shows the ATM font Korinna) and size from the toolbar, choose the text tool (the button with the letter "A"), click in the workspace, and type the first word, **Creating**.
2. Click on the arrow tool, click on the word Creating to select it, and then select Object⇨Bevel to display the Bevel dialog box shown in Figure 14-2. Then select a bevel that you like to apply a sculpted edge to your lettering and click OK.

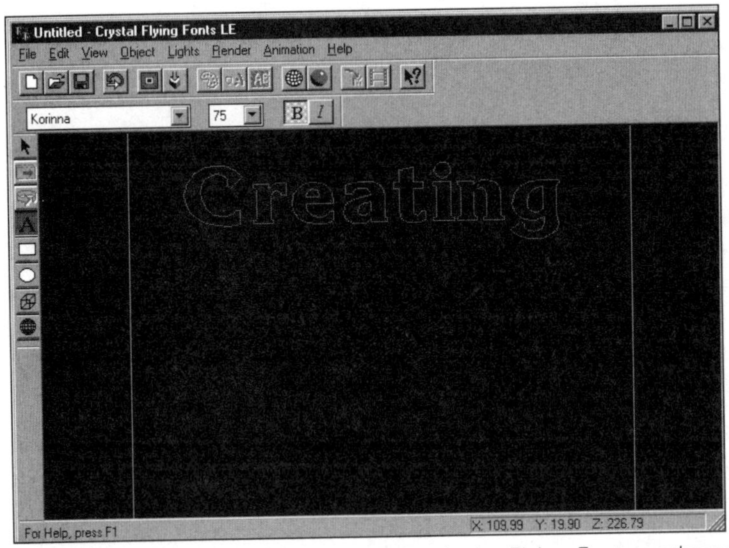

Figure 14-1: You can create a text object in the Flying Fonts workspace with any TrueType or Adobe PostScript font.

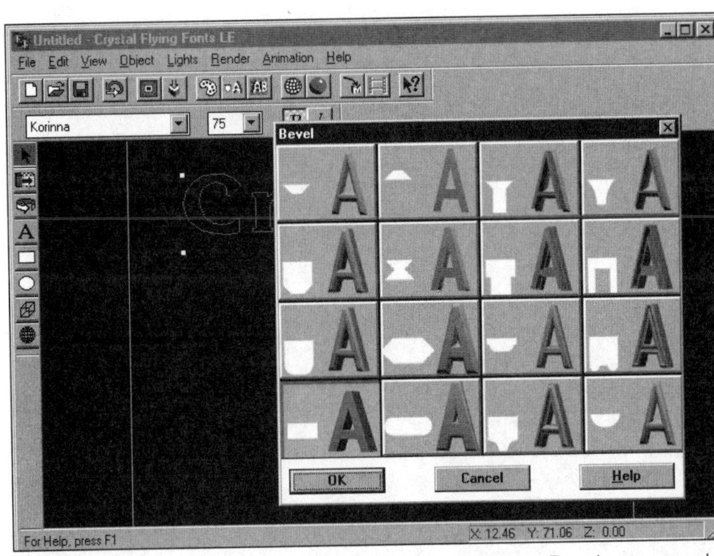

Figure 14-2: Give the text a 3-D effect by using the Bevel command.

3. Now that you have the shape you want, apply a material to it with Object⇨Apply Material. Figure 14-3 shows the available options; select Brushed Chrome for an elegant texture.

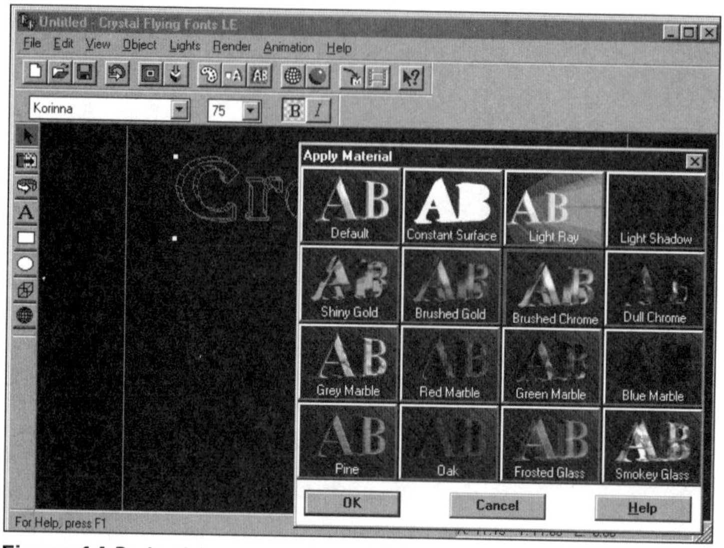

Figure 14-3: Applying a preset material texture to complete the text object's design.

4. Repeat Steps 1 through 3 to create the additional text objects **Cool** and **Presentations**. Use Shiny Gold for the word Cool, so that it stands out for emphasis. The workspace now looks like Figure 14-4.

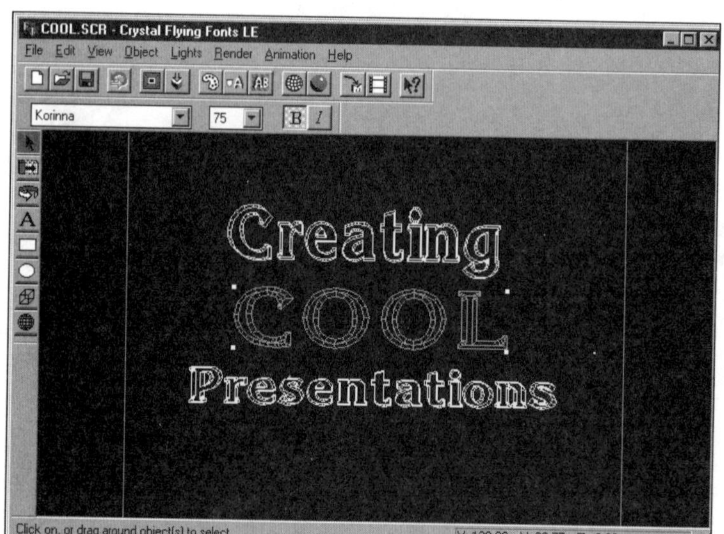

Figure 14-4: You create the other text objects in the same way, using a dramatic gold material for the key word "Cool."

5. So far, all of the activities have been performed in wireframe mode, in which only object "skeletons" appear on screen, for speed. To make sure that you're on the right track, select Render⇨Full Render to see what the image looks like after Flying Fonts applies the textures and scene lighting to flesh out the objects (Figure 14-5).

Figure 14-5: Rendering the scene to verify that the bevel and texture choices look good in the final animation.

6. Now for the *really* cool stuff. Flying Fonts makes it very easy to apply preset motions; you don't have to worry about key framing or tweening. Just click the word Creating to select it, choose Animation⇨Assign Motion, and click Orbit (Figure 14-6).
7. Assign the Orbit motion to the word Presentations in the same manner. To emphasize the word Cool, give it a different motion: Stretch is a fun one.
8. We've now created a great animation, but let's make it even better by creating a *compound motion* for the individual letters in the word Cool. As the word itself is stretching from nowhere up to full size, you can make the individual letters rotate simultaneously. Alt-click each letter to select them separately and apply the Spin motion. The workspace now shows motion paths for each animated object, as in Figure 14-7.

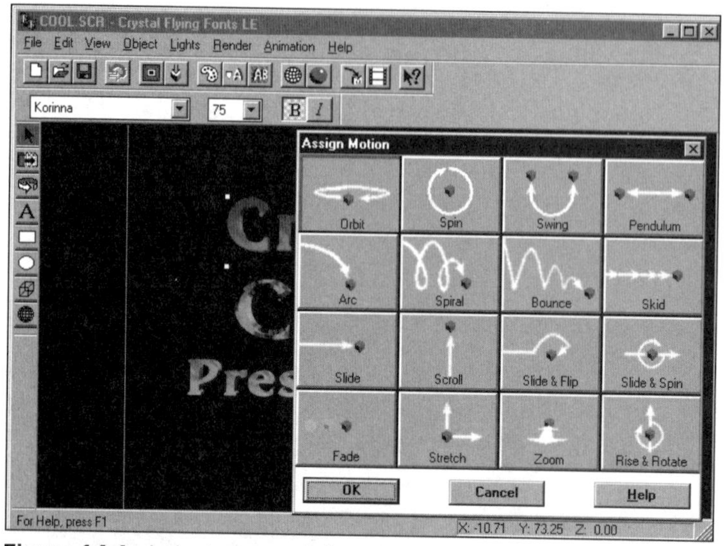

Figure 14-6: Assigning a predefined orbital motion to the word "Creating."

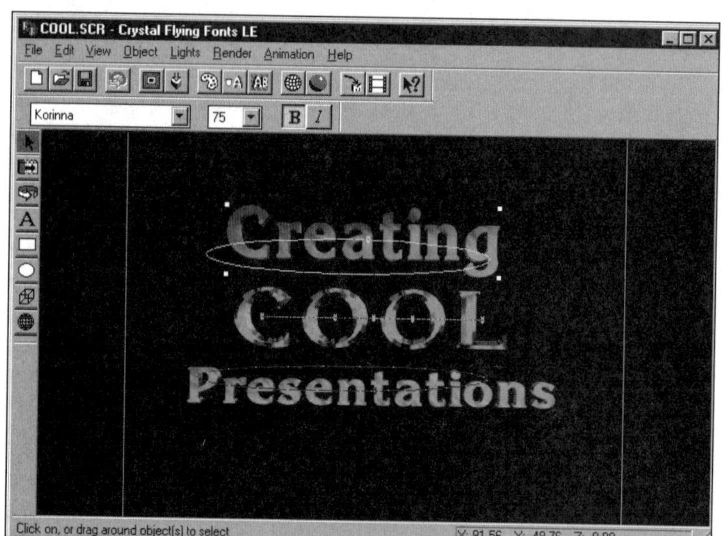

Figure 14-7: The workspace shows motion paths for every object to be animated.

9. Instruct Flying Fonts to create the FLC or AVI file by selecting Animation⇨Make Movie. As Figure 14-8 illustrates, you can specify many options; we've chosen the FLC file format, a size of 560 x 420 pixels, a duration of 4 seconds, and a frame rate of 30 frames-per-second.

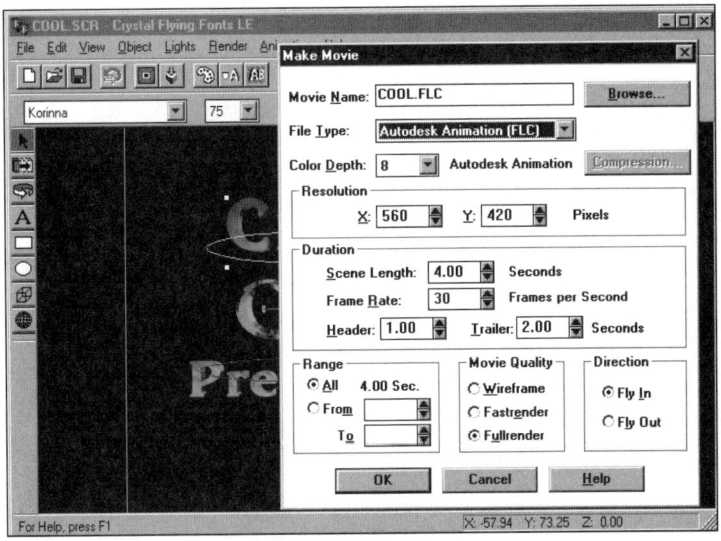

Figure 14-8: The final step is to specify animation file settings, such as file format, screen size, duration, and frame rate.

10. Go to lunch. The program needs some time to render each individual frame, applying the defined motions and calculating all the angles of the beveled text objects. When it's finished, the file COOL.FLC is ready to run. We've included this file on the enclosed CD-ROM in the \BOOK\TUTORIAL directory so that you can see the finished animation. No one would ever guess that we designed it in half an hour!

Animation "gotchas"

warning

The biggest mistake amateur computer animators make is to try pushing more data through the PC than it can handle. You will have to experiment, but having a somewhat smaller window and smoother motion usually is better than using a larger window with hesitation on playback.

warning

The FLC format uses *differential encoding* to store the pixels that change from one frame to another. Differential encoding works well when the number of changing pixels is small but poorly when that number is large. We once tried to do a cool animation effect in which we morphed from one complex, Corel Draw! fractal bitmap background to another as a text title sequence displayed in the foreground. It was a neat idea, but so slow on playback as to be utterly unusable, because just about every single pixel in the playback window changed between frames.

You may read that FLC files are limited to standard VGA sizes, such as 640 x 480, 800 x 600, and 1024 x 768. Not true! If you have a video editing program, such as Premiere, or a graphic manipulation tool, such as DeBabelizer (alas, Macintosh only), you can crop FLC files to whatever dimensions you want — the AutoDesk player will handle it.

Both FLC and Microsoft AVI with RLE compression limit you to 8-bit color. Therefore, don't use backgrounds with too many different colors, especially if you're animating foreground materials (such as reflective metals) that have subtle color gradations that you'd like to capture. This is one reason why we used a black background for COOL.FLC in the preceding example.

Installing the FLC Player

Once you've created an animation, you need some way to play it back from within PowerPoint. If you're using AVI, no problem; the Windows Media Player supports the AVI format without any special configuration. The FLC format is another story.

Several good FLC players are available for DOS and Windows, but the freeware AutoDesk player is the only one we've seen that permits OLE linking into PowerPoint via Media Player and an MCI driver. To install the AutoDesk Animation Player for Windows (AAWIN) and the Media Control Interface driver, follow these steps:

1. Download WINPLA.EXE from CompuServe (it's in the ASOFT/Utilities forum as of this writing). You don't want the older version, NEWPLA.ZIP.
2. Put WINPLA.EXE in its own directory and run it; it's a self-extracting archive file.
3. Run the AASETUP program to install the Animation Player for Windows. Among other tasks, this setup program modifies the WIN.INI [extensions] section to include entries for *.FLI, *.FLC, and *.AAS file types.
4. Follow the instructions in MCIAAP.DOC to install the MCI driver. The key steps are to copy MCIAAP.DRV to the \WINDOWS\SYSTEM directory and add the line **Animation1=mciaap.drv** to the [mci] section of SYSTEM.INI.
5. Restart Windows and fire up Media Player. You should see Autodesk Animator™ Animation as a new entry in Media Player's Device menu (Figure 14-9).

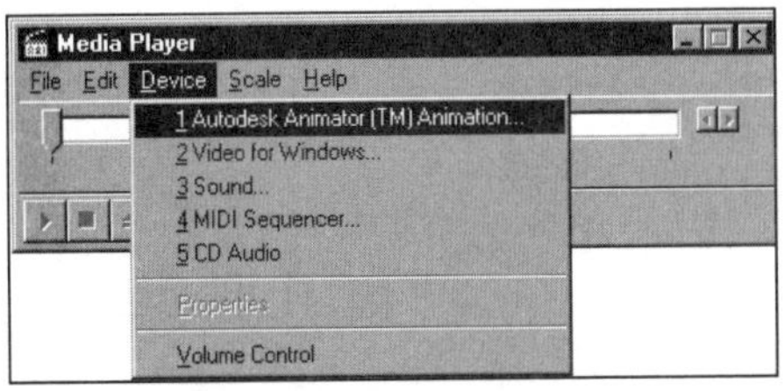

Figure 14-9: Media Player can become an OLE server for FLC animations after installing all the software in the freeware file WINPLA.EXE.

Customizing FLC Playback with Scripts

versions 4, 7 & 8

Scripting is a cool capability of the AutoDesk Animation Player for Windows that's not available for AVI or QuickTime playback unless you have a sophisticated digital video editing program — another reason why we like to use FLC files. With a script, you can modify the animation's speed, specify bitmap images for the first and final screens, pause at the end for a specific number of seconds, string several animations together, specify full-screen playback, and even add sound files! (The sound feature sometimes doesn't work under Windows 95, however.)

When you run AAWIN and open a FLC animation, you can select File➪New Script to customize the way your animation plays and even add a few special effects.

The screen in Figure 14-10 shows some of the things you can do with a script. This example shows a FLC file named S.FLC, but notice the S, N, M, and P codes on the left of the window, under Settings. These codes indicate that some changes have been made in the Settings window to modify the playback speed (S), incorporate a MIDI sound file (N), load the animation file completely into memory for smoother playback (M), and pause at the end (P). Figure 14-11 shows the Settings window where you can specify these parameters.

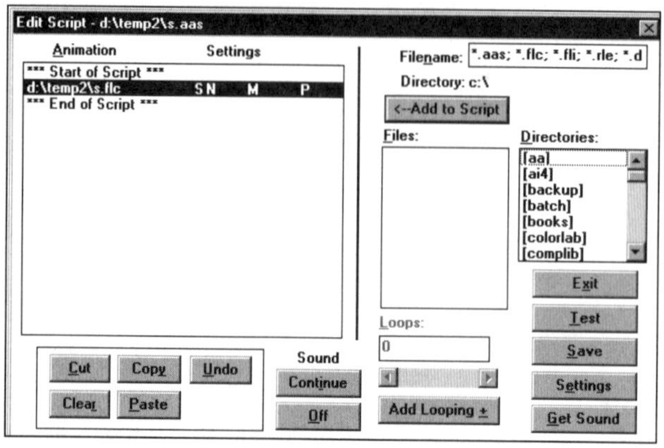

Figure 14-10: Creating a script to play an animation with special settings for greater control.

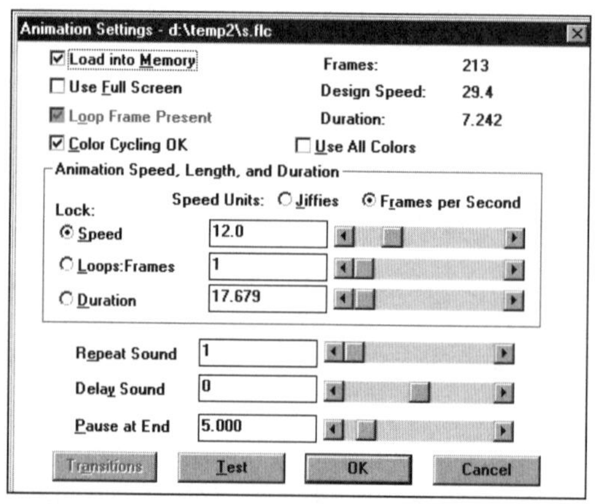

Figure 14-11: Modifying FLC animation playback settings for the script.

After you're done creating your script, select File⇨Save Script to create a file with the extension *.AAS (for AutoDesk Animator Script). This file is nothing more than an ASCII text file with the options you've chosen. You can load and run scripts from the Animation Player for Windows just as you load and run FLC files directly.

Bringing Animations into PowerPoint

After you've created an animation, you need to link it into a PowerPoint slide show. The procedure varies depending on whether you use FLC/AAS files or AVI files.

Importing FLC and AAS files

versions 4, 7 & 8

The following list describes the procedure for bringing a FLC file or AAS script into PowerPoint. (As with all OLE operations, you can start either with the client or the server; this procedure assumes that you want to start with PowerPoint, the client.)

1. Start PowerPoint, load your presentation, select View⇨Slides to get into slide view, and move to the slide where you want the animation to play.
2. Choose Insert⇨Object and select Media Clip. Make sure that both Create New and Display as Icon are checked (Figure 14-12).

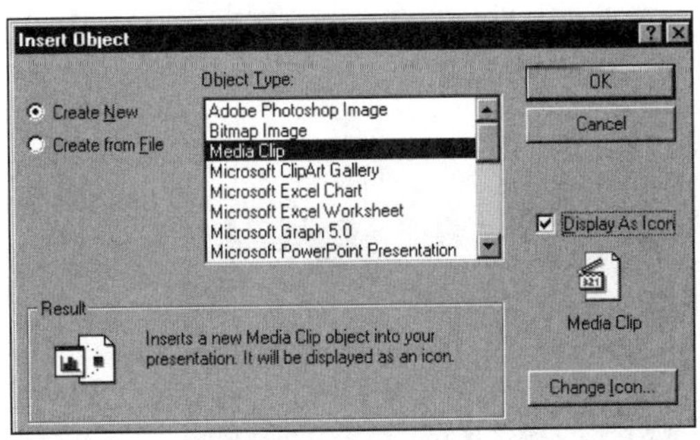

Figure 14-12: Proper settings for inserting a FLC or AAS Media Clip object into PowerPoint.

3. In the Media Player window, select Device⇨AutoDesk Animator™ for Windows. In the File Open dialog box that appears, locate the *.FLC or *.AAS file you want. (Remember, if you want full-screen playback, specify this option in a script file, as described earlier.)
4. Select File⇨Exit and Return to Presentation to link the media clip into PowerPoint.
5. Select Slide Show⇨Custom Animation (Version 8), Tools ⇨Animation Settings (Version 7), or Tools⇨Play Settings (Version 4) to provide PowerPoint with the details it needs to determine whether to play the animation as soon as possible, when the object is clicked, or after a preset delay. You can also choose to hide the icon when the animation isn't playing.

You've just created an OLE link between PowerPoint and Media Player. When the animation runs, Media Player passes control to the MCI driver for the AutoDesk Animation Player for Windows.

If your animation plays hesitantly rather than smoothly, go back to AAWIN and edit the script to specify a slower playback speed. You're looking for the fastest frame rate that doesn't introduce skips during playback.

Where you put the Media Player icon doesn't matter; the animation will always be centered on the screen during playback.

One side effect of playing FLC files in a window is that they always display a title bar showing the filename at the top of the playback window (Figure 14-13). The title bar doesn't appear if you use a script to specify running the FLC full-screen; by using that method, however, you may get a bit of video flicker before and after full-screen animations run. These problems are minor cosmetic points and generally good trade-offs for the speed of FLC file playback, but if you find them unacceptable for a particular slide show, use the AVI or QuickTime format instead of FLC.

Figure 14-13: The title bar that always appears when playing FLC files in a window on a PowerPoint slide.

Importing AVI files

The procedure for importing AVI format animations is the same as the one for importing AVI digital video files, which the next chapter examines in depth. You follow most of the same steps, but there are a few variations. For one thing, if you don't want to run an AVI file full-screen, you can leave the Display as Icon check box cleared and place your AVI window wherever you like on the slide.

Summary

Animation means more than just builds and transitions: It means the capability to put just about anything into motion that you can draw with an illustration tool. The following are some of the important points discussed in this chapter:

The few 3-D animation tools that were available for the PC cost thousands of dollars only a few years ago (we know, we paid), but several fine, reasonably priced programs are available today, and some of these tools are very easy to use.

The usual technique for creating animations is to build your objects' shapes, colors, and textures, define motion paths or patterns, create key-frame "snapshots," and let the software fill in the intermediate frames via tweening.

Some tools, such as Flying Fonts, don't require you to create key frames but use predefined motions instead.

You can use AVI or QuickTime file formats, but, in most cases, the FLC format offers better speed if you can do without synchronized audio. You can also easily create scripts with FLC files to customize playback options.

PowerPoint plays animations via OLE links to Media Player, in much the same way that it plays sounds using Media Player and Sound Recorder. To link FLC files, however, you must install the appropriate MCI driver so that Media Player can understand them.

Computer-generated animations are a great deal of fun and very cool, and you can create some impressive ones yourself in a couple of afternoons. At other times, though, you will want to incorporate real-world video footage into a PowerPoint slide show, and that's where the next chapter on digital video comes in handy.

Digital Video: AVI and QuickTime

15

In This Chapter

Understanding the basics of video capture boards

Setting up your PC with the proper digital video software drivers

The AVI and QuickTime digital video formats

Compressing videos to save space

Creating video clips for your presentation

Linking your video clips to PowerPoint slides

Customizing playback settings to get the effects you want (and avoid the ones you don't!)

Digital video design tips

If your delivery hardware can handle it, digital video clips can really snazz up your slide show. This chapter tells you how to link these most demanding of multimedia files.

In the preceding chapter, we talked about creating computer-generated animations, AutoDesk animation (FLC) files in particular, and linking them to PowerPoint with tools such as the AutoDesk animation player. In this chapter, we extend our discussion to computer-based videos based on *real-life* images — that is, anything that you can film with a camcorder.

If PowerPoint slide shows containing sounds or animations are fairly rare, those with digital video clips are even rarer — and for good reasons. The biggest one is *performance*. Simply put, you need a pretty powerful PC to play back digital video files at anything close to an acceptable size and speed. You can often get away with using a limited number of colors when making computer-based animations, because no one expects them to look "real." Audiences tend to be less forgiving when you are showing video clips of real people, places, or things, however: They know what these things are supposed to look like and are accustomed to seeing TV- or movie-theater-quality images.

Other reasons explain the dearth of video-enhanced slide shows also. Creating, editing, and optimizing video clips requires more expensive hardware and software than performing the same tasks with sound or animation clips. The technology is also more complex because video clips combine the elements of visual motion and audible motion (sound). And the learning curve for working with digital video products is steeper; mastering a video editing program such as Adobe Premiere isn't something you do over a weekend (although the program is not as confusing as it first looks).

In many respects, then, this chapter is the most challenging in the book. We begin with video basics: the hardware, software, and file formats you need to understand. Next, we give you some inside information on making and editing your own video clips based on our own video experiences. Finally, we look at how you add videos to PowerPoint and control how they play back.

Getting Ready for Video

The following is a brief introduction to digital video technology, which consists of the following three key elements:

- Video capture boards and drivers
- Windows digital video file formats
- Media Player, Movie Player, and digital video

Let's examine these key elements in detail.

Video capture boards

Video capture boards, which translate an analog video signal (such as from a camera or VCR) to a digital video file on the computer's disk drive, can provide several functions:

- Hardware-based, real-time video compression to achieve bigger, smoother video clips than possible with software compression
- Audio-in capability, so that you don't need a separate sound card to record audio and video simultaneously
- Pass-through capability for your existing Windows graphics board, so that you won't have to flip cables around as much

Some capture boards also do double duty as Windows video accelerators, so you don't need a separate graphics board in the PC to drive the monitor when running everyday Windows programs, although using these products always involves a degree of compromise in terms of performance. We recommend using a board optimized for digital video only. You can get a pretty good one for $200–$300 these days.

When shopping for capture boards, evaluate the capture specifications. What is the largest size window that the board can capture, and at what frame rate (number of frames per second) and color depth (256 colors, 32K colors, 65K colors, true 24-bit color)? Keep in mind that anything you capture at less than 24 frames-per-second (fps) will probably look a little jerky when you play it back.

Also look at the accompanying software utilities for ease of configuration and diagnostics tools. Video cards can be a pain to configure because they typically need their own interrupts, base memory addresses, and upper memory addresses. If the configuration utilities enable you to change these settings without you having to yank the card out of the PC and move jumper blocks around or flip switches on the card, so much the better.

Finally, check which software the video card supports. Most video cards work with Adobe Premiere, but if you're using a different video capture-and-editing utility, verify that the card will work with it. Many video cards don't have Windows 95 drivers yet, so that may be another factor for you to consider.

tip

You can install video-card drivers by using procedures similar to those outlined in Chapter 13 for installing sound-card drivers.

Digital video file formats

You have two main choices for digital video files in the PC world:

- *AVI*, or *Audio-Video Interleave*, is the Microsoft standard supported by both Windows 3.*x* and Windows 95 (and also known as Video for Windows). With Windows 3.*x*, you generally have to add or upgrade the Video for Windows run time files. These files are downloadable from Microsoft, and the version you want is Version 1.1e. With Windows 95, Video for Windows is built into the operating system, so you don't have to download anything to play AVI files.
- *QuickTime* is the Apple standard. It was the first format on the block for small computer video. You have to get the QuickTime for Windows support files from Apple (at http://quicktime.apple.com); they usually are bundled with any good video-editing software, too. The standard QuickTime file extension is MOV. QuickTime for Windows has its own separate control panel (Figure 15-1).

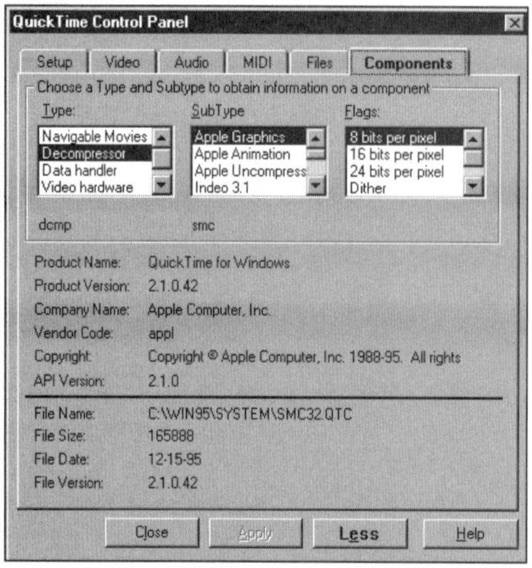

Figure 15-1: The QuickTime for Windows 95 control panel provides details on driver versions, options, and installed components.

Which format should you use? Both technologies are capable of doing what you need. If you want cross-compatibility with the Macintosh world, go with QuickTime. If that doesn't matter to you, AVI is probably the better choice because most PCs don't have the Apple-supplied QuickTime for Windows support.

As you saw with sound files in Chapter 13, a number of compressor-decompressor (codec) techniques are available for these multimedia files. In fact, compression is probably more important for digital video than for sound files because your computer has to manage much more data per second of material. Table 15-1 provides an overview of the codecs available for Video-for-Windows (VFW) and QuickTime (QT).

Table 15-1: Video-for-Windows and QuickTime Codecs

Codec	Description
Apple Animation (QT)	The best codec for computer-generated images because it supports greater color depths than Microsoft RLE.
Apple Video (QT)	Use for moderate- to high-quality analog video capture and compression at 64K colors. Can recompress without much degradation.
Cinepak (VFW, QT)	Use for compressing 24-bit analog video (16.7 million colors). Better end result than Video 1 but much slower to compress. Recompressed files have degraded quality.

Table 15-1: Video-for-Windows and QuickTime Codecs

Codec	Description
Intel Indeo R3.2 (VFW, QT)	Comparable to Cinepak.
Intel Indeo RAW (VFW, QT)	Use for capturing uncompressed video with smaller resulting disk files than "no compression."
Microsoft RLE (VFW)	Use for computer-generated images and animations at 256 colors only.
Microsoft Video 1 (VFW)	Use for compressing analog video at 256 or 64K colors. Faster to compress than Cinepak, but lower playback quality.

There is another codec that seems poised to enter the mainstream of PC video: MPEG, named after the International Standards Organization's Motion Picture Experts Group. It has not been widely adopted since its debut in 1993. Microsoft's endorsement of MPEG in its own ActiveMovie specification, the solidification of standards, and the precipitous price drop in the cost of boards for both movie creation and playback, however, all bode well for MPEG's future. MPEG is rarely used for slide shows compared to other codecs, so we won't explore it further here, except to note that PowerPoint 8 can play MPEG movies. However, the technology bears watching.

What do we recommend you use for a video codec? It varies by type of material:

- For computer-generated animations, which typically have clean lines and precise boundaries, a *lossless* compressor such as Microsoft RLE or the Apple QuickTime Animation codec is a good choice. (We prefer the Apple codec for most jobs.)
- For real-life digital video clips, Cinepak and Indeo usually are good choices.
- You get maximum quality with no compression, but most PCs can't handle the required data rates or file sizes.
- Most video cards have some form of hardware compression built in, such as Orchid's AURA chip on its Vidiola card, which you can use if the delivery PC has the same video board as your development PC.

Most codecs are updated from time to time, and we recommend running your own tests on a small video clip to see which codecs work best for you.

Media Player and Movie Player

The Windows Media Player applet is compatible with AVI files and is the usual method for getting them into PowerPoint via OLE. You should be familiar with Media Player by now in the context of MIDI and FLC files.

Apple's Movie Player applet, which comes with the QuickTime for Windows software, is an OLE server and therefore can act much like Media Player for inserting QuickTime videos into PowerPoint. It also has a useful Movie Info feature that provides details on the loaded file (Figure 15-2).

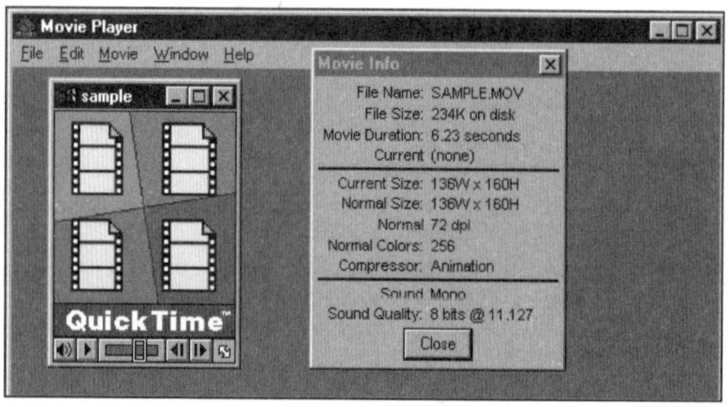

Figure 15-2: Apple's Movie Player acts as an OLE server for QuickTime videos.

tip

If you're using the 16-bit version of QuickTime (such as on a Windows 3.*x* machine), the file MCIQTW.DRV provides a Media Control Interface for QuickTime movies so that you can play them with Media Player. The 32-bit QuickTime for Windows 95 does away with this file, however, so you should use Movie Player rather than Media Player.

version 8

Chapter 13 pointed out that PowerPoint 8 can play sound files *natively*; that is, without an OLE server. The same goes for AVI and MOV files, but this capability is an even bigger advantage here than with sound files. When PowerPoint 4 or 7 loads Media Player to play a movie, you will notice a delay of a few seconds, but movies start playing almost immediately in Version 8.

Making Movies

Although the Windows Sound Recorder is an adequate no-frills application for creating your own sound files, neither Windows 3.*x* nor Windows 95 come with a similar application for creating digital videos. You have to buy a third-party application to make movies. Fortunately, many video capture cards come bundled with such software.

Several programs are available for making and editing movies, with varying degrees of cost, complexity, and sophistication. These include In:sync Corp.'s Razor Pro, U-lead Systems Inc.'s MediaStudio Pro, and Asymetrix's

Digital Video Producer. We've spent most of our time working with Adobe Premiere, a capable midrange program that does most of what we need to do and doesn't have a price tag that breaks the bank. Premiere also is the utility most often bundled with midrange video capture cards, so we use this program here for discussion purposes.

Capturing video

The procedure for capturing analog video to a digitized file is pretty standard no matter what software you use. You connect the video-out port of your source device, be it a camcorder or VCR, to the video-in port of your capture card. You need a phonograph-type plug cable for composite video or a DIN-plug cable for S-Video (SVHS). Other options may be available on higher-end equipment.

tip

Use the highest-quality source signal your equipment can generate. For example, if you're capturing from a VCR that has both VHS and S-VHS capability, use the S-VHS connectors. The better your source signal, the better your final product will look. Capturing at the higher resolutions of an S-VHS signal creates larger data files. In the video world, however, scaling down by discarding data is always a better method than scaling up by *interpolating* (guessing what the extra pixels should be when you increase the window size, for example).

If your video clip contains audio, you can either connect the source device's audio-out port to the audio-in port of your video capture board or to the audio-in port of a separate sound card.

Once you're all connected, you have to make some decisions about the resolution, frame rate, and compression technique you want to use. You preset your capture utility for all of these options (Figure 15-3). The following paragraphs present a few guidelines.

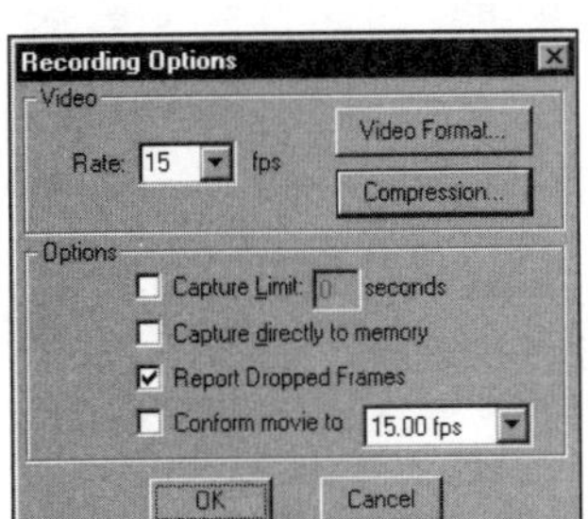

Figure 15-3: Setting video capture options in Premiere has a major impact on the video's final quality.

warning

Capturing full-screen, full-color, 30-frames-per-second video isn't feasible without hardware compression on the video capture card. High-end capture cards such as the Targa 2000 can manage the task, but they are still expensive (thousands of dollars), although costs are coming down. Midrange capture cards with an onboard hardware compressor can usually grab one-quarter-screen video at 24 fps. You also need a fairly fast disk that can store the data streaming in from the capture card without choking — good choices are Fast SCSI (Small Computer Systems Interface) and Fast/Wide SCSI or, even better, high-performance disk arrays.

tip

The best results come from experimenting with a given hardware setup. Start out ambitiously, with no software compression, hardware compression, the size of window you want, a 30-fps frame rate, and full-color capture. Check whether your capture program reports *dropped frames*, which occur when the capture settings are more than the hardware can handle, and then back off your settings one by one. Try a smaller window, a slower frame rate, and fewer colors. When you can capture the video clip with no dropped frames, you can be comfortable that you've done as well as you can do with that particular PC.

Once you've done some experimenting and settled on your capture settings, creating the digital video is a simple matter of starting your source device and activating the video-capture command in your program (for example, File⇨Capture⇨Movie Capture in Premiere). After you're done, you have a nice big AVI file on disk – and it's time to edit it for your slide show.

Editing video

In its most basic form, video editing consists of cutting out footage you don't want and compressing your movie to a manageable size for delivery.

Cutting excess footage is a simple task in all video-editing programs — just mark the sections you want to cut and delete them. Compression, however, is another matter.

We said earlier that when capturing a video, you want to achieve the greatest window size, frame rate, and color depth that your hardware supports. Generally, though, when editing your clip for production, you have to trim one or all of those settings to a level that your delivery PC can handle and to achieve a manageable file size. (Your delivery PC may not have a 2GB hard drive or 64MB of RAM!)

tip

As with sound files, archive your original video clips to a suitable storage device, such as a ZIP drive or Syquest cartridge, so that you can go back to them later without having to re-create your movie.

Typically, you set your window size and compression options right before you save the edited movie, as shown in Figures 15-4 and 15-5. Executing the Make Movie command then instructs Premiere to go through your original clip, apply the new frame rate, window size, and compression settings you've specified, and create a new, smaller clip that you can import into PowerPoint.

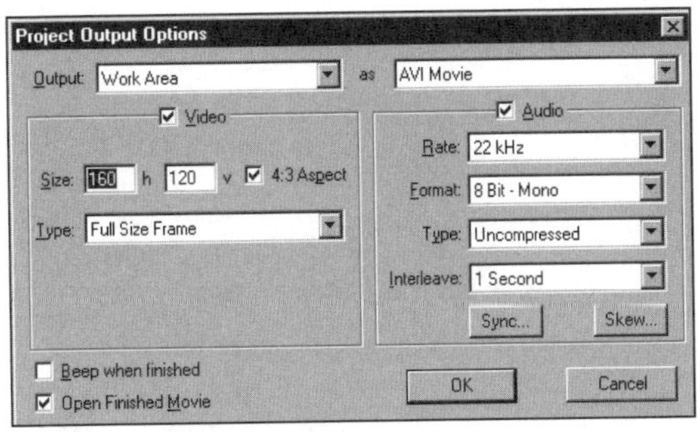

Figure 15-4: Set final resolution and file type options in Premiere before saving the edited file.

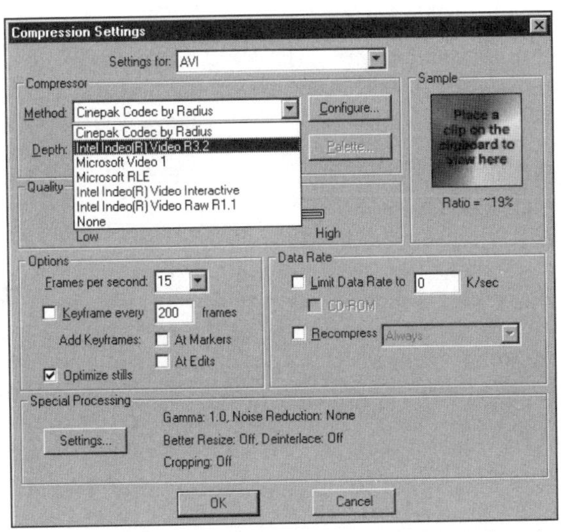

Figure 15-5: Set final compression options in Premiere before saving the edited file. Compression creates a smaller file suitable for playback in PowerPoint.

warning

Making your edited movie can be a time-consuming process because the video editor has to go through every single frame and massage the data to your specifications. In particular, *asymmetric* codecs such as Cinepak can take a long time to compress, even though they don't take long to play.

Therefore, experiment with small portions of your video before making the entire movie. Also, use the fastest, most RAM-rich PC you can get your hands on — preferably one with a power backup!

Special effects

If you want to get a little fancier, you can use your video editor to create various special effects before saving your edited movie. Some of the effects you can add include the following:

- Fades in and out
- Titles (either static or moving)
- Splices and transitions between different video clips
- Superimposed graphics

We could write an entire book about all the special effects available in Premiere. For example, you can take many of the Photoshop graphics filters and apply them to a video clip progressively over time. Most readers of this book won't be creating MTV-style videos, however, so we'll keep it fairly basic here.

Fades are always nice for bringing in and taking out a video clip. Usually, you want to fade in from black and fade out to black. The usual technique is to add a black "matte" frame in your video editing program and specify a transition to or from it and your main video clip, as is done in Figure 15-6. This simple step adds a professional touch.

Titles can be created two ways: on the PowerPoint slide itself (such as just below the video window border) using the standard PowerPoint text tools, or on your video clip. If you're not showing a video clip full-screen, creating your title on the PowerPoint slide is probably the easier method. If you're showing a video clip full-screen, use your video editor to superimpose a title that stays for two or three seconds and then fades out. We favor static titles over the fancier rolling titles for most uses, due to the difficulties of playing back titles of a legible size in a small video window, although Premiere enables you to assign motion to your titles — it's an impressive effect if you have powerful playback hardware.

Transitions between clips are slick when, for example, you show two "talking heads" interviews one after the other. The general technique is to drag and drop the first clip onto the A bar of Premiere's construction window, drag and drop the second clip onto the B bar, and then drag and drop the desired transition from the Transitions window to the bar in-between (Figure 15-6).

Premiere offers dozens of transitions, but just like PowerPoint's transitions, some work better than others on typical PC hardware platforms. Do some experimenting with small clips at low resolution to see which ones you like.

Superimposed graphics can be cool if you want to, say, add a company logo to a corner of the video, in much the same way most TV stations do with their station logo nowadays. Just remember that your playback window will probably be fairly small and that putting such a graphic element on the PowerPoint slide itself may be easier.

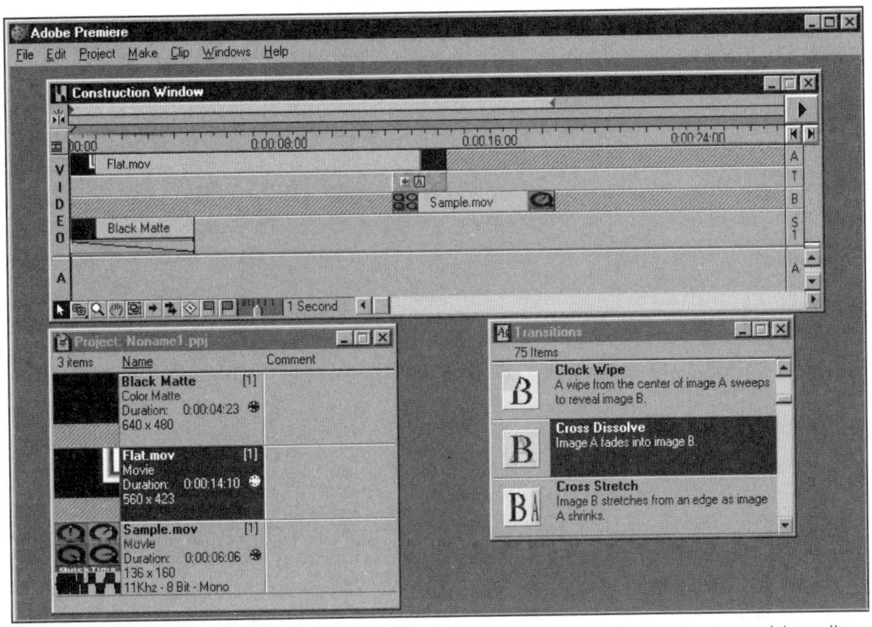

Figure 15-6: Creating a fade-in from black and a transition between two video clips in Premiere is performed in the Construction Window.

Importing Video Clips into PowerPoint

You've created, edited, and compressed your digital video clip. Now it's time to bring it into PowerPoint. For Versions 4 and 7, the procedure is very similar to that described earlier for importing a sound or animation file. For Version 8, it's even easier, as the new PowerPoint can play movies without Media Player.

Creating the OLE link

As usual, you can start in PowerPoint and select Insert⇨Object (or Insert⇨Movie in Version 7 to save a step) or you can start from Media Player (or Movie Player for QuickTime), do an Edit⇨Copy operation, and then move to PowerPoint for the Edit⇨Paste operation. We won't rehash the details here; the process is almost the same as the one for sound files.

warning

Movie Player is slow as molasses when used as an OLE server. Don't give up on it; updating the PowerPoint slide show sometimes takes more than two minutes.

version 8

Drop a movie onto a PowerPoint 8 slide with the command Insert⇨Movies and Sounds, and choose Movie from File or Movie from Gallery (the new Clip Gallery can manage movies as well as graphics and sounds). You've created a link to the data file — remember, movies are never embedded into PowerPoint — but PowerPoint 8 plays the movie without invoking an OLE server, so technically it's not an OLE link. This method bypasses Media Player, so the movie won't have the usual control bar on screen.

Specifying play settings

version 8

Right-click the linked or embedded movie and select Action Settings, if you want the movie to play when you click on it or when you move the mouse over it. To play the movie automatically — either immediately, after a preset delay, or in an animation sequence — right-click it, select Custom Animation, and then set options under the Timing and Play Settings tabs as described in Chapters 11 and 13. You can even have the video clip "fly in" by specifying an animated build effect for it on the Effects tab. The Hide while not playing option on the Play Settings tab keeps the video clip placeholder out of sight.

versions 4 & 7

By clicking on the linked or embedded movie and selecting Tools⇨Animation Settings (Version 7) or Tools⇨Play Settings (Version 4), you can tell PowerPoint to play the video as soon as possible or to wait until it is clicked or a preset delay elapses. The Hide while not playing option keeps the video clip placeholder out of sight.

You can hide the playback window's border and control bar much the same way as you did for Media Player MIDI clips. Click on the clip, activate Media Player, and select Edit⇨Options. Deselect the check boxes labeled Border around object and Control Bar on playback.

Note that the playback options for QuickTime movies in Windows 95 are different and more elaborate than for AVI clips, as shown in Figure 15-7. Right-click on the movie and select Play Options...QuickTime Movie Object.

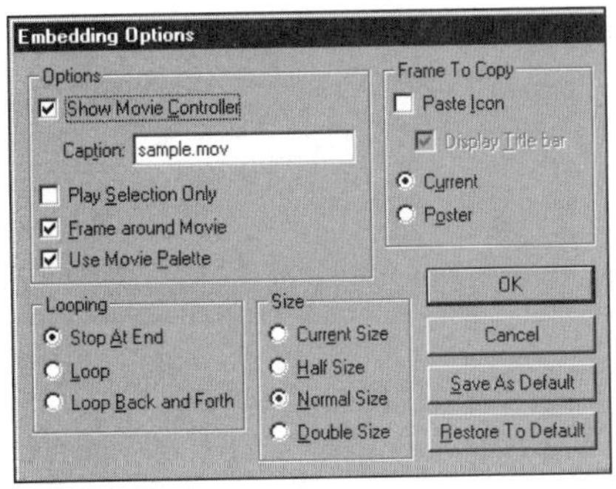

Figure 15-7: QuickTime playback options in Windows 95 appear in the Embedding Options window.

Normally, you want your AVI video clips to play in a window on an existing PowerPoint slide. (In fact, that's the only way you can play them in Version 8, unless you use Media Player.) At times, however, you may want to play a clip at full-screen size. The procedure for doing so is not at all obvious in either PowerPoint 4 or 7, so follow these steps and save yourself some time:

1. Click on the Media Clip object and select Edit⇨Media Clip Object⇨Edit to open Media Player.
2. Select Edit⇨Options and clear the Play in client document checkbox.
3. Select Device⇨Configure⇨Full Screen.
4. Click on Set Default and Enter and then select File⇨Exit & Return to Presentation⇨Yes.

The easiest way to get a Media Player AVI clip to play at full-screen size is to insert it as a Media Clip object, not as a movie, and select the Display As Icon checkbox (Figure 15-8).

Load the file into Media Player and select Device⇨Properties⇨Full Screen. Then click File⇨Exit and Return⇨Yes. Now when you click on the icon during your slide show, the movie plays back at full-screen size.

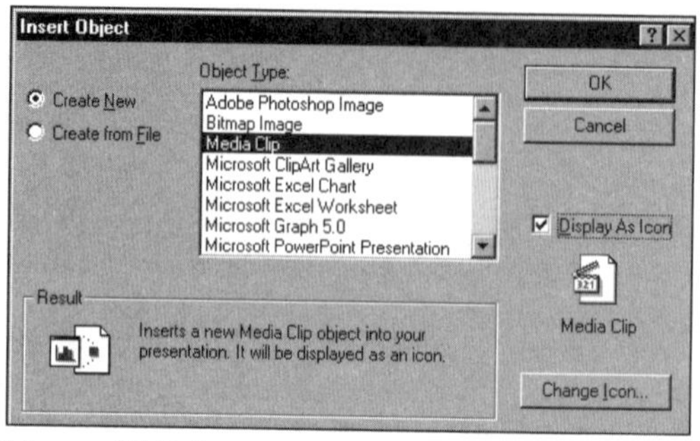

Figure 15-8: Importing a video as an icon permits full-screen playback in PowerPoint 7.

tip

Microsoft recommends that you let PowerPoint determine the best size for your digital video's playback window, given the desired screen resolution, to minimize jerkiness:

- In Version 8, select Format⇨Picture⇨Size⇨Best scale for slide show and choose the appropriate resolution.
- In Versions 4 and 7, select Draw⇨Scale⇨Best Scale for Slide Show and choose the appropriate resolution.

Video-clip "gotchas"

version 4

If you use digital video clips in a PowerPoint 4 slide show and set the slide show to loop continually, the PC will eventually crash with an error such as `General Protection Fault in module OLE2.DLL at 000B:000A.` The cause of the crash is that a special Windows 3.*x* memory pool called *system resources* is being depleted gradually over time. Moral: Don't loop slide shows that contain digital video clips, or upgrade your system to at least Video-for-Windows Version 1.1a with the help of your friendly Microsoft support technician.

Also in Version 4, you may notice that your AVI clips seem to rewind to the first frame after playing back from PowerPoint. The reason is that Media Player puts the first frame of the clip on the screen as a placeholder, or *poster image*. When the clip is finished, the poster image is displayed again on the screen. The easiest way around this problem is to click on the AVI clip, select Tools⇨Play Settings, and check the Hide while not playing option.

Summary

In this chapter, we covered the following points:

To get started with digitized video, you need a fairly fast PC, a capture/editing program, and a video capture card that can accept analog signals from camcorders or VCRs and turn them into disk-based files.

Most Windows PCs support the *AVI* format, also known as Video for Windows, but you can also use Apple's QuickTime for Windows if you need cross-platform compatibility or if the clips you want to use are already in QuickTime format.

When creating a digital video, use the highest-quality settings you can without dropping frames. Then edit your video by trimming, splicing, and adding special effects as you like; we favor simple fades and transitions, preferring to create titles and graphics on the PowerPoint slide's border area surrounding the playback window.

Save your edited video to disk with an appropriate codec, resolution, speed, and color depth to achieve a file that's manageable in size and looks good when played back. Experiment a little with a brief excerpt of your video to get the best overall compromise.

Link the file into PowerPoint 4 or 7 using Media Player as your OLE server for AVI files and Apple's Movie Player for MOV files. If you have PowerPoint 8, you don't need an OLE server unless you want to play a movie full screen. Finally, set your playback options and you're ready to go!

After reading the last four chapters, you may be eager to load up your current PowerPoint project with sound, animation, and video clips. But before you do so, take five extra minutes and read the next chapter. It helps you walk the often fine line between the bold and the garish, the impressive and the intrusive, the pleasing and the distracting — and helps your presentations come off as professional and polished rather than amateurish and rough.

Enough Versus Too Much

16

In This Chapter

- Relating the uniqueness of a special effect with the frequency of its use
- Looking at a slide show from the audience's perspective
- Considering limitations of the underlying hardware when deciding how much multimedia to use
- Evaluating the appropriateness of delivering multimedia content through PowerPoint versus other means
- Deciding whether you'll have enough access to the right kind of equipment to still present your multimedia content if something goes wrong

Part III ends with a short chapter on when too much "cool" becomes "uncool." In Chapters 12 through 15, you read about how you can use multimedia to add flash and style to your PowerPoint shows. Before moving on to Part IV (on presenting your shows), take a deep breath and spend a few minutes learning how to avoid going overboard with multimedia — that is, how to distinguish "enough" from "too much."

Berlioz and the Triangle

Hector Berlioz was a classical composer and an expert at orchestral color — that is, combining instruments to produce different tonal textures. Even if you're not a classical music fan, listen sometime to a few minutes of Berlioz' *Symphonie Fantastique*. It's remarkable how many different sounds and moods Berlioz was able to evoke in this piece of music.

One of the techniques Berlioz used, and passed on to his students, was to reduce the playing time of particular instruments the more unusual or distinct their sound was. For example, not everybody can instantly identify a viola, but everybody can instantly identify the sound of a triangle. So,

Berlioz said, you should use the triangle very sparingly, much less often than the viola. Similarly, don't give the piccolo, tuba, or gong much playing time. Berlioz knew that audiences quickly tire of hearing a very distinct and somewhat unusual sound over and over.

What does this have to do with PowerPoint? Your composing a PowerPoint slide show has a great deal in common with Berlioz composing an orchestral piece of music. In both cases, the "composer" is fashioning a sensory experience designed to convey ideas and feelings to a group of people and must choose from a variety of tools and effects to achieve that end.

Moral: Consider taking a page out of Berlioz' book and adopting a rule that the more unusual an effect (whether a sound clip, digital video, animation, or transition), the less often you should use it. Your special effects will grab the audience's attention more effectively if you don't overuse them. Too many animated builds, too many startling sound clips, and the media starts to get in the way of the message, rather than enhancing or underlining it.

The Audience Viewpoint

You may be saying to yourself, "Why should I learn how to integrate multimedia effects with PowerPoint if I'm not going to use them?"

Well, you *are* going to use them — you're just not going to become *infatuated* with them and use them without good reason. Part of maintaining a good, aesthetic perspective on multimedia bells and whistles is to consider the audience viewpoint. Here's an example.

Show a quarter-screen, true-color, 24fps digital video clip running on a fast Pentium PC with a late-model video accelerator card to someone who's been using PCs for 10 years and remembers technologies such as CGA video, and that person is likely to react with a statement such as "Wow! That's great!" or "I didn't know a PC could do that."

Show the same video clip to a businessperson who has never used a PC before. You're likely to get a response such as "Well, it sure isn't TV-quality, is it?" or "Can't you make it bigger?"

The multimedia capabilities of today's PCs impress those who are aware of how far PCs have come in this area. They still look weak, however, to many of the people who will be in your audience, compared to the effects you can see any evening on TV science-fiction shows. Therefore, putting a digital video clip onto a PowerPoint slide may make *you* go "Wow! Cool!," but your audience may find it somewhat less astounding.

Moral: Resist the temptation to do cool things with PowerPoint just because they may have some technical appeal to you. Use multimedia clips where they serve a valid purpose. Ask yourself: Is this sound or video clip communicating something that I couldn't get across with text and bullets? If so, great; if not, you may be going past "enough" and into the "too much" zone.

The Hardware Factor

What looks great on your desktop PC may not look so great on the slower notebook machine that you'll use to deliver your talk. In Chapter 18, you learn to interpret some PC hardware specifications that will help you evaluate your delivery platform; and, in Chapter 19, you learn some tips on improving PowerPoint speed.

As the old saying among car enthusiasts goes, however, "There's no substitute for cubic inches." (A variation for foreign-car enthusiasts is that the only substitute for cubic inches is cubic money.) In other words, you can use some tricks to squeeze more power out of delivery PCs, but you just can't display effective AVI clips on an 80386DX with a slow, frame-buffer display circuit. Similarly, a music clip may sound good on small multimedia speakers in a noisy office, but when you hook up an old, 8-bit sound card to an auditorium's PA system, the audience hears all the background noise and distortion from the sound card's limitations.

Moral: Too much multimedia is *any* multimedia that the supporting hardware can't handle easily.

The Appropriateness Test

To determine the right amount of slide show multimedia content, ask whether it is appropriate to deliver that multimedia content through PowerPoint, considering the quality of other available alternatives.

Here's an example. Suppose that you're revamping a customer service seminar in which you use a PowerPoint slide show throughout the daylong session. You want to add a 10-minute videotape that demonstrates service attitudes in a humorous way, so you buy limited rights for the clip. You're licensed to present the material digitally, so you think about capturing the video into an *.AVI file and playing it back from one of your PowerPoint slides. In doing so, you wouldn't have to set up a great deal of new hardware (such as a VCR, projection unit, or big-screen TV).

In this situation, however, using PowerPoint to deliver a 10-minute video clip doesn't meet the appropriateness test; it would fall into the category of "too much" multimedia for a slide show to handle. The VCR would present the video clip at a greater color depth, at a full frame rate, with a full screen, and with high-fidelity, perfectly synchronized sound. To achieve similar results with PowerPoint and an AVI file, you would need a $20,000 delivery computer and a massive external hard disk array. You'd also have to spend a fair amount of time capturing and compressing the analog tape to a digitized video format.

The better way to deliver longer video clips (the definition of "longer" changes as PC hardware continues to advance) is through a vehicle other than a PowerPoint slide show using digitized AVI files. Slide show moral: Consider whether your presentation will be more effective by delivering demanding multimedia content in more traditional ways, without funneling it through PowerPoint.

The SNAFU Factor

Look back at the example in the previous section. You may wonder if you could use PowerPoint to control the VCR (through an MCI driver), as discussed in Chapter 12. This would be more appropriate than digitizing the video, but you still have to ask yourself what the benefits and risks would be.

Is it a big deal to pause your PowerPoint slide show and hit the Play button on an actual (versus a virtual) VCR? Probably not. Are you guaranteed compatibility between the MCI driver on the notebook PC and the particular VCR you'll be using to present? That could be a tough question to answer, especially if you're renting or borrowing the VCR. And what if the VCR goes out on you? Can you obtain a same-model replacement easily?

To determine whether you may have too much multimedia content in a PowerPoint show, think about the SNAFU factor. (SNAFU stands for Situation Normal, All Fouled Up. Actually, it stands for something slightly different, but you get the idea.) How many elements in your multimedia presentation have to come together perfectly for everything to work?

If you plan to connect your delivery PC's sound card to a meeting room's amplifier and speaker systems, not too much can go wrong if you carry along a couple of different cables and connectors. If, however, you plan to play back AVI clips on an active-matrix LCD panel and overhead projector (both of which you're renting for the day), you could have problems. The LCD panel may not have a video input; it may not be fast enough to handle your frame rate; and, it may not handle enough simultaneous colors for the video to look good. (Chapter 18 considers such issues in more detail.)

We observed a good example of the SNAFU factor at a demonstration in Denver, held by a high-end graphics workstation company known for their capable hardware and confident marketing attitude. The presenters had a van-load of equipment to demonstrate (probably half a million dollars' worth), a roomful of potential customers for their $70,000 computers, some very sophisticated multimedia demos, and highly trained technicians — and those technicians couldn't get *any* of it to work right, after making the audience wait two hours while they doggedly tried to synchronize the audio and video. We took this as an important lesson in how *not* to make a presentation! (And Emily decided to keep her Macintosh.)

You can minimize the SNAFU factor's importance by allocating more setup time before your presentation and by carrying spares of key multimedia components (sound card, video card, cables, and so on). If your setup time is limited, however, and you won't necessarily have access to replacement hardware that meets your PC's demands, don't rely too heavily on multimedia clips in your slide show. Ask yourself this last question: If the multimedia support hardware won't work at all, can you still present an effective slide show? If you're using multimedia for accents, you will. If you're relying on it almost exclusively to convey your primary message, you won't.

Finally, here's a design tip: Put "big" multimedia content (such as AVI clips) on their own slides. That way, if you do hit a SNAFU right before show time, you can quickly hide those slides so that PowerPoint will skip over them, and the audience may never know what they've missed.

Summary

Use multimedia by all means! But use it sparingly, wisely, and prudently. Remember, though, that Microsoft didn't design PowerPoint for multimedia playback; you're better off playing to PowerPoint's strengths (text and still graphics) while you apply multimedia clips as accents.

The more unique or startling a special effect, the less frequently you should use it if you want to achieve maximum impact when you do.

Remember that your audience isn't as impressed with PC multimedia technology as you may be, so never use video clips just for the sake of adding video to a presentation — only use them when they truly help communicate a message!)

Keep in mind that presentation hardware may limit the effectiveness of any video, animation, or sound clip you use, and that the delivery hardware's limitations can be magnified by an auditorium's big screens and heavy-duty sound systems. Is alternative analog technology more appropriate for more demanding multimedia selections? How many different pieces of equipment have to work just right for your slide show to present its multimedia clips without a hitch? Can you still deliver your message if your sound card dies midway through the show? The answers will help you determine the difference between "too much" and "just enough."

Championship basketball coach Pat Riley wisely observed that although a team needs to develop its own approach (or philosophy) to the game at game time, it all comes down to execution — putting the pieces together and delivering when it counts. A great-looking PowerPoint slide show can still flop if you don't carry it off with efficiency, confidence, and panache. In Part IV, therefore, we focus on execution: preparing and delivering the cool slide shows that you've created so that all your hard work up to that point truly pays off.

PART IV

PRESENTING YOUR SLIDE SHOWS

Part IV concerns itself with preparing and delivering your presentation. This part covers moving PowerPoint files between computers, getting your presentation hardware ready for action, tuning PowerPoint for speed, handling troubleshooting situations, and applying some presentation tips for the day of the show.

Transporting PowerPoint Files

17

In This Chapter

Transporting a slide show to a PC that doesn't have PowerPoint installed

Using PowerPoint 7 and 8's Pack-and-Go wizard

Handling different versions of PowerPoint and Windows on development and delivery PCs

Transporting a slide show to a Macintosh user

Using a delivery PC with a different graphics display configuration

Transporting a slide show that's too big to fit onto a single diskette

This chapter offers several tips for moving your finished slide show from a *development* PC (that is, one you use to create the presentation) to a *delivery* PC (one you use to deliver your show).

Rarely is the development machine the same as the delivery machine for a PowerPoint slide show. As a result, you must move your work from one computer to another. You also may occasionally have to send your slide show to colleagues, customers, or managers, so they can view it directly on their PCs.

You'll meet a few challenges when moving your PowerPoint presentations between computers:

- The delivery machine may not have PowerPoint installed already, or it may not have enough disk space to load a full version of PowerPoint.
- The delivery machine may run a version of PowerPoint that is different from the version you run on the development PC.
- The delivery machine may run a different version of Windows. You may have created your presentation with Windows 95, but many notebooks still run Windows 3.*x*. The opposite situation is also possible.

- The delivery machine may be a Macintosh, running PowerPoint 4 for the Mac.
- The graphics setup may be different. For example, you may develop your presentation at 800 × 600 resolution, but the delivery notebook may only be capable of 640 × 480 resolution.
- Your PPT file may not be able to fit onto a single diskette. (You can almost bank on this being the case with Versions 4 and 7!)

Fortunately, with some planning and a little sleight of hand, you can meet these challenges gracefully. In this section, we look at them one at a time.

The Delivery PC Doesn't Have PowerPoint

If the delivery PC doesn't have PowerPoint, you'd think the easiest solution would be to install it. Delivery PCs, however, are often notebooks with limited (and expensive) disk space. You may not want to purchase another PowerPoint license for the delivery PC or spend the time installing it.

Fortunately, you don't need to install the complete PowerPoint program onto the delivery machine. Just install the appropriate PowerPoint Viewer utility, which is much smaller than the full program and also easier to use.

The Version 4 Viewer

version 4

To install and run the PowerPoint 4 Viewer on the delivery PC, follow these steps:

1. Create a copy of the original Viewer diskette (number 11). Don't put anything else on the copied Viewer diskette. You have Microsoft's blessing to use it on as many machines as you want.
2. Put the diskette into the delivery PC's disk drive and run VSETUP from that drive to install the Viewer application onto the delivery PC's hard drive.
3. Double-click the Viewer icon to run the program. Choose the PPT file you want and then click the Show button (Figure 17-1).

tip

The PowerPoint 4 Viewer can't handle branched presentations. You can, however, automatically run several PPT files in succession by creating a text file with the name format *.LST. This "list file" should contain the full filenames of the PPT files you want to run one after another, each on a separate line. Specify the list file you want to run in the Viewer dialog box instead of a PPT file.

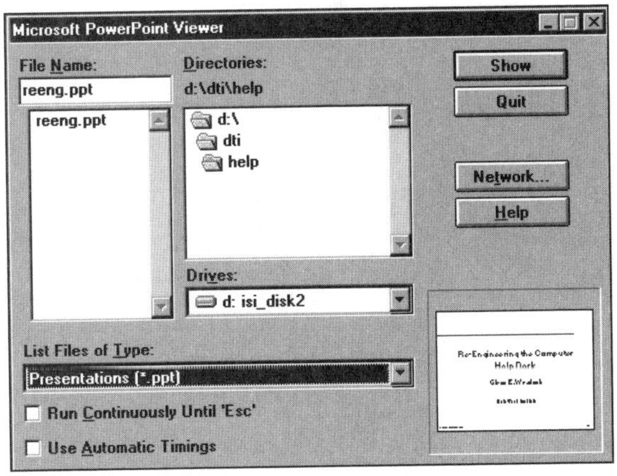

Figure 17-1: Running the PowerPoint 4 Viewer.

The Version 7 and 8 Viewers

With PowerPoint 7 and 8, you don't have to go through a separate step to install the PowerPoint Viewer. Just run the Pack-and-Go wizard; it conveniently bundles the Viewer with the slide show.

To run the Pack and Go wizard, follow these steps:

1. Select File⇨Pack And Go.
2. Follow the prompt screens to specify the presentation you want to transport and the destination device (for example, drive A).
3. Decide if you want to choose the Include Linked Files option (Figure 17-2). You don't need to do this if you only have text and graphics; you *do* need to do this if you have one or more linked AVI movies in your slide show, as they're not part of the PPT file.
4. Decide if you want to choose the Embed TrueType Fonts option (Figure 17-2). The safest choice is to check this option just in case the delivery PC doesn't have all the fonts you've used, but doing so will increase the file size somewhat.
5. At the next screen, click Include PowerPoint Viewer (or Viewer for Windows 95 or NT in Version 8).
6. At the final screen, click the Finish button. If you're saving to diskette, add diskettes as prompted by the wizard.

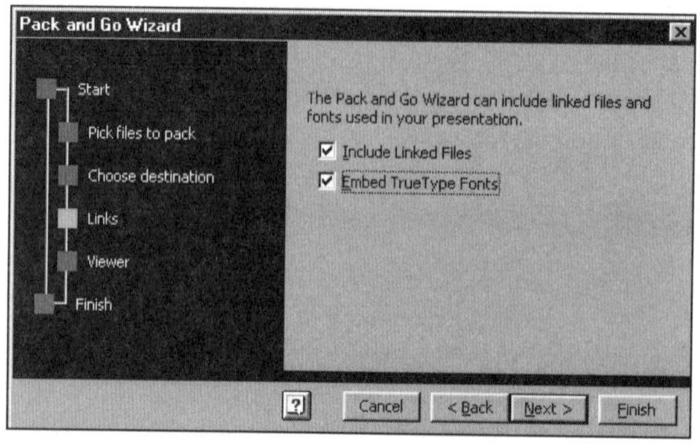

Figure 17-2: Running Version 8's Pack-and-Go wizard makes it convenient to include linked multimedia files and to embed TrueType fonts.

At the delivery PC, installing the presentation and the Viewer is a simple affair. The diskette contains a file named PNGSETUP.EXE, which, when you run it, automatically installs both the Viewer application and the presentation (which is stored in a *.PNG file).

tip

Microsoft has released an updated, faster, and more reliable 32-bit version of the Version 7 Viewer (Figure 17-3); it's available free as PPTVW32.EXE from Microsoft's online sources. To automatically have the Pack-and-Go wizard bundle the new Viewer with your slide show files, install this version over the old Viewer.

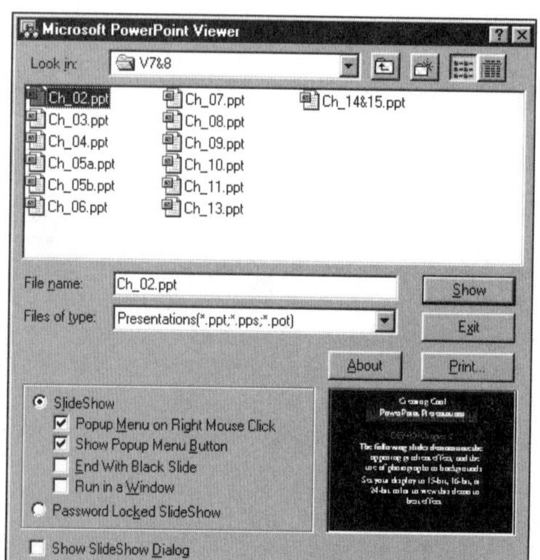

Figure 17-3: Version 7 Viewer's 32-bit release is faster and free for the downloading. Clicking the About button reveals options only available through command-line switches, such as /L for continuous looping.

warning: The Version 7 Viewer does not have the list file capability of the Version 4 Viewer.

version 8: PowerPoint 8's Pack-and-Go wizard bundles the PowerPoint 7 Viewer, if you tell it to include the viewer, and saves your PPT file to Version 7 format. Watch for the Version 8 Viewer, which should be available by mail and on Microsoft's Web site 90 days after Office 97 ships. After you install the Version 8 Viewer, the Pack-and-Go wizard will use it instead of the older one and will save your PPT file in the Version 8 format.

The PowerPoint Versions Are Different

If different versions of PowerPoint run on delivery and presentation PC's, problems can arise. Consider the following four scenarios.

From Version 8 to Version 7

You develop a slide show on PowerPoint 8 and need to present it on a delivery PC running Version 7. You have two options:

- Select File⇨Save As and specify **PowerPoint 95 & 97 Presentation (*.ppt)** in the Save as Type: field. This special dual format is designed for cases where Version 7 users only need to open the file — not edit it.
- Select File⇨Save As and specify **PowerPoint 95 (*.ppt)** in the Save as Type: field. You can open, edit, and save the file from Version 7, but features unique to Version 8 will be lost.

In either situation, features unique to Version 8 won't work when the show is played back in Version 7. These features include animated chart elements, custom shows, Bézier curves (PowerPoint will approximate these with small straight lines), picture fills, perspective shadows, complex hyperlinks, and action settings. Therefore, it's smart to perform a trial run using Version 7, to see if any of the restrictions affect your particular slide show.

From Version 4 to Version 7 or 8

If the delivery machine is running PowerPoint 7 or 8, and you used PowerPoint 4 on the development machine, don't worry. PowerPoint 7 and 8 can read and display Version 4 files directly and will display a conversion message upon opening the file, as shown in Figure 17-4.

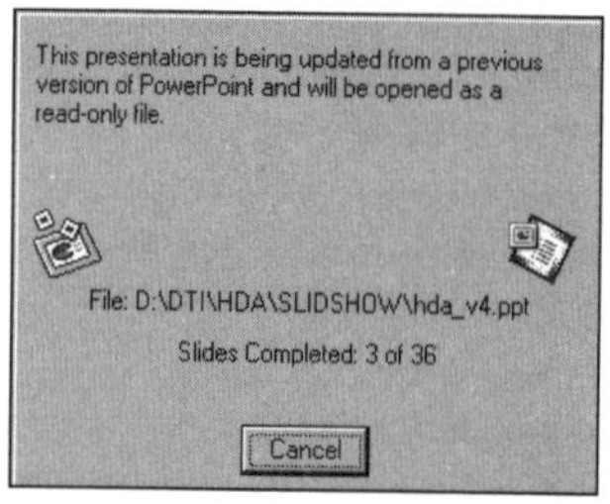

Figure 17-4: PowerPoint 7 (shown) and 8 can read PowerPoint 4 files directly with the File⇨Open command.

Although Versions 7 and 8 do a fairly good job of translating Version 4 files, they doesn't always get the positioning and alignment of text and graphics right. If possible, try to open your slide show from a PowerPoint 7 or 8 machine before you send it off, and then see if you have any problems.

From Version 7 or 8 to Version 4

If the delivery PC is running Version 4 and you've developed your presentation with Version 7 or 8, converting versions is a bit trickier. Version 4 can't read Version 7 or 8 files directly, so you must save your presentation as a Version 4 file before you transport it. Select File⇨Save As and specify **PowerPoint 4.0 (*.ppt)** in the Save as Type: field.

If you've used any features unique to Version 7 or 8 (such as any of the new gradient fills, two-color gradients, semi-transparent fills, 3-D effects, or animation effects), they won't make it into your Version 4 file. The only way to get these features to work right is to upgrade the delivery machine to Windows 95 and PowerPoint 7 or 8. Also, font embedding won't work.

From Version 7 or 8 to Version 3

If the delivery PC is running PowerPoint 3, we strongly suggest that you upgrade it to Version 4. If you can't upgrade, follow these steps (if the development machine is running Version 7):

1. Save the slide show from Version 7 in Version 4 format, as previously described.
2. Find a machine with PowerPoint 4 and then load the Version 4 slide show.
3. Save the Version 4 slide show to the Version 3 format.
4. Clean up any formatting problems on the delivery PC before giving your presentation.

If the development PC is running Version 8, the solution is easier: Select File⇨Save As and specify **PowerPoint 3.0 (*.ppt)** in the Save as Type: field.

Expect a fair number of clean-up problems when you go back two versions in this manner.

The Windows Versions Are Different

If you've developed a slide show with PowerPoint 4 and Windows 3.*x*, and the delivery PC is running Windows 95, you can run PowerPoint 7 or 8 on the delivery PC and open the Version 4 slide show read-only file as previously described. You may, however, want to install PowerPoint 4 (or at least the PowerPoint 4 Viewer program) on the delivery machine — that is, if you have the disk space. Windows 95 can run PowerPoint 4, and by configuring your PC this way, you won't have to learn the nuances of PowerPoint 7 or 8 when you deliver your slide show.

Make sure that you install PowerPoint 4 in its own directory if you already have PowerPoint 7 or 8 installed on the delivery PC.

The Delivery PC Is a Macintosh

When the delivery PC isn't a PC but is, instead, a Macintosh, you can still supply a PC-format slide show; the Mac version of PowerPoint should be able to read it. You have two challenges here: to get your file over to the Mac hard drive, and to get PowerPoint/Mac to read it properly.

Moving the file between PC and Mac

If the slide show fits onto a single diskette, moving it between PC and Mac platforms is rather easy. Newer versions of the Mac operating system can read PC-format 1.44MB diskettes directly. Earlier versions of the Mac OS may require the Mac user to copy the file from diskette by using Apple File Exchange (supplied with the original system software diskettes).

If you cannot fit the slide show onto a single diskette, you can use the preceding approach, but cut up the slide show into smaller slide shows and then have the Mac user reassemble it in PowerPoint for the Mac. You can also copy the file over the network (that is, if the target Mac is on the same LAN as the development PC) or over an information service (such as CompuServe).

Getting Mac PowerPoint to read the show properly

PowerPoint for the Macintosh Version 4 can read Windows PowerPoint 4 files, so if your development PC is running PowerPoint 7, you have the following two choices:

- Save the slide show as a PowerPoint 4 format file with File⇨Save As and then specify **PowerPoint 4.0 (*.ppt)** in the Save as Type: field.
- Provide your Mac user with the translator that enables PowerPoint 4 for the Mac to read PowerPoint 7 for Windows 95 files. This file is available on the *Office 95 Resource Kit* as Convert\Mac\Powerpnt\PP7TRANS.HQX; you must decompress it with the BinHex 4.0 utility. (A similar translator for PowerPoint 8 should be available 120 days after Office 97's ship date.)

Because Windows and the Mac OS use different fonts, the fonts in your presentation may not translate properly. You can avoid this problem the following ways:

- Use only *standard* Windows TrueType fonts, such as those in Table 17-1, which PowerPoint/Mac will convert to near-equivalents.
- Use PostScript fonts (with Adobe Type Manager) that are also present on the Mac computer.

Table 17-1: Font matching between PowerPoint/Mac and PowerPoint/Windows

Windows Font	Macintosh Font
Arial	Helvetica
Arial Narrow	Helvetica Narrow
Book Antiqua	Palatino
Bookman Old Style	Bookman
Century Gothic	Avant Garde
Century Schoolbook	New Century Schoolbook
Monotype Corsiva	Zapf Chancery
Monotype Sorts	Zapf Dingbats
Times New Roman	Times

The only sure way to avoid font problems is to load your Windows slide show onto a Macintosh yourself and then change font types as necessary on the Mac before you send your slide show to the Mac user.

The Graphics Setup Is Different

Slide show development PCs are usually full-featured desktops that run monitors at resolutions of 800 × 600 or 1024 × 768. Notebook delivery PCs, however, are often limited to a resolution of 640 × 480 .

Although PowerPoint is supposed to adjust for different screen resolutions, this adjustment can be imperfect. Therefore, we suggest you change your development PC's screen resolution to 640 × 480 through Windows SETUP (Version 3.*x*) or the Display control panel (Windows 95 — see Figure 17-5), and then see how your presentation looks. (You may have to restart Windows after you make the resolution change before it takes effect.) Make any adjustments necessary, save your file with a new name, and it will look good on the notebook system.

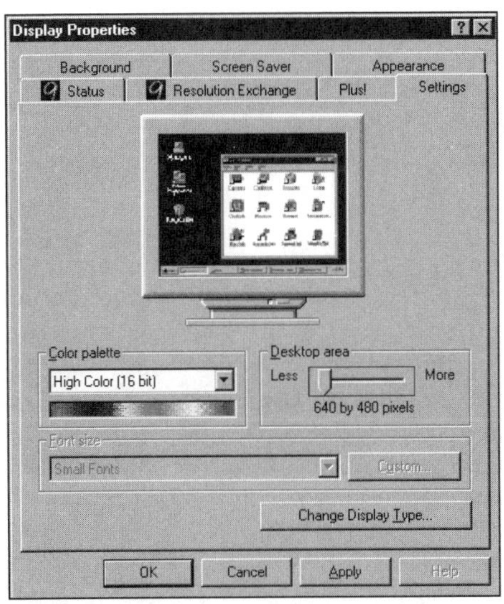

Figure 17-5: Changing the development machine's display resolution in Windows 95.

If you send the file to another person, you may want to include a *read-me* file, suggesting that he or she set the machine to 640 × 480 before viewing the show.

If the delivery PC can't display 256 colors, your gradients (and other graphic elements) probably won't look good. Most notebooks today can handle 256 colors, but they may be set at the factory with a plain old 16-color driver. Change drivers as directed by the notebook user manual or technical support, or add this suggestion to your "read-me" file (that is, if you're sending the slide show out for someone else to view).

The File Won't Fit on a Diskette

If you've applied almost any of the ideas in this book for jazzing up your presentations, chances are your PPT file will be too large to fit onto a single diskette, because it contains bitmap graphics, sound files, movies, and so on.

If you have PowerPoint 7 or 8, the solution is simple. Use the Pack-and-Go wizard as described earlier in this chapter. The wizard spreads your slide show over as many diskettes as necessary, and it reassembles everything on the destination machine when you run PNGSETUP. Version 8 compresses files automatically, resulting in smaller files than the Version 7 Pack-and-Go wizard creates.

PowerPoint 4 doesn't have the Pack-and-Go wizard; you'll have to figure out another way to get your slide show onto diskette. The easiest way is to use the shareware PKZIP and PKUNZIP utilities (see Appendix A).

Sometimes, simply compressing the PPT file with a command such as **PKZIP -A SHOW.ZIP SHOW.PPT** produces a compressed archive that fits onto one diskette. Then you can just copy the archive to the delivery PC (via diskette) and decompress it on the hard drive with a command such as **PKUNZIP SHOW**.

If the compressed file is still too large for a floppy, you can create a multiple-diskette archive in PKZIP (a cool trick that many people don't know).

We discovered this technique when Glenn was on the road in New York and needed a file in Emily's office in Denver. The file was far too large to send via modem. We used PKZIP (Version 2.04g) and overnight mail; it worked like a charm. Just use the "-&" parameter on the PKZIP command line to enable diskette spanning. For example:

PKZIP -A -& A:\SHOW.ZIP C:\PPTFILES\SHOW.PPT

If you don't have PKZIP and you're in a crunch situation, break up your slide show into smaller pieces and save them as individual PPT files (each of which can fit onto a single diskette). Then, on the destination machine, you can reassemble the pieces into a single slide show (again using cut-and-paste). This approach is tedious, but it'll work in a pinch.

You can also use CompuServe (or another information service) to mail the PPT file to yourself (as a binary attachment to an e-mail message), and then retrieve it from CompuServe directly onto the target machine's hard drive. This technique presumes that you have CompuServe software and a modem on both the development and delivery machines.

Summary

In this chapter, you learned the following:

There are various ways to get your slide show from where you created it to where you'll present it (or to other machines for colleagues or customers to view).

Setting up the delivery machine to run the same version of PowerPoint is always preferable, but if you can't do so, be aware of possible conversion glitches and try to correct them before you make your presentation or pass the file off to others.

Use the PowerPoint Viewer and (with Versions 7 or 8) the Pack-and-Go wizard to reduce disk space requirements on delivery PCs without the full PowerPoint program.

In the next chapter, we take a closer look at the delivery PC's hardware setup and clue you in on some cool accessory hardware that can make your presentation more effective and convenient to deliver.

Presentation Hardware

18

In This Chapter

Why most portable PCs aren't up to the PowerPoint challenge

What to look for in PC presentation hardware

How to "hot-rod" a PC to boost performance

Pros, cons, and tips regarding large VGA monitors, TVs, LCD panels, and direct-projection devices

How to have 35mm slides made and how to make your own

Ways to break free of the stationary mouse

This chapter looks at the hardware setup of your presentation PC, as well as some equipment that you may connect to it at show time.

There's no way around it: The success of your show depends on the hardware you use — that means your presentation (or *delivery*) PC and everything you connect to it.

The biggest equipment problem PowerPoint presenters face is that although portable (laptop or notebook) PCs are convenient for delivering a slide show, they are usually less powerful than desktop computers in many characteristics, including CPU, RAM, disk, video, and so on. Whereas underpowered machines are fine for word processing, scheduling, and e-mail, they can really drain the "cool" out of a PowerPoint show, especially a show using some of the fancier features we explore in this book. This chapter offers some suggestions about what you need in a portable PC to start with and how you might be able to "hot-rod" notebook hardware if you can't get the PC you really need.

The second equipment concern is this: Will everything you connect to your PC work as it should? A wide variety of hardware is available on both the purchase and rental markets for everything from pointing devices to projection equipment. Even if you don't have much choice about what you'll be plugging into your notebook's ports, having a grasp of presentation gear is important, so that you can make the most of it. And if you *do* have some choices in the equipment you use, this chapter will help you evaluate your needs and make appropriate equipment selections. Appendix A provides contact information for the vendors mentioned here.

Presentation PCs: The Nerve Center

The little portable you probably will use for your slide presentation has several limitations from the start:

- The portable wasn't designed to run taxing software such as PowerPoint, but rather more mundane and less demanding programs, such as word processing, e-mail, modem communications, and Solitaire.
- The high cost of miniaturization is usually offset by major compromises in performance to achieve a reasonable total cost.
- Your notebook probably isn't very accommodating when it comes to upgrading hardware components to higher-performance alternatives. And if such upgrades are even possible, they're likely to cost you much more than they would on a desktop PC.

We look at notebook hardware from two viewpoints: what you should try to obtain in terms of *base capabilities,* and what you can try to add through *hardware upgrades.*

tip

If you're using PowerPoint 8's View on Two Screens feature (Slide Show⇨View on Two Screens), you'll be running the slide show on your notebook but using another PC (notebook or desktop) to drive the display your audience sees. This feature is handy because you can set up your PC to display screens that the audience won't see — such as speakers' notes, Meeting Minder, and Slide Meter — by right-clicking your screen in Slide Show mode to bring up the Stage Manager.

View on Two Screens mode requires that both PCs be running PowerPoint 8 and have a null-modem serial cable connecting their COM ports. From the hardware speed standpoint, the PC controlling the slide show is more important than the one driving the audience display.

Base capabilities

Base capabilities are the notebook's sales-sheet specs — what the portable consists of as a *stock* machine, before any upgrades. These capabilities include the following:

- **CPU.** To run PowerPoint at a reasonable speed, you need at least a quick 80486DX (66 MHz or higher) or a Pentium CPU. You do NOT need a

Pentium Pro; this microprocessor is optimized for a full 32-bit environment such as Windows NT and, when running Windows 3.*x* or Windows 95, doesn't perform much better than the regular Pentium at the same chip speed.

- **RAM.** You need RAM for several things. First, you have to load the operating system; plan on needing approximately 4MB for Windows 3.*x* and 6MB for Windows 95. Next, you have to load PowerPoint, which is a big program; plan on 3MB for Version 4, 6MB for Versions 7 and 8, and 2MB for either version of the PowerPoint Viewer. Third, PowerPoint loads upcoming slides into memory so they can appear more quickly and smoothly. Allow an extra 2–4MB for this purpose. Fourth, you'll want some disk caching, especially if your slide show plays multimedia files; plan on using 1–2MB for this purpose. Add it all up, and you're looking at 16MB as a base requirement and 24–32MB as the desirable amount of RAM to have.
- **Disk.** Capacity isn't normally your biggest concern here; you can always offload some unnecessary software to a network or backup device to free up the room you need. Here you're more worried about speed, especially if you have digital video or animations linked into your slide show. Look for a disk with at least 128K of onboard cache memory, an 11-millisecond or lower average access time, and an EIDE (Enhanced Integrated Drive Electronics) rather than IDE interface for faster transfer rates.
- **Video.** Video is the biggest downfall of most notebooks, which cut corners by offering unaccelerated graphics. Here you are looking for a graphics accelerator chip, such as an S3 or Mach processor, to turbocharge your display operations. Avoid a simple (and slow) *frame buffer* video circuit.
- **Power Supply**. If you plan to travel outside the U.S., be sure your notebook has either a *universal* power supply that automatically adjusts to local line voltage, or a separate 220V power supply.

The preceding description sounds like a pretty expensive machine, and it probably is. If you are buying a notebook primarily for presenting, though, you can make some other tradeoffs to keep the cost down.

- **Weight.** Weight really won't be that much of a concern for a presentation PC; after all, you won't be holding it while you're presenting. You can save money by avoiding the ultra-light machines and working out a little to beef up the arm muscles for carrying the notebook on your trip, if you're traveling. (Don't ever check a notebook as baggage on a trip! Remember, the notebook is your presentation's nerve center.)
- **Size.** Being able to fit the delivery PC into a briefcase is secondary to raw speed, so you can get a machine that is a little bigger and clunkier to cut the price tag.
- **Battery Time.** You don't need a machine that will run for six hours on a single battery charge. The meeting room will have AC outlets! (But do take the battery along to serve as a cheap power backup while you are presenting.)

Also, consider the cost of the notebook in light of the importance of your presentation. If you are trying to raise money for a stock offering, win management approval for a $500,000 project, or sell a five-year consulting contract, spending $10K on a notebook is a drop in the proverbial bucket. Put it into perspective, take a deep breath, convince whoever holds the purse strings, and do it.

tip Don't overlook the leasing option. A week-long or month-long rental of a high-powered notebook may fit the budget better than an outright purchase. And finally, consider the "beg-or-borrow" approach: Sweet-talk a colleague with a fast portable who can spare it for a few days.

Hot-rodding possibilities

The preceding information is well and good, but suppose the boss has decreed that you will use a specific notebook, and the budget has no room for a new one with the base specifications you really need. There may be some ways you can finagle one or two "aftermarket" hardware components that the boss will approve to hot-rod that clunker:

- **CPU.** Check whether your notebook supports a CPU upgrade chip (Intel calls them *OverDrive* processors). For example, you may be able to upgrade an 80486DX/66 to a Pentium/83, which provides approximately 30 percent better performance, with a $200 OverDrive chip. Such an upgrade requires performing surgery on your machine, so get someone with experience to help if you've never worked on a circuit board.
- **RAM.** It's unfortunate that many notebooks have a fairly low physical limit on how much RAM they can hold. Unfortunate fact number two is that notebook RAM often uses a proprietary design that limits you in terms of the notebook vendor you can use (and the vendors, capitalists that they are, price their RAM upgrades to take full advantage of the situation). If your notebook can hold more memory, however, and if it can use off-the-shelf RAM modules from a mail-order supplier, adding RAM is a great idea.

tip If the PC supports *Static RAM* (also known as SRAM, or CPU cache), you may be able to add 64K or 128K for as little as $50 – $100 and enjoy a speed boost of 10 – 25 percent.

tip If you buy RAM by mail, use a credit card to avoid refund or replacement hassles if you receive defective merchandise.

- **Disk.** Again, your choices from the notebook vendor may be very limited, but don't let that fact stop you. Open your notebook's case and note the manufacturer and model of the hard drive. Then call a good mail-order disk drive house and ask what it can sell you that will fit and add speed. You may also be able to use a PCMCIA hard drive as an add-on, instead of replacing the notebook's primary disk.

- **Video.** About your only option in terms of upgrading video circuitry is to add an industry-standard video accelerator card, if the notebook provides an expansion slot. If your machine has no slot, there may be a docking station or bus expander available that you can buy to provide that flexibility. You'll probably have to get the docking station from your notebook's manufacturer and pay a premium for it, but you'll save big on the video board, which can be a type that works with any desktop PC. Always test new video drivers in advance. Also, taking along an assortment of drivers (including plain VGA) to the presentation is smart insurance.

Projection and Pointer Options

The equipment you use to display the slide show's image and navigate from slide to slide can either enhance or undermine your presentation.

Projecting a professional image

You can get your slide show up where your audience can see it in several ways:

- Connect your PC to a very large computer monitor.
- Connect your PC to a television screen by using a *scan converter,* a device that translates the VGA signal to television's NTSC signal.
- Use an LCD panel and overhead projector together to throw an image onto a white screen.
- Hook up the PC to a direct-projection device that works much like a big-screen projection TV. Projectors may be portable or built-in to the meeting room or auditorium.
- Have 35mm slides made from your PowerPoint file and use a standard slide projector.
- Use a Local Area Network to present your show on audience PCs.

TV screens and large monitors

The first two choices are suitable only for smaller groups (a dozen or so). ViewSonic, NEC, Sony, and others make very large (29-inch to 42-inch) VGA presentation monitors, and some even have built-in stereo speakers for connecting to your PC's sound port. Alternatively, you can go with a big-screen TV (such as those made by Mitsubishi) and put a scan converter (for example, VideoLogic) between your PC and the television to translate the video signals to television signals. The VGA presentation monitors almost always provide a clearer picture than the TV-plus-converter solutions, although they may be less readily available than big TVs.

When selecting large VGA monitors, consider the following seven criteria:

- **Brightness.** The brighter the monitor, the better. You can always turn the brightness down, but you can't always get the monitor as bright as you'd like. Monitor brightness (measured in footlamberts) is very important when working in rooms that are already very bright.
- **Contrast.** Contrast is the difference between pure black and pure white as displayed on-screen. The minimum acceptable ratio for a professional graphics user is 7:1, though greater contrast levels are available and desirable.
- **Tracking.** Tracking is the balance between the strength (or luminance) of the red, green, and blue electron guns that light up the screen. If you feed each gun the same signal, they should all illuminate the screen phosphor to the same extent. Tracking problems show up as a color cast favoring one color or another. Look for less than a 4 percent variance between R, G, and B at the worst point in a good monitor.
- **Linearity.** Linearity measures how well the monitor follows orders to display a particular color at a particular intensity level. For example, if the PC tells the monitor to display a 25-percent gray, does it actually do that or does it display a 30-percent gray that's 5 percent too bright? High-quality monitors don't vary more than 4 percent between signal intensity and displayed intensity.
- **Convergence.** Ideally, the R, G, and B guns should hit the same exact point on the screen for every pixel. In reality, however, the points where they hit don't perfectly coincide. Misconvergence is measured in tenths of millimeters; the less misconvergence, the better.
- **Distortion.** That is, *geometric* distortion — are lines straight, are squares square, are circles round? Distortion needs to be measured at the corners of the screen as well as in the center. You want a monitor that has less than 1⁄16-inch distortion at the worst point (usually the corner).
- **Glare.** Glare can be minimized by manipulating the placement of the monitor and of any local light sources, but filters can help if glare persists.

LCD panels

If you get more than 15 or 20 people in a room, large monitors and TVs just aren't large enough for everyone to see what is taking place. You can achieve a much larger image with an *LCD panel* that connects to your notebook's VGA port and then sits on top of an overhead projector.

LCD panels have come a long way from the pioneering Kodak Datashow used several years ago, which projected a pale yellow image that faded into oblivion when the panel heated up. They're brighter, more colorful, and much lighter. Tremendous variation exists between models, however. Most good ones ($2K to $6K; vendors include nView and Sharp among others) can handle a wide range of analog colors (from *high* color, or thousands of colors, to *true* color, or millions of colors). The big differences are in brightness and image size.

tip

Brightness and image size are actually *inversely related* to each other. That is, you can always achieve a bright image by placing the projector close to the screen and making the image very small. So, when comparing LCD panels, set them up on the same model overhead projector and position them to project the same size image. This way, you can get a true luminosity comparison.

Here are a few tips for LCD panel users:

- Get the highest-intensity overhead projector you can lay your hands on, but in no event get anything less than 400 watts. Even the best LCD panels cut the projector's intensity way down by the time light gets through the panel. There is no such thing as too bright an image.
- Make sure that the LCD panel uses active-matrix technology. These panels are faster, brighter, and more colorful. They also use three separate transistors (RGB) for each pixel, so they're more expensive.
- If you can arrange for a power conditioner (such a small battery backup unit), put your LCD panel on it. LCD panels seem to be sensitive to voltage fluctuations.
- Position the projector so that it doesn't block anyone's view. Sit in every chair ahead of time to verify clean lines of sight.
- You will always make a compromise between image size and brightness. Put the projector and LCD panel on a separate, small table so that you can move them in and out relative to your screen. Set the distance so that the image is just big enough to be easily seen by viewers in the back of the room. If you make it too large, the luminosity per square foot goes down, and you end up having to turn off all the lights for people to see it, at which point they won't be able to take any notes.
- If the LCD panel controls run on a battery, take along a spare battery. And always know where you can get a replacement lightbulb for the overhead projector.

Direct projection devices

Direct projection devices, which shoot an image onto a screen much in the same way that front-projection big-screen TVs do, can offer the biggest and brightest images, but they have their "gotchas" as well. We were doing a technical seminar in London a year ago and had a fairly large group, about 45 people, so we rented a couple of roll-around Barco projection units. The image quality was great, but it took the technician about an hour and a half to make all the adjustments (alignment, focus, conversion, pincushioning, and so on) to get it ready. Then, at lunchtime, somebody bumped one of the units and moved it a few inches out of position, and we never did get the display just right after that. We have had similar experiences in the United States with other Barco and Sony projectors.

Our suggestion is that if you're going to use direct-projection devices, find out whether they require a great deal of delicate fiddling to set them up correctly — and whether they require another round of fine-tuning if they get bumped slightly out of position. The latest generation of portable projectors from companies such as Epson, Panasonic, Proxima, and Sharp produce good images without a great deal of fussing. Although these products are much bulkier than LCD panels and usually more expensive, too, they throw more light on the screen, and you don't have to worry about getting a separate, high-intensity overhead projector.

Of course, you may be presenting in a venue that has projectors built into the ceiling or permanently installed in a projection booth at the rear of the room. Barco and Electrohome are common brands. Focus and alignment shouldn't be a problem with permanent projectors; just make sure that a standard VGA cable is available for you to use.

tip

Whatever method you choose for a computer-based presentation, make sure that your delivery PC can handle *simultaneous output* to the built-in screen and to an external projection device. Sometimes you need to issue a special command to activate both video "ports" on a notebook. One Compaq Contura that we've used has the annoying habit of automatically disabling the internal screen if it detects an external display device, so we have to manually activate both displays with every reboot.

35mm slides

The best non-computer-based presentation format is *35mm slides.* If you want the best possible picture quality in terms of resolution and brightness and don't care about giving up the elements of integrated motion and multimedia, no substitute compares with color slides. A 35mm slide presentation also frees you from the details of computer-to-projector interfacing and practically guarantees hardware compatibility because everyone has a slide projector.

versions 4, 7&8

Setting up PowerPoint to use 35mm slides as your presentation format is easy. Select File⇨Slide Setup (Versions 4 and 7) or File⇨Page Setup (Version 8) and choose 35mm Slides in the Slides Sized for: field to size your slides properly (Figure 18-1). You may have to do some reformatting because the aspect ratio of 35mm slides isn't the same as the aspect ratio of a VGA computer screen. Set PowerPoint's zoom factor to 100% and work in Slide view — things won't look right in Slide Show view.

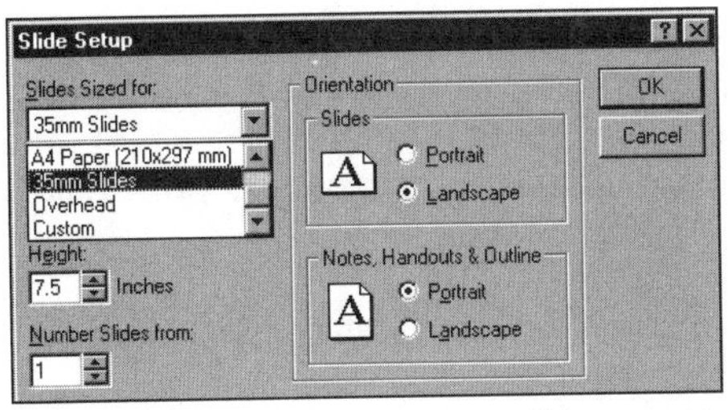

Figure 18-1: Sizing for 35mm slide output.

Many graphics-service bureaus throughout the country can create slides directly from your PowerPoint files. You pay more for faster service, but typically plan on spending around $5 per slide for a two-day turnaround. We like to modem files over to the service bureau to save time. We've been happy with Imagers in Atlanta, but you can use the Genigraphics wizard built in to PowerPoint if you want to use that service bureau — just select File➪Send to Genigraphics (Version 7) or File➪Send to➪Genigraphics (Version 8) and follow the prompts (Figure 18-2).

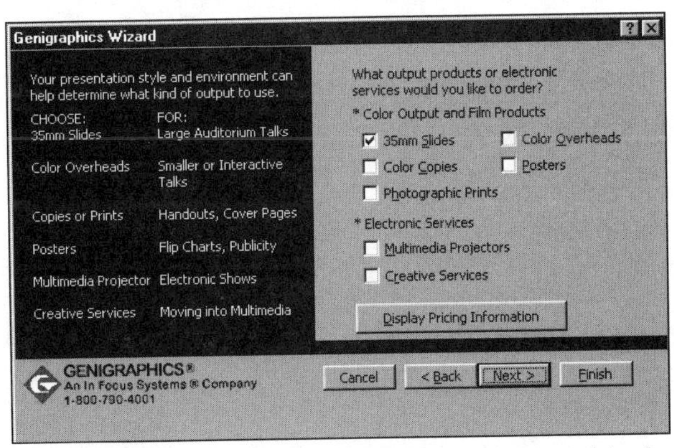

Figure 18-2: Sending your slide show to Genigraphics for processing is easy with the supplied wizard. The PowerPoint 8 version (shown) now provides pricing information.

You can also create your own slides if you have a *film recorder*. These devices create slide transparencies from digital files. They are built from a high-quality monitor and a 35mm camera in one enclosure. Film recorders make transparencies in a three-pass process, one pass each for the red, green, and blue components of the image. The process may take anywhere from two minutes to two hours, depending on resolution, image complexity, manufacturer, and file format. The resolution of the resulting transparencies is very high: *4K* resolution is 4096 x 2732, and *2K* resolution is 2048 x 1300.

These devices vary widely in both size and cost, but $5,000 is a good estimate for the smallest desktop units, whereas $40,000 gets you a high-end model the size of a medium-capacity photocopier. If you do a lot of slide shows or deal with extremely confidential information, a film recorder may be a good investment. Vendors include Agfa, Lasergraphics, Management Graphics, Mirus Industries, and Polaroid.

tip

Let the film recorder warm up for a few minutes before making your slides, for better color fidelity and consistency.

tip

When creating slides with a film recorder, use 2K rather than 4K resolution. These slides print four to five times faster and look just as good, unless you have some radial or linear gradient fills in your image, in which case the lower resolution causes banding — edges where colors change abruptly.

Networked presentations

versions 7&8

For the sake of thoroughness, we should mention the presentation conferencing capability in Versions 7 and 8. The presenter connects to audience PCs on the same local area network and then launches the slide show, which the audience can then view on their machines.

Although it sounds slick, this method of presentation is fairly time-consuming to set up and is limited in some serious ways. For example, you can't play any sound or video files on the audience PCs, though they play on the presenter's PC. And with Version 7, your LAN must be running the TCP/IP protocol, which rules out most NetWare sites. PowerPoint 8 can run presentation conferencing on NT Server networks but not on NetWare, and multimedia playback is still not available because of the considerable technical difficulties in synchronizing multimedia across the LAN.

Making your point

The better presenters don't plant their feet behind a podium and grow roots there. Rather, they walk around the front of the room and even wander up and down the aisles, especially during a long presentation. If that is your style, you don't want to be cramped by having to run back to your keyboard every time you want to advance a slide.

One of the presenter's best friends is the remote or *cordless* mouse, trackball, or tablet. These devices typically have two components: a receiver, which connects to the PC via the serial or mouse port, and a transmitter, which roams with you and runs on batteries. The transmitter and receiver communicate either by an infrared or a radio link. These devices are not terribly expensive (approximately $100) and they enable you to control your slide show from wherever you happen to be in the room. Here are some things to look for when shopping:

- **Range.** If you're presenting in a large room, you don't want a range-limited device inhibiting your clicking. Seventy-five feet isn't as far as you think it is.
- **Directionality.** Most remote mice nowadays don't require a direct line of sight to the host PC, but some infrared devices do. Radio-frequency (RF) devices never have a directionality problem.
- **Compatibility.** Modern notebooks often come with a built-in infrared port. Will the remote device work with it to simplify configuration and reduce cabling?

Some remote-control pointing device vendors include MindPath's Remote Control, Gyration's GyraPoint Pro, and Interlink's Remote Point Plus. The MindPath and Interlink products include programmable buttons in addition to the usual mouse movement and click controls.

Summary

Presentation hardware falls into two categories: the PC you use to deliver your show, and the projection and pointing equipment you connect to your PC's video and communications ports. The type of presentation hardware that you use can greatly influence your success, so keep the following factors in mind when choosing your hardware:

PowerPoint is a demanding program that taxes the capabilities of most notebooks. Try to beg for, borrow, buy, or rent a notebook with a Pentium CPU, at least 16MB of RAM, an 11ms EIDE hard drive, and accelerated graphics.

If you can't get the machine you want, upgrade the one you're with by adding an OverDrive processor, CPU cache, more RAM, and a faster hard drive.

If you use PowerPoint 8 and have access to two PCs, explore the View on Two Screens feature, so that you can see screen elements that your audience can't. Just remember to use the faster PC to control the slide show.

Connect your notebook to a high-luminosity projector, preferably one that doesn't require a great deal of fiddling, or use a combination LCD panel and high-intensity overhead projector. Then test the projection by viewing it from the back of the room. You will strike a compromise between image size and brightness.

35mm slides sacrifice motion and multimedia elements for great picture quality.

Use a pointing device that doesn't tie you to the PC but enables you to roam the room.

Now that you have a clear idea of what sort of delivery computer you need, how to rev it up a little by grafting in some hardware horsepower, and what to look for when considering projection and pointing equipment, take a look at the next chapter for how to tune the delivery PC for speed from the *software* standpoint.

Improving PowerPoint Speed

19

In This Chapter

Configuring DOS and Windows memory setups

Removing network support to free memory

Optimizing Windows disk performance with proper drivers and caching

Tuning the presentation PC's display settings

Activating Windows print spooling

Optimizing PowerPoint's bitmap and vector graphics

Changing PowerPoint transition speeds

Speeding up file conversion, spell-checking, and printing within PowerPoint

Upgrading to PowerPoint 7 and 8

This chapter provides several tips for coaxing the most speed from your development and presentation systems.

For all PowerPoint's great capabilities, it has become infamous among slide show creators for its sluggishness. On a recent video shoot (during which we were capturing graphics directly from a PC), we spent 10 percent of our time waiting for PowerPoint to load slide shows and move from one slide to the next. Delays are expensive in a TV studio, but they're deadly when you're trying to create a presentation that flows smoothly from one idea to the next. The last thing you want is for you and your audience to have to wait for PowerPoint to catch up to you. Cool slide shows must be fast.

Although presentation speed is the most important aspect of improving performance, your time *developing* slide shows is valuable, too. Some of the tips in this chapter apply equally to presentation and development platforms; some specifically target one or the other.

The chapter begins with a discussion of hot-rodding the underlying Windows platform, and the second part of this chapter deals with specific PowerPoint tips.

Turbocharging Windows

To a large extent, PowerPoint's speed is Windows' speed. If you don't tune Windows for performance, you can't do much to make PowerPoint go fast. This first section presents the most important step you can take to make sure that PowerPoint is running on a finely tuned Windows platform. Here's a list of the areas the section covers:

- DOS memory
- Virtual memory
- Network drivers
- Disk drivers and caching
- Display configuration
- Print configuration

This chapter covers *software* setup; if you're skipping around in the book, you may want to read the preceding chapter too, which covers hardware issues.

DOS memory

Windows 3.*x* runs faster if you have at least 580K RAM free in conventional memory. Open a DOS window and type **MEM** to see how much is free on your system. If you have less than 580K, try to free up some memory by loading EMM386.EXE in CONFIG.SYS and using the DEVICEHIGH and LOADHIGH commands to move drivers and TSRs out of conventional memory and into upper memory. Although you can read entire books on this subject (see Appendix A), you can also run an automatic memory optimization utility (such as DOS 6's MEMMAKER program). Such utilities often get you to where you want to go.

For Windows 95, however, *don't* run EMM386 in CONFIG.SYS unless you have some special reason to do so. It isn't as necessary here because Windows 95 doesn't use as much conventional memory as Windows 3.*x*, and our tests suggest that EMM386 can slow down disk performance up to 10 percent under Windows 95.

Virtual memory

Windows uses a disk-based *swapfile* as a substitute for RAM when physical RAM is exhausted. Swapfile optimization is key for good Windows performance, especially on PCs that have less than 16MB of memory.

In Windows 3.*x*, use a permanent swapfile rather than a temporary one. Permanent swapfiles cause Windows to load faster, run faster, and exit faster. When you size the swapfile for PowerPoint — a famous memory hog — a good rule of thumb is that you should end up with a total of 24MB total memory (RAM plus swapfile space). For example, if you have an 8MB PC, you would create a 16MB permanent swapfile. Large slide shows may need more: To set the swapfile size and type, select Control Panel⇨386 Enhanced⇨Virtual Memory⇨Change.

Windows 95 dynamically resizes its swapfile as necessary, and you don't need to choose between temporary versus permanent. Make sure, though, that you have virtual memory turned on. In the System control panel's Performance tab, click the Virtual Memory button and Let Windows manage my virtual memory settings (recommended). You may need to change the setting that specifies which hard drive Windows 95 will use, if you have a PC with two local hard drives. Windows 95 defaults to the drive from which Windows 95 starts, which may not be the faster drive. You can also specify a minimum swapfile size of 8MB or more if you have plenty of disk space; doing so allows Windows 95 to run a little faster, as the reserved minimum swapfile area acts like a "permanent" swapfile and cannot become fragmented.

Network drivers

Both Windows 3.*x* and Windows 95 run fastest when they load only the minimum number of drivers necessary for the tasks at hand.

If you won't be using a network during your slide show, configure Windows so that it's not loading network drivers. Windows for Workgroups puts these settings in a Network Setup icon; Windows 3.1 enables you to rerun SETUP.EXE and choose No Network Installed; and Windows 95's Network control panel lists all the loaded network software in the Configuration tab, where you can click on a component and then the Remove button (Figure 19-1). Reloading network support later is simple, but you want to reserve as much memory as possible for the PowerPoint program and your slide show to minimize the use of slow virtual memory.

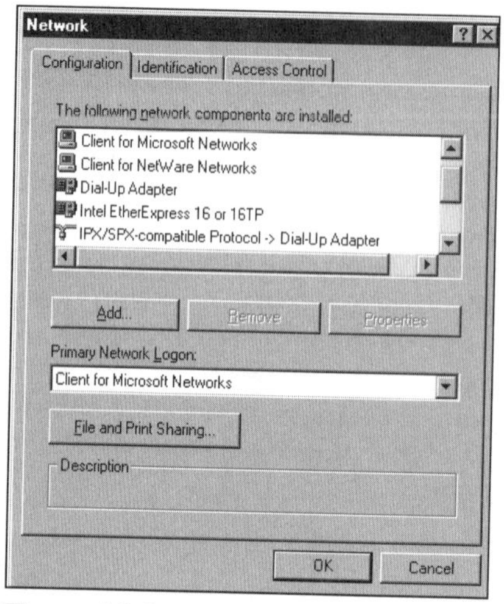

Figure 19-1: Network drivers appear on the Configuration tab in Windows 95's Network control panel.

Disk drivers and caching

Disk performance is important because PowerPoint's data files are usually large and you want your PC to be able to read them as quickly as possible. PowerPoint also uses many Dynamic Link Libraries (DLL's) that it must read from the disk. Here are three tips on Windows 3.*x*, three more on Windows 95, and one that applies equally to both.

If you run PowerPoint 4 on Windows 3.*x*, use the following disk performance tips:

- Run SmartDrive
- Use FastDisk
- Use 32-bit file access

SmartDrive, the cache program that comes with both DOS and Windows, can help PowerPoint read your PPT files more rapidly, but you don't want to allocate too much memory to SmartDrive because you'll starve PowerPoint. Usually, SmartDrive's default sizes work just fine; just make sure that you have a line in AUTOEXEC.BAT that runs SMARTDRV.EXE.

If you use Windows 3.1, make sure that your PC is compatible with Windows' FastDisk (or 32-bit disk access) feature; you can do this by checking your PC's documentation or calling the vendor. If it is compatible, activate FastDisk; it's hidden in the 386 Enhanced control panel in the Virtual Memory window. FastDisk allows Windows to use the disk controller more efficiently.

If you use Windows for Workgroups 3.11, try using 32-bit file access, as well. This setting is also in the Virtual Memory window (Figure 19-2). Nearly all IDE and EIDE disk drives work with these features activated. Set the cache size to a value that works well for you; 1024KB usually works well on an 8MB machine and 2048KB usually works well on a 16MB machine. Don't load SmartDrive in AUTOEXEC.BAT anymore; the 32-bit file access cache is faster.

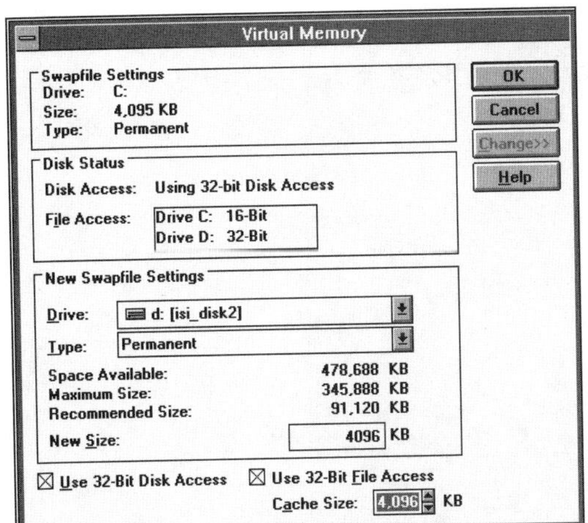

Figure 19-2: Using 32-bit disk and file access provides better speed in Windows for Workgroups 3.11.

versions 7&8

Here are three disk performance tips for readers who use PowerPoint 7 or 8 on Windows 95:

- Use protected-mode disk drivers
- Set the file system profile to "desktop"
- Reduce the CD-ROM cache size

First, check your Windows 95 system to see if you're using a 32-bit, protected-mode device driver for your disk drive. Run the System control panel's Performance tab and look for the notation `Your system is configured for optimal performance`. If you don't see this message, but you see a warning stating that `compatibility mode paging decreases performance`, then Windows 95 is *not* running your hard drive at maximum speed. Contact your disk drive manufacturer for a Windows 95 driver diskette.

Windows 95 has a little-known bug that reduces disk performance if you set the file system profile to anything but *Desktop*, so verify this setting, too. Run the System control panel's Performance tab, click File System, and set Typical role of this machine to Desktop Computer. You should also set the Read-ahead optimization to the maximum value.

If you won't use a CD-ROM for your presentation, but your notebook has a built-in CD-ROM drive, tell Windows 95 to use the least possible memory for caching the drive. Click the System control panel's Performance tab, click the File System button, and then choose CD-ROM. Set the Supplemental cache size to the smallest value, and then set Optimize access pattern to No read-ahead (Figure 19-3).

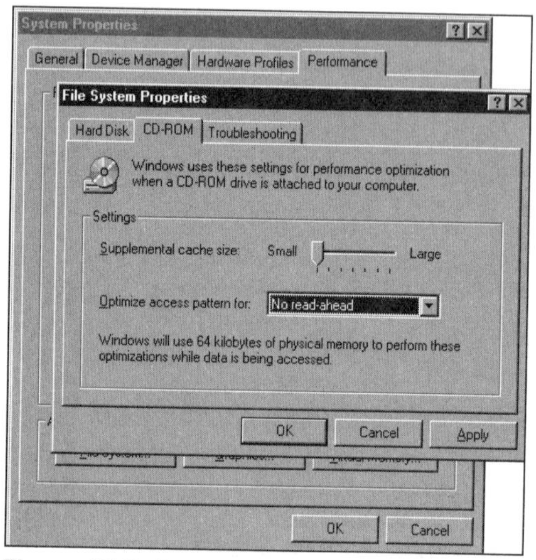

Figure 19-3: From the File System property sheet, you can reduce the memory Windows 95 uses for CD-ROM caching.

Although *disk compression* schemes (such as DriveSpace, Stacker, and so on) are commonplace on notebook machines (where hard drive space is more expensive), they exact a performance toll on the order of 5 to 15 percent. Upgrade notebook hard drives to higher capacities, if necessary, but *don't* use disk compression. And *don't* buy those bigger drives from the notebook manufacturer: they will cost two to three times what the same model costs from a reputable mail-order house.

Display configuration

Notebook PCs come with displays that can run at different color depths. The color depth is simply how many colors the display can show at one time. Your options may include the following:

- 4-bit color (16 colors at a time, or "VGA" color)
- 8-bit color (256 colors at a time)
- 15-bit or 16-bit color (thousands of colors at a time, or "high" color)
- 24-bit color (16.7 million colors at a time, or "true" color)

You can change these options in Windows 3.*x* with the SETUP program, or in Windows 95 with the Display control panel. Generally, the greater the color depth, the slower the display, so run the minimum color depth that makes your slides look good. For most PowerPoint presentations, that's 8-bit color.

Make sure that you use the latest display drivers for your presentation computer. For notebooks, use the drivers specifically designed for your PC, and you'll usually get the best speed. For example, if you're using a Toshiba notebook, download the latest video drivers from Toshiba's BBS, CompuServe forum, or Internet site. Windows video drivers (shipped with a notebook "out of the box") almost always run slower than the latest downloadable ones.

Print configuration

In Windows, "fast" printing means one of two things: fast return-to-application time (that is, how quickly you can resume working with your program), and fast total-elapsed time (that is, how many seconds go by between the moment you click Print and the moment the page emerges from the printer).

To get the fastest possible return-to-application time, activate Windows' spooling feature; it creates a disk file first and then copies printer data from the disk file to the printer in the background. Here's how to activate spooling:

- Under Windows 3.*x*, run the Printers control panel and make sure that you select the Use Print Manager check box.
- Under Windows 95, right-click the relevant printer and choose Properties⇨Details⇨Spool Settings⇨Spool print jobs so program printing finishes faster. For best speed, the Spool Data Format should be RAW for PostScript printers and EMF for most other types (see Figure 19-4).

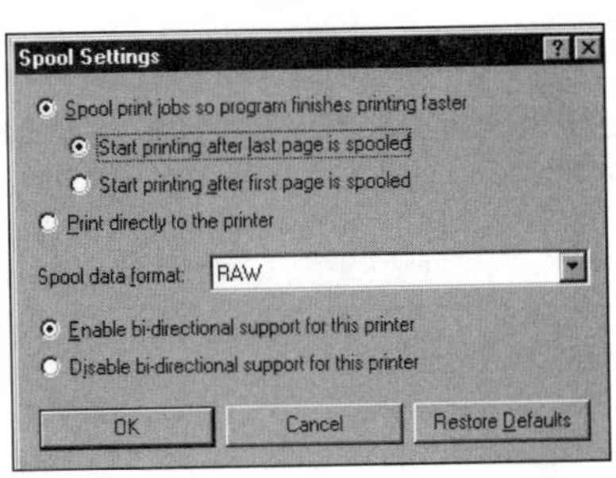

Figure 19-4: Setting Windows 95 print spooler options improves return-to-application time.

Turbocharging PowerPoint

Now that you know the essentials of tuning Windows 3.*x* and 95, you can concentrate on the PowerPoint settings that affect speed, in these five areas:

- Bitmap graphics
- Vector graphics
- Transitions
- Slide show development
- Upgrading

Bitmap graphics

versions 4, 7 & 8

Although bitmap graphics look great, too many of them (in a slide show) will slow down PowerPoint. You can use the following tricks to speed up such shows:

- If the show's looks don't suffer for it, try setting each bitmap to the same 256-color palette. If PowerPoint doesn't have to reset the palette for each slide, it runs faster. The best tool for this purpose is Equilibrium Technologies' DeBabelizer (see Appendix A). Because it only runs on the Macintosh platform, though, you'll have to do some file transfers over a network or via floppy. It's worth the trouble.
- If you use a bitmap for a gradient background, see if you can duplicate the effect with PowerPoint's gradient color tools (see Chapter 2). If you can, use the PowerPoint gradient instead of importing the bitmap.
- Break up the slide show where feasible. For example, if you know you'll be taking a break midway through your presentation, create two PPT files rather than one giant one. If PowerPoint can fit the whole PPT file into RAM, it runs much faster.

If you have some slides that you may not need to display, use the *branching* approach to break up the slide show. With branching, you include *hot links* (not the edible kind!) on certain slides from which you may want to jump to another set of slides. Chapter 21 looks at branching in more detail. For now, don't use branching in Version 4 if you know you will display all the slides in your presentation; PowerPoint takes its sweet time loading the slides in a branched PPT file. You have an excuse for the delay if someone in the audience asks for more details on a particular topic — "It so happens I have a few slides on that subject, if you can bear with me a moment" — but branching is too slow for general use. If you have Version 7 or 8, there are ways to speed up branching operations, as Chapter 21 explains.

Vector graphics

Complex clip art or drawing objects can drastically slow down PowerPoint. For example, we imported a detailed vector graphic of a network interface card for a networking seminar slide show, and it took PowerPoint 7 about 20 seconds to move to that slide. Very uncool! We simplified the graphic by ungrouping it and deleting objects (chips, traces, and so on) that were too small to see anyway. The slide now appears in 2 or 3 seconds. Moral: If it's too small to see, delete it!

Transitions

To control the speed of transitions, select Slide Show⇨Slide Transitions (Version 8), Tools⇨Slide Transitions (Version 7), or Tools⇨Transitions (Version 4). Often you can improve slide-to-slide performance on a slow computer by setting the transition speed to the maximum. Even then, however, you may find some transitions unacceptably slow, so do your own testing and use only those transitions that perform briskly.

Slide show development

This section helps you speed up the slide show development process in the following areas:

- Converting old PPT files to PowerPoint 7 or 8
- Spell-checking slide shows
- Printing speaker's notes, handouts, and slide-sorter thumbnails

versions 7&8

You've just upgraded from PowerPoint 4 to PowerPoint 7 or 8 for Windows 95, and you have dozens of PPT files you'd like to convert to the new version. Don't waste time converting those files one by one, by loading and resaving. Rather, use a little batch conversion utility from Microsoft; in Version 7, it's called PPCONV.EXE (Figure 19-5). The file you want for Version 7 is WT1230.EXE, available from the usual Microsoft sources (Internet, CompuServe, Microsoft Network, and so on), or you can copy the file PPCONV.EXE from the Office 95 Resource Kit CD-ROM. Put PPCONV.EXE wherever you want, and put THREED.VBX and VBOA300.DLL in your Windows SYSTEM directory. Then run PPCONV, make your list of files, specify a destination, and let 'er rip. For Version 8, a new version of the conversion utility is included in the Office 97 Resource Kit.

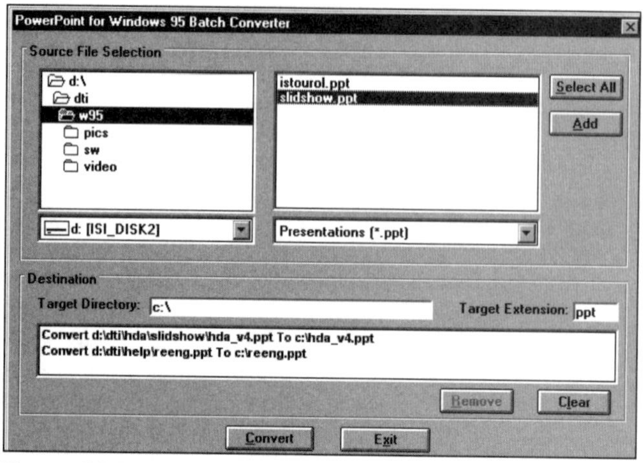

Figure 19-5: Converting PowerPoint 4 files en masse becomes possible with PPCONV.EXE.

If you're a good speller, you may want to improve the speed of your spell-checker. To do so, turn off Always Suggest in Tools⇨Options⇨Spelling (Version 8), Tools⇨Options⇨Edit (Version 7), or Tools⇨Options (Version 4). All you need is for the spell-checker to flag misspelled words so you can fix them on your own. Consult a good dictionary if you have any doubt.

Printing from PowerPoint can be painfully slow, especially slide show thumbnails (handouts). Here are some ways you can minimize delays.

If you want to simplify your slides for printing, Version 4 makes it easier than Version 7. You have two options in the Print dialog box: Black and White and Pure Black and White (Figure 19-6). Both options eliminate backgrounds, simplify color fills, outline borderless objects, and simplify text and lines to black; and both can cut your printing time in half. The only significant difference is that Black and White uses grayscale fills and Pure Black and White uses white for filled areas.

Here are some tips to speed up slide printing:

- If you print to a monochrome device (such as a black-and-white laser printer), check the box labeled Black and White; it optimizes printout appearance and, as a bonus, runs about 5 percent faster. Don't be confused; this option does *not* force all colors to black and white, as it did in Version 4. Perhaps Microsoft should have labeled it "Optimize for monochrome printer."

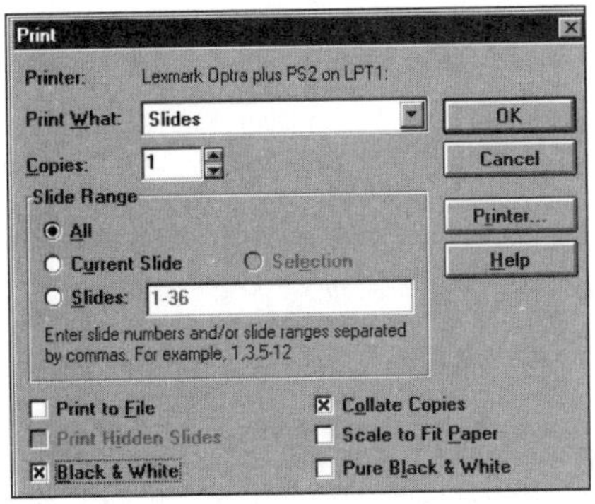

Figure 19-6: Simplifying slides improves printing speed in PowerPoint 4.

- Activate the Black-and-White View option in the Slide View mode by choosing View⇨Black and White (you can also use a toolbar button). Your presentation shifts to a black and white color scheme and a thumbnail of your original color presentation appears. Now, select Edit⇨Select All, right-click on any object, choose Black and White from the context menu, and choose an option that simplifies your slide (such as Black with White Fill — see Figure 19-7). Repeat this process for each slide you want to print and your PC will generate printouts much faster.

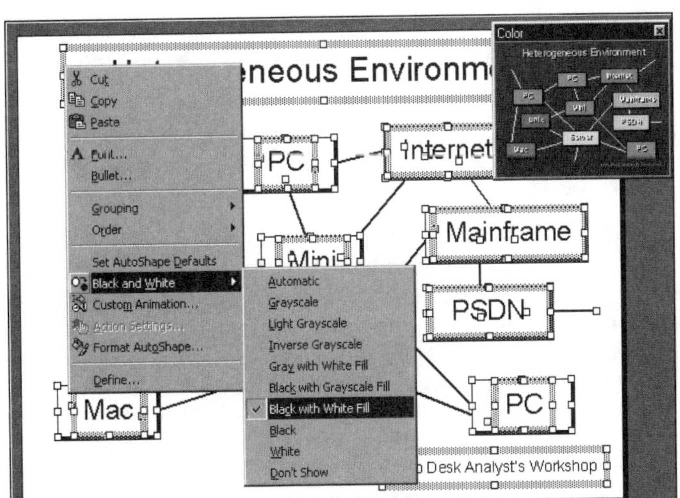

Figure 19-7: Removing fancy gradients in PowerPoint 8 by using Black and White Fill for faster printing.

Frustrated that PowerPoint 7 doesn't have the Pure Black and White printing option that was so convenient in Version 4? So were many other people, apparently, as Microsoft has provided an add-in for Version 7 that corrects the omission. The file is WT1249.EXE from the usual Microsoft online sources, and it adds the new print option to the File menu. (Yes, it would be more convenient on the Print dialog box, but at least it's available!) Version 8 builds this capability into the Print dialog box.

Here are a few more printing speed tips:

- Don't check the Collate option (it's Collate in Version 4) in the Print dialog box when you must print multiple copies; it's quicker to collate copies by hand. For example, two copies of a three-page printout requires *six* page downloads to the printer with the collation function on; the same printout only requires *three* page downloads with collation off because the printer can "remember" each page while it's printing multiple copies of it.
- Print at 300dpi rather than 600dpi, 800dpi, or 1200dpi for all drafts and for documents that your audience won't see. For example, 300dpi printing is typically 15 percent to 25 percent faster than 600dpi printing. Set the resolution in the Printer Setup dialog box in Windows 3.*x* and the printer property sheets in Windows 95.
- Go to the Slide Master and remove any defined background.
- If your printer supports both PCL and PostScript modes, you can generally get faster output using PCL, and you probably won't notice any difference in quality.

Upgrade

We'd be remiss in any discussion of speed if we didn't encourage you PowerPoint 4 users to take the plunge and upgrade to Windows 95 and PowerPoint 7 or 8. Both PowerPoint 7 and 8 run noticeably faster in almost every area (except clip art cutting and copying), but especially in the areas of printing and Slide Sorter view redraw (see Table 19-1 — it includes data reported by Microsoft, as well as some of our own testing). Versions 7 and 8 have implemented both functions in a separate "thread" of execution — that is, the functions run faster and you can do other things while they're processing.

If you've ever gnashed your teeth waiting for PowerPoint 4 to draw your slides in the Slide Sorter view, or print slide thumbnails, you'll appreciate the new versions' speed improvement in these areas.

The latest PowerPoint version loads and saves files incrementally, so that when you open a slide show in Version 8, you can begin work on early slides while the later slides are still loading. In addition, like most other Office 97 programs, Version 8 loads noticeably faster than Version 7.

Table 19-1: PowerPoint 7 speed improvement over Version 4 on the same hardware

Operation	% Faster
Open Typical Document	-7%
Open Complex Document	100%
Save Typical Document	184%
Save Complex Document	109%
Slide View Redraw (Typical Document)	57%
Slide View Redraw (Complex Document)	263%
Slide Sorter View Redraw (Typical Document)	189%
Background Print (Typical Document)	495%
Background Print (Complex Document)	4034%

tip

If you use the PowerPoint Viewer to present your slide shows, you may not know that the Viewer program that shipped with PowerPoint 7 is a slower, 16-bit program. In January 1996, Microsoft released an updated, 32-bit version of the Viewer; it's available free as PPTVW32.EXE from Microsoft's online sources. If you install the new Viewer, your presentations will be both quicker and more reliable (Figure 19-8). If you install it over the old Viewer (which we recommend), the Pack-and-Go wizard will automatically bundle the new Viewer with your slide show files. The same will be true for the Version 8 Viewer, expected to be released shortly after the commercial release of Office 97.

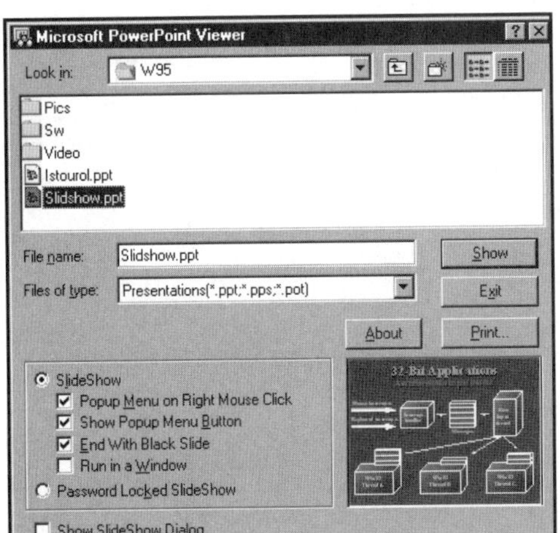

Figure 19-8: PPTVW32.EXE is the new high-performance viewer for PowerPoint 7.

Summary

This chapter discussed ways to fine-tune Windows and PowerPoint for better speed.

In Windows 3.*x*, provide at least 580K of conventional memory; use a permanent swapfile rather than a temporary one; unload network drivers; use FastDisk and SmartDrive, or even better, FastDisk and 32-bit file access; set the display to the lowest color depth that looks good; and use print spooling.

In Windows 95, avoid EMM386; let Windows manage the swap-file's maximum size, but set a minimum size if you have plenty of disk space; unload network drivers; use protected-mode disk drivers; set the file system profile to "desktop"; shrink the CD-ROM cache; set the color depth as low as you can; and use EMF spooling with PCL printers.

In PowerPoint itself, make presentations faster by breaking up the slide show where feasible; standardizing bitmaps to the same 8-bit color palette unless you need more accurate color; using PowerPoint gradients instead of bitmaps where they look the same; and adjusting transition speeds for your hardware.

For slide show development work, use PPCONV to speed up file conversions; turn off the spell-checker's suggestion feature; print as black-and-white where possible; and upgrade to PowerPoint 7 or 8 for faster printing and Slide Sorter redraws.

The next chapter provides several troubleshooting tips to help you out when PowerPoint doesn't do what you want or expect.

Troubleshooting PowerPoint

20

In This Chapter

Mending master, template, and outline problems

Correcting text problems

Fixing slide show display glitches

Solving clip art and graphics dilemmas

Troubleshooting sound and video difficulties

Fixing production and presentation glitches

Bugs, glitches, and problems aren't cool, but fixing them quickly is. This chapter covers 50 of the most common PowerPoint problems and their solutions, so that you can recover from them gracefully whether you are in the midst of developing a new slide show or are about to present one in the field.

We have culled this list from the previous chapters and have added some new tips as well, so you won't have to page through the whole book to get a quick answer to a common problem.

Masters, Templates, and Outlines

version 4

Version 4

PROBLEM: Applying a template doesn't seem to be reversible.

SOLUTION: In PowerPoint 4, you can't reverse a template application. Save your file before applying a template, in case you want to go back. Alternatively, upgrade to PowerPoint 7 or 8, which enables you to "undo" a template application.

Versions 7 and 8

PROBLEM: Selecting Insert⇨Slides from Outline causes PowerPoint to present an error message that says the file is currently in use.

SOLUTION: You only get this message when the outline file is open in Word. Close the file in Word and try again.

Versions 4, 7, and 8

PROBLEM: Suppose that the Slide Master includes several graphic elements. For a particular slide, you want to use some of the graphics but not others; however, PowerPoint doesn't give you that option.

SOLUTION: Select Format⇨Custom Background (or, in Version 8, Format⇨Background) and check Omit Background Graphics from Master and then re-import the graphics you want on that slide.

PROBLEM: You added a cool background graphic to the Slide Master, but it doesn't appear on all slides.

SOLUTION: Check the Title Master. The Title Master is independent from the Slide Master, so title slides usually do not reflect changes made to the Slide Master after the Title Master has been created.

PROBLEM: Inserting slides from an existing document creates more slides than you want but no bullet items.

SOLUTION: Go back to the original outline document and make sure that bullets are preceded by tabs, not spaces.

Text

Versions 4, 7, and 8

PROBLEM: Text bullets do not look right on the presentation PC.

SOLUTION: Make sure that the Monotype Sorts font is installed on the presentation PC. PowerPoint uses this font frequently for creating bullets.

PROBLEM: Bullet lines are too close together, but you don't want to change the font size.

SOLUTION: Select the slide text, choose Format⇨Line Spacing, and reset the value to 1.25 or 1.50 (or whatever looks good to you).

PROBLEM: PostScript fonts aren't working.

SOLUTION: Upgrade to the latest version of Adobe Type Manager (3.02 for Windows 3.*x* and 4.0 for Windows 95 as of this writing). In Windows 95, make sure that the video acceleration slider is not set to None and that ATM is not installed in the Fonts folder.

PROBLEM: WordArt won't work with PostScript fonts.

SOLUTION: If you have PowerPoint 8, use the new built-in WordArt tool on the Drawing toolbar instead of Insert⇨Object⇨Microsoft WordArt 2.0. If you have PowerPoint 4 or 7, use another program, such as Adobe Typealign or CrystalGraphics' Flying Fonts, to create the text warping effects you need, save the results as a graphic, and then import the file into PowerPoint.

PROBLEM: You selected TrueType font embedding when saving your PPT file, but the fonts still do not show up on the presentation PC.

SOLUTION: Font embedding is iffy technology. Always install the TrueType fonts you need on the presentation PC in the usual way (but make sure that you won't violate the license agreement by doing so).

PROBLEM: When you move a slide show between Macintosh and Windows platforms, the fonts come out all wrong.

SOLUTION: Make sure that you only use the TrueType and PostScript fonts that are supported on both platforms when designing a cross-platform presentation.

PROBLEM: When you add text, it won't justify.

SOLUTION: In Versions 4 and 7, choose Format⇨Text Anchor and select Word-wrap Text in Object. In Version 8, choose Format⇨AutoShape⇨Text Box and select Word-wrap text in autoshape.

PROBLEM: Getting the figures in a table of data to line up vertically is nearly impossible.

SOLUTION: Use a column-based approach instead of a row-based approach. Draw a text box around the column and set it to align however you want. Then insert all of the figures for that column in the text box.

PROBLEM: You can't select just individual letters within a word; PowerPoint forces you to select the entire word.

SOLUTION: Select Tools⇨Options⇨Edit and clear the Automatic Word Selection check box.

Display

version 7

Version 7

PROBLEM: When changing between different views in PowerPoint 7.0a, objects are redrawn improperly or not at all, and an "out of memory" error sometimes appears.

SOLUTION: Download and apply the Microsoft fix PPREDRAW.EXE or upgrade, either to PowerPoint 7.0d or 8.0.

versions 4, 7 & 8

Versions 4, 7, and 8

PROBLEM: When you import a graphic that you have precisely sized for the screen (for example, to fill 640 x 480), the image doesn't fill the entire slide.

SOLUTION: The simplest approach is to drag the graphic's selection handles so that the graphic fills the screen, although doing so may distort your image. You can also try changing the bitmap's resolution (in Photoshop, for example). The unwritten rule for PowerPoint 4 and 7 is to divide the screen width by 10. For example, for a 640 x 480 display, set the image resolution to 64dpi; and for an 800 x 600 screen, set it to 80dpi.

In Versions 4 and 7, you may have to set the Draw⇨Scale setting to 100% (PowerPoint sometimes leaves it at 99.9%, which causes an annoying line to appear at the bottom or right border). Finally, if you're using Version 8, be sure to use the BMP format rather than the TIFF format (the TIFF graphic filter ignores physical size information), set the image resolution as described in the previous paragraph, and verify that the imported image scale is set to 100% (it may come in at an odd value, such as 83%).

PROBLEM: Your cool gradients exhibit *banding* on the delivery PC.

SOLUTION: See if you can increase the number of colors for the delivery PC's video in the Windows control panel. Testing the slide show with your development PC set to the same color depth as the delivery PC is a wise precaution. Many notebooks only permit 256-color displays, which can't handle many fancy gradient fills.

PROBLEM: You are making a videotape of a PPT slide show, but the screen borders are being clipped.

SOLUTION: For the short-term, beg, borrow, or rent a professional scan converter that can zoom down your slide area. For the long-term, always leave a "safe area" of at least 25 pixels on each border.

PROBLEM: Your slide show looked great at a resolution of 800 x 600, but doesn't look great at 640 x 480, which is the only resolution the laptop you're using supports.

SOLUTION: Save two versions of your show, one for each resolution. If you have been working at a higher resolution, reset the PC's video configuration to edit the 640 x 480 version and manually correct any alignment problems.

Clip Art and Graphics

Version 4

PROBLEM: A networked PC won't run the ClipArt Gallery without displaying the error message "The ClipArt Gallery cannot create an index file."

SOLUTION: The problem has to do with running Windows 3.*x* off a shared network drive. Either run Windows 3.*x* off the local drive or update to PowerPoint 4.0c.

PROBLEM: PowerPoint 4 doesn't permit you to use build effects with graphics.

SOLUTION: Simulate the build by creating multiple slides with progressively more objects and use suitable (that is, fast) transitions.

Versions 4, 7, and 8

PROBLEM: Double-clicking a particular clip art image doesn't bring up the ClipArt Gallery as it usually does.

SOLUTION: The image has most likely been disassembled, so PowerPoint no longer considers it to be a true clip-art image. Select Insert⇨Clip Art (or, in Version 8, Insert⇨Picture⇨Clip Art) to open the ClipArt Gallery.

PROBLEM: Diagonal lines (such as those in a right triangle) vanish when embossed.

SOLUTION: The embossing parameters (direction, color) in PowerPoint aren't adjustable, so the best approach is to avoid 45-degree angles in any object that will be embossed.

PROBLEM: You have created a drawing object that obscures another graphic and can't get that graphic back.

SOLUTION: Select the foreground object and click Draw⇨Send Backward

(Draw➪Order➪Send Backward in Version 8) or Draw➪Send to Back (Draw➪Order➪Send to Back in Version 8). When you have everything the way you want, move objects forward or backward a step at a time to get the effect you desire.

PROBLEM: PowerPoint won't allow you to move or place a drawing object precisely, pixel by pixel.

SOLUTION: Uncheck Draw➪Snap to Grid (Draw➪Snap➪To Grid in Version 8).

PROBLEM: PowerPoint can't import the graphics files you have created in other programs.

SOLUTION: Install all the graphics filters onto the PC, using the PowerPoint or MS Office Setup program. (Some graphics filters are omitted in a Typical installation.) If the graphics files still won't come in, save them in a different format that PowerPoint can import. If you can't do that, use a graphic conversion utility such as Quarterdeck's Hijaak to create importable files. As a last resort, do a Windows copy-and-paste operation.

PROBLEM: Imported bitmap graphics look terrible — all the colors are off.

SOLUTION: Go back to the application you used to create them and *dither* the file down to fewer colors (such as to a 256-color palette). Then re-import the graphic files.

PROBLEM: PowerPoint produces a "white box" effect around the picture outline when you import a graphic. You want that area to be transparent.

SOLUTION: Don't import the graphic as a bitmap. Save it as a WMF or CGM vector file and then import it into your slide show. Alternatively, if the graphic has a solid monochromatic background, use the "Set Transparent Color" button on Version 8's Picture toolbar.

Sound and Video

version 4

Version 4

PROBLEM: AVI clips seem to rewind to the first frame after you play them from PowerPoint.

SOLUTION: The easiest way around this problem is to click on the AVI clip, select the Tools➪Play Settings, and check the Hide while not playing option.

PROBLEM: You cannot insert a large WAV file.

SOLUTION: This problem is a bug in the Windows 3.1 Sound Recorder. Try recompressing the WAV file using a different codec or different compression options.

Versions 7 and 8

PROBLEM: Sounds won't play from PowerPoint 7 or 8, and movies play without sound.

SOLUTION: Check the Volume Control accessory by double-clicking on the Taskbar's speaker icon or by selecting Start➪Programs➪Accessories ➪Multimedia➪Volume Control. Make sure that the Mute All and Mute check boxes are cleared and that the sliders are set to the middle.

Make sure that you have a sound card installed!

PROBLEM: When you play back a sound from PowerPoint 7 or 8, it produces an error message that says a sound device is not installed.

SOLUTION: Add the line

```
drivers=MMSYSTEM.DLL
```

to SYSTEM.INI's `[boot]` section.

Versions 4 and 7

PROBLEM: Sounds and movies won't play in PowerPoint.

SOLUTION: Install Media Player through the Windows 3.*x* SETUP program or the Windows 95 Add/Remove Software wizard. Make sure that you have copied any Media Player objects to your delivery PC; they are linked, not embedded.

PROBLEM: AVI movies play fine, but QuickTime movies don't.

SOLUTION: Install Apple's QuickTime for Windows on the presentation PC. The program probably came bundled with your video editing program; if not, you have to download it from Apple.

PROBLEM: When videos and animations play, a border and control bar appears that you don't want to see.

SOLUTION: In Media Player, select Edit⇨Options and deselect the checkboxes labeled Caption, Border around object, and Control Bar on playback. Then select Edit⇨Copy Object, go to PowerPoint, and choose Edit⇨Paste.

PROBLEM: You can't seem to get digital video clips to play in full screen mode in PowerPoint.

SOLUTION: The easiest way to get a Media Player AVI clip to play in full screen mode is to insert it as a Media Clip object, not as a movie, and to select the Display as icon check box. Load the file into Media Player and select Device⇨Properties⇨Full Screen. Then select File⇨Exit and Return⇨Yes.

versions 4, 7 & 8

Versions 4, 7, and 8

PROBLEM: AVI animations created in other programs have fuzzy edges and do not look crisp.

SOLUTION: Compress the AVI files with a *lossless* compressor, such as Microsoft RLE or QuickTime Animation.

PROBLEM: You installed the Autodesk animation player, but it doesn't show up on the Media Player menu.

SOLUTION: You also have to install the MCI driver for Autodesk animations. Download MCIAAP.ZIP from CompuServe's ASoft forum and install it according to the bundled instructions.

PROBLEM: You need to play a sound automatically but don't want to see it on-screen, and the Hide While Not Playing option doesn't work.

SOLUTION: Reduce the size of the sound icon and put it behind another object by using the Draw menu. In Version 7, associate the sound with a transition by using the Tools⇨Slide Transition command; in Version 8, the command is Slide Show⇨Slide Transition.

Production and Presentation

version 4

Version 4

PROBLEM: The PowerPoint Viewer doesn't work with branched presentations.

SOLUTION: The best you can do is to create an LST file that names different PPT files in succession and then load the LST file into the Viewer instead of a PPT file.

PROBLEM: Your delivery PC completely locks up from time to time, sometimes displaying a message about "low system resources."

SOLUTION: Don't run any other programs while PowerPoint is running, disable Windows wallpaper (a good idea anyway to avoid intermittent font problems), turn off screen savers, and restart the PC right before making the presentation. A long-term solution is to upgrade to Windows 95.

Version 7

PROBLEM: You can't get the presentation conferencing feature to work.

SOLUTION: This feature only works with TCP/IP networks in Version 7; upgrading to Version 8 permits presentation conferencing with NT Server networks also but (alas) still not with NetWare. Multimedia file playback isn't supported on audience machines in either Version 7 or 8.

PROBLEM: The PowerPoint 7 Viewer is slow and somewhat buggy.

SOLUTION: Update it to the new 32-bit version. Download PPTVW32.EXE from any Microsoft online source.

PROBLEM: After changing Windows 95's user profiles configuration, several PowerPoint commands are missing.

SOLUTION: Auto ClipArt, Meeting Minder, Style Checker, and other commands use Registry settings on a per-user basis, rather than a per-machine basis. Turning user profiles on or off, or logging in as a different user, can create this problem. Reinstall PowerPoint with the SETUP /Y /R command while logged in as the desired user.

Versions 4, 7, and 8

PROBLEM: You sent your PPT file to a service bureau to have 35mm slides made, and everything came back misaligned and distorted.

SOLUTION: Select File⇨Slide Setup (it's File⇨Page Setup in Version 8) and choose 35mm Slides under the Slides Sized for: window to size your slides properly. Then go back and reformat your slides so they look good in Slide View with zoom set to 100%.

PROBLEM: Certain slides with complex illustrations take unacceptably long to draw during the presentation.

SOLUTION: Zoom in on the offending drawing objects, ungroup them, and delete components that you don't really need and that aren't noticeable on screen. And make sure that tiny objects do not use gradient fills.

PROBLEM: Some transitions are really slow, even on a fast PC.

SOLUTION: Avoid the worst offenders, including the various *cover* transitions.

PROBLEM: The delivery PC's built-in display goes dark when you connect it to an LCD projector.

SOLUTION: Usually, a function-key command unique to each notebook is available that toggles internal, external, and simultaneous display modes. Watch out, though — some notebooks won't "see" an external display device unless it is connected when you power up the notebook.

PROBLEM: The remote mouse isn't working.

SOLUTION: Replace the batteries in the transmitter. Check to see if you are out of range or out of the infrared device's line of sight.

PROBLEM: A slide show developed on PowerPoint 7 or 8 but saved as a PowerPoint 4 file doesn't look right — the gradients are wrong, for example.

SOLUTION: Upgrade the presentation PC to Version 7 or 8, if that is what you used to create the slide show. Or go back to the original file and remove all two-color gradients before saving the file as a Version 4 file.

PROBLEM: You need to transport a large PPT file that won't fit onto a single diskette.

SOLUTION: Copy the file over a network if one is available, or use PKZIP with the -A option (for archiving).

Summary

After reading to this point in the book, you now know the following:

- How to move slide shows from machine to machine
- How to tune up your hardware and software for maximum speed
- What to do in the face of the more common PowerPoint problems

All that remains now is to provide some tips to guide you as you take the stage and deliver your shows.

Tips for Presenters

21

In This Chapter

- Performing a design review of your show
- Spell-checking your slides
- Tailoring your presentation to the audience
- Managing the presentation environment to minimize distractions
- Rehearsing your show to set timings and build confidence
- Choosing a presentation mode based on the size and needs of the audience
- Using the Pen, Meeting Minder, and Slide Navigator tools during the show
- Using branching and hidden slides for ad-hoc elaboration
- Refining your presentation style to achieve a polished, professional delivery

This final chapter prepares you for the moment of truth: when you're on stage, making your presentation.

You've done your homework and put together a great slide show that conveys the information you want to convey; it looks professional, clean, and aesthetically pleasing. Your files are ready and your computer is ready. Good job! Don't get too comfortable, though; you have a little more work to do. Now you must prepare for and deliver the actual presentation.

Whether you're presenting directly from a computer or from 35mm slides made from your slide show, the execution of your delivery is crucial. The good news is that if you have a solid, beautiful slide show behind you, you won't be nearly as nervous. The slides, however, can't completely speak for themselves. This chapter presents a few tips from experienced presenters to help you polish your act and guide you through the execution phase.

If you follow the ideas presented here, your fears will disappear. If you can't incorporate all the ideas into your show, practice bringing together two or three at a time until you feel comfortable adding more. Then weed out the ones you don't need and keep the ones that suit your style.

This chapter has two main sections: preparing for the show and presenting in front of your audience.

Preparing for the Show

Consider the following four key elements when you prepare for a successful slide show presentation:

- Design review and spell check
- Type of audience
- Presentation environment
- Timings and rehearsal

Design review and spell check

Give your slide show one last sprucing up with a design review and spell check.

Design checklist

When you're designing a slide show, you're too close to the details to perform an overall design review. Take a break from the presentation for a couple of days, if possible, and then perform the review. Run the entire presentation through on your PC and think about the following design elements (discussed in earlier chapters):

- Text consistency (capitalization, typestyle, tense, end punctuation, and so on)
- Location of charts, graphs, and clip art
- Color scheme blending (including foreground and background elements)
- Slide element balance (top-heavy, lopsided, and so on)
- Clutter

Simplify and shorten the slide show as needed. It's not a bad idea to view the show with a colleague who hasn't seen it before (don't comment on it as you watch it!) in order to get a second opinion. Remember though, it's *your* show, and you make the final decisions.

version 8 Colleagues reviewing your slide shows on their own PCs can attach digital "sticky notes" by using Insert⇨Comment, without modifying the actual slides.

An opening hello and a finishing touch

Part of your design review should include consideration of an opening hello and a finishing touch — that is, special slides that can open and close your presentation.

Before you even open your mouth, you can deliver a good impression with a "hello" slide. This slide can welcome the audience and introduce you and your company or department. Thirty minutes before we begin our technical seminars, we display a "hello" slide with a list of registration instructions so that early arrivals can get their paperwork out of the way instead of waiting idly.

Remember the artistic style of the other slides you've created and be consistent with the overall look. However, the "hello" slide is a time to think cool. Make your audience smile with an image from the ClipArt Gallery, or calm their jitters (and yours) by placing a beautiful landscape in the background.

At the end of the show, finish with a "finale" slide that lets your audience know the visual presentation is over. The finale slide not only puts closure on your slide show, it also draws your audience's attention back to you. You can then thank people for their time, open the floor for Q&A, or present a verbal closing statement with their full attention.

warning If you don't create a finale slide, PowerPoint may throw you back into Slide View when you click past the last slide in the show. It's a shame to end a great presentation on a klutzy note!

versions 7&8 To end with a black slide, choose Tools⇨Options, click the View tab, and then check End with Black Slide (Figure 21-1).

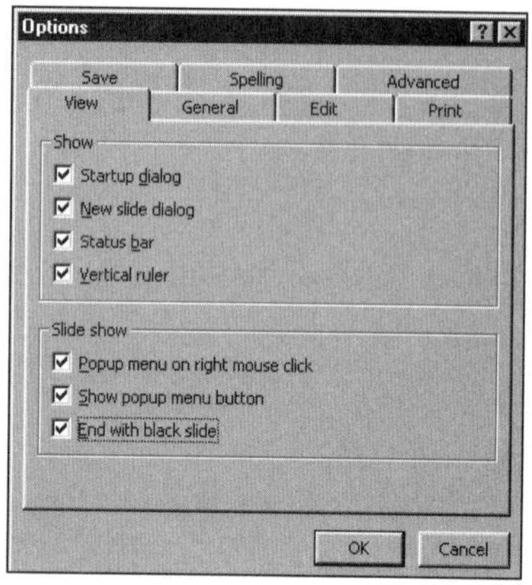

Figure 21-1: Ending with a black slide is simple in Version 8 (shown) and 7, but a little more involved in Version 4.

To end with a black side in Version 4, you must add a blank autolayout to the end of the slide show as follows:

1. From Slide View, place the blinking cursor after the last slide.
2. Select Insert⇨New Slide.
3. From the New Slide dialog box, scroll down and select the blank slide.
4. Select Format⇨Slide Background; ensure that Display Objects On This Slide is not selected.
5. Under Shade Styles, select None. Click Change Color, choose black, and then click Apply.

Although you can end your presentation with a black slide, this kind of finale is a little boring. You may want to create a beautiful background with a simple legend such as "Questions and Answers," "End of Presentation," or just a polite "Thank You." Creating unique, memorable backgrounds for the first and last slides is a stylish way to polish your show and bracket it with visual bookends.

Spel chek

Nothing can be quite as embarrassing as when you project a beautifully laid-out slide on the screen and a misspelled word (full size and in living color) jumps out at you and your audience. Of all the mistakes you can make, spelling errors are the easiest and most common; you become so captivated with the cool slides you've created that spelling completely slips your mind. Don't let it!

Fortunately, PowerPoint supplies a built-in spell checker. Just select the Spelling button from the standard toolbar, or press F7. The Spelling dialog box appears if PowerPoint thinks you may have misspelled a word (Figure 21-2).

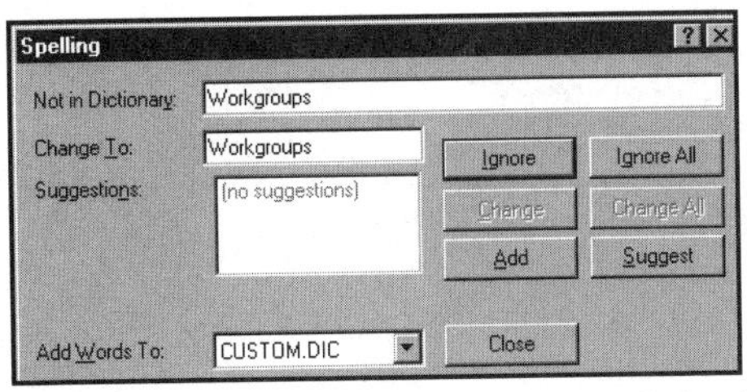

Figure 21-2: PowerPoint's built-in spell checker can save you embarrassment.

Version 8's spell checker works like the one in Microsoft Word: It flags spelling errors with a wavy red underline as you type text onto a slide. You can then right-click a misspelled word for a menu of alternate spellings or to bring up the Spelling dialog box. If you find the wavy underlines distracting, as they could be in a slide show with many proper nouns, disable them by selecting Tools⇨Options⇨Spelling and clearing the Spelling check box under Check spelling as you type. You can still spell-check the slide show by pressing F7.

No spell checker is foolproof, and PowerPoint's is no exception. For example, you intend to use the word *for,* but you mistakenly type **foe**. Because *foe* is actually a word, the spell checker will skip it. Further, the spell checker will not recognize names or words that aren't in its main dictionary, although it may make suggestions. When in doubt, use a print dictionary or a good, electronic, standalone dictionary (such as the one that ships with Microsoft Bookshelf, supplied with the Office Professional). If some know-it-all corners you after your presentation, and (trust us) it will happen, you can say with confidence, "I looked that one up and it surprised me, too."

Take advantage of the *custom dictionary* facility. If you often use a particular name, term, or abbreviation, add it to the dictionary with the Add button. The spell checker won't flag it again.

Keep in mind that text created in WordArt — even the built-in WordArt facility in Version 8 — is an object and not recognized as text. The spell checker will not check WordArt objects. This warning applies to any imported pictures with integrated text.

Type of audience

The type of audience you address sets the mood for your presentation. A presentation to the board of directors regarding the company's annual budget is formal, whereas a presentation to the PTA regarding the Spring carnival is not.

If the audience is *informal*, you may want to use bright colors, unusual fonts, lively animations, and cool sound effects in your show. You may also want to relax your own personal style by dressing down, walking around the room, and allowing yourself a little time to digress and crack a few jokes.

If your audience is *formal*, you may need to tone down your color schemes, use more conventional and sophisticated fonts (for example, with serifs), and skip animations that may take up too much time. Dress conservatively, but don't be too boring; if you wear a conservative suit, add a splash of color somewhere (for example, a colorful necktie). Keep the jokes, digressions, and offhand comments to a minimum. Most formal meetings last too long anyway, so make your points with efficiency. We once worked months on a presentation that only took five minutes to deliver to a room full of high-octane Washington lawyers, but that presentation helped decide a multimillion-dollar lawsuit.

Presentation environment

To be a good presenter, you must control your environment with seemingly effortless aplomb — and to do so, you must learn about that environment ahead of time. In a successful presentation, your audience members should barely notice the environment, but achieving that goal takes work on your part. The following is a list of some items to check. Although the list may seem long, remember, smooth presentations don't just happen!

- Is the room the proper size for your audience? If it's too large, set up chairs in a group instead of trying to fill up the room, and remove unused chairs so it doesn't look as if attendance is low.
- If your audience needs to take notes (and most do), have tables available and position chairs so people aren't straddling table legs with their human legs. Make pads, pens, and (if you plan to pass out printed handouts) highlighters available; someone always forgets and will appreciate the convenience.
- Have extra chairs and tables available (for example, in a nearby closet) in case more people show up than you anticipated.
- Have a coat rack available, regardless of the weather. (Business jackets or suit coats draped on chair backs get wrinkled and stained.)
- Provide water for everyone (including yourself!). Depending on the length of your presentation, have sodas, coffee, tea, and fruit juice available, too.

- If you present your show in a hotel meeting room, find out in advance whom to contact if you need anything (such as chairs, tables, pitchers of ice water, adjustments to climate control, and so on). Coordinate with the hotel manager to make sure staff won't be vacuuming next door during your talk. If there's a noisy meeting going on in the next room, see if you can move, or at least have a friendly chat with the meeting leader and moderate the microphone volume.
- Be sure everyone can see the screen by placing your equipment so that it doesn't block anyone's view. Don't put chairs where building columns can obstruct your visuals.
- If you worry about latecomers disturbing you and your audience, set up chairs and tables to face the front of the room, which should be opposite the doorway.
- Do you have control over heating and cooling? If so, where is the thermostat? Try it out ahead of time; half the thermostats on the planet don't connect to anything anymore — if they ever did. Set the room temperature to slightly cool so that everyone doesn't nod off.
- Check the number of electrical outlets available for your hardware, projector, and so on. You may need to bring an extension cord or multiple outlet attachment, and make sure that it's grounded.
- Many meeting rooms have lighting controls by the doorway, in which case you may want to designate an attendee at the back of the room to work the dimmer switch or switches. If you have more than one switch, figure out which ones you need to control and which you can leave preset.

tip

It's tempting to take meeting room details for granted, especially when someone else is supposed to attend to them. Don't! *You* are the one on stage, and any problems will reflect on *you*, no one else. If possible, get the room set up at least an hour before your presentation. Allow time for the *X* factor: the high-intensity projector bulb that burns out, the broken light switch, the wobbly table.

Timings and rehearsals

versions 4, 7 & 8

PowerPoint provides rehearsal features that become invaluable once learned. The rehearsal feature varies slightly between versions, but the purpose is the same: to ensure that you can work within your time constraints, and to develop confidence.

Whether you have all the time in the world or are limited because you must follow other speakers or because they must follow you, be aware of your time frame. The time frame must include equipment setup and teardown, the time you're actually speaking, Q&A at the conclusion, and a buffer zone for any snags you may encounter.

By practicing your presentation, you will develop a level of confidence that will radiate to your audience. A confident speaker is a pleasure to watch and will allow the audience to concentrate on the message rather than the messenger.

If you stumble only occasionally, your audience will be surprisingly forgiving — especially if you shake your head and briefly laugh at yourself instead of becoming flustered. Although no audience expects a letter-perfect oratory, watching a presenter continually correct or reverse himself is a painful experience.

Practice using the actual hardware you plan to use for the show. Your desktop Pentium will run the slides faster than your 486 notebook. If possible, arrive early at the site and do a run-through with your notebook or the meeting room's PC before your audience arrives.

To use PowerPoint's rehearsal feature, follow these steps in Version 7:

1. Select View⇨Slide Show. The Slide Show dialog box appears.
2. Click Rehearse New Timings and Show.

In Version 8, just select Slide Show⇨Rehearse Timings.

You can now advance manually from slide to slide while you rehearse your presentation, and PowerPoint will time each slide for you. (A good rule of thumb is to speak for no more than two to three minutes per slide — audiences appreciate a presentation that moves along.) To advance your slides, click the mouse or press Spacebar. During the rehearsal, you can always press Esc to end before the last slide. When you finish rehearsing, PowerPoint asks if you want to save the timings; if you do, the recorded time will appear below each slide in the Slide Sorter View.

Take a closer look at the Slide Show dialog box, and its options, in Figure 21-3.

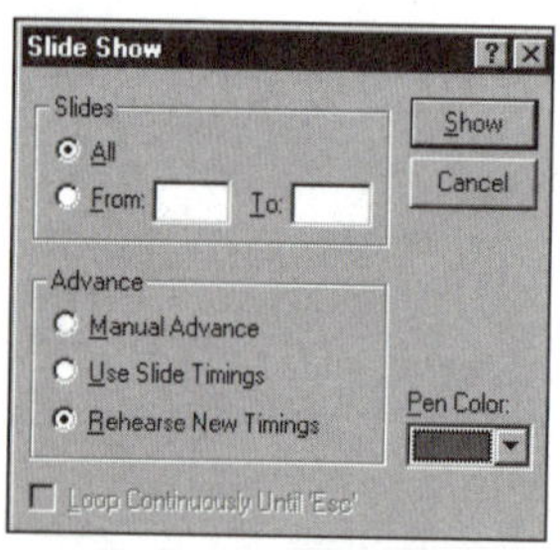

Figure 21-3: The Slide Show dialog box offers several options for presentation mode in PowerPoint 4 and 7.

Remember, you can use the Slide Show dialog box for interactive presentations as well as for rehearsals. The options are as follows:

- You can choose All to run through the entire show, or you can specify slide numbers in the From and To fields.
- Manual Advance is usually the correct choice for the actual presentation, when a mouse click or keystroke will advance to the next slide.
- Use Slide Timings automatically runs the slide show according to timings already stored in the presentation template from a previous rehearsal.
- Rehearse New Timings enables you to run through the slide show and record a new set of slide timings over any old timings that may be present.
- Loop Continuously Until Esc (Run Continually Until Esc in Version 4) makes the presentation repeat until you press Esc. (This choice is grayed out if you've chosen Rehearse New Timings.)

version 8

The Slide Show dialog box from Versions 4 and 7 has been moved to a new dialog box called Set Up Show (Figure 21-4), which you can access by selecting Slide Show⇨Set Up Show.

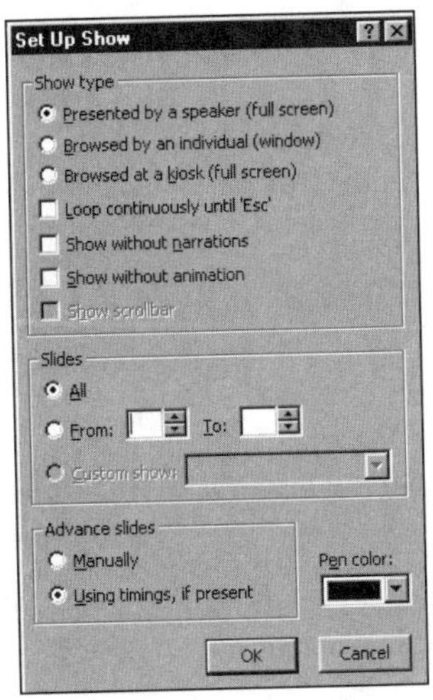

Figure 21-4: PowerPoint 8 relocates slide show options to the Set Up Show dialog box. Most options work as they did in previous versions, but several new choices appear under Show type.

Many settings in the Set Up Show dialog box are the same as in Versions 4 and 7, but a few new options are available:

- Browsed by an individual (window) is useful if your audience will be viewing the slide show on a PC. New controls and menus simplify the PowerPoint interface in this mode.

- Browsed at a kiosk (full screen) is preferred if you're setting up a PC to run unattended, for example, at a trade show or in a shopping mall. PowerPoint's usual slide navigation tools are disabled, and users can perform actions only through predefined Action Buttons and Action Settings.
- Show without narrations turns off voice narrations that you may have previously recorded.
- Show without animation deactivates build effects, which is preferable for users browsing the slide show on a PC.
- Custom show enables you to select a custom version of the slide show you may have previously created with Slide Show⇨Custom Shows. This useful new feature permits you to create variations of the same basic presentation for different customers, for example, and save them in a single PPT file.

version 4

When you rehearse a slide show, the timer appears in the lower-left corner. To reset or re-rehearse, click the timer button once. To move to the next slide, click anywhere but on the timer. PowerPoint allows you only one reset.

versions 7&8

When you rehearse a slide show, the timer appears in the lower-*right* corner and includes extended controls (such as Pause and Repeat). This timer indicates how much time has accumulated for the entire presentation, on the left; and for each slide, on the right (Figure 21-5).

Figure 21-5: PowerPoint 7 and 8's Rehearsal timing window.

warning

PowerPoint 4, 7, and 8 share the same problem: When you use the annotation tool, the timer stops dead. When you finish a "chalk talk," you can click the annotation tool again and the timer resumes, but it doesn't add back the time from your chalk talk. Moral: If you want your chalk-talk time included in the rehearsal timings, don't use the annotation tool. Wave a pencil in front of the screen or sketch on a piece of paper so the timer keeps ticking.

tip

Rehearsing slide shows is an iterative process; you won't get it right on the first try. When you've rehearsed the show and recorded timings at least once, choose Use Slide Timings in the Slide Show dialog box (Version 7) or Using timings, if present in the Set Up Show dialog box (Version 8). The show automatically runs and you can see whether you're comfortable with the speed.

versions 7&8

PowerPoint 7 and 8 offer a cool tool for getting your iterations right the *Slide Meter* (Figure 21-6). This tool doesn't appear on the Slide Show or Set Up Show dialog box (where it belongs). Instead, you must choose Manual

Advance in the Slide Show dialog box (Version 7) or Advance slides Manually in the Set Up Show dialog box (Version 8), and, as soon as the show starts, right-click the mouse and choose Slide Meter. The "gas gauge" display tells you whether you're advancing the slides too soon or too late, based on the most recent set of timings.

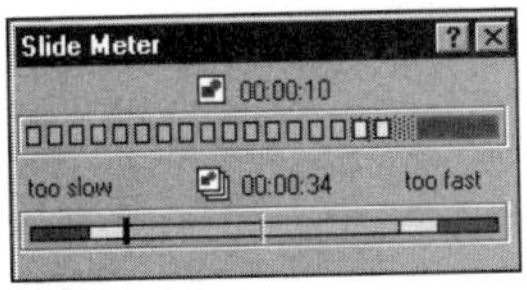

Figure 21-6: PowerPoint 7 and 8's Slide Meter window for pacing rehearsals.

Presenting the Show

By now, you've performed your design review, spell-checked your slides, made appropriate plans for the type of audience you'll have (formal versus informal), prepared the presentation environment, and gone through your rehearsals to get the timing down and build your confidence. It's time to present!

This section discusses PowerPoint's presentation tools and how to branch from one presentation to another for a more flexible show. It also provides many tips on delivery and presentation style.

Presentation tools

You may want to use these three tools during your presentation: the Pen, the Meeting Minder, and the Slide Navigator. Let's take a closer look at each one.

The Pen tool

PowerPoint's Pen tool works much like the chalk-talk feature you often see during broadcast football games. Use this tool to indicate motion, circle particular slide elements, and so on, but note that it looks more like a crayon than a fine-point pen. Rehearse with the Pen tool before you present.

In PowerPoint 7 and 8, you can get to the Pen tool no less than three different ways once you're in Slide Show View:

- Move the mouse anywhere to pop up the translucent icon in the lower-left corner, click that icon, and select Pen from the expanded menu. If you choose Pointer Options and Pen Color, you can set the color that you prefer, as shown in Figure 21-7.

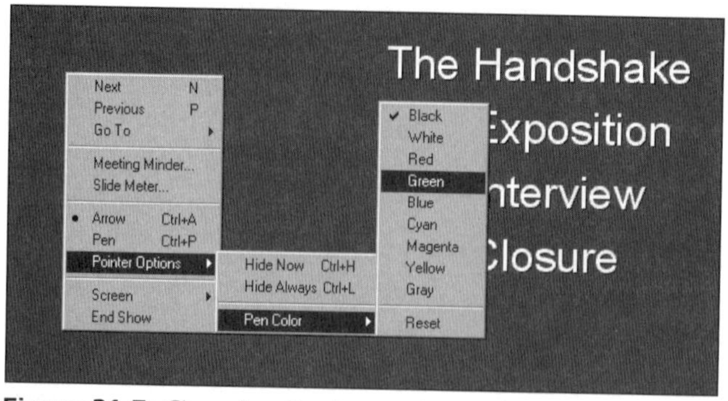

Figure 21-7: Changing the Pen tool color in PowerPoint 7. The procedure is the same in Version 8.

- Right-click the screen and then select Pen from the expanded menu.
- Press Ctrl-P to go directly to the Pen tool instead of going through the menu. You can't change the Pen color this way, but it's our favorite method once you've already chosen a Pen color you like via the pop-up menu; it's less distracting to the audience. You may want to select your Pen color at the first slide before you begin your presentation, so the audience never sees the menu.

tip

Though you may think you can choose from only the colors that appear in the pop-up menu, you actually have more flexibility than that. You can use the standard or custom color palettes to create your own cool pen color, but you can only get to it one way. In Version 7, don't start the show with the slide show toolbar icon, but rather start it from the View⇨Slide Show menu. In Version 8, select Slide Show⇨Set Up Show. Click the Pen Color drop-down menu and choose Other Color. Now choose any color you like off the palette you prefer. When you run the show and press Ctrl-P, the Pen tool uses your custom color. If you change colors during the presentation, you can get back to your custom color by right-clicking and choosing Pointer Options⇨Pen Color⇨Reset.

version 4

Move the mouse in Slide Show View, and the pen icon appears in the lower-right corner. Click the icon to perform your chalk talk. You cannot choose your pen color: If the background is dark, the pen will be yellow; if it's light, the pen will be green.

warning

In PowerPoint 4, don't right-click the screen to bring up the Tools menu as you would in PowerPoint 7 or 8 — the right mouse button moves you back to the previous slide.

versions 4, 7&8 The following Pen tool tips apply to all three PowerPoint versions:

- When you finish with the Pen tool and want to return to the arrow cursor, press Esc.
- Clear your Pen tool markings by pressing E (for Erase). You can clear away the pen markings and make new annotations any number of times per slide.
- Our second favorite cool pen tip: You can draw perfectly straight horizontal or vertical lines by holding down Shift while dragging the mouse. This technique is great for underlining or indicating motion. Unfortunately, though, you can only draw one line at a time, so if you need to surround a screen element, circle it freehand instead of trying to box it in.

The Meeting Minder

versions 7&8 The Meeting Minder debuted in Version 7; it permits the presenter to take notes during the presentation on individual slides, as well as view previously recorded notes. Microsoft responded to customer requests from presenters who had to jot down meeting minutes or action items on a piece of paper during a PowerPoint 4 presentation and transcribe them later. Meeting Minder saves the transcribing step and organizes notes on a per-slide basis. To use it, follow these steps:

1. During your presentation, right-click the screen or click the lower-left icon to display the pop-up menu and then choose Meeting Minder. In Version 8, you can leave Meeting Minder on screen while you proceed through the show.
2. Select either Meeting Minutes, Action Items, or Notes Pages (Version 7 only) from the available tabs.
3. Click OK to remove the Meeting Minder window so you can go to the next slide.

Meeting Minutes is for noting comments or discussion that come up during the slide show but that don't necessarily require action.

Action Items is for noting comments that suggest or require a follow-up of some kind. Version 8 adds fields for task owner and due date.

Notes Pages (not available in Version 8) is not editable while the presentation is running; it just displays whatever notes you've made on slide note pages while building the slide show.

tip You can edit Meeting Minutes and Action Items by highlighting text and using Ctrl-X to cut, Ctrl-C to copy, and Ctrl-V to paste.

Meeting Minder offers no "undo" capability.

When your meeting is over, you can merge your Meeting Minutes into your presentation's slide notes with Meeting Minder's Export button (Figure 21-8). (Unfortunately, you can't do this with Action Items, making them less useful.) You can also create a new Word document listing both Meeting Minutes and Action Items, again with the Export button. PowerPoint will automatically launch Word and create the document for you; you can reformat it as desired and save it with a new filename.

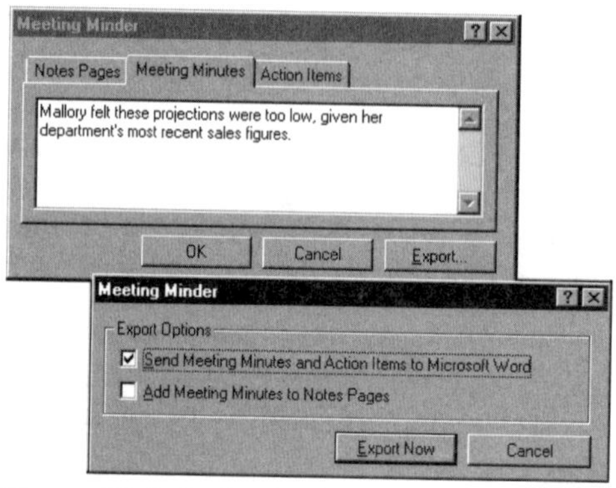

Figure 21-8: *Saving interactive notes with Meeting Minder (Version 7). In Version 8, you have the option of exporting Action Items to Outlook, for e-mail distribution later.*

The Slide Navigator

PowerPoint 7 and 8's Slide Navigator permits you to jump to any slide in your presentation by slide number or title. From the Slide Show mode, right-click the screen and then choose Go To⇨Slide Navigator. A list of your slides appears in a scrolling window (Figure 21-9). Find the one to which you want to jump and double-click it.

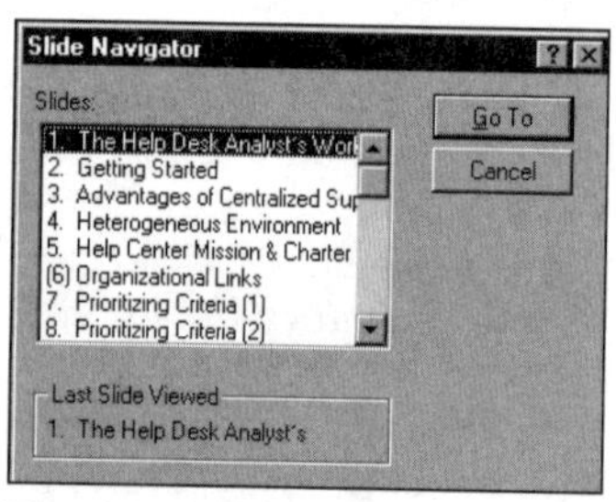

Figure 21-9: *Jumping to a specific slide from the Slide Navigator.*

If the slide number is enclosed in brackets (such as Slide 6 in Figure 21-9), it's a hidden slide. You can, however, still select and display it.

Slides that you create with the blank autolayout (such as pure graphics slides) don't have titles that show up in Slide Navigator. Further, according to Microsoft, you cannot name such a slide. You can, however, apply a simple autolayout with just one title line. You can then create the title as you want it to appear in Slide Navigator, give it a color that matches the background and no outline, and then shrink it to a tiny size and scoot it off in one corner of the screen. The title won't be visible, but the slide will have a name. Awkward? You bet, but at least it works.

If you are working from speaker's notes and know the number of the slide to which you want to jump, type it in during the slide show and press Enter. This approach is *much* quicker than Slide Navigator.

Branching slide shows

Branching is a useful technique when you have a slide series that you don't think you'll need but that you may want to show if someone asks for more particulars on a given topic. Here's the traditional way to set up a slide show branch in any version of PowerPoint:

1. In Slide View, display the slide from which you want to branch.
2. Select Insert➪Object and then choose Microsoft PowerPoint Presentation from the list under Object Type.
3. Click the Create from File radio button and then select Browse to choose your new *.PPT file.
4. Click Display as Icon and then click OK.

Not only does the presentation icon appear on your slide, but the name of the destination slide show appears beneath it. You can define the method of playback by clicking the icon and choosing Slide Show➪Action Settings (Version 8), Tools➪Interactive Settings (Version 7), or Tools➪Play Settings (Version 4). You can also have multiple slide show icons per slide. The only drawback to this OLE branching technique is slow performance.

If you have just a handful of slides that you may want to use for elaboration, you may prefer to implement these as *hidden slides* instead of using the branching technique. Just select the slide (or slides) from Slide View and then click Tools➪Hide Slide.

Remember, you can either use the Slide Navigator or you can just type the slide number and press Enter to get to a hidden slide. You can also type **H** to advance to the next hidden slide in sequence.

As a variation on the hidden slide technique, you can use interactive settings with drawing objects in Version 7, or with "action buttons" in Version 8, to accomplish smoother, faster branching than creating an OLE link. Here's how:

- In Version 7, draw an arrow (for example, with AutoShapes) on the slide from which you want to branch. Choose Tools⇨Interactive Settings⇨Go To: and select the target slide from the drop-down list (it can be a hidden slide).
- In Version 8, select Slide Show⇨Action Buttons, pick a shape, and click and drag on the slide to create the button; when the Action Settings dialog box appears, choose Hyperlink to: and specify the target slide.

In either version, you can put an arrow at the end of your branched list to return you to the "main" presentation.

Delivery tips

This final section lists several suggestions for delivery style and procedure. Use only the tips that make sense for your presentation situation.

- When you start a presentation, make a preliminary "let's get started" announcement, and then allow enough time for attendees to take their seats. Always introduce yourself, your company (if appropriate), and the reason for the gathering. This introduction should usually last no longer than five minutes.
- Provide an opportunity for brief questions ("How long will this meeting take?" and so on) before you launch into your show. If you don't have much time, tell your audience to hold their questions until the designated Q&A session at the end of the show.
- If you use handouts, explain their purpose.
- Use arm and hand motions to underline your points, but don't make repetitive, nervous, meaningless motions (such as rocking from one foot to the other).
- Address your audience, not the slide on the screen. Make eye contact rather than focusing on the back of the room.
- Don't be afraid of silence; it's much better than "ahhs" and "umms." Use the silence either after or before a key point to add emphasis. (Listen to Paul Harvey on the radio to hear how one expert communicator uses silence for emphasis.)
- In a longer presentation, avoid monotone. Vary your voice volume somewhat, especially at moments where you sense the audience is drifting or where you want to add some drama.

- Keep the audience involved by asking rhetorical questions or describing situations that they can project themselves into as you speak. These are especially good techniques for meetings where you explain a new process or idea.
- During the Q&A session (or during the show if you've allowed it), if one individual asks specific questions that are not of interest to the general group, politely ask that person to join you after the meeting for further discussion; you don't want to slow down the group.
- Keep your answers to audience questions brief.
- If you use speaker's notes, you may want to introduce the next slide a moment *before* you bring it up on screen. The moment you display a new slide, the audience may be reading it instead of listening to you.

versions 4, 7 & 8

If you must pause during a slide show, press **B** to black out the screen or **W** to white it out. If the room is heavily dimmed, using **W** will provide enough light for everyone to see each other (and you). Practice it first, though, to make sure that you don't blind your audience! Press **B** or **W** again to resume the slide show.

Summary

This chapter has laid out the steps you can take to make sure the execution of your presentation is as sharp, impressive, and persuasive as the slides themselves.

Do a design review and spell check to finalize your slide show.

Learn the details of the presentation environment so that you can make both yourself and your audience comfortable.

Use PowerPoint's rehearsal feature (preferably on the same hardware you'll use to present) to minimize the jitters.

Master the Pen tool for annotating slides and making the presentation come alive.

Prepare hidden slides for particular audience questions, and set up a branched slide show if there are more than a handful of such slides.

When speaking, engage and involve the audience, keep your energy level high, and keep a brisk and steady pace.

This chapter has covered live presenting, but you can also perform *virtual* presentations by publishing your slide shows on the Internet or on a corporate "intranet" that uses Web server technology. The next (and final) chapter tells you how.

Publishing Presentations on the Internet

22

In This Chapter

Discovering PowerPoint's three Internet features

Installing Internet features on a Windows 95 or Windows NT PC

Using Internet Assistant to publish "still" slide shows

Using Animation Publisher to publish slide shows with builds, transitions, and multimedia effects

Finding out tips for optimizing presentations to appear on a Web server

So far in this book, we've assumed that you're presenting live PowerPoint slide shows, but you can also present slide shows over the Internet via the World Wide Web, or even over corporate *intranets* that use Web technology. This capability is built into Version 8, and you can retrofit it to Version 7 with simple (and free) software upgrades, but it's not available for Version 4. (In all versions of PowerPoint, you can place your PPT files and the appropriate version of the PowerPoint Viewer on an FTP or HTTP server and make them available for downloading. Using the PPS file format in Version 8 forces the presentation to open in Slide Show mode.)

Three Internet Features

PowerPoint's Internet-publishing features consist of the following:

- The *Internet Assistant* (part of the Save as HTML wizard in Version 8) creates Internet-publishable "stills" of PowerPoint slides in GIF or JPG formats. It creates both a text version and a graphics version of your slide show and builds a home page Hypertext Markup Language (HTML) file that most Web browsers can play. HTML files created by the Internet Assistant do not contain animations, transitions, builds, or multimedia effects, but they do support interactive, "jump-to" slide settings (*hyperlinks*) and they can be read by users running Windows 3.*x*.

- The *Animation Publisher* (also part of the Save as HTML wizard in Version 8) enables PowerPoint to create full-featured Web animations that you can publish on a Web site you control. Slide shows modified for Web publishing contain the same builds, transitions, and sound effects that they would have in an interactive presentation. The file type is different, however: PPZ files are *compressed* for better performance across the Internet and can't be opened by PowerPoint itself; only by Web browsers equipped with the Animation Player.
- The *Animation Player* empowers a Web browser to play PowerPoint animations created with the Animation Publisher. The Animation Player works in-line with Netscape Navigator 2.0 or later or with Microsoft's Internet Explorer 3.0 or later. It can only display PowerPoint presentations full-screen as a "helper" program (that is, a program that extends a Web browser's basic HTML functionality) with Navigator 1.2, Internet Explorer 1.0, or any browser that supports helper programs. The Animation Player requires Windows 95 or Windows NT.

Installing the Software

This section explains how to install PowerPoint's Internet features.

version 8

Internet Assistant and Animation Publisher are installed when you run the PowerPoint or Office 97 setup program, as long as you specify Web publishing features (one of the options in the Custom setup procedure). You access both Internet features from PowerPoint with the built-in File⇨Save as HTML command.

version 7

The Internet Assistant is contained in PPTIA.EXE, which is available from http://www.microsoft.com/mspowerpoint. Running this file does not install the Internet Assistant; it just expands the archive. You have to run IA4PPT95.EXE to perform the installation. The best way is to run this file from your PowerPoint program directory. The installation will create the new command File⇨Export as HTML (or File⇨Export for Internet⇨As HTML, if you also install the PowerPoint Animation Publisher).

warning

The Internet Assistant may not work unless you've already installed an Internet browser on your PC.

Both the Animation Publisher and Animation Player add-ins are contained in the file AXPUB.EXE, which you can also download from http://www.microsoft.com/mspowerpoint. (If you want to install the Animation Player only, use AXPLAYER.EXE, available from the same location.)

Install the software simply by running the file and specifying a target directory; the usual choice is C:\Program Files\Common Files. AXPUB.EXE modifies the Windows 95 Registry to add a single new PowerPoint command: File⇨Export as PowerPoint Animation (or, if you've already installed the Internet Assistant, File⇨Export for Internet⇨As PowerPoint Animation).

You can conveniently uninstall the Animation Publisher and Player by using the Add/Remove Programs wizard in the Control Panel. Uninstall the Internet Assistant by manually deleting the files PPT2HTML.PPA, PPT2HTML.DLL, PPT2HINTL.DLL, SLIDEDMP.EXE, IMAGE.TPL, and TEXT.TPL from your PowerPoint program directory.

Using the Internet Assistant

versions 7&8

You run the Internet Assistant two different ways, depending on the PowerPoint version. The Internet Assistant is the program PowerPoint runs when you select either GIF or JPEG in the Graphic Type stage of Version 8's Save as HTML wizard (Figure 22-1). In Version 7, you run the Internet Assistant with the File⇨Export as HTML or File⇨Export for Internet⇨As HTML commands.

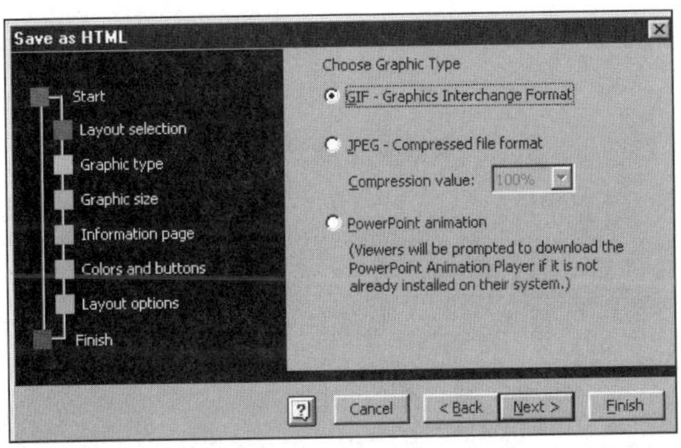

Figure 22-1: Choose a still graphic file type in PowerPoint 8's Save as HTML wizard to run the Internet Assistant.

You should use the Internet Assistant rather than the Animation Publisher in the following cases:

- If you want Windows 3.*x* or Macintosh users to be able to view your slide show
- If you want Windows 95 or NT users who don't have the PowerPoint Animation Player to be able to view your slide show
- If your slide show doesn't contain many animated effects or multimedia elements

Here are a few tips on using the Internet Assistant that apply to both Versions 7 and 8:

- If your slide show contains hidden slides that you don't want to include in the HTML presentation, delete them and save the slide show with a new name, such as "Introduction to PowerPoint (Internet)."
- If you haven't already done so, define slide titles. These appear as hyperlinks on the slide show index page that your audience sees. If you used the blank AutoLayout, you may want to change your slides to use an AutoLayout with a title. You can hide the title by specifying a font size of 1 point, rescaling the title to a tiny size, and pushing it off to a corner of the slide.
- If you want your slides to appear with 100 percent accuracy, choose the GIF format. If you want your slide show to occupy less space, choose the JPEG format and specify the degree of compression (more compression equals less quality). Be careful — specifying too low a compression setting for JPEG output causes text and lines to appear fuzzy.
- When finished, test your presentation in your Web browser; for example, by using Explorer to open the folder you've created and by double-clicking the file INDEX.HTM, which is your presentation's "home page." Clicking the first slide in the hyperlink list opens a window such as that shown in Figure 22-2. You can then navigate your slide show with the arrow buttons.

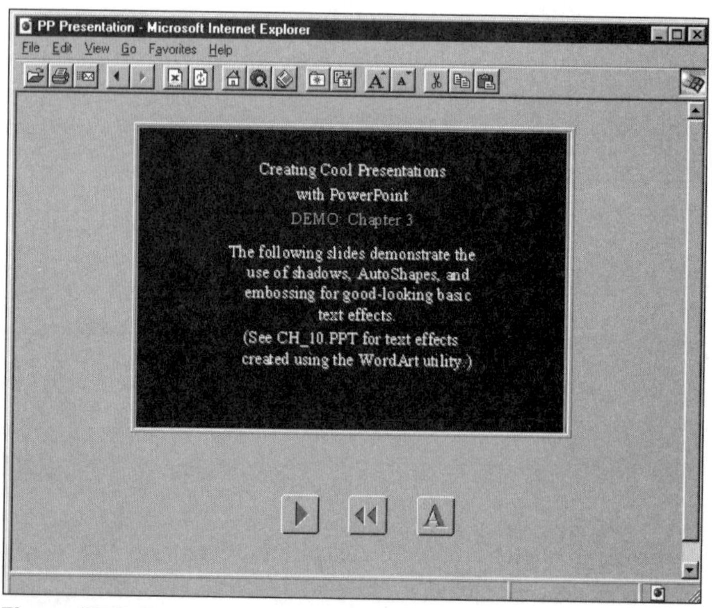

Figure 22-2: *Test your slide show by playing it with your Web browser. This figure shows a presentation running in Microsoft Internet Explorer.*

In Version 8, the Save as HTML wizard conveniently walks you through all the steps. Experiment with the different options and view the results in your Web browser. In Version 7, the procedure is more involved, so we provide the steps here in detail:

version 7

1. Run PowerPoint, open your slide show, and move any floating toolbars (including the Windows 95 Taskbar) away from the upper-left corner of the screen.
2. Disable pop-up menus by selecting Tools➪Options➪View and clearing Show Popup Menu Button.
3. Set your monitor to its maximum possible resolution (such as 1024 x 768) to create the largest possible images. Internet Assistant provides no other convenient mechanism for specifying image size.
4. Select File➪Export as HTML if you don't have the Animation Publisher installed, or File➪Export for Internet➪As HTML if you do. The dialog box in Figure 22-3 appears.

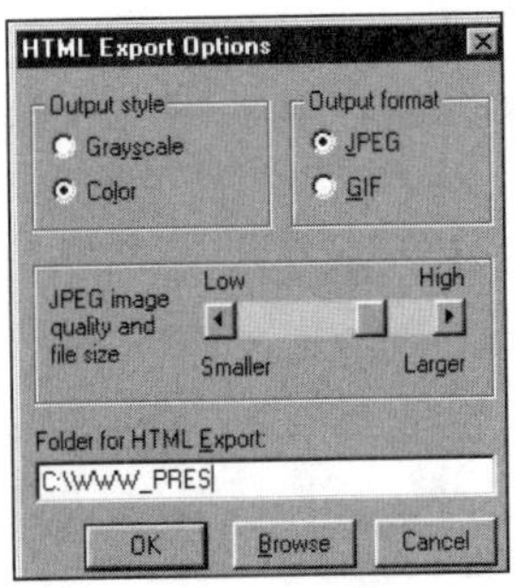

Figure 22-3: Specify color versus grayscale, image file format, compression quality, and destination folder in the HTML Export Options dialog box.

5. Choose the graphic format (GIF or JPEG) in the HTML Export Options dialog box.
6. Name the destination folder for your HTML presentation in the HTML Export Options dialog box. Specifying a new folder is wise, to make sure that no leftover files from previous presentations clutter the folder.
7. When all the options are set to your liking, click OK and go get a cup of coffee. Internet Assistant takes a few minutes to create the HTML files. If you want to watch the process in action, you can see Internet Assistant build a window in the upper-left corner and process your slides one by one. Wait for the message that your presentation has been successfully exported.
8. Test your presentation in your Web browser. If you're happy with the results, give your Internet guru (or *Webmaster*) the folder with your

HTML presentation in it, and ask him or her to place it on the Web page you specify. (Each presentation should have its own folder, if feasible; otherwise, you must rename files and edit the HTML scripts to differentiate your presentations, as PowerPoint reuses many of the same filenames for each slide show.) You're done!

Using the Animation Publisher

versions 7 & 8

As with the Internet Assistant, you run the Animation Publisher two different ways, depending on the PowerPoint version. The Animation Publisher is the program PowerPoint runs when you select PowerPoint Animation in the Graphic Type stage of Version 8's Save as HTML wizard. You run the Animation Publisher in Version 7 with the File➪Export as PowerPoint Animation or File➪Export for Internet➪As PowerPoint Animation commands.

You should use the Animation Publisher in the following situations:

- If your intended audience has Windows 95 or Windows NT, and it's not important that Windows 3.*x* and Macintosh users be able to view your slide show
- If your audience has access to the PowerPoint Animation Player
- If your slide show contains a number of animated effects or multimedia elements

Here are a few tips for using the Internet Assistant that apply to both Versions 7 and 8:

- If your slide show contains hidden slides that you don't want to include in the HTML presentation, you don't have to delete them; Animation Publisher will skip them automatically. If you do want to include hidden slides, you must unhide them by toggling the Tools➪Hide Slide (Version 7) or Slide Show➪Hide Slide (Version 8) menu options.
- Test your presentation in your Web browser; for example, by using Explorer to open the folder you've created and by double-clicking the file slideshow.HTM, where *slideshow* is the filename you selected in the previous step. If you have Netscape Navigator 1.*x* or Microsoft Internet Explorer 1.0 or 2.0, you see a screen such as Figure 22-4, and you can play the presentation in full-screen mode. If you have Navigator 2.*x* or Internet Explorer 3.*x* or later, you see a screen such as Figure 22-5, and you can play the presentation within your browser.

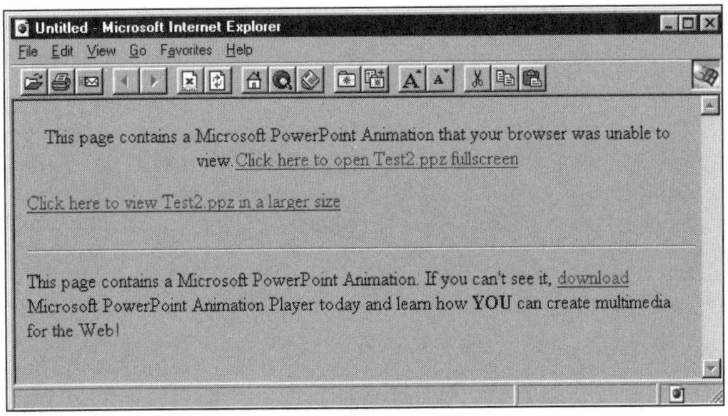

Figure 22-4: Test your slide show by playing it with your Web browser. This figure shows a presentation running in Microsoft Internet Explorer 2.0, which must run the presentation in full-screen mode. Note the option for downloading the Animation Player.

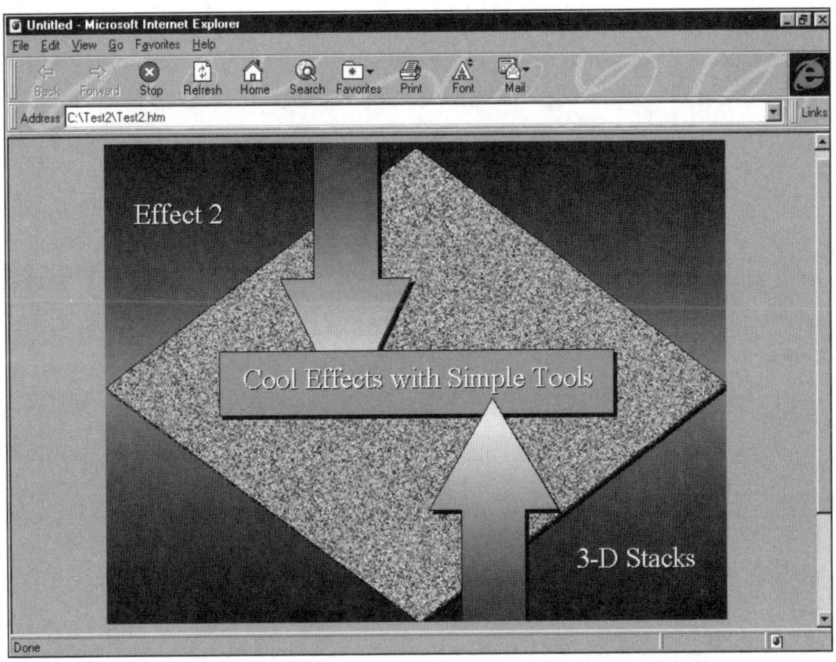

Figure 22-5: This figure shows a presentation running in Microsoft Internet Explorer 3.0, which can run the presentation inline within the browser window.

- You cannot play PPZ files with the standalone PowerPoint Viewer but only with a Web browser that has the Animation Player. Use PowerPoint Viewer for making live presentations only.
- When viewing PPZ files by using Internet Explorer 3.0 or higher or Navigator 2.0 or higher, you can right-click the animation and choose either Full Screen to have the animation fill the screen or Full Window to have the animation fill the browser window.
- If you want to add the animation to an existing Web page, advise the Webmaster to copy the contents of your HTM file between and including the <OBJECT> and </OBJECT> tags.

In Version 8, the Save as HTML wizard walks you through all the steps, as with the Internet Assistant. In Version 7, as before, the procedure is not quite so straightforward:

1. Run PowerPoint and open your slide show.
2. Set the dimensions of the slide show by using File⇨Slide Setup. (This method is much more convenient than Internet Assistant's method of changing your display resolution!) You can also change dimensions by using Draw⇨Scale.
3. Select File⇨Export as PowerPoint Animation if you don't have the Internet Assistant installed, or File⇨Export for Internet⇨As PowerPoint Animation if you do.
4. Name the destination folder for your HTML presentation in the Export as PowerPoint Animation dialog box and click the Save button. As with the Internet Assistant, specifying a new folder is wise, to make sure that no leftover files from previous presentations clutter the folder.

Animation Publisher is much faster than Internet Assistant, but you won't get a confirming dialog box when Animation Publisher is finished. Give it a couple of minutes, depending on the size of your slide show. Animation Publisher creates two files: the compressed animation file (format *.PPZ) and the HTML file that runs the animation (format *.HTM). PowerPoint 8 creates several other support files for screen elements such as buttons.

5. Test your presentation in your Web browser.
6. If you're happy with the results, give your Internet guru (or *Webmaster*) the folder with your HTML presentation in it and ask him or her to place it on the Web page you specify. (Each presentation should have its own folder, if feasible; otherwise, you must rename files and edit the HTML scripts to differentiate your presentations, as PowerPoint reuses many of the same filenames for each slide show.)

Internet and Intranet Tips

Here are a few tips for publishing PowerPoint slide shows on Web servers:

- In PowerPoint 8, you can create a new presentation that already has some Web-formatting features by using the AutoContent wizard. Simply select Information Kiosk as the Presentation Type and choose Internet, kiosk when prompted.
- You can associate links to other Web pages with PowerPoint objects, and both the Internet Assistant and the Animation Publisher will maintain those links. For example, if your slide show demonstrates the virtues of your company's product, you may want to include a link to your Web server's order entry page on the last PowerPoint slide to make it easy for a customer viewing the presentation to place an order.
- The technique in Version 7 is to create a drawing object for the interactive "button" and select Tools⇨Interactive Settings⇨Run Program. In Version 8, choose Slide Show⇨Action Buttons, pick a shape, and draw it on the slide. Then type the link's Uniform Resource Locator (URL) into the Run Program field (Version 7) or the Hyperlink to: field (Version 8); for example, http:\\www.abc.com. (In Version 8, you can also assign a hyperlink to an existing graphic object with Insert⇨Hyperlink — see Figure 22-6.) When the user clicks the drawing object, he or she jumps to the specified Web page.

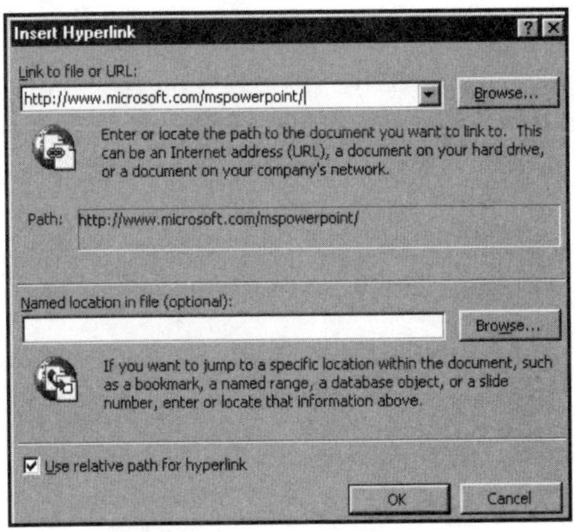

Figure 22-6: PowerPoint 8's Insert⇨Hyperlink feature enables your audience to click on any object and jump to a URL you specify.

- Making PPZ files smaller enables faster downloading across the Internet or an intranet. Omit the preview picture by selecting File⇨Properties⇨Summary and clearing the Save Preview Picture check box. Don't use long sound effects (WAV files). Use 256-color bitmaps instead of true-color or high-color image files.

- If you're familiar with HTML, you can customize the files PowerPoint uses to create Internet presentations. Internet Assistant uses IMAGE.TPL to control the creation of graphical slide shows, and TEXT.TPL for text versions. Animation Publisher uses TEMPLATE.HTM to create compressed, animated Internet presentations.

Summary

This chapter has laid out the steps you can take to publish your PowerPoint slide shows on the Internet or on a company intranet that uses a Web server.

For PowerPoint 7, install the Internet Assistant to add the capability to publish still presentations. Install the Animation Publisher to add the capability to publish presentations with builds, transitions, and multimedia effects intact.

For PowerPoint 8, make sure that the Web publishing feature is installed along with PowerPoint. The Internet Assistant and Animation Publisher are both activated with the Save as HTML wizard, which provides additional formatting options.

We've come to the end of our journey to create cool presentations with PowerPoint. We hope we've provided some tips and techniques that you won't find in any manual or any other "how-to" book. More importantly, we hope this book helps you create great-looking slide shows that will make your audience ask "What did you use to create that presentation?" so that you can then enjoy watching their jaws drop when you tell them you did it in plain old PowerPoint! Have fun, and happy presenting!

PART V

APPENDIXES

Part V consists of two appendixes. Appendix A provides detailed information on companies mentioned in the book, as well as on books and magazines of interest. Appendix B provides information on what's included on the enclosed CD-ROM.

Appendix

References and Resources

A

Throughout this book, we mention several companies that make hardware and software products to enhance the "cool" quotient of your presentations. If you'd like to contact any of them, this appendix will help. Here we also reference some magazines and books that you may like to investigate as you become a more experienced slide-show artist.

Companies Mentioned in the Text

3D/Eye, Inc. (Trispectives)
1050 Craft Road
Ithaca, NY 14850
800-946-9533, 607-257-1381,
607-257-7335 (fax)
`http://www.eye.com`

Adobe Systems Incorporated (Adobe Type Manager, Gallery Effects, Illustrator, Photoshop, Premiere, TypeAlign)
1585 Charleston Road, P.O. Box 7900
Mountain View, CA 94039-7900
415-961-4400, 415-961-3769 (fax)
`http://www.adobe.com`

Agfa (film recorders)
100 Challenger Road
Ridgefield Park, NJ 07660-2199
800-227-2780, 201-440-2500,
201-440-8187 (fax)
`http://www.agfahome.com`

Apple Computer (QuickTime for Windows, Movie Player)
1 Infinite Loop
Cupertino, CA 95014
800-776-2333, 408-996-1010
`http://www.apple.com`

Autodesk, Inc. (Kinetix Division) (Windows Animation Player, Animator Studio)
111 McInnis Parkway
San Rafael, CA 94903
800-879-4233, 415-507-5000,
415-507-5314 (fax)
`http://www.ktx.com`

Barco (video projection devices)
1000 Cobb Place Boulevard
Kennesaw, GA 30144
770-590-7900, 770-590-8836 (fax)

Caligari Corporation (TrueSpace)
1959 Landings Drive
Mountain View, CA 94043
800-351-7620, 415-390-9600,
sales@caligari.com

Corel Corp. (Draw!, PhotoPaint)
1600 Carling Avenue, The Corel Building
Ottawa, ON CANADA K1Z 8R7
800-772-6735, 613-728-8200,
613-728-9790 (fax)
http://www.corel.com

Creative Labs, Inc. (sound cards)
1901 McCarthy Boulevard
Milpitas, CA 95035
800-998-1000, 408-428-6600,
408-428-2394 (fax)
http://www.creaf.com

CrystalGraphics, Inc. (Flying Fonts, Topas Professional)
3350 Scott Boulevard, Suite 14
Santa Clara, CA 95054
800-979-3535, 408-496-6175,
408-496-0970 (fax)

Diamond Multimedia Systems, Inc. (video capture cards)
2880 Junction Avenue
San Jose, CA 95134-1922
800-4-MULTIMEDIA, 408-325-7000,
408-325-7070 (fax)
http://www.diamondmm.com

Electrohome, Ltd. (projectors)
809 Wellington Street N.
Kitchener, ON CANADA N2G 4J6
800-265-2171, 519-744-7111,
519-749-3136 (fax)
http://www.electro.com

Epson America, Inc. (scanners, projectors)
20770 Madrona Avenue, P.O. Box 2842
Torrance, CA 90509-2842
800-289-3776, 310-782-0770,
310-782-5220 (fax)
http://www.epson.com

Equilibrium Technology (DeBabelizer)
Three Harbor Drive, Suite 111
Sausalito, CA 94965
415-332-4343, 415-332-4433 (fax)
http://www.equilibrium.com

Fractal Design (Painter, Ray Dream Studio)
P.O. Box 2380
Aptos, CA 95001
800-297-2665, 408-688-5300,
408-688-8836 (fax)
http://www.fractal.com

Gyration, Inc. (cordless mice)
12930 Saratoga Avenue, Building C
Saratoga, CA 95070
800-316-5432, 408-255-3016,
408-255-9075 (fax)
http://www.gyration.com

Image Club Graphics (clip art, fonts)
729 Twenty-fourth Avenue SE
Calgary, Alberta, CANADA T2G 5K8
800-661-9410, 403-262-8008,
403-261-7013 (fax)
http://www.imageclub.com

Imagers (35mm slide service bureau)
Atlanta Technology Center
Building 400, Suite 490
1575 Northside Drive NW
Atlanta, GA 30318-4211
404-351-5800, 404-351-9020 (fax)

Intel Corp. (OverDrive processors)
5200 NE Elam Young Parkway
Hillsboro, OR 97124-6497
800-538-3373, 503-629-7354,
503-629-7580 (fax)
http://www.intel.com

Interlink Electronics (cordless mice)
546 Flynn Road
Camarillo, CA 93012
800-340-1331, 805-484-8855,
805-484-8989 (fax)
http://www.interlinkelec.com

LaserGraphics, Inc. (film recorders)
20 Ada Avenue
Irvine, CA 92718
800-727-2655, 714-753-8282,
714-727-9282 (fax)
`http://www.lasergraphics.com`

Management Graphics, Inc. (film recorders)
1401 East Seventy-ninth Street
Minneapolis, MN 55425
612-854-1220, 612-851-6159 (fax)
`http://www.mgi.com`

MetaTools, Inc. (Kai's Power Tools, Kai's Power Photos, KPT Convolver)
6303 Carpinteria Avenue
Carpinteria, CA 93013
805-566-6200, 805-566-6385 (fax)
`http://www.metatools.com`

Micrografx (ABC Graphics Suite)
1303 East Arapaho Road
Richardson, TX 75081
800-733-3729, 214-234-1769,
214-994-6227 (fax)
`http://www.micrografx.com`

Microsoft Corp. (Word, Excel, PowerPoint)
One Microsoft Way
Redmond, WA 98052-6399
800-426-9800, 206-882-8080,
800-936-4100 (fax-back)
`http://www.microsoft.com`

Mind Path Technologies, Inc. (cordless mouse)
12700 Park Central Drive, Suite 400
Dallas, TX 75251
800-736-6830, 214-233-9296,
214-233-9308 (fax)
`http://www.mindpath.com`

Mirus Industries Corp. (film recorders)
3350 Scott Boulevard, Building 48
Santa Clara, CA 95054-3123
800-942-9770, 408-980-6600,
408-980-6601 (fax)
`http://www.mirus.com`

Mitsubishi Electronics America, Inc. (presentation monitors)
5665 Plaza Drive, P.O. Box 6007
Cypress, CA 90630-0007
800-843-2515, 714-220-2500,
714-229-3854 (fax)
`http://www.mela-itg.com`

The Music Bakery (sound clips)
7522 Campbell Road, Suite 113-2
Dallas, TX 75248
800-229-0313
`http://www.musicbakery.com`

NEC Technologies, Inc. (presentation monitors and projectors)
1414 Massachusetts Avenue
Boxborough, MA 01719-2298
800-615-5566, 508-264-8000,
508-264-8488 (fax)
`http://www.nec.com`

Network Music, Inc. (Presentation Audio)
15150 Avenue of Science
San Diego, CA 92128
800-854-2075, 619-451-6400,
619-451-6409 (fax)
`http://www.networkmusic.com`

nVIEW Corp. (LCD panels)
860 Omni Boulevard
Newport News, VA 23606
800-736-8439, 804-873-1354,
804-873-2153 (fax)

Orchid Technology, Inc. (video-capture cards)
45365 Northport Loop West
Fremont, CA 94538
800-767-2443, 510-683-0300,
510-490-9312 (fax)
`http://www.orchid.com`

PhotoDisc, Inc. (stock digital photography)
2013 Fourth Avenue, Suite 402
Seattle, WA 98121
206-441-9355, 206-441-9379 (fax)
`http://www.photodisc.com`

Polaroid Corp. (film recorders)
565 Technology Square
Cambridge, MA 02139
800-225-1618, 617-386-2000,
617-386-9339 (fax)
`http://www.polaroid.com`

Proxima Corp. (LCD panels and projectors)
9440 Carroll Park Drive
San Diego, CA 92121-2298
619-457-5500, 619-457-9647 (fax)
`http://www.prxm.com`

Publisher's Depot - Picture Network International, Ltd. (digital art on the Web)
2000 Fourteenth Street North
Arlington, VA 22201
703-312-6247, 703-522-1236 (fax)
`http://www.publishersdepot.com`

Sharp Electronics Corp.
(LCD panels and projectors)
Sharp Plaza
Mahwah, NJ 07430
800-BE-SHARP, 201-529-8731,
201-529-9636 (fax)
`http://www.sharp-usa.com`

Sonic Foundry (Sound Forge)
100 South Baldwin, Suite 204
Madison, WI 53791-8062
608-256-5555, 608-256-7300 (fax)
`http://www.sfoundry.com`

Sony Electronics, Inc.
(presentation monitors)
3300 Zanker Road
San Jose, CA 95134-1901
800-352-7669, 408-432-1600,
408-943-0740 (fax)
`http://www.sony.com`

Turtle Beach Systems (sound cards)
5690 Stewart Avenue
Fremont, CA 94538
800-884-0190, 510-624-6200,
510-624-6291 (fax)
`http://www.tbeach.com`

VideoLogic, Inc. (scan converters)
1001 Bay Hill Drive, Suite 310
San Bruno, CA 94066
800-578-5644, 415-875-0606,
415-875-4167 (fax)
`http://www.videologic.com`

ViewSonic Corp. (presentation monitors)
20480 E. Business Parkway
Walnut, CA 91789
800-888-8583, 909-444-8800,
909-468-3756 (fax)
`http://www.viewsonic.com`

Books

Bulletproofing Windows 95
Glenn E. Weadock
McGraw-Hill/Computing, 1996

Fundamental Photoshop
Adele and Seth Greenberg
Osborne/McGraw-Hill, 1995

The Illustrator Wow! Book
Sharon Steuer
Peachpit Press, 1995

The McGraw-Hill Multimedia Handbook
Jessica Keyes, editor
McGraw-Hill, 1994 (hardback)

The Photoshop Wow! Book
Linnea Dayton and Jack Davis
Peachpit Press, 1993

Photoshop 3 for Windows 95 Bible
Deke McClelland and Robert Phillips
IDG Books Worldwide, Inc., 1996

Point, Click, and Wow! A Guide to Brilliant Laptop Presentations
David Fine and Claudyne Wilder
Pfeiffer & Company, 1996

Power of... PowerPoint 4
James Karney
MIS Press, 1995

The Presentations Kit
Claudyne Wilder
Wiley, 1994 (hardback)

Using PowerPoint for Windows 95
Rich Grace, Pamela R. Toliver, Nancy Stevenson, Rick Darnell
Que, 1995

Windows 3.1 SECRETS
Brian Livingston
IDG Books Worldwide, Inc., 1992

Magazines

Computer Artist: Digital Imaging, Illustration, Design
10 Tara Boulevard, Fifth Floor
Nashua, NH 03062-2801
918-831-9405, 603-891-0123

Computer Graphics World: Modeling, Animation, Multimedia
10 Tara Boulevard, Fifth Floor
Nashua, NH 03062-2801
918-835-3161, 603-891-0123

Digital Video: Video, Audio, Multimedia, Authoring, Animation
600 Townsend Street, Suite 170 East
San Francisco, CA 94103
800-998-0806, 415-522-2400

Multimedia Producer: For Creators and Developers of Interactive Media
701 Westchester Avenue
White Plains, NY 10604-3098
914-328-9157, 818-397-6839

New Media
901 Mariner's Island Boulevard, Suite 365
San Mateo, CA 94404
609- 86-4430, 415-573-5170

Presentations: Technology and Techniques for Effective Communication
50 S. Ninth Street
Minneapolis, MN 55402
800-707-7797, 800-328-4329

Windows Magazine: Your #1 Independent Windows Resource
One Jericho Plaza
Jericho, NY 11753
800-294-0198, 516-733-8300

Appendix B

CD-ROM Notes

You're in for a treat! We've included more than 300MB of software on the enclosed CD-ROM for you to explore. Although most of the directories have their own documentation files, this overview summarizes the CD-ROM's contents. All the companies represented on the CD-ROM appear in Appendix A of the book, with full address and phone information.

The CD-ROM that accompanies this book will work with Windows 3.*x* and Windows 95.

For Windows 3.*x*, you need to have a CD-ROM driver in your CONFIG.SYS file and the MSCDEX.EXE program in AUTOEXEC.BAT. Your CD-ROM drive probably came with a manual and a diskette that explain how to set up these files on your computer.

For Windows 95, you don't need a device driver in CONFIG.SYS, nor do you need MSCDEX.EXE in AUTOEXEC.BAT. No AutoRun feature is available, so we suggest that you use the Windows 95 Explorer or My Computer to explore the CD-ROM's contents.

We suggest that you set up a new subdirectory on your hard drive to install any of the demos or tryout programs on this CD-ROM. Some of the programs create a large number of files when you run the SETUP command. Also, some of the self-extracting archives in *.EXE format expand into a large number of files.

We've taken every precaution in creating this CD-ROM, but, as always, scanning all new files for viruses before running them is a good idea.

\3DEYE

A demo of the 3-D illustration program for Windows 95 called Trispectives.

NOTE: This program will *not* run under Windows 3.*x*.

\BOOK\TUTORIAL

Some PPT files that illustrate concepts in the book. The filenames indicate the relevant chapter. You will see many of the examples used for the book's screen snapshots. These files look best at display settings of 800 x 600 resolution and more than 256 colors.

NOTE: Directory "V4" contains PowerPoint 4 files, whereas directory "V7&8" contains PowerPoint 7 files that you can also read with Version 8.

\BOOK\BKGRNDS

A collection of 118 slide backgrounds that Emily created using Photoshop and filters from MetaTools and Adobe. Feel free to use these in your own slide shows!

\FLYFONTS

A demo of Crystal Graphics' Flying Fonts, the program used in the book tutorial for Chapter 14. You can use Flying Fonts as a 3-D modeler or as an animation engine for creating FLC and AVI files.

\FREEWARE

The AutoDesk Animation Player for Windows, in the form of the freely distributable file WINPLA.EXE. This file also contains the MCI driver to make FLC files compatible with Windows' Media Player.

\IMAGCLUB

Thirty-one sample clip art images from Image Club.

NOTE: The originals are in EPS format; we used Micrografx Designer to convert them to WMF format as well, for direct importing into PowerPoint.

\KPT\DEMOS

Demos of Kai's Power Tools, specifically the fractal designer, gradient designer, and texture explorer. We mention these MetaTools filters in Chapter 7. Copy the *.EXE files to your hard disk and run them directly. Delete them when done.

\KPT\IMAGES

Sample images created with Kai's Power Tools.

\KPT\TRYOUT

A trial version of Kai's Power Tools you can install if you already have a filter-compatible program such as Photoshop, Picture Publisher, or Painter.

\KPTCONV\DEMO

A demo of KPT Convolver, a convenient filtering application from MetaTools.

\KPTCONV\IMAGES

Sample images created using KPT Convolver.

\PAINTER

A demo version of Fractal Design's Painter 4 illustration program.

\PHOTDISC

35 sample images from PhotoDisc. The versions included here are "low-res" and suitable for using on PowerPoint slides. When you buy photos from this vendor, you also get hi-res JPG files that you can crop or scale down for use in PowerPoint.

\PHOTOSHP

A tryout version of Adobe's popular image editing program. Many examples in the book mention Photoshop, especially in Chapter 7.

\PREMIERE

A tryout version of Adobe's digital video editing application. The book contains some discussion of Premiere in Chapter 15.

\STRMLINE

A tryout version of StreamLine, Adobe's tracing utility for converting bitmap images to vector format.

\TS2TRIAL

A trial version of Caligari's TrueSpace 2 program for 3-D illustration.

Index

Page numbers in *italics* refer to illustrations.

NUMBERS

A

IDG BOOKS WORLDWIDE, INC.
END-USER LICENSE AGREEMENT

Read This. You should carefully read these terms and conditions before opening the software packet(s) included with this book ("Book"). This is a license agreement ("Agreement") between you and IDG Books Worldwide, Inc. ("IDGB"). By opening the accompanying software packet(s), you acknowledge that you have read and accept the following terms and conditions. If you do not agree and do not want to be bound by such terms and conditions, promptly return the Book and the unopened software packet(s) to the place you obtained them for a full refund.

1. License Grant. IDGB grants to you (either an individual or entity) a nonexclusive license to use one copy of the enclosed software program(s) (collectively, the "Software") solely for your own personal or business purposes on a single computer (whether a standard computer or a workstation component of a multi-user network). The Software is in use on a computer when it is loaded into temporary memory (i.e., RAM) or installed into permanent memory (e.g., hard disk, CD-ROM or other storage device). IDGB reserves all rights not expressly granted herein.

2. Ownership. IDGB is the owner of all right, title and interest, including copyright, in and to the compilation of the Software recorded on the CD-ROM. Copyright to the individual programs on the CD-ROM is owned by the author or other authorized copyright owner of each program. Ownership of the Software and all proprietary rights relating thereto remain with IDGB and its licensors.

3. Restrictions On Use and Transfer.

(a) You may only (i) make one copy of the Software for backup or archival purposes, or (ii) transfer the Software to a single hard disk, provided that you keep the original for backup or archival purposes. You may not (i) rent or lease the Software, (ii) copy or reproduce the Software through a LAN or other network system or through any computer subscriber system or bulletin-board system, or (iii) modify, adapt or create derivative works based on the Software.

(b) You may not reverse engineer, decompile, or disassemble the Software. You may transfer the Software and user documentation on a permanent basis, provided that the transferee agrees to accept the terms and conditions of this Agreement and you retain no copies. If the Software is an update or has been updated, any transfer must include the most recent update and all prior versions.

4. Restrictions on Use of Individual Programs. You must follow the individual requirements and restrictions detailed for each individual program in Appendix E of this Book. These limitations are contained in the individual license agreements recorded on the CD-ROM. These restrictions include a requirement that after using the program for the period of time specified in its text, the user must pay a registration fee or discontinue use. By opening the Software packet(s), you will be agreeing to abide by the licenses and restrictions for these individual programs. None of the material on this CD-ROM or listed in this Book may ever be distributed, in original or modified form, for commercial purposes.

5. <u>Limited Warranty</u>.

(a) IDGB warrants that the Software and CD-ROM are free from defects in materials and workmanship under normal use for a period of sixty (60) days from the date of purchase of this Book. If IDGB receives notification within the warranty period of defects in materials or workmanship, IDGB will replace the defective CD-ROM.

(b) IDGB AND THE AUTHOR OF THE BOOK DISCLAIM ALL OTHER WARRANTIES, EXPRESS OR IMPLIED, INCLUDING WITHOUT LIMITATION IMPLIED WARRANTIES OF MERCHANTABILITY AND FITNESS FOR A PARTICULAR PURPOSE, WITH RESPECT TO THE SOFTWARE, THE PROGRAMS, THE SOURCE CODE CONTAINED THEREIN, AND/OR THE TECHNIQUES DESCRIBED IN THIS BOOK. IDGB DOES NOT WARRANT THAT THE FUNCTIONS CONTAINED IN THE SOFTWARE WILL MEET YOUR REQUIREMENTS OR THAT THE OPERATION OF THE SOFTWARE WILL BE ERROR FREE.

(c) This limited warranty gives you specific legal rights, and you may have other rights which vary from jurisdiction to jurisdiction.

6. <u>Remedies</u>.

(a) IDGB's entire liability and your exclusive remedy for defects in materials and workmanship shall be limited to replacement of the Software, which is returned to IDGB at the address set forth below with a copy of your receipt. This Limited Warranty is void if failure of the Software has resulted from accident, abuse, or misapplication. Any replacement Software will be warranted for the remainder of the original warranty period or thirty (30) days, whichever is longer.

(b) In no event shall IDGB or the author be liable for any damages whatsoever (including without limitation damages for loss of business profits, business interruption, loss of business information, or any other pecuniary loss) arising out of the use of or inability to use the Book or the Software, even if IDGB has been advised of the possibility of such damages.

(c) Because some jurisdictions do not allow the exclusion or limitation of liability for consequential or incidental damages, the above limitation or exclusion may not apply to you.

7. <u>U.S. Government Restricted Rights</u>. Use, duplication, or disclosure of the Software by the U.S. Government is subject to restrictions stated in paragraph (c) (1) (ii) of the Rights in Technical Data and Computer Software clause of DFARS 252.227-7013, and in subparagraphs (a) through (d) of the Commercial Computer—Restricted Rights clause at FAR 52.227-19, and in similar clauses in the NASA FAR supplement, when applicable.

8. <u>General</u>. This Agreement constitutes the entire understanding of the parties, and revokes and supersedes all prior agreements, oral or written, between them and may not be modified or amended except in a writing signed by both parties hereto which specifically refers to this Agreement. This Agreement shall take precedence over any other documents that may be in conflict herewith. If any one or more provisions contained in this Agreement are held by any court or tribunal to be invalid, illegal or otherwise unenforceable, each and every other provision shall remain in full force and effect.

IDG BOOKS WORLDWIDE REGISTRATION CARD

Visit our Web site at http://www.idgbooks.com

Title of this book: Creating Cool™ PowerPoint® 97 Presentations

My overall rating of this book: ❑ Very good [1] ❑ Good [2] ❑ Satisfactory [3] ❑ Fair [4] ❑ Poor [5]

How I first heard about this book:

❑ Found in bookstore; name: [6] ❑ Book review: [7]

❑ Advertisement: [8] ❑ Catalog: [9]

❑ Word of mouth; heard about book from friend, co-worker, etc.: [10] ❑ Other: [11]

What I liked most about this book:

What I would change, add, delete, etc., in future editions of this book:

Other comments:

Number of computer books I purchase in a year: ❑ 1 [12] ❑ 2-5 [13] ❑ 6-10 [14] ❑ More than 10 [15]

I would characterize my computer skills as: ❑ Beginner [16] ❑ Intermediate [17] ❑ Advanced [18] ❑ Professional [19]

I use ❑ DOS [20] ❑ Windows [21] ❑ OS/2 [22] ❑ Unix [23] ❑ Macintosh [24] ❑ Other: [25]________________ (please specify)

I would be interested in new books on the following subjects:

(please check all that apply, and use the spaces provided to identify specific software)

❑ Word processing: [26] ❑ Spreadsheets: [27]

❑ Data bases: [28] ❑ Desktop publishing: [29]

❑ File Utilities: [30] ❑ Money management: [31]

❑ Networking: [32] ❑ Programming languages: [33]

❑ Other: [34]

I use a PC at (please check all that apply): ❑ home [35] ❑ work [36] ❑ school [37] ❑ other: [38] ________________

The disks I prefer to use are ❑ 5.25 [39] ❑ 3.5 [40] ❑ other: [41]________________

I have a CD ROM: ❑ yes [42] ❑ no [43]

I plan to buy or upgrade computer hardware this year: ❑ yes [44] ❑ no [45]

I plan to buy or upgrade computer software this year: ❑ yes [46] ❑ no [47]

Name: Business title: [48] Type of Business: [49]

Address (❑ home [50] ❑ work [51]/Company name:)

Street/Suite#

City [52]/State [53]/Zipcode [54]: Country [55]

❑ **I liked this book!** You may quote me by name in future IDG Books Worldwide promotional materials.

My daytime phone number is ________________

IDG BOOKS WORLDWIDE

THE WORLD OF COMPUTER KNOWLEDGE®